W9-BXE-511

WITHDRAWN

EFFECTIVE
SPEECH

EFFECTIVE SPEECH

SPEECH

Fourth Edition

ROBERT T. OLIVER

The Pennsylvania State University

RUPERT L. CORTRIGHT

Wayne State University

HOLT, RINEHART AND WINSTON

New York • Chicago • San Francisco

Toronto • London

13649

For ROBERT and DENNIS, RUTH and HELEN
Representatives of a generation confronting
unrivaled communicative opportunities
and problems

PN
4121
.O55
1961

7 8 9

PREFACE

FROM THE FIRST APPEARANCE of this book in 1939 through the present revision an unchanging aim has been to help students attain a more complete self-realization. In its fullest sense, of course, this has always been the aim of education. It is the primary aim of speech training. In Athens twenty-three centuries ago, Isocrates taught:

The power to speak well is taken as the surest index of a sound understanding; and discourse which is true and lawful and just is the outward image of a good and faithful soul.

In our time, Harry Overstreet writes: "When we begin to understand the role that speech plays in life, we cannot dismiss the prevalent immaturity of speech. . . . Our lives are in good order only if the communicative linkages between us and our world are relatively mature and becoming more so."

The last revision of this book appeared ten years ago. In this new edition, which remains eclectic in approach, our concern has been to retain those features whose worth a decade of successful use has proved, while at the same time utilizing recent research; to take advantage of the helpful suggestions from many users of the previous edition; and to bring to date illustrative materials and references.

It is our conviction that speech, already pre-eminent among means of communication, is to have a role of increasing importance in tomorrow's life. Effective speech is a means of making truth dynamic and personality more effective through the wise and skilled use of idea, language, voice, and the visible aspects of speech. We know from our own observation and experience that there is no short and easy way to effective speaking; speech, like any other skill, is achieved only through basic understanding and thorough training, including persistent, guided practice.

Since the arts of expression, oral communication, and listening constitute the essence of man's social adaptation, the focus of this book is upon effective interaction of speaker, viewer-auditor, and situation. Because these arts are composite achievements we have sought to harmonize and coordinate the contributions from such separate areas as written composition, oral composition, communication, public speaking, and speech fundamentals.

Every college student has an obligation to develop his own special abilities by means of his educational opportunities. Every student is going to face, if he has not already, occasions in which the right words, spoken with the finest skill and with that courage which ought always to uphold truth, will be decisive in moving men to right decisions. To help him meet such situations is a principal aim of this book.

As the long task of rewriting this book is completed we gratefully acknowledge our indebtedness to hundreds of teachers and thousands of students whose experiences with former editions have given us many practical suggestions for improvement; critics and editors who have added clarity and vigor to ideas and their expression; colleagues who have contributed generously of their illustrations and exercise materials; many pioneers as well as contemporary leaders of our field whose influence and inspiration are evident throughout the book; and members of our families who have been patient in neglect and tolerant of the role of critic when it was thrust upon them.

Like so many books that have enjoyed the privilege of wide and long use, *Effective Speech*, 1961, is genuinely the result of collective effort. Authors and readers may be grateful for the warm-spirited helpfulness of human nature.

January, 1961   R.T.O.
                                                                    R.L.C.

CONTENTS

Part Two. SPEECH IN GROUP ACTIVITIES

Part Three. PREPARING THE SPEECH

Production of a Single Act: Conclusion, 2??. Persuasion and Manipulation, 2??. THE SPEAKER WRITES: Manuscript...

Part One

THE NATURE OF SPEECH

CHAPTER 1

CONTENTS

This course in speech will help bring to your public speaking the natural communicativeness of your best conversational manner. (Black Star)

YOUR NEED TO
SPEAK EFFECTIVELY

Y ou are in college to get the best education possible to fit you for
living the kind of life you wish. There is much to learn. This is a
demanding world in a time of rapid change. No other generation has
encountered so great a need for effective self-expression. "We may
regard education," writes social psychologist Floyd Allport in his book
Institutional Behavior, "not primarily as a transmission of the cultural
heritage (though this aim is not precluded), but as a process of helping
individuals to find and to express themselves. It is a method of revealing and liberating their potentialities for various forms of experience."
The Curriculum Committee of the English Department of a large
eastern university reported in 1950: "One test generally applied to
determine a man's educational level is that of language. If he can
extract the correct meaning from a standard sample of oral or written
literary symbols, and if he can turn his thoughts into understandable
symbols of speech and writing, we feel that he has attained a certain
degree of human skill." As a psychologist Kurt Goldstein has pointed
out, "The change of personality which accompanies some defect of
language reveals the close relationship between the self-realization
of man and the use of language."

The importance of skill in speech has been increased by the development and wide use of radio, television, the motion picture, and the
telephone. There are more American homes with television sets than
with bathrooms; and the time that the average family spends in front
of its set has been found to be more than five hours daily.[1] Of all our
time devoted to communicative activities, it has been estimated that
we spend 9 percent in writing, 16 percent in reading, 30 percent in
talking, and 45 percent in listening.[2] More than fifty-five million of

[1] Based on a study made by the American Broadcasting Company Television Network in 1958, cited by Oliver Treyz, President of the ABCTV, in his "Broadcasting
as an Instrument of Commerce," in *Re-establishing the Speech Profession: The First
Fifty Years,* published by The Speech Association of the Eastern States, 1959.

[2] A CBS study, reported by David C. Phillips, University of Tennessee *Extension
Bulletin,* November, 1948.

4

our homes have telephones, and well over a hundred million radios are in use in the United States. Speech pours upon and around us in an endless flow, to a degree unimaginable in any earlier period of history. The need for both the ability to speak well and the ability to listen discriminatingly has been accentuated.

WHAT SPEECH IS

A Form of Symbolism

Language is *symbolic representation*. It is a means of grasping reality, of comprehending the world about us, and of sharing that understanding with others—both receiving and giving. Only man, among all living beings, has the power to do these things. A mother hen can cluck to her chicks of the danger of a hovering hawk; but she cannot, in the safety of the chicken house, talk to them of that danger and tell them how to avoid it. For chickens possess no ability to symbolize. This tremendous ability belongs to man alone. It gives to language its power. It makes man unique.

Try to imagine man deprived of language and it will be evident how he would sink below barbarity to mere animalism. It is through our use of language that we formulate purposes, express our personalities, represent our thoughts and feelings, achieve cooperation, coordinate activities, plan for the future, analyze the past, stimulate mutual feelings, and achieve understanding of elements lying beyond our immediate sensory perception. Without the power to symbolize, man would lack almost every characteristic we think of as distinctively human. With that power only haphazardly or incompletely developed, then, how short we must fall of the full realization of our inherent potentialities.

Our symbolic power expresses itself in many ways. Mario Pei, in *The Story of Language,* estimates that there are over 700,000 gestural and postural meanings which may be produced, transmitted, and understood. The unabridged dictionaries contain almost as many words. Variations of vocal and tonal pattern provide still another wide range of meaning units. Differing methods of thought analysis and of organization of ideas, as well as differing means of expression through examples, through forms of logic, through types of facts, and through grammatical and stylistic forms, all comprise means of speech communication. Furthermore, our speech activities include such diverse forms as conversation, discussion, dramatics, debate, public speaking, and reading aloud and such vocal expressions as cheering, booing, chuckling, and singing. The forms of speech are infinitely various, but all serve to symbolize thought and feeling.

A Composite of Thought, Language, Voice, and Action

This book includes a wide range of topics because the interrelationships of all the varied speech elements are complex. As a *Report of the National Commission on Cooperative Curriculum Planning* emphasizes, "*a concept of speech which focuses attention on one or more such limited aspects of the total process . . . comes dangerously near to mere academic abstractions. . . .* In using the term *speech processes,* we refer to the means by which any act of speaking is accomplished. They include knowing, thinking, believing, and analyzing speech content; using oral language; using voice and articulation; using visible symbols; and integration of attitudes and adjustments." It is clear that thinking is the essential counterpart of talking; or, as the psychologist Norman Munn puts it, thinking in itself is "restrained speaking" or "subvocal talking."

Four essential skills comprise the process of speech. There must first be a *thought* to communicate. It is obvious that the speaker must have command of his ideas. Once he has a thought, he must be able to formulate it in words. *Language,* both written and spoken, enables us to share, develop, preserve, and pass on the experience of each generation, so that sustained thinking on human problems is possible. Linguistic communication is the carrier of our human heritage. It is the carrier, too, of thought itself. We think in language symbols. *Action,* another essential element of speech, is constantly intermingled with language. We speak to the eye as well as to the ear. We convey many meanings entirely with postural movements, or gestures. A shrug of the shoulders, a lift of an eyebrow, a tilt of the head often says much that can be interpreted in words only with great difficulty. Similarly, tones of the *voice* may greatly modify the meanings of words uttered. Voice and action combine in speech to be the carriers of meaning.

These nonlinguistic means of communication are products of our social experience just as surely as is our language. Every group tends to develop its own gestural and tonal characteristics, and in that sense these become veritable attributes of the language of the group. Every individual develops habits of voice and body that serve the kind of society in which he lives. In moving out of the social groups of child-hood and adolescence into those of maturity, it is just as necessary to revise and adapt our nonverbal methods of communication as it is to make changes in our use of language. We must master all the means of communication.

A Product of the Whole Personality

In a larger sense, speech training is the unfolding and development of a person's resources. Its aim is to make outwardly effective his inner strengths. It attempts to teach each student to make the most effective use, in his dealings with other people, of his ideas, knowledge, and feelings. We can use with maximum effectiveness only that knowledge which we can communicate. Our communicative abilities depend for their development upon training and correct practice. A course in speech is a course in self-development. The students enrolled are the real subjects of study.

Look around at the other students in your class. Today they are strangers whom you may not even recognize when you meet them next. Yet by the end of the semester you will know a great deal about all of them. You will have firmly fixed opinions about their personalities, characters, and abilities. You will know a good deal about their attitudes and interests, their preferences and prejudices. These things you will learn as part of the process of adapting and adjusting to your classmates. You have much to learn from them, and they have much to learn from you. And each will be learning a great deal about himself. In a broad sense, you will be learning what you have to know of human nature in order to talk effectively. It is difficult even to start a conversation with a stranger. We must first find experiences, attitudes, and understandings in common. Without these even a common language is inadequate. Just as a good salesman studies his prospect, so every good speaker studies his listener.

The necessity of knowing as much as possible about our listener is borne out by the phonetic and semantic approaches to speech, which stress sounds and meanings. It is generally realized that when a person pronounces a word incorrectly, the mispronunciation is an impediment to the listener's understanding. You know how difficult it is to understand a speaker who uses a dialect with which you are unfamiliar. Yet far more prevalent than errors and variations in pronunciation are differences in the meanings attached to words. What is your definition, for example, of each of the following words: educated, American, old-fashioned, collegiate, good, religious, democratic? Do you think that everyone in the class would agree with you? This is one of the major problems of speech: how to make ourselves clearly understood when the words we must use are inexact in their meaning. Obviously, then, the more we know about our listeners and the more experiences we have had in common with them, the more likely is it that they will understand our words as we mean them—hence the more easily we can communicate with them.

In summary, then, speech is a form of symbolism; a composite of thought, language, voice, and action; and a product of the integrated personality. In its full, functional sense, speech is used almost constantly to satisfy our needs, wants, and desires. It is essential to our adaptation to other individuals and to all of society about us.

SPEECH IN THE AMERICAN COMMUNITY

Speech as a Part of General Education

General education is concerned fundamentally with stimulating and assisting students to enrich their minds, clarify their understandings, improve the quality of their judgments, and enhance their appreciation of moral, social, and esthetic values. This means that the purpose of learning (as of living) is basically the enrichment of personality— when personality is properly understood to include all the intellectual, moral, esthetic, and social qualities that go beyond the mere life-sustaining and reproductive activities of nonhuman beings. When this aim of education becomes your own goal, you will find that your work in speech will not be merely "another course," but a means through which all you learn, all you believe, and all you feel can be identified, analyzed, organized, interpreted, and communicated.

You study history and chemistry, mathematics and music, sociology and cost accounting, philosophy and physics. Whatever courses you take can be simple quantities of isolated facts to be learned and for a time remembered. Or, out of the whole educative process (outside as well as inside school), you can integrate what you know into a dynamic unity of convictions and skills. You can also learn the methods of acquiring, interpreting, and applying new knowledge through ever-expanding experience. Unless education becomes a continuing habit that will be lifelong—a way of thinking and applying what you know to new situations—it fails to accomplish its real goal. And unless speech helps you to achieve this kind of self-mastery, you will not have attained its most significant values.

The study of speech is as old as civilization. Indeed, the oldest book ever discovered, the precepts of an Egyptian sage named Hotep, who lived over two thousand years before Christ, is a speech textbook, written especially for the guidance of a young pharaoh. Both Aristotle and Plato were concerned with how individuals can attain understandings and communicate them honestly and effectively to others. Quintilian, the greatest of the ancient teachers of speech, about A.D. 90 wrote *The Institutes of Oratory,* which was the basic educational textbook in the Roman Empire. In it he advised students to learn everything they could (of history, literature, mathematics, and politics); then to integrate their understanding of the whole world of knowledge into their own personalities. The test of whether they succeeded in this high aim, he taught, must lie in their ability to communicate their

Your need to speak effectively: these college students, recognizing their need for effective speech, are preparing to participate in a great debate tradition. (Bates College News Bureau)

thoughts and feelings meaningfully and purposefully to their associates; not only, we may add, in public speeches, but even more urgently in conversation and discussions.

Your course in speech constitutes a challenge to your own thinking and to your relations with others. A mind that is empty of facts or careless in handling them cannot produce talk that "makes sense" to intelligent listeners. Someone who is selfish or unconcerned about the needs or feelings of other people will never succeed in developing the reciprocal relationship necessary to true communication. A conscientious student who hungrily absorbs facts but fails to consider their relationship or significance cannot think effectively with the fund of knowledge he has accumulated. One way of avoiding these common pitfalls is to apply three questions to any area of study: (1) Can I satisfy myself that it is true? (2) How does it relate to me personally? (3) What ought it to mean to other people—to those with whom I associate, and to whom I talk from day to day? The application of these criteria should guide your approach to either casual or prepared speaking.

Speech and Good Citizenship

We Americans and some of our allies are engaged in a great experiment in democracy. In the long view of history, popular democracy has emerged only recently, and it is today (as always) challenged strongly by opposing philosophies of totalitarian dictatorship. Whether democracy proves meaningful and valuable to any people depends upon how effectively they make it work. Should we fail in citizenship, democracy can hardly succeed as a way of government. For it to succeed, the people who have the opportunity must exercise their right of free speech with skill and responsibility.

To vote by secret ballot is but the culmination of the total task of citizenship. Preceding this must have come the vital prerequisites of knowing, considering, and evaluating the issues. This is why our democracy always has been characterized by a vast amount of community talking, from the days of the colonial town meetings in New England to the multitude of luncheon clubs, study groups, community meetings, and radio and television forums of today. Democracy is no stronger than the extent and quality of active participation in it. Those who stay at home on Election Day have deserted their citizenship obligation. Those who stay away and let a minority group run the PTA, or a union, or a school district meeting, or any other community session, are contributing to the weakening of democracy. Most important of all, perhaps, they are neglecting their own personal education and growth. The ability to think critically and clearly, and the ability to give effective oral expression to one's thoughts, are developed just as any other skill is developed: only as a result of diligent and right practice. This is why speech training has so substantial a contribution to make to good citizenship. It is an essential element in the strengthening of democracy itself. Of what value is our boasted freedom of speech to those who lack the confidence to speak? Or to those who lack the ability. Healthy and strong democracy depends upon discussion, debate, and talk for the education of its citizens as well as for the wise solution of its problems. Good speech has a basic contribution to make to good citizenship.

Speech in Vocational Training

By general agreement it appears that vocational success depends upon acquiring special technical skills as well as developing skill in various speaking situations. Testimony to this effect comes from many sources.

The personnel manager of the Owens-Corning Fiberglass Company wrote: "Is training needed in speech? Indeed! Effective speaking is needed by practically every employee who has any ambition whatsoever."[3] A United States Steel Company executive declared, "One of the specific criticisms directed toward engineering personnel indicates a deficiency of training in this [speech] field." Robert F. Moore, Director of Personnel for Columbia University, said in 1950: "There will be 50,000 graduates in engineering from the nation's colleges this spring. About 35,000 of them will get jobs in their chosen profession. They won't necessarily be the best in technical training; they'll be the ones who best know how to speak. By and large, the greatest weakness in technical education today is lack of training in communications and human relationships." And P. W. Boynton, who had interviewed some 75,000 job applicants in hiring from 100 to 500 annually for the Socony-Vacuum Oil Company, commented, "In all my experience I have never interviewed an engineer who has been a college debater. If I ever meet such an applicant, he'll doubtless get a job."

On February 12, 1959, the United States Army distributed a directive to all ROTC officers which said: "The inability of an officer to express himself clearly detracts from his overall value to the military

[3] See Harold P. Zelko, "Adult Speech Training," *Quarterly Journal of Speech*, February, 1951, pp. 55 ff. for many additional judgments of this nature.

service. The service school commanders have been directed to place additional emphasis on oral expression at Army service schools." The personnel manager of Johns-Manville reports: "We are placing more emphasis, particularly for our sales people, on their ability to *think on their feet*. Speech training is incorporated in our sales training program." To inquire what college courses they felt were indispensable, the dean of the Purdue University Engineering College polled 3,800 engineers who had graduated from Purdue between 1911 and 1956. The replies indicated first speech, then English composition, psychology, and economics.

YOUR MAJOR USES OF SPEECH

Speech serves many purposes in our everyday lives. We talk in order to cement friendships, to exchange information, to give or ask for orders, to buy or sell, to entertain ourselves and others, sometimes even to display our wit, intelligence, or information. Yet, basically we are always seeking to satisfy some need, want, or desire, and we find speech not merely helpful but essential to that end.

The functions of speech may be made clear by a brief examination of how and why speech has developed in the history of the race and in the life of the individual. How did you happen to learn to speak? If you are now studying, or have studied, some foreign language, you realize that learning to speak a language is no simple task. How, then, did you learn to speak your native language so early in life? At a remarkably early age you began to acquire a working vocabulary in your mother tongue because you found the words which were essential to your well-being. It was quite unsatisfactory, for example, to rely any longer than absolutely necessary upon that universal language of crying, because it was too often misinterpreted. Imagine your dismay at having a cry inspired by a pricking pin interpreted as a desire for food! Many such experiences played an essential part in motivating you to wish to learn to speak.

Three theories as to the fundamental needs which motivate the development of speech have been widely held and strongly supported. Speech has been traced to the needs for *expression*, for *communication*, and for *social control*. According to the first view, speech is primarily the means of manifesting outwardly the inner workings of the mind. The second view—that language exists for communication—carries this interpretation a step further. It emphasizes a receiver as well as an expresser: communication is not complete until the expression has been received and understood. The third theory is well summarized in the words of Grace Andrus de Laguna in *Speech: Its Function and Development*: "Speech is the great medium through which human cooperation is brought about. It is the means by which the diverse activities of men are coordinated and correlated with each other for the attainment of common and reciprocal ends. Men do not speak simply to relieve their feelings or to air their views, but to awaken a response in their fellows and to influence their attitudes and acts." In the light of these three theories, we may now describe the *functions of speech*.

Speech as Self-Expression

Man, alone among all living creatures, is highly conscious of himself as a distinct entity. He has "personality." Man remembers his past acts, meditates upon the present, and dreams of the future. He regards his whole life as something of a unity. He is keenly aware of his differences from other men and from all other creatures. Man is certain that he has a "self" to be expressed. When he speaks, he "announces" himself, as it were. Children, too, interrupt conversations between adults simply as a reminder of their own presence.

If you analyze your judgments of your fellow students or of your friends of longer standing, you may be surprised at the extent to which you judge them by their speech. Their personality and character, their culture and general intellect, the extent of their knowledge, as well as the nature of their feelings, emotions, and general attitudes, you measure and evaluate largely through their speech. Thus you have long recognized the importance of speech as an indication of all that the individual is.

There are at least three levels upon which self-expression may exist. On the lowest level is *the mere desire to attract attention;* it is open and avowed among children and perpetual adolescents, but is camouflaged by normal adults. Then, there is *the desire to relieve the pressure of extreme emotional states.* This is a substitute for the physical reaction that might have been expected from primitive men. It has been found in convalescent hospitals that there is great therapeutic value in discussion. It permits men who are struggling to rehabilitate themselves and to adjust to new modes of living necessitated by the loss of a limb or by invalidism to express their concerns, their worries, and their discouragements. Expression is important to everyone in times of emotional stress. It is an indispensable part of mental and emotional health. Finally, there is the kind of expression which springs from the enthusiastic possession of an idea, from *the desire to express an intense conviction*. Some poems and some speeches, such as Francis Scott Key's *The Star-Spangled Banner* and Patrick Henry's famous appeal for liberty or death, seem to spring almost spontaneously into being, so great is the depth of feeling which gives them birth. We must never underrate the importance of expressive speech as a contributor to mental and emotional health and as an outlet for creative impulses.

Speech as Communication

Since man is gregarious, it is not unusual for him to speak only to attract the attention of others. "Hello" spoken in passing an acquaintance on the street has this function. But man also talks because he has much to communicate. And by listening to others he in turn can

Whether you are talking over the day's assignment with a fellow student or meeting any of the other numerous opportunities and demands for effective speech, your aim is to make certain that you and your ideas are properly and fully understood. Clear thinking, genuine feeling, and communicative speaking are daily requirements for us all.

profit. Through this communicative function of speech man is able to learn what has been discovered by his predecessors and by his contemporaries. It is useful to be able to explain processes, objects, or situations to another person or to hear them explained. In an age in which the telephone, the motion picture to which the dimension of sound was added many years ago, radio, and television are so much a part of daily life, the increasing importance of communicative speech is evident.

The number of misunderstandings in our daily living—at home, at work, and at play—is evidence of our shortcomings in speech. All too many of these misunderstandings lead to unpleasant family relations, loss of friends, and failure to win promotion on one's job. Communication makes fairly constant and important demands upon us. Certainly each of us could greatly increase his effectiveness in daily living by becoming a more skilled communicator.

Speech as Social Control

In prehistoric times, before man developed a language, physical might must have been the chief means of controlling the activities of others. The strong dominated the weak. In time the weak came to understand the will of the strong as it was expressed in threats, commands, and questions. Thus the necessity for physical force diminished. With this change there developed the curious situation that skill in speech became of itself a weapon by which human behavior could be controlled. The pen—or tongue—became mightier than the sword. The symbol became more powerful than the thing it had at first symbolized. This is far from being universally true, but it is shown in the numerous ways in which "brain" commands "brawn." It is apparent that normally we get others to do what we wish by argument, persuasion, suggestion, or simple request much more frequently than we do by resort to physical violence. Thus children and even infants exercise amazing control over the behavior of their parents!

Leadership depends upon speech for social control. In *The Silent Billion Speak*, Frank C. Laubach has written of the twelve hundred million people—over half of the human race—who cannot read or write: "You think it is a pity they cannot read, but the real tragedy is that they have no voice in public affairs; they never vote; they are never represented in any conference; they are the silent victims, the forgotten men, driven like animals mutely submitting in every age . . . ."

But before we expend too much sympathy upon those who have no voice in their own affairs we should consider what use those of us who are able to read and write make of our multiple opportunities. It is small wonder that Lee De Forest, inventor of the audion, by which long-distance radio was made possible, exclaimed in despair over the poor quality of the programs presented through the miracle of world-wide radio broadcasting. And the President's Commission on Higher Education observed: "We have worked wonders by the application of technology to the problems of our physical environment, but we have scarcely touched the fringes of its possibilities in the realm of human relations." In the United States, one adult in every ten has had some period of study in college. Yet our use of our native tongue remains woefully inadequate.

Our own experience teaches that what we say and how we say it has much to do with how well we get along with others. "With speech we govern men," said Benjamin Disraeli. Gustave Le Bon, the great French pioneer sociologist, believed that "the memorable events of history are the visible effects of the invisible changes of human thought." Those *invisible changes* occur as man speaks to man, earnestly, thoughtfully, convincingly. Yet all the unsolved problems that plague our community and national relationships combine to remind us how pitifully unsatisfactory are the words we use and the ways in which we use them in the realm of human relations. Today we may exclaim with Job, "How forcible are right words!" And now even more than then we must be aware of the tragic result for humanity of the right words being spoken in the wrong way or for wrong ends.

THE VALUES OF SPEECH TRAINING FOR YOU

You naturally desire to become as effective as possible in the ordinary speech situations with which you will be confronted. You will wish to add to your knowledge and convictions such skill in their expression as will give them maximum effectiveness. In order to achieve this goal, it is important first of all to discover your specific speech problems and then to work toward solving them. Consider the following brief statements written by students during their first-semester speech course. As you read these self-analyses, check them against your judgment of yourself. How do your needs compare with the needs of these students? How do you differ markedly from them? Can you see any means by which the study of speech can remedy the weaknesses they discuss?

STUDENT A

When I try to make an analysis of my own speaking, I find that it is both hard and easy to do. In the first place, I am too self-conscious and have a great feeling of inferiority. I think that this is my main trouble. If I could get rid of this feeling, I think it would be easy to get rid of the rest of my faults. For instance, when I get up in front of a group, even if it is a group with whom I am acquainted, I always feel a little lower than the rest. I think they are looking down on me and inwardly making fun of me. I have this trouble in everyday life, as well as in school life. When I get this feeling I get excited and lose all my nerve. I pitch my voice too high, look out the window to get away from the faces of my audience, clasp my hands (thus preventing myself from making gestures that really do come to me), and many other such things. As for force, I think sometimes I have too much, for I nearly shout when I get excited. If I pause for emphasis, I forget what I have said and have to stumble around finding some words. When I do find the words, I cannot open my mouth to say them—my lower jaw just won't work.

However, I think that in spite of these troubles, I can overcome them a little bit if I speak on a subject that I really like or know very well. Although I sometimes get my words mixed in this type of speech, it is easier to substitute other words.

STUDENT B

In the beginning of my speech course, here is the way I figured. I would get up and say my talk in the allotted time given, always be prepared to give my speech at the time assigned to me, then let it go at that. Then I began to realize it was more than just having the nerve to get up in front of the class and say something that didn't amount to much. I then began to make an outline and choose my topic so that I would be interested in it, because if I wasn't interested in it, how could I present it to the class and make them interested in it? The next thing I tried to do was to sell myself to the class by humor, personality, etc., and then try to take command of the situation. For me it was rather hard to do because my eyes were always wanting to look out of the window. When I did this it showed that perhaps I was getting disinterested in the subject, hence the audience would lose its interest, and all my work had gone for naught.

Another factor which is quite important is how you look to the audience. Are you unshaven, is your hair combed, etc.? I believe the only way in which I can become a better speaker is by more practice, because, as I see it, the more you do a certain thing, the more you realize how imperfect you are. When you get to this stage you can really pick out your mistakes one by one and correct them one by one.

You have noted that these students were concerned with both direct and indirect speech problems. They wanted to be able to stand before a group and deliver a plain, simple, unpretentious speech which would hold their audience's attention and interest and win agreement

Sincerity, directness, and the urge to communicate—taken for granted in such informal gatherings as the one pictured here—result in good public speaking.

with their points of view. But they were also concerned with acquiring social ease and confidence sufficient for the purposes of their ordinary daily life. The advertisers of patent remedies had not quite convinced them that their inadequacies and failures were all due to bad breath, fallen arches, or athlete's foot. These students wanted to be able to enter easily and confidently into all sorts of conversations, to be free of self-consciousness in groups, to overcome the bogy of stage fright, and to be able to express themselves effectively in their talks before an audience. They realized that speech is a tool which they must use in almost every area of their lives, at work and at play, and that they need more skill in its use.

SKILLS YOU WILL NEED

A conscientious study and practice of public speaking should develop many of the skills mentioned and perhaps some others besides. Here are some of the things you can hope to accomplish:

1. Primarily, of course, *you will improve in the art of speaking.* You should become a better conversationalist and more effective in discussion. You should develop the ability to stand on your feet before an audience and express your ideas clearly, effectively, and with mastery over fear. It is toward this basic goal that much of the work of this course is directed. As inevitable outgrowths of the work, however, the following results should also be sought.

2. *You will come to a much clearer understanding of yourself:* how well your mind responds to the demands you make upon it, how your personality affects others, how vivid your imagination really is, how much you may expect to accomplish through self-discipline and concentrated effort. Will this be of much value to you? The three greatest thinkers of ancient Greece believed so. Plato declared that it is more difficult (and more important) to govern oneself than to govern a city. Socrates suggested "Know thyself!" as the guiding motto of human lives. Aristotle said that our true selves are not what we are, or what we have achieved in the past, but what we are capable of becoming. To these three, and to most later thinkers, self-knowledge is the starting point to self-mastery.

3. *You will gain a better understanding of other people* as you develop greater sensitivity to their reactions and deeper knowledge of common human motives. This enlarged understanding is the key not only to effective speaking but to effective social living. It presupposes, first, a genuine interest in other people; second, a keen sense of observation; and third, a willingness to adapt yourself readily and unobtrusively to changes in the moods and interests of those about you.

4. *You will evolve clearer, more logical thought processes and more orderly habits of thinking.* Many people admit that they understand their own thoughts best when they explain them to others. Doubtless all of us have had this experience at one time or another. Writing out your thought is probably the best way to clarify it; for when you have it down on paper you can examine it critically. But it is impossible for us to do this most of the time—when we are explaining something to a friend, over the telephone, on a street corner, or across the bridge table. We must develop orderliness and fluency in the spontaneous expression of our thoughts, and a very effective method of achieving this skill is found in the discipline of speaking before an audience.

5. *You will develop a deeper appreciation for the character traits of generous human sympathy, earnest sincerity, genuine enthusiasm, and straightforward honesty*—qualities without which no speech can really succeed. Emptiness, pretense, pronounced egotism, and bluff

are nowhere so easily revealed as in speech. More than two thousand years ago the elder Cato defined the true orator as "a good man skilled in speaking." Ralph Waldo Emerson made the same point more forcefully when he said, "What you are stands over you . . . and thunders so that I cannot hear what you say to the contrary." You will find yourself warming to speakers who are unquestionably sincere and paying little attention to those whose enthusiasm is artificially generated to suit the needs of the hour.

6. *You will learn to observe the world around you with keener vision, to respond to it more sensitively, and to take a more intelligent interest in the course of events.* The good speaker, like the good reporter, must have the ability to see in any situation those details which are fundamentally important and interesting. To the extent that you develop the psychological characteristics of the public speaker, you will find yourself weighing and assessing situations and events for their speech value; that is, you will attempt to discover their true significance and the elements of interest which they hold for you and for other people.

7. *You will increase your aptitude for evaluating what you hear.* You should become not only a better speaker but a better listener. Knowing what to look for and what to expect, you will derive far greater enjoyment from hearing good speakers, and you will be much better able to guard yourself against the appeals of demagogic and self-seeking pleaders. This is of particular importance in the present era, when we are exposed as never before to propaganda and to pressure groups of all sorts. It has been charged that the great danger of mass education is that it produces a population literate enough to read and to listen widely but insufficiently discriminating in its choice of what to believe. As you study the technique of influencing audiences, you should increase your ability to discriminate between true sentiment and mere sentimentality, between honest patriotism and jingoism, between logic and rationalization, between sincerity and skillful pretense. You should progress in what some have called the basic aim of all education—the ability to tell the difference between a truth and a lie.

To conclude this discussion, the following statement is offered. It deals with but one kind of speaking, but the author would doubtless agree to the extension of his remarks to include careful training in general speech skills. Alexander Meiklejohn, college president and progressive educator, in his book *The Liberal College*, declared:

. . . when I try to single out from the long line of students one group which will stand forth as intellectually the best—best in college work and best in promise of future intellectual achievement . . . much as I should like to do so, I cannot draw the line around my own favorite students of philosophy, nor the leaders in mathematics, nor those successful in biology; nor could I fairly award the palm to the Phi Beta Kappa men who have excelled in all their subjects. It seems to me that stronger than any other group, tougher in intellectual fiber, keener in intellectual interest, better equipped to battle with coming problems, are the college debaters—the boys who, apart from their regular studies, band themselves together for intellectual controversy with each other and with their friends of other colleges.

YOUR ETHICAL OBLIGATIONS AS A SPEAKER

Thus far we have been considering the positive values and uses of speech to the individual and to society. But speech, like any other skill, may be used for evil or for good. The ancient Sophists were accused of teaching their students "to make the worse cause seem the better." Is this still an art which speakers desire to learn? Are speech skills sought so that supersalesmen can sell inferior products, designing politicians win votes, and promoters ensnare the gullible? Is it true that public speaking is ordinarily regarded as an instrument of power over others for the achievement of personal ends? How universal is the view expressed by Sinclair Lewis's Babbitt: "It certainly is a fine thing to be able to orate. I've sometimes thought I had a little talent that way myself, and I know darn well that one reason why a four-flushing old back number like Chann Mott can get away with it in real estate is just because he can make a good talk, even when he hasn't got a doggone thing to say."

This rather dismal picture does not, of course, represent a complete view of speech training. What it does do is warn against unethical practices which the sincere speaker must avoid. Speech is power, and before it is acquired it is highly proper to ask how that power is to be used.

Thomas Carlyle raised a crucial question when he asked, "For if a good speaker—an eloquent speaker—is not speaking the truth, is there a more horrid kind of object in creation?" Among Carlyle's contemporaries, the question was answered by Thomas Babington Macaulay: "We see doctrines, which cannot bear a close inspection, triumph perpetually in drawing rooms, in debating societies, and even in legislative or judicial assemblies." In our own day the problem is just as pressing, and most of us would agree with Professor Carl Dahlstrom that "society does not need more individuals who have ways and means of selling themselves, of taking advantage of the ignorant and the sentimental, of putting something over on gullible people, of vainly seeking even a noble end *via* stinkingly corrupt means; but society is sadly in need of men and women who can become proficient and known in their professions without loss of personal integrity or sacrifice of self-respect."

There is an important positive point here for college men and women. If in our time demagogues succeed in making the weaker cause appear the stronger, it will be evidence that educated persons who know the truth lack the training and ability to present it more effectively than the demagogues present their half-truths or even untruths. If there are those who misuse the power of speech and turn it to unethical ends, then it is truly imperative that those who serve truth be highly skilled in speech.

The Speaker and His Audience

Audience adaptation offers one of the crucial problems in the ethics of speech. There is one type of adaptation in which the speaker tries to "give his audience what it wants"—to tell it what it wishes to hear, whatever that may be. The speaker who does this varies his politics, his religion, and his convictions and beliefs to suit whatever hearers he happens to be addressing. He is liberal for the liberals and conservative for the conservatives. He is the platform "yes man," who does not lead his audience, but is driven by it, to the conclusion which his speech upholds. In politics this kind of speaker is known as a faithful wheel horse, who can be expected to veer in whatever direction is deemed necessary by party policy makers.

A contrast with this abject surrender to audience demands is Socrates, who asserted his independence of spirit when, at the trial which resulted in his condemnation and death, he told his judges, "I would rather die having spoken after my manner, than speak in your manner and live."

There is, of course, a desirable mid-point between subservience to an audience and the refusal to meet it on its own terms. The ethical responsibility of anyone who attempts to influence other people is to try to do for them what they most need. If they are prejudiced, try to make their thinking more objective; if they are indifferent through ignorance, try to arouse their interest by showing them the significance of the facts. A good speaker neither rejects his audience nor panders to it, but seeks to lead it where he sincerely believes it ought to go.

The Speaker and His Subject Matter

Many students of ethics have called attention to the concept of "moral thoughtfulness," or "the moral obligation of being intelligent." There is, they declare, a moral obligation to be properly informed concerning the urgent questions of general public interest. Certainly a speaker has a "moral obligation of being intelligent" about any subject which he elects to discuss before an audience. To present an argument or explain a situation in vague generalities, rather than with specific facts, is a form of deceit. The speaker pretends to an authority and a thoughtfulness which he does not possess. A speaker who denounces governmental policies which he has not taken the trouble to understand is indulging in a form of malicious platform gossip. There is no substitute for knowing what you are talking about. Cocksure assertion cannot take the place of careful research. As much harm may result from ignorant misstatement as from deliberate lying, and an audience has the right to expect that whatever a speaker asserts as fact is true.

A speaker should be especially careful when citing authorities in support of his ideas. If he is quoting directly, he should make sure (1) that he has quoted exactly and without any misleading omissions and (2) that the quoted matter is fairly representative of the whole attitude of the authority. Upton Sinclair pointed out in one of his lectures that the Bible *could* be quoted as directly stating that "there is no God." It is only necessary to omit a portion of the verse "The fool sayeth in his heart that there is no God." Using such a method, one might misrepresent any authority as saying the precise opposite of what he really means. It is frequently possible also to find isolated passages which, when lifted out of their context, give a wholly false view of the authority's position.

The use of illustrative stories presents another ethical problem. Speakers have always told humorous stories as true experiences of their own, and most audiences have learned to accept this as a conventional device. However, it is easy to slip from this practice to another which is not so easily excused: the invention of illustrative stories which are cited as "proof" of a point the speaker is making. Thus, a speaker who is urging a reform of living conditions in the slums might invent several illustrative stories which he presents to the audience as being true. They may truly reflect his conviction as to what the situation is like. This does not alter the fact that he is trying to "prove" his contentions by fabricated evidence. Whenever a speaker cites specific instances in support of his argument, he should be as careful of their authenticity as he would be of statistics or other facts.

Rhetorical exaggeration presents another problem in discrimination. Sometimes it serves as a merely conventional form of courtesy, as in the opening sentence of a speech by Chauncey Depew, the late lawyer, orator, and politician, to a group of his New York Central Railroad Company associates: "The pleasantest day to me of all the year is the day that I meet you on my annual return from Europe." Sometimes it serves as a humorous device, for which purpose all humorists have freely used it. Frequently rhetorical exaggeration is used to emphasize a point. When this is done, the question arises whether or not the point itself has been misrepresented in the process. Consider, for example, the following extract from a speech on government in business: "When the Shipping Board wishes to hire or fire an office boy, it must take a referendum of 110,000,000 people." This, of course, is an obvious overstatement; but without offering any proof beyond this assertion the speaker went on, "Is it any wonder, then, that the Shipping Board operation costs us something like $25,000,000 a year for the experiment?" It is evident that the speaker intended his audience to be influenced by his exaggeration, in which case it ceases to be rhetorical and becomes simply a misrepresentation of fact.

The Speaker's Character

Aristotle pointed out that all persuasive speaking must arise from one of three sources: facts and logic, emotional appeals, or the confidence which listeners have in the character of the speaker. Just how powerful an influence is exercised by the last of these three factors may be indicated by popular reaction to three great leaders of the immediate past. In 1933, President Roosevelt's buoyant optimism and confidence gave persuasive power to his assurance that "the only thing we have to fear is fear itself." In the same way, unfortunately, did German faith in the sincerity and patriotism of Adolf Hitler help build the Nazi strength which led to World War II. Similarly, the typical cry "Good old Winnie!" indicated how Winston Churchill's wartime audiences placed confidence in his character and personality. When a speaker commands such confidence in his honesty, his effectiveness in winning an audience to his point of view is greatly strengthened. How different is the effect of those speakers who have, as Shakespeare said, "that glib and oily art to speak and purpose not!"

As his perfect public speaker, Quintilian sought one who would be "utterly noble alike in thought and speech." It is demonstrated in our everyday relationships that character is a requirement for good speaking. We all know how readily we take upon trust the word of some people, whereas we scarcely believe others even when their statements are thoroughly bolstered by evidence. A businessman knows that his reputation is his most precious asset. It is likewise an invaluable asset for a speaker to be known as honest, reliable, and trustworthy.

A speaker who is willing to sacrifice his convictions for the advantage he may gain in addressing a particular audience faces a grave danger. Insincerity will almost always betray itself, for it is no easy matter to keep from stumbling and hesitating when one's words contradict one's thoughts. But whether or not the speaker is a clever enough actor to conceal his duplicity, we must agree with Demosthenes, who said in his "Oration on the Crown," "What greater crime can an orator be charged with than that his opinions and his language are not the same?"

CONCLUSION

The role of speech is vital and functional in the present and future life of each college student. Speech is good or bad in terms of how well it serves our needs as members of society. Speech serves an individual well when his mastery of it is sufficient to permit him to express his variety of moods, attitudes, feelings, and ideas; when it provides a satisfactory means of communication with his fellows; and when it enables him to exercise a desirable degree of social influence and control. Through a study of the nature and functions of speech, you will develop many personal and social values that go far beyond the conversational and public-speaking situations.

As you seek to develop your potentialities as a speaker, you should not lose sight of ethical implications. You have a personal integrity that should never be sacrificed. You should use speech not as a means of achieving that will-o'-the-wisp popularity, but as a tool for helping to establish your own ideas and ideals.

EXERCISES AND BIBLIOGRAPHY

Exercises

1. Prepare a three-minute speech on one of the following topics:
    a. Why I am proud (or ashamed) of my home community.
    b. What I expect to get out of college.

    c. Why I am planning to be a doctor (or lawyer, teacher, merchant).
    d. The kind of speaker I admire most (or least).
    e. Why I am interested in politics (or literature, sports, music, dramatics, debate).
    f. The most interesting (or exciting, adventurous, embarrassing, humorous) experience I have had.

These topics are merely suggestive. You yourself are the only one who can decide what you wish to talk about. Take one of these suggestions and narrow it down to a phase which will fit well into a three-minute talk. You could not expect to tell us all about your home town, for example, in that time. If you choose this topic, decide which *one* feature of your home town is most admirable or deplorable, and center your thoughts upon that. Decide precisely what your point of view is to be, such as, "I am proud of my home town because of its progressiveness." Then select the illustrations, facts, and arguments with which you will support this assertion. Any of the other topics should be similarly limited in scope. Develop your topic in such a way as to draw heavily upon your experience and interests. Once you have determined your point of view, be sure to use only such materials in your speech as will help you to establish it.

2. Introduce yourself to the other members of the class in a statement requiring not more than three minutes. Tell them interesting highlights of your life, including your education to date, your plans, hobbies, interests, favorite sports, favorite recreations, travel experiences, and the like. Tell them the things about yourself that you would find it interesting to know about them.

3. Give a three-minute talk on some pet peeve—something about which you feel keenly. This might be some type of radio program, some public figure, or some motion-picture actor or actress.

4. Write an analysis of your own potentialities as a speaker. What experience have you had, both as a speaker and as a listener? What personality traits do you have which you feel will help you in becoming an effective speaker? Do you have any which will handicap you? How can you best go about developing the desirable traits and eliminating the undesirable?

5. Prepare to speak in class on the uses which you would like to make of increased skill in public speaking. How can you utilize this skill to benefit both yourself and society? How should training in speech improve both your citizenship and your vocational success?

6. As you listen to the first round of speeches by your classmates, write a one-sentence characterization of each speaker's personality as revealed in his speech. Keep your characterizations for later reference, to see

how your opinions change as the students gain increased skill in revealing and utilizing their abilities, ideas, and attitudes.

Bibliography

Emerson, Ralph Waldo, "Eloquence," in *Society and Solitude*.

Jacks, L. P., "Government by Talk," *Hibbert Journal,* XXII (October, 1923), 5–19.

Jones, Edgar De Witt, *Lords of Speech* (Willett, Clark, 1937).

de Laguna, Grace Andrus, *Speech: Its Function and Development* (Yale University Press, 1927).

Laird, Charlton, *The Miracle of Language* (Premier Books, 1957).

Langer, Susanne K., *Philosophy in a New Key* (Pelican Books, reprinted from Harvard University Press, 1942 edition).

Lippmann, Walter, *Public Opinion* (Macmillan, 1922).

Quintilian, *Institutes of Oratory,* Book I and Chapters 15–21 of Book II.

ILLUSTRATIVE SPEECH

Ben Kuroki, of Japanese ancestry, was born and reared on a farm in Hershey, Nebraska. The day after Pearl Harbor he went into the United States Air Force. In a B–24 he flew 30 missions, blasting Nazi targets in Europe. There was a rule against trusting a Japanese-American in the Pacific. Through the intercession of Representative (later Senator) Carl Curtis, of Nebraska, and others, Secretary of War Henry Stimson granted Kuroki special permission. Flying 28 bombing missions over his parents' homeland, he was a gunner in a B–29 which bombed his mother's home town, Yokohama. He wanted no doubt of his loyalty. With two medals, he returned at war's end. So did his four brothers.

Ben remembers most vividly his nervousness at the luncheon preceding his delivery of the following speech before the New York *Herald Tribune* Forum in 1945. There was an imposing array of distinguished folk present, including a general who might be very critical. Ben remembers, too, the warm handclasp of that general after the speech. In a few years Ben Kuroki had graduated in journalism from the University of Nebraska. In its June 12, 1950, issue *Time* described as "The 59th Mission" his purchase of a newspaper. Five years ago he moved to Michigan, where he became owner and editor of the *Williamston Enterprise*. Here, near the state's capital, he now lives with his wife and three young daughters. Already he has doubled his paper's circulation and won a position of respect and affection in his community's religious, fraternal, business, and governmental life. Headlined *The Detroit Free Press* in a feature article on newspaperman Kuroki, May 6, 1960: "He Writes His Editorials as He Fought—with Gusto."

As you read this speech, ask yourself the questions: Why is the message of this speech so unanswerable? What gives this speech its power?

Nebraska Boy Over Japan

BY BEN KUROKI

The town I came from is called Hershey, Nebraska. It's near the Platte River, between Cozad and Ogallala, about twelve miles down the road from North Platte. We've got a farm there—my father and mother and my brother George and I. We raise sugar beets and seed potatoes. Dirt farming isn't a very easy life, but it suits us fine.

I never traveled much. I'd go down to North Platte for feed, or go fishing up in the mountains over in Colorado or down to Chicago to see my sister. I figured some day I'd get to New York, but I didn't plan on visiting Tokyo. Japan is the land of my ancestors, but I never had any desire to go there. And yet, one morning like a lot of other American boys, I started out down the road from my house and I was headed for Tokyo. And like a lot of other American boys, I got there the hard way.

The day after Pearl Harbor my kid brother and I piled in the Chevrolet and drove 150 miles down to Grand Island and enlisted. I remember, after we were sworn in and before we got our uniforms, we were on a train headed for camp. There were some people on the train and they stared at me and said, "What's that Jap doing in the Army?" They said it good and loud, so I'd hear. It just knocked me off my feet. After coming from a town where I knew everybody, I suddenly realized that no matter where I was born or what was in my heart, to these people I was an alien. All the way to camp people kept looking at me, staring at me. I'll never forget that train ride.

I went into the air force and applied for flying. Somehow my papers got lost; they always seemed to be lost, or held up somewhere or going through channels. When I finally got overseas it was as a clerk with the 93d Bomb Group. It was quite an outfit—the newspapers called it Ted Timberlake's Flying Circus.

Those were the early days in England and things weren't going so good. Liberators were getting knocked off like flies, and there was a shortage of gunners. I remember one day in England, I picked up a magazine and read about an organization called the Native Sons and Daughters of the Golden West. They had a plan to isolate all Japanese-Americans down in the swampland somewhere. I kind of blew my stack when I read the article. I volunteered for gunner. I had five days of training, and then the outfit pulled out for Africa.

I flew my first bombing mission over Bizerte. Our tail gunner got it on that mission and I moved back to the tail turret and that's where I stayed. We tagged some rough missions those days—Naples, Wiener-Neustadt, Rome. We had a saying, "On the way to the target you're flying for Uncle Sam. On the way back, you're flying for yourself."

My twenty-fourth mission was to Romania, to a place called Ploesti. It was the first low-level raid on that target. It was murder. Two out of nine planes in my squadron came back.

I finished my tour of missions and our outfit was set to go home, but I volunteered to stick around and fly five more. My kid brother still wasn't overseas and so I figured I'd just check off five missions for him.

The last mission was Muenster, where flak ripped open my turret, the plexiglass cut my face, and the blast ripped off my oxygen mask. A gunner named O'Connel from Superior, Wisconsin, got a mask and held it to my face and everything came out okay.

Then I came back to the States, back to Nebraska. I felt like a kid on Christmas morning. Everybody looked at my ribbons and shook my hand. It was wonderful to know that people appreciated what I'd done and respected me for it.

When I reported back to the Army in California, they asked me to go on a radio program. That was still pretty early, when returned veterans were something special. I really felt like a big wheel. I invited some of my buddies to see the show, and they all sat there in the front row. And then an hour before we were to start, word came through that I couldn't go on. They didn't object to my being a tail gunner. They didn't mind my having two D.F.C.'s. But it seemed I was a Japanese-American and that made it a controversial issue.

In California I met a boy I'd flown with in Europe, Ed Bates, a kind of rough-and-tumble kid. He'd had his fingers frozen off on a mission. It didn't seem to bother him. Nothing bothered Bates, except his brother. His brother had just been killed in the Pacific. He went half crazy when he heard the news. Bates wanted another tour in the Pacific, but they wouldn't let him go on account of his hand. Maybe that was when I first got the idea I wasn't through with this war. And when I got to Denver, that cinched it. I started to get into a taxicab with somebody, and he said he wouldn't ride with "no lousy Jap." I was wearing my wings and all my ribbons, but it didn't matter. I almost cried, I was so mad.

After that, it was Tokyo or bust. I wanted to fly in a B-29 and for about three months I listened to people tell me, no, it was impossible; there were regulations against it. But I also ran into some people who were willing to go to bat for me—Dr. Deutsch, vice-president of the University of California; Chester Rowell, of the San Francisco *Chronicle,* and Ray Lyman Wilbur, of Stanford University—a lot of people all over the country who believed my record earned me the right to be trusted. A Congressman from Nebraska, a former commander of the American Legion from Wisconsin, the head of the War Relocation Authority—they all put up a holler, and the next thing I knew I was training for B-29's. It gave me a little courage to meet people everywhere who didn't judge a man by his grandfather's nationality or the color of his skin.

It was just before I left for the Pacific I heard about Gorden Jergeson. I guess he was the closest friend I ever had. Back in Hershey we played together since we were kids. We were on the basketball team. In high school he was president of the class and I was vice-president. I got a pass and went to see his folks. We sat there and his mother remembered how we used to go duck hunting and I'd come by at 3 in the morning and honk the horn and wake everybody up. Gorden was killed in the Solomon Islands. That was another reason for going to Tokyo.

We flew out of an airfield on Tinian in the Marianas. The name of our bomber was "Honorable Sad-Saki." I flew twenty-eight missions in the Pacific, over Kobe and Osaka and finally Tokyo. I even had a crack at my mother's home town—Yokohama.

When the boys in my outfit found out I'd flown a tour over Europe they figured I had holes in my head for volunteering again. I used to kid around and tell them that communications were all cut off from Japan and that this was the only way I could visit my Uncle Nagasaki. I never talked much about my real reason for being over there.

Not only did I go to war to fight the fascist ideas of Germany and Japan, but also to fight against a very few Americans who fail to understand the principles of freedom and equality upon which this country was founded.

I'm no authority; I'm not an expert or a big wheel. I don't know anything that any boy from Nebraska couldn't tell you. But I know this: I fought with a lot of men in this war, all kinds—a Polish gunner, a Jewish engineer, a German bombardier and even a full-blooded Dakota Indian. I saw men wounded, and whatever land their grand-fathers came from, their blood was always the same color. And what-ever church they went to, the screams of pain sounded just about the same.

I've had fifty-eight bombing missions now, and I'm still tired enough so my hands shake, and plenty of nights I don't sleep so good. I'd like to go home to Nebraska and forget the war, and just lie under a tree somewhere and take it easy. It's hard to realize that the war is not over for me. Not for a lot of us, Jewish-Americans, Italian-Americans, Negro-Americans, Japanese-Americans. While there is still hatred and prejudice, our fight goes on. Back in Nebraska on our farm, when I planted a seed, I knew that after a while I'd get a crop. That's the way it was with a lot of us in this war: we went to plant the seeds to bring in a crop of decency and peace for our families and our children.

Back in high school in Nebraska, one of the things they taught me was that America is a land where it isn't race or religion that makes free men. That's why I went to Tokyo. I went to fight for my country, where freedom isn't color but a way of life, and all men are created equal until they prove otherwise. That's an old idea we have in Hershey, Nebraska, just down the highway from Cozad, which is near North Platte.

CHAPTER 2

CONTENTS

Senator Hubert Humphrey is known for the vitality of his convictions and the vividness of his speaking. (Wide World Photos, Inc.)

HOW TO SPEAK
COMMUNICATIVELY

As a listener you have doubtless heard much speaking that is
distressingly uncommunicative. Perhaps some of your professors,
when they are lecturing, dull the effect of what they are saying by
speaking in a flat monotone, or by keeping their eyes fixed on their
notes; or they may speak with a great deal of vigor, gesture freely,
keep their eyes fixed on the class, yet all the while pour out the lecture
material without any indication that it has any kind of special meaning
to the particular students who compose their class. Surely you have
also heard lectures in which the speaker genuinely "talked over his
ideas with his audience," making you and your classmates feel as
though he were eager to share with you ideas and facts which would
be helpful to you in your own thinking.

There are many differences between good speaking and bad—
but the fundamental difference is really between *communicating with*
an audience and merely *talking at* it. This is a distinction you make
when you are a listener, even though you may make it unconsciously.
It explains why you are interested in some speeches and bored by
others. The genuinely communicative speech may or may not be clear
and purposive; you may or may not understand just what point the
speaker is trying to make. Further, it may or may not be convincing;
you may agree or disagree with the speaker's point of view. But you
do feel that the speaker is talking to you. The qualities of clarity and
persuasiveness are other attributes that distinguish good speaking from
bad, but whenever you hear someone talking your first reaction is
this: *Is he actually talking to me?* Only when the answer is clearly
"Yes" is there an effective speaker-listener relationship established.

This chapter should help you identify the factors necessary to
communication—and show you how you may make steady progress
toward improving your own talking, whether in conversation, in
discussions, or in public speaking.

THE COMMUNICATIVE QUALITY

Perhaps you have memorized the Gettysburg Address, and have read others of Lincoln's magnificent speeches. You have probably admired the greatness of his spirit, the clarity of his thought, and his command over a style that could vary from colloquial intimacy to elevated grandeur. These are among the reasons why his speeches are regarded as masterpieces of the art of public address. But when his principal biographer, Carl Sandburg, undertook to describe in *Abraham Lincoln: The Prairie Years* the one factor which in his judgment constituted the special quality that gave greatness to the speaking of Lincoln, this is what he said: "Was this oratory? debating? The man, Abraham Lincoln, was speaking to thousands of people as if he and another man were driving in a buggy across the prairie, exchanging their thoughts."

Booker T. Washington, speaking throughout the North and the South on behalf of better race relations in the closing years of the nineteenth century, appeared in thousands of packed auditoriums and was highly praised for his factual soundness and calm reasoning; yet the commendation that he valued most highly was the comment of one listener: "If I were seated in the third balcony behind a pillar, Mr. Washington still seemed to take me by the lapels of my coat and speak directly and personally to me." This characteristic of speaking so that every auditor will feel that the talk is aimed "directly and personally" at him is what we mean by the communicative quality.

Communicative speech is not addressed *at* or *toward* its hearers; it is talk *with* and *to* its listeners. The difference (to steal a phrase from Mark Twain) is the difference between the lightning and the lightning bug.

Communication is, first of all, a *two-way process*. It is essentially "conversation" in that it requires a flow of meanings that go from the speaker to the listeners, then back to the speaker (as interpretations of their responses) and then once more back to the listeners (with the manner of speaking now changed to take account of those responses). Sometimes this process is called *circular response*. Details of how to achieve these results will be discussed later in this chapter.

Second, communication does not *deliver* a message to listeners, but *arouses* responses in them. If you hold a bag of peanuts in your hand, you can physically give a peanut to each of your auditors. But when

Both interest and concentration are shown by this group at the Discussion Leadership Center, Syracuse University.

you are speaking *about* peanuts, you can only utter words and use gestures and vocal tones that will *stir up* in their minds their own thoughts on the subject—thoughts that will resemble what you are saying, but that will be different because the listeners' experiences with and attitudes toward peanuts are not the same as yours. Thus, for you to continue speaking sensibly about peanuts to your listeners, you have to respond alertly to the cues they give you indicating what kinds of meanings are being aroused. This problem, too, will be discussed more fully later.

Third, communication is *creative* as well as *reproductive.* In part you speak to your audience what you have prepared; you remember and reproduce. But in part you create new approaches; you may spend more time than you had planned on one phase of your talk (if the audience fails to understand, or seems to resist your reasoning), and this means you must inevitably reduce what you had planned to say on another part. Instead of parroting words you had memorized, you make instant decisions on phrasing as you go along—precisely as you do in conversation. Thus communication has life, vitality, and immediacy—once again reflecting the essential fact that it is a live process of *exchange* between you and your listeners.

Rapport and Circular Response

Rapport is a sympathetic relationship of mutual understanding and feeling. When the speaker and the audience are *en rapport* they are agreed on the importance of the subject being discussed; they are both interested in it—whether or not their views agree; and they feel mutual respect for one another's intelligence and sincerity. Such cooperation is impossible unless the speaker cares what his listeners think about what he is saying and makes his concern evident to them. Perhaps by the use of questions, or personal illustrations, or the personal pronouns, or by the communicative quality of his voice and gestures, he will speak in a manner that makes them know beyond any doubt that he is not merely "telling them" but is also "considering with them" the merits of the topic. Once again to quote from Sandburg's description of Lincoln as a speaker: "He used words natural to farmers shucking corn in a cold November wind or carpenters putting the adze to oak rafters." This goes far beyond using words that are familiar to the listeners; it has more to do with attitudes in common, with a sympathetic understanding of their problems, with the speaker's assurance that he is with them in their problems and aspirations.

Circular response is a mechanism through which rapport is established and maintained. The speaker must not be so self-centered, so intent on "remembering" what he plans to say, that he is oblivious of the reactions of his listeners. When he mentions a fact which seems to him important, a speaker should watch his listeners intently to discover whether they also consider the fact of significance; then he modifies his subsequent remarks in response to what he interprets their reaction to be. If he thinks they have not grasped the importance

A good storyteller always has an attentive audience. (Library of Congress)

of his fact, he may repeat it, or amplify it, or use an illustration. If he thinks they do not accept it, he may cite an authority or support it with another fact that they will accept. This kind of speaking is possible only when the speaker is so attentive to his audience that he is stimulated by its reactions, just as he tries to stimulate his listeners by what he is saying.

Circular response requires alertness while the speaker is delivering his speech. However, preparation may be made for audience responses, unpredictable though they may be. For one thing, while preparing the speech, the speaker should by all means take account of the experience of his audience. He will plan to say "you and I," rather than merely "I"; he will prepare illustrations familiar to his audience; for example, recent or current well-known events; and he will build upon what his audience already knows about his topic. Thus his preparation is actually a circular response, for he will be making an anticipatory response to his audience.

Message and Response

As the second characteristic of communication, we said that a speaker does not merely deliver a message but stirs up thought about it. It is obvious that if you praise religion to skeptics, they will not accept what you say, but will examine and perhaps modify or reject your statements while you are speaking. They cannot talk back (unless there is a question period or an opportunity to heckle the speaker), but nothing can prevent them from thinking back. What takes place is a two-way conversation, even though the speaker may do all the talking, while the audience has to make its retorts silently to itself. All of us have had such an experience while listening to a speech with which we disagreed.

To clarify the difference between messages that stir up and messages that deliver let us assume that a speaker tells his auditors something they did not know, say, that Sigmund Freud died in England in 1939 at the age of eighty-three. This statement would seem to have been delivered; it would seem that it could not be stirred up, for the information was new to the listeners, not lying dormant in their minds waiting to be aroused.

Whenever you speak you set in motion both light waves and sound waves that impinge on the eye and ear receptors of your auditors, thereby sending neural impulses to their brains which result in their forming certain concepts—whether or not these are what you intended.

There is no need to stress this process (which means that nothing you say can be "delivered" but that meanings can only be "stimulated"); but it is important to stress the fact that what is *aroused* in the mind of the listener will never be precisely what you intended. You may present new information, which may be accepted by the listeners as accurate; but listeners will not agree either with you or with one another as to its significance. Some may say to themselves, "So what?" Others may respond by thinking, "How interesting!" or "Can this be reconciled with what was said a few moments before?"

The message you want to present to your audience should be measured by three criteria: Are your statements accurate? What is the purpose of your presentation? How can it be best conveyed to the audience? You can enhance your ability to stir up the meanings you wish in the minds of your audience as you attain increasing skill in analysis, in research, in the use of various forms of support, and in the organization or synthesis of your subject matter so that you will be able to represent your topic accurately; as you learn to determine your purpose in speaking on your chosen topic to a particular audience at a particular time; and as you learn more and more about how to analyze an audience both to guide your preparation and to affect your behavior while speaking. These are the ways in which you can make your message and the audience's response to it come to correspond more nearly.

Memorized and Extemporaneous Speeches: Reproduction and Creativity

One of the troublesome problems for inexperienced speakers is how to *prepare* their talks so that they can easily adapt to their audience while they are speaking. Should they deliver the speech as they have prepared it? Or should they change and adapt it according to the audience's response while they are speaking? If the speaker is supposed to respond to his audience's reactions, as the principle of circular response suggests, is it not a positive handicap to be too well prepared? The problem is real, but there is also a real solution for it.

Reproduction of what has been prepared may take one of several different forms. The speaker may write out his speech and then read it—or he may memorize it. In either case, there is little room for *creativity* on the platform. Nevertheless, skillful readers of manuscripts can do a great deal with voice and gesture to make an audience feel that the words being read are intended very specially for them and for the particular circumstances; moreover, the speech should be written so that it fits its intended audience, and none other. When a speech is memorized, it may, but need not, sound stilted and unreal. Successful actors memorize their lines, but they deliver these memorized speeches with such naturalness that the lines *sound* like spontaneous utterances. Speakers who have memorized their talks can perhaps learn this same skill; but if they do they cannot change, elaborate, or condense their remarks to fit the reactions of their listeners.

Successful *extemporaneous* speaking is the result of careful preparation and even memorization of facts and ideas, but not of the precise words to be used. This preparation is *idea-centered,* not *word-centered.* When you give this kind of speech, you have the maximum opportunity to "reproduce" the line of thinking that you have carefully prepared while you "create" the verbal-gestural pattern in which it is given. Your preparation consists in mastering your facts until you *know* them and do not have to strain to *remember* them—just as you may *know* various styles of modern music, or the characteristics of your favorite movie stars or athletes. Your preparation also involves organizing your facts into a pattern that suits your purpose. This pattern, like your facts, you will *know,* for it has resulted from your careful consideration of how best to arrange the sequence and relationships of your facts. Trying to remember only words makes you little more than a machine, a phonograph. Then when you forget some of the words, your mind goes blank. You have been remembering instead of thinking, but if you have your facts and your organization solidly mastered and are formulating your actual words and sentences out of the speaking situation, you have achieved the ideal combination of reproduction and creativity. It is the speaking method that, particularly for the inexperienced, is most likely to result in genuine communication.

HOW PATTERNS OF SPEECH DEVELOP

An entire series of problems in the use of speech as oral communication arises from the fact that speech is a process of social adaptation. That is why it is futile to seek to become a "good speaker" as an end in itself. Speech is never an end in itself, but a means by which our social purposes may be accomplished. Speech is a method of social communication, the most important means by which we conduct our relationships with others. It is a way of imparting and gathering information, of persuading and being persuaded, of creating and changing opinions, of entertaining and being entertained, of inspiring and being inspired.

The word "society" means the common understandings shared by persons living and working together in their daily occupations, and in the family group, the church, and the community, state, and nation. As we seek to establish a world society, one great problem we encounter is that of evolving a method by which peoples of different languages and cultures can communicate with one another. In every social activity we attempt to share understandings. This sharing process is at the very heart of the meaning of *communication*.

But even within a single language there are many varying patterns of good speech. Speech that is highly acceptable in one section of our nation seems strange in another. The slang that was popular in high school is considered out of place in college. The way you talked among your fellows on your summer job probably would not be sanctioned in your English class. Your diction, articulation, sentence structure—your whole manner of speaking—change as your hearers change. You speak quite differently, for example, in a conference with the dean from the way you speak with other members of "the gang" at the corner soda fountain. It is apparent that a *basic requirement of good speech is that it be appropriate to the social situation in which it occurs.*

Your present speech habits have developed out of your environment and associations. You have tended to develop speech patterns that have served your purposes up to the present time. If your speech has been careless, highly colloquial, and loud, that in itself is a revelation of the kind of associates you have had and the kind of speech you have thought they have expected of you. The lisp of one student, the thin, high-pitched voice of another, the careless slang of a third have been tolerated in the intimate environment of childhood and of the immediate neighborhood. But uncritical school friends and all-too-tolerant family are left behind as you move on into the more impersonal and extensive life of the college campus. Soon college, too, will be left behind as you go into the highly competitive realm of business or the professions. Speech mannerisms that once seemed "smart" will come to be regarded as peculiar. Once assets, they may come to be damaging handicaps, even before you realize it. One aim of your speech course is to make you aware of different patterns of speech in your own life, how these patterns have become established, what serious handicaps wrong patterns can be to your future success, and how to develop and improve the best possible patterns of speech for a pleasing personality, professional proficiency, and a happy, well-adjusted life.

Your patterns of speech must go on developing. A new adjustment is required for almost every social situation. As was true in your past experience, no single type or pattern of speech will serve all the varying requirements of adult life. In most purely social circumstances and in many vocations the highest success comes to the individuals who are most sensitively responsive to the communicative elements in each situation in which they are involved.

By the time you entered college, you had already acquired speech patterns typical of your region. You had learned the speech of your own economic and social group, and developed some characteristics of speech peculiar to your own circle of intimate friends. To feel that any one pattern of speech is *better* than another is only another way of indicating a preference for customs among which we have grown up and with which we feel at home. Such expressions as "he talks like a professor," or "like a high-pressure salesman," or "like a politician," or "like an Army man" are common-sense observations of differences that actually do exist. Farmers and city dwellers are conscious of differences in each other's speech patterns. The differences in the speech of residents of the United States, England, Canada, and Australia are the subject of jokes and comments that indicate attitudes of superiority, inferiority, amusement, or curiosity.

Language diversities are, however, being modified by the changes in transportation facilities. Railroad, steamship, automobile, and airplane have greatly increased the mobility of our population. Millions of people travel long distances for the sake of a vacation away from home. Besides these transients are other millions who have moved from one section to another. This enormous population shift is doing much to destroy our provincialism and to make us familiar with patterns of speech other than our own. As we travel about and learn how many speech variants exist, we come to take them for granted. More important still, this very mobility of population will do much to diminish the variations.

The change in communication facilities may be expected to have an even greater influence upon our speech. The radio, the movie, and television are bringing to all of us one fairly uniform or "standard" pattern of speech. Since these media reach millions of people daily, there is a general tendency for persons in all sections and social groupings to imitate the kind of speech they hear.

This conception of speech as a set of customs transmitted to you from your associates should allay the fear many college students have that they can never become "good" speakers. The speech pattern you now possess you learned because it served fairly well your need of coordinating and cooperating with your previous social groups. Just as surely as you learned that pattern, you can now learn new ones. Speech training merely expedites and assists by orderly methods and counsel a process of speech growth that is constant throughout life.

Fine insight into the purpose of speech training was revealed by one freshman when he said that the speech course is "a familiarization of a green, inexperienced student with a situation of leadership, control, and influence." Another student doubtless had much the same thing in mind when he wrote, "I think speech will prove invaluable training for the future if its only accomplishment is to add one iota of self-confidence to my personality." To conclude, speech training allows every student to progress in his own way toward the goal of acquiring speech skills that will help him to make adjustments to the larger and more impersonal society of his mature world.

HOW SPEECH SKILLS DEVELOP

The first screams and kicks of infants are responses to biological needs, such as the need for air, water, or food; they are also reactions to painful conditions or they are manifestations of physical well-being. These activities are not communicative in themselves, but meaning is attached to them by watchful parents. The parents respond by picking the infant up, or in some other way impressing upon his mind the kind of response he may obtain by repeating the activity. In this way, a full cycle of communication is completed and the child eventually learns to use speech symbols.

Acquisition

At every stage of acquiring speech skills, from the first babbling of an infant to the acquisition of conventionally accepted speech symbols (such as words and gestures), the child depends on others to indicate to him what kinds of speech are effective. Out of the great variety of sounds that he makes as random vocal play, his parents respond with special delight and attention to such sounds as *da-da* and *ma-ma*. Naturally, the infant repeats them and gradually comes to accept the meaning that others attach to the sounds. So it goes with every addition to his vocabulary, until he is old enough to engage in a conscious study and practice of linguistic skills. He follows the same process in developing communicative skill with gestures. Certain random bodily movements produce negative responses and are dropped; others produce favorable reactions and are continued. The type and extent of developments of vocabulary and gestures are determined by the intelligence of the child as well as by the kinds of stimulation and response he receives.

Social Interaction

From the nursery through maturity it is evident at every stage that speech is always a social product and reflects the individual's total social environment. The example of an American youth who was reared in China illustrates the social nature of speech. Upon the boy's arrival in New York some years ago, the newspapers reported that his vocal intonations, his manner of walking, his gestures, his postural patterns were typically "Chinese." All these characteristics were ways of communicating meaning. And the ways developed in one environment naturally seemed strange when transferred to another. Similar differences in communicative patterns are evident as one moves from section to section in the United States.

The development of skill in speech depends upon an individual's ability to secure attention and establish relationships with others. Thus the strongest characteristic of speech in its early and pliant stages is its adaptability to the reactions of its audience. Whatever proves effective is tried again and gradually becomes fixed as a habitual manner of expression. In time every child develops a large range of symbols, which become more or less definitely fixed in his mind. If the child has a narrow circle of stable human relationships—that is, if he has few associations aside from his parents and perhaps two or three playmates—his use of speech symbols becomes relatively limited. He finds that a certain few symbols always receive the desired response, so that he comes to have full confidence in their use. Naturally, such a child will have "speech difficulties" when he moves into a wider social environment and encounters situations in which these responses are not so uniform.

Another child, let us say, develops in a wide and variable environment. He encounters many different people who respond to him in different ways. His speech pattern becomes broader, less definitely fixed, and consequently is much more readily changed to meet new situations. Such a child is said to have developed social ease and the ability to adjust.

Images

In either of the hypothetical circumstances just described, the child builds up images of himself by interpreting the responses of his close associates. He becomes aware that he is a person, something alive, new, and different. If he is often described as "bad," he comes to think of himself as being so and acts accordingly. If he is called "artistic," his activities tend to develop in that direction. Just as surely as the communicative skills and habits are established by social responses, so are the images every individual comes to have of the kind of person he is. The nature of these images becomes a positive force that in turn helps to shape the further development of speech patterns. Vocal intonations, gestural patterns, and word choice are all linked to the images an individual holds of himself. The girl who thinks of herself as shy and retiring will develop speech that conforms to that image. The boy who thinks of himself as inferior will use communicative methods appropriate to that image. Both individuals will, however, have other images that also exert influence on their speech.

The child develops early a whole series of images of himself. In interacting with members of the family, he may speak in a nasal tone and pronounce words sibilantly when with his mother, use submissive, nonassertive tones when with his older brother, and speak slowly but precisely when with his father. The speech patterns he uses on the playground and in school will be still different. But in each situation the images he forms of himself and the speech he uses as a result are all predicated upon his interpretation of how best to "get along" with his associates and to gain attention and approval—or at least to avoid criticism and rejection. In every social situation, the child uses the speech he believes will be most effective in his relationships with others.

Roles

The child establishes various relationships with people he meets frequently. The stability of these relationships provides the security the child seeks. One of the causes of much personality maladjustment is the unpredictability of the behavior of some parents, teachers, or others in authority, so that the child finds his relationship patterns undependable. In such circumstances, the speech of the child becomes typically apologetic, uncertain, and badly developed. On the other hand, a child whose relationships present no uncertainties tends to develop confident, fluent, precise speech. Charles H. Cooley called the process by which a child's speech is developed in accordance with the expectations of others "the reflected looking-glass self"; another sociologist, George H. Mead, called it "role-taking." Both terms emphasize the fact that the way we talk is a key to, as well as an outgrowth of, the relationships that have been established for us in a social group.

Out of this process of role-taking, however, arises one of the major causes of speech problems. Our basic speech habits are established in childhood, when our relationships are formed primarily in the home. These early speech characteristics survive in persistent patterns of speech behavior. No matter how we try to adjust our speech to our new roles in society, there is always a partial carry-over from the earlier, firmly fixed habits. Consequently, our speech adaptation to new situations is never complete. Vocal, gestural, postural, and facial mannerisms that proved effective in dealing with parents, brothers, and sisters tend to persist when, much later, we communicate with fellow students, professors, and employers. One cause of the uneasiness and lack of confidence commonly experienced in speech situations is a half-conscious awareness of our internal conflict as we strive to cast off former roles and to assume the one appropriate to our present relationship.

A clear understanding of these factors of interaction, image, and role-taking will help you to make the new adjustments that are continually demanded in our highly individualistic and changing society. In brief summary, a social situation is composed of individuals who have roles in the groups and their own images of what those roles are; whose activities, influences, and attitudes are continually interacting with those of the other group members. Every member of the group finds his speech—indeed, his whole self—shaped to a large extent by the nature of the other members and their interrelationships. The more similar the members' experiences, attitudes, values, and sentiments the more communication is possible. The more dissimilar the individuals, the more difficult it is for them truly to understand one another. Consequently, there is always some barrier to communication between student and professor, day laborer and banker, army private and captain, or professor and businessman. The ideal speech situation is to be found in a home, where the members' roles are clearly defined and where all are bound together by many common experiences and strong ties of sympathy. The ideal kind of speech in normal situations is the speech that adapts most closely to the elements the group holds in common. A frequent cause of failure in speech is the inability or unwillingness to make the adaptation required by every change in the social situation.

SPEECH AS PERSONAL ADJUSTMENT

We have pointed out that speech is basic to the individual's adjustment to society. This topic will be continued in greater detail in the next chapter, which discusses speech as a major factor in personality and shows how personality itself is the measure of an individual's adjustment to his social environment. Social ease is part of good speaking. Social ease means, for the most part, readiness and versatility in shifting into the roles demanded by new situations.

The individual who withdraws into himself, who is constantly preoccupied with satisfying his own personal wishes and desires, who is not interested in others, and who is content to rely upon a limited number of familiar roles will never become an effective speaker. The better we can understand people, the better we shall be able to make ourselves understood by them. In a democratic society, effective speaking and effective living, which have much in common, require a degree of ability to lose one's self, or, more correctly, to *find* one's self, in an expanding interest in others. This, of course, assumes a high degree of social adaptiveness.

As your personality was being developed in response to your social relationships and to your interpretation of your successive roles in your home, church, and school, a similar change was occurring in other members of your speech class—and in every other individual everywhere. This means that you must talk and listen to individuals who, like you, are products of their past and of their social relationships. "Speak that I may know you" needs to be interpreted as meaning "Speak that I may know what you have been taught" and "Speak that I may learn what you wish to become." Our speech always reflects the tendencies we carry over from the past, which are intermingled with influences from the direction in which we are seeking to go.

Your speech is thus an index of what you are and of how you react to everything around you. When you seek to improve your speech, therefore, you undertake a task which involves the study of your whole

self and the re-evaluation of all the adjustments you make to your
fellow human beings. If you have clear and firmly held convictions,
then these, to a degree, qualify you to communicate with others concerning them. The wider your experience with people has been, the
more easily you will be able to exchange understandings with new
groups. The more successful you have been—in studies, in athletics,
at social affairs, with your hobbies, or in your family, church, and
work relationships—the more confidently and easily you will speak
with others, in either a conversational or a larger audience situation.
Success in a wide variety of activities is not necessary for success in
speaking but it helps. Certainly speech is one subject which cannot
be studied in a social vacuum; rather, the study of speech is a study
of our whole social selves. When we increase the number and variety
of our friendships, when we throw ourselves energetically into new
groups and situations and improve our facility in adapting to them,
when we take every reasonable opportunity to talk with others, to
learn more about them, and to discover why they hold ideas different
from our own, we are using one of the most effective methods of improving our speech.

CONCLUSION

The aim of speaking, as we have pointed out, is *communication.*
This means talking *with* your listeners, in a two-way exchange (differently but not essentially less in public speaking than in conversation).
This two-way process, sometimes called "circular response," depends
upon your achieving *rapport,* or a sympathetic relationship of mutual
understanding, with your listeners. Furthermore, communication
means that you will induce your listeners to accept *your message* by
presenting it in a manner that accords with *their* conceptions of the
facts. In order to speak in this manner, you must prepare in a way
that will allow you to say what you have planned to say with extemporaneous creativity—adapting to your listeners' reactions, rather than
trying to deliver a set speech to them.

We have noted that the speech each individual uses has been determined largely by the kinds of social relationship he has experienced
and by the customs of the groups in which he has lived. Out of these
considerations should emerge a new understanding of the nature of
speech and of the meaning of "good," or effective, speech. Whatever
speech problems you may have should be interpreted as arising in

part from the general need of adjustment to the new circumstances attending adult responsibilities. But even more important is the fact that every speech situation we encounter is to some extent unique, and the highest speech skill is the ability to sense and react to the needs, moods, and attitudes of the social situation in which we are conversing, discussing, or giving a speech.

EXERCISES AND BIBLIOGRAPHY

Exercises

1. As a term speech project, join some organization, on the campus or in the town, in which discussion and speaking are common. This might be a club devoted to photography or to discussion of race relations, current social problems, politics, or religion. Make an active and continuing analysis of the role you play in the group and of the ways in which you exercise influence. Try to determine by what means and to what degree you are in turn influenced by other members of the group. By the end of the term, write a report on the kinds of interaction you observed in the group and the role you occupied in it. Evaluate your role in terms of speech effectiveness.

2. Prepare a five-minute speech for delivery to your class on the importance of role-taking in some group you know well. Suggestive of the kinds of topic you might select are the following:

   a. My fraternity brother as student, son, and athlete.
   b. Members of this class as speakers, as listeners, and as students taking exams.
   c. My experience in answering a summons in traffic court (or in interviewing the dean, in helping to buy a new car, in working on a farm, or in taking a trip on the subway).
   d. Changes in our family when my brother was born (or when my sister was married, or when my cousin came to live with us).

   In your speech, whatever topic you choose, the important thing is to show clearly what relationship existed among the various people concerned and how the social interaction that developed was affected by the various roles.

3. Prepare for a discussion in class of the meaning of the following terms: interaction, image, role-taking, adjustment, society, customs, and "reflected looking-glass self." Be prepared to illustrate each of these terms with reference to college life.

4. Read George Bernard Shaw's *Pygmalion*. To what extent do you believe he was serious in his representation of an entirely transformed person-

ality resulting from improvement in speech? Criticize the process of "personality readjustment" as represented in the play.

5. Any considerable reading of book reviews reveals how frequently the critics refer to whether or not an author has "caught the inflections of real talk." Prepare to tell the class what you have noted about the speech patterns of some book or play you have recently read.

Bibliography

Hayakawa, S. I., "A Semantic Parable," in *Language in Thought and Action* (Harcourt, Brace, 1949), pp. 1–7.

Lippmann, Walter, "The World Outside and the Pictures in Our Heads," from *Public Opinion* (Penguin Books, 1946), pp. 1–22.

Linton, Ralph, *The Cultural Background of Personality* (Appleton-Century-Crofts, 1945), Chap. 1.

Rogers, Raymond, "The Gonks and the Tiger," in *Language, Meaning, and Maturity*, S. I. Hayakawa, ed. (Harper, 1953), pp. 303–14.

Sapir, Edward, "Communication," in *Encyclopedia of Social Sciences* (Macmillan, 1942), Vol. IV.

ILLUSTRATIVE SPEECH

Read and discuss the following speech. What relationships do you find between its content and form and the ideas discussed in Chapters 1 and 2? Note that the language is recorded just as Mrs. Roosevelt spoke it. Do you think it must have sounded better than it reads? Why would there be a difference? Must there be?

Language Difficulties Are Barriers to Confidence[1]

BY ELEANOR ROOSEVELT

As Member of the United States Delegation to the General Assembly of the United Nations

I was to talk to you about what you could do for the United Nations. One thing I feel very strongly. You've just heard about the crisis at present in college education. Well, you know that crisis

[1] Delivered at the New York *Herald Tribune* High School Forum, New York City, 1946.

points up a great deal that we are constantly hearing about. We're always meeting crises because nobody has enough imagination to look a little bit ahead and realize that we're going to have these crises, that they're coming inevitably.

Now young people should develop imagination, and while you are in high school is a very good time to develop it, and while this happens to be a very small crisis from my point of view, nevertheless, it points to the fact that you need to have imagination in every field, and you need to have it in the future of the world. Now I heard the end of a speech which was very interesting to me, because it pointed up something that I wanted to say to you in your relation to the United States. What you do in your own communities and in your own lives is vital, because the United Nations are fifty-one nations, and they have to be brought together and understand each other and work together, and each one has to recognize the good things about the other and the things that they don't understand they must try to gain an understanding of, and that's going to require imagination.

And it's going to require, for the future, a vision and a vision above everything else of our responsibility as individuals, to accept the fact that what we do at home, in our community, builds the kind of a nation we have and the kind of influence that nation is going to have in this group of fifty-one nations now, but which will later be even greater.

One thing that I kept thinking about in London was the fact that always we compared other people to ourselves, as we were now. We seemed to have so little perspective on the growth of nations and the development of nations, and we seemed to forget what we ourselves had been in our own development.

Now you are learning history. Don't just learn history as a question of dates and wars. Try to make this history that you learn come alive. Think of it in terms of people, of different stages, and when you meet people from other nations think of your contacts as historic contacts, contacts in which you are making history for the future.

Sometimes I think that one of the things that excites us most today is how we are going to get on with the countries in Europe and in Asia that we don't know much about and that are handling their problems in a different way from the way we handle ours today.

Well, if we will remember the way we handled problems a hundred years ago it'll help us a great deal. And that's one of the things that I think while you are in high school you can do. Another thing is that we in the United States have always looked down, really, upon people from other parts of the world. We haven't wanted to learn their languages. Now I happen to believe that the best thing we could do for peace is to find a language—and I know all the political difficulties attached to choosing a language—but if we could overcome them through the United Nations and find a language which all over the world all of us will learn, besides our own, it would mean a great deal for better understanding in the future. That language barrier was one of the things that struck me over and over again.

I wanted to talk to a woman from Byelo-Russia. Well, first of all, I had to find out what part of Russia was Byelo-Russia, which shows how bad my own geography was. When she told me Minsk was the capital, why then I knew, because I remembered watching what happened around Minsk. But I knew very little about Byelo-Russia.

We could get along all right with an interpreter when we were just talking to each other, but when it came to a discussion, she was way behind, because no interpreter can interpret fast enough to tell you what a lot of people are talking about all round.

So, you young people, talk to other young people whenever you get a chance, from other countries, and try not to look down on foreign languages, and try to come to some agreement that all of you everywhere will gradually be learning one language through which you can talk to each other without interpreters. That's one of the greatest barriers.

The woman from Byelo-Russia had a lot to tell me that I really needed to know, and a lot that made it clearer why certain things were felt in certain parts of the world, but it took a long while for me to find out. It would have been much easier if I had been able to really talk.

And I think one little story which will amuse you, but which illustrates this language trouble, will help to clarify it for you.

I served on a committee which discussed the rights of individuals to self-determination, and in the course of it a subcommittee was appointed because our Russian representatives felt sure we would come to some better agreement than we had reached in the whole committee. And we'd argue for days on a phrase. And finally, one day, my adviser handed me a phrase he thought might do—it was just a couple of sentences—and I read it out to the committee. Before I had finished reading it the British representative, who was typically British Foreign Service trained, with generations of training behind him, spoke. We used to be worried by that kind of British diplomat— we always felt we were inferior. Nowadays we don't feel that any you expect a great deal, people will often live up to it. So the approach of youth is a valuable approach, both in international relations and in our own domestic relations, and you want to feel that you have a real job to do, a job which you can do day by day.

You can be preparing yourself with what you learn through your understanding for the responsibilities which will fall upon you as you grow older. But in everything you do, day by day, you're getting ready for those responsibilities and you are helping to create public opinion.

What you feel and how you do things will have an effect even on your elders. So you have a responsibility already in the community as a whole. Be courageous in approaching responsibility. Have imagination about it. Have vision. People will tell you that you dream dreams. Well, remember that every step forward is the result of somebody who dreamed dreams. Never be afraid of wanting to go forward too fast. You'll be slowed up by circumstances anyway. Have your beliefs clearly in mind and have the courage to live up to them. Have heroes and follow them and you'll find that they will be stronger and better because of your trust.

Good luck to you and God bless you.

more because we're grown up. But he was on his feet immedi
He said, "Mrs. Roosevelt, in the interest of good English, I
we should say that thus and so," and he put in about a hundred w
for my twenty. I was quite willing to accept it, but before he
finished the Russian delegate was on his feet. He was Dr. Arutiui
professor of economics in Moscow, and he said, " I have been ca
by Sir George's good English before." Sir George promptly c
back with "I have been caught by Dr. Arutiunian's tricks before,"
I promptly said, "Gentlemen, it means the same thing. Mine's g
American, his is good English." And Dr. Arutiunian said, "I
good American. I can understand it."

You see, all agreements and all peace are built on confidence. Y
cannot have peace and you cannot get on with other people in
world unless you have confidence in them. You know that just
well as I do. Now, what we are building in the United Nations
what we're trying to build—is confidence. Now, if they look at
in our communities in this country—and remember that all rac
and all religions are represented—if they look at us and find us prej
diced, doing things without regard to our Constitution and our B
of Rights, they wonder whether what we say about democracy
what we really mean or whether it's just a kind of lip service. Or
of the things I noticed was the fact that so many of our young peop
in the Army were not always able to say really what they believe
democracy meant in action. They'd heard a good many things ii
schools, but they had never translated it into the way you live, da
in and day out. And, after all, your government is the expression o
the way you live and believe.

Now sometimes it's awfully hard to live up to the beliefs and the
things that you have read about and accepted, just taken for granted.
But when you come to actually live up to them, those things sometimes lead you into difficult situations.

The best thing, I think, that you young people can do is to face up
to your difficult situations at home. You will be much better prepared to support the United Nations and face up to the difficult situations that arise between nations. There are always going to be difficulties among human beings. Now, young people have a great
advantage. They've had no disappointments to speak of about human
nature. As you grow older you have more disappoinments. But when
you're young you have more courage, more confidence, because you
haven't had so many disappoinments, and that is a very good thing,
because very often people live up to what is expected of them, and if

CHAPTER 3

CONTENTS

Note how something of the personality of each of these men is revealed by facial expressions in this panel discussion conducted by members of the Steelworkers Union at the Pennsylvania State University.

THE PERSONALITY
OF THE SPEAKER

WHAT type of personality do you most admire? If you could have your personality refitted like a suit of clothes, just what changes would you wish to have made? No doubt each of us has been made keenly aware of the importance of his own personality, yet few of us have analyzed carefully just what personality is, or exactly how to go about changing it.

If you will reflect briefly upon what you mean when you refer to another person's personality, you are likely to find you mean that person's characteristic behavior, his usual reactions to others, and how he usually adapts to the situations in which he finds himself. For instance, you say that one person has a pleasing personality because, no matter what the situation, you can count on his being pleasant. The world has need of people who are well adjusted, who get along effectively with their fellows. But it has more need of another type of personality—the individualist, the nonconformist, the person who has the courage of his convictions, the capacity for independent thinking, and resolute integrity.

It is mainly through speech that you reveal your personality. A principal purpose in speaking is to share with others those ideas and feelings that are uniquely your own. And it is largely what you say and how you say it that determine how successfully you get along with others.

Your study of various methods of improving personality will give you new insights into the personalities of others and should enhance your understanding of and adaptations to your audience. No one possesses a single, rather fixed, describable, and unvarying personality. Quite the contrary, each of you possesses more "personalities" than a good golfer has clubs. And you choose which personality to be in each situation much as a golfer selects which club to use. It was this which Oliver Wendell Holmes had in mind as he observed, in *The Autocrat of the Breakfast Table,* that there are three Johns for each one who bears that name: "1. The real John, known only to his Maker. 2. John's ideal John; never the real John, and often very unlike him. 3. Thomas's ideal John, never the real John, nor John's John, but often very unlike either."

Actually, each of you possesses not just three "personalities" but as many as there are distinctive types of situations in which you find yourself. In this sense, each of you has one personality at the dinner table at home, but quite another at lunch with a campus group. You may be quite a different personality at worship on the Sabbath from that which you have been the evening before at some social event. These, of course, are surface variations, and only slight modifications of a deeper pattern of personality behavior which characterizes each person.

PERSONALITY FACTORS IN SPEAKER-AUDIENCE RELATIONS

Standards of Public Speaking

On questions of etiquette, on manner of dress, and on most other phases of organized human activity, including what constitutes good speaking, a general agreement exists. A speaker is expected, for example, to stand on the floor rather than to sit or lie on the table. Of course, it is possible that he might be a successful speaker even while standing on his head, but he would find it much easier to keep his audience's attention concentrated on what he had to say if he stood easily erect. Similarly, he is expected to look at his audience, rather than away from it; to be neatly and appropriately dressed; and to speak clearly enough so that he can be heard and understood. These and other characteristics of effective speech are discussed elsewhere. It is sufficient at this point to remark that there is no value in being so bent upon being individual and "different" that you find yourself struggling against the pattern of expectation of your audience. It is important to remember that different audiences have different patterns of expectation, and that what pleases and influences one might be offensive or at least ineffective with another.

The Speaker's Individuality

The fact that audiences do have standards by which they prejudge speakers does not mean, on the other hand, that every speaker should attempt to force himself into a mold and to follow the anticipated pattern precisely. As a matter of fact, one of the chief expectations of the audience is that a speaker will be himself. When you are invited to speak, it is because the audience wants to hear you. Your special points of view, cultural achievements, or distinguishing characteristics are probably among the chief reasons you were invited to speak. When a college professor was invited to address a farmers' organization, he made the serious mistake of being "folksily" ungrammatical and of drawing his illustrations largely from the farm. As the farmers were leaving the meeting, several were heard to complain, "He can't be much of a professor if that's the way he talks!" The fact that everyone tends to change his personality as he shifts from one social situation to another is no reason for a speaker to imitate the chameleon by trying to change color to match the group which he happens to be addressing. Instead, the basic characteristics of the speaker, modified though they must be to the particular circumstances of each speech, should always be apparent.

The best balance between conformity with the audience's pattern of expectation and maintenance of his own intrinsic characteristics will be achieved by the speaker who has developed self-respect, flexibility, and security. Anything that has limited one's emotional life and experience—too much poverty or too much wealth, too much or too little parental care and supervision, too few friends or too little variety in type of friends—may tend to affect success in speaking. The individual whose childhood has seemed to him to have been normal and who has developed many and varied satisfying social relationships is apt to have the self-respect and the feeling of security that make him insist upon being and expressing "himself." Moreover, the diversity of his friendships will make it relatively easy for him to make flexible adjustments to audience situations.

But those of you who come to your speech classes from backgrounds that have been less than ideal for creating the kinds of personality most easily adapted to speech training need not feel excessively handicapped. What you need is to realize that your personality should have two distinct characteristics, both of which you can attain. The first is a healthy consistency; and the second is a sensitive adaptability. For the first, you should clarify your own understanding of what you feel and believe. For the second, you should alert yourself to the small but vital cues in the behavior of your associates by which they signal a wide variety of responses to what you say and how you say it. We may summarize these two characteristics by saying that the speaker should be self-respecting but not self-centered.

PERSONALITY AS GOOD HEALTH

Everyone wants to have a "good personality." By the very term "personality" we seek to indicate the factors in behavior which are socially desirable and successful. Difficult as personality may be to define, we recognize it as comprising the various ways in which individuals manifest their reactions to one another. "Poor personalities," on the other hand, is a term used to describe people who are selfish, antisocial, withdrawn.

Dr. Harry Stack Sullivan, speaking to the American College of Physicians at Johns Hopkins University, listed four characteristics which frequently marked the beginnings of mental upsets: (1) withdrawal from social activities, (2) abstraction and daydreaming to the neglect of waiting obligations, (3) suspicion of what others may be thinking, and (4) complaints of a variety of imaginary ills. We are not suggesting that any or all of these personality traits invariably lead their possessor to the psychiatrist's couch. In fact, all normal people exhibit these traits to some extent. But assuming that you want to take constructive steps in shaping an effective personality you should assess yourself thoroughly. Sullivan's list is a good point from which to start: Do you participate enjoyably in a reasonable number of social activities? Do you avoid daydreaming about impossibilities when you ought to be attending to present duties? Do you avoid both stage fright and other more troublesome inhibitions by not worrying unduly about what others may be thinking of you? Do you give your ailments (and failures) as little self-pity as you can? Tensions, fears, inferiority complexes, and extreme nervousness are as detrimental to good mental health as to effective speaking and a pleasing personality.

Effective speakers are usually healthy, mentally and physically. Conversely, increased success in speaking will have a marked tendency to improve the healthy personality of the speaker.

PERSONALITY AS HABIT

Both our speech and our personality are composed of habit systems. As we look from this point of view upon personality as it is exhibited in speaking, it ceases to be some mysterious abstraction which we can scarcely define except as "good" or "bad" and becomes instead a series of definite items which we can change if we wish. You might make a list of elements in your own speaking which you feel ought to be changed, noting opposite each the quality with which it should be replaced. Following is a sample list:

Habit to be changed	*Quality to be sought*
Careless preparation	Thorough investigation and practice
Boastfulness	Accuracy or understatement
Fault-finding	Appreciation and constructive criticism
Unsupported assertions	Marshaling of facts
Dull voice	Enthusiasm and tonal variety
Nervously rapid speech	Calm, deliberate rate

No such listing, even when followed by conscientious effort to make the desired changes, will re-create a personality in a short time. The habits which make you what you now are have developed over a period of years. Some of them you can alter in a matter of months or even weeks; others may take much longer. To an extent that may surprise you, your habits will change unconsciously in response to the demands and standards of the new social situations of which you become a part. But in dealing with habits, as with specific skills, much can be accomplished by concentrating on the precise changes you wish to make.

FACTORS OF PERSONAL ADJUSTMENT

It is highly important to keep in mind that the personality we exhibit on the speaking platform is not basically different from the one we display in all types of social situations. Giving a speech does not change us, except insofar as it broadens the range of our personalities. To improve our conduct on the platform requires some examination and change of our habits of personal adjustment. Those who are poor speakers may want to eliminate the causes, not primarily to become better speakers but to improve their general social adaptability. They should examine themselves in the two aspects of personality emphasized in the introduction to this chapter.

Recognition of One's True Worth and Ability

The individual ought to strive to accept himself as he really is. Moreover, he should do so without brooding over the facts. One who is too conscious of his personality and intellectual status is known as an introvert; one who is insufficiently conscious of himself is known as an extrovert. The speaker is most likely to be effective if he can maintain a mid-position between these extremes, accepting himself as he is with a calm determination to make the most of those abilities which he has.

Criticism in the speech class should be sought and welcomed as an aid toward proper evaluation of one's ability and toward the development of increased ability in objective self-criticism. After classroom days are over, fair, honest, and reliable criticism will seldom be available.

One of the more reliable personality-rating scales lays great stress upon balance between overconfidence and self-distrust. At one extreme is the individual who is too domineering; but no less unhappily adjusted is the too submissive person. Each human being normally begins life in a quite submissive role. His parents make most, or all, of his decisions. Later on, teachers and perhaps church leaders exert dominating influences on the evolving personality. This is normal and proper. Yet it is also normal and proper for an individual gradually to grow in self-reliance, to come to make decisions for himself, to drop complete reliance upon parents, teachers, or any others.

Different individuals achieve this in varying degrees. Adolescents, as they first become aware of the extent to which parents have necessarily dominated their early years, frequently swing to unwise extremes of assertive self-reliance. They go about flaunting unconventionalities. They noisily declare their opinions on every subject. They must have their own way. They are selfishly inconsiderate of others and of the wishes of others. They resent all criticism, because criticism makes conceit uncomfortable. They stick to decisions, even defend wrong answers, long after they know they are wrong. They monopolize conversations. And they inevitably lose friends, since such traits become increasingly intolerable.

We are interested in the speech personality because speech is the most important means by which we achieve our social adjustments. And because speech is so largely a product of one's whole personality it would be most inadequate indeed to study language, thought, voice, and action without relating these to the personality of which they are but essential parts. What shall it profit a student to perfect his mechanics of speech if, for example, every time he gets up in class he speaks with a chip on his shoulder? Or if his arrogance makes his hearers forget all his good qualities? Or if he is so painfully shy and retiring that no one feels he can possibly have something worth while to say?

Your ego ought not to be completely static. Although there are times when a low estimate of yourself is desirable, there are also times when it is advisable to estimate yourself very highly. In other words, egotism is not always undesirable. As a student of speech you will find the desirable kind of egotism of great assistance at certain times. Underestimate yourself when you are preparing a speech. Be modest then. Assume that the task is going to be a difficult one and that you will need all possible preparation in order to accomplish it well. Assume that your speech technique is weak and that you ought to consider carefully the advice of your text and your instructor. But the effective delivery of your speech calls for an expansion of your ego. That is the time to be confident. Remind yourself of your careful preparation; assure yourself of your ability to do as well as, or better than, your associates. Unleash your full power for use in the immediate task of "selling" your ideas and personality as effectively as possible.

It is an important task of the speech class to show you how to make an objective evaluation of your own personality. Improvement is, of course, the goal; but improvement will be accelerated as you come to a keener appreciation of your own worth, ability, and integrity. This can add authority to what you say. This can win listener respect. This can give you solid foundation for needed and deserved self-confidence as a speaker and as a personality.

Establishment of Satisfactory Relations with Others

We realize that it is necessary to be properly aware not only of ourselves but of other people. They have egos too. And just as we like to expand ours, so do they like to expand theirs. Indeed, there is no more effective way to "win friends and influence people" than to see to it that anyone in our presence has an opportunity to feel pleased with himself. You may be tempted to exalt your own ego and to neglect those of others, even when you are most desirous of making a good impression, for then you feel that you must show the best side of yourself in order to be properly appreciated. As a matter of fact, although you ought not to lose self-esteem or become hypocritical, it is principally through appreciation of others that you will win appreciation for yourself. Get the other fellow to tell of his fishing exploits or his high bowling score and he will respond with a warm interest in you.

This awareness of others has to be cultivated; it is not a natural growth. The preadolescent child is strongly egocentric. He is seldom aware that other people have feelings which must be considered and wants which ought to be satisfied. He expects all plans to center about him and his desires. During the period of adolescence there ought to be a gradual growth of egoistic balance, so that he is finally able to view himself almost as objectively as he views the people and objects around him. This objectivity is one of the necessary characteristics of maturity. Respect for, and ability to get along with, others must balance self-respect.

PREVENTING STAGE FRIGHT

Stage fright is very much like other kinds of fear. It can be pampered and nursed along until it grows in intensity, just as can the fear of the dark, or of dogs, or of cancer. It can be encouraged by constant yielding and by failure to face the fact that it is a form of fear. On the other hand, by a bold facing of the problem, by a determination to eliminate it, by a refusal to yield, it can be overcome. The cure, of course, is not merely to say, "I hereby refuse ever to have stage fright again." No personality problem is ever quite as simple as that. The remedy lies, rather, in an orderly, systematic effort to destroy the causes of the problem and to eliminate the habitual responses which have become associated with it.

We all know that prevention is more effective than the best remedy for any physical malady. So it is with stage fright. Two types of preventive measures may be recommended: Try to develop favorable mental attitudes. Be sure to prepare your speeches adequately. These two steps must, of course, be undertaken long before the delivery of the speech.

Favorable Mental Attitudes

The development of favorable mental attitudes constitutes a general readjustment of the speaker's personality. This change involves, first of all, an analysis and understanding by the speaker of his stage fright. The preceding pages should help in this, but the essential need is for the speaker to ask himself just which of the symptoms that have been described are most noticeable in himself and to determine for his own satisfaction the precise cause of his stage fright. Sometimes he may discover that wholly personal and extrinsic factors—such as a background of poverty or family unhappiness or a physical deformity—have caused him to develop feelings of general inferiority and to lack social ease and poise.

Once the speaker has determined the specific causes of his feelings of inadequacy and inferiority, a self-administered program of mental hygiene is in order. This consists for the most part in assuming a positive, affirmative, and optimistic outlook concerning his ability to meet and overcome his problems. For the beginning speaker the following mental attitudes are suggested. There is nothing startlingly new about them. In fact, they are so old they sound like platitudes. However, it should be remembered that they are familiar simply because they have been found so helpful through successive generations that they have continued to be practiced and advised.

1. "I must make the most of what I have and what I am." If others have been endowed with higher intelligence or greater wealth, you cannot alter the situation. But as William James, the famous psychologist, pointed out, most people use only about 20 percent of their potential ability. This means that an enormous field for improvement is open to everyone, whether his IQ or his personality rating be high or low. Any football coach knows how important it is for his players to hold to this attitude and how dangerous it is for them to lose it by feeling either so overconfident or so inferior that they fail to do their very best.

2. "Nothing succeeds like a successful attitude." If you show by your manner that you expect to succeed, others are unconsciously led to expect success of you. This, in turn, leads you to expect more of yourself. This does not imply that the individual should develop braggadocio and arrogance; these sham attitudes usually cover up fear of failure, and are likely to be recognized by your audience. Furthermore, they inevitably arouse the audience's resentment and dislike. The really successful attitude is a calm assurance that, taking success for granted, has no need of obtrusive and offensive overconfidence.

3. "It is better to have tried and failed than never to have tried at all." The excessive fear of failure which some students have is abnormal. It actually has an egotistical basis. The student feels himself to be in the center of the consciousness of his associates, and he is sure that if he does anything foolish it will be not only noticed but long remembered and commented upon. As a matter of fact, most people are too busy concentrating on their own affairs to occupy their minds very long or very seriously with other people's failures. Even if your speech did turn out to be an unsuccessful performance, most members of your audience will think no more of it than to hope that they will do better themselves when their turn comes. You should use this speech as a steppingstone to a better one the next time, to be based

upon analysis of your failure. Above all, never pass up an assigned speech in order to save yourself the anticipated embarrassment and stage fright. This technique of avoidance of difficulties is easy to follow and hard to discontinue after it is once tried. Be assured that no matter how badly the speech may go, the mere fact of having stood up before the audience will make it easier to stand up the next time, and each step of improvement in a spech will make the next step more sure.

4. "The only real failure is a failure to do my best." In this sense a very good speaker can fail as completely as a poor one. You should develop the habit of competing not with your associates but with yourself. Decide what your true potentialities are, and then try to reach that standard in every speech. Judge your degree of success in terms of that competition rather than by comparing your speech with the speeches of others. An interesting application of this procedure occurred in the college life of Albert J. Beveridge, one of the best-known senators of the early years of this century. His oratorical reputation was so formidable by the time he reached his senior year in college that his classmates refused to compete if he were allowed to take part in the annual oratory contest. The director of oratory thereupon had Beveridge compete against himself, with a board of judges to decide whether he achieved a standard sufficiently high, in comparison with his previous performances, to justify their awarding him the prize. This is an ideal practice for each speaker to follow in judging the success or failure of his own speeches.

5. "My problems are very similar to the problems of all the rest of the class members." In other words, all beginning speakers are in the same boat; the things that are most difficult for one are difficult for the rest, too. Your special problems bulk so large in your own eyes that perhaps you do not observe how similar are the problems confronting the other speakers. It is exceedingly helpful to establish firmly the habit of regarding yourself as normal. There is always a temptation to think, "None of this discussion applies to me, because I am different from other people." In most basic respects human beings are all very much the same. All the students enrolled in a college speech class are certain to have much more in common than most of them suspect. One thing, at least, that all have in common is their concentration upon the problems of speech improvement. The class sessions are, in effect, laboratory periods in which experiments in speaking are carried on. Occasionally you conduct the experiment;

at other times you observe it. At all times you and your associates
are engaged in a common task and are pursuing a common goal. If
your attitude toward your audience is one of respect and good-
fellowship, the audience is certain to be sympathetic toward you. You
will have just the type of atmosphere you need for conducting a reorganization of such personality traits and speaking habits as you
find ought to be changed.

6. "The listeners are interested not only in me but in my subject
and in what I have to say." When you speak you may be exceedingly
self-conscious about your gestures, your dress, your facial expression.
You may feel that everyone is looking at your hands and thinking
how awkward you look. It is helpful to remember that the audience
is not especially interested in you as the speaker. You are the only
one who thinks you are the center of attention. The audience is there
to hear what you have to say and to judge how pertinent it is.
If you keep your attention on your audience and subject, on the ideas
you wish to communicate—and thus wholly away from your egotistical self—you will be surprised at the ease with which you can
speak before an audience.

Adequate Preparation

Adequate preparation of your speeches—the second preventive
measure—ought to require little comment. Yet as many students come
to the end of their speech courses, they freely make such admissions
as the following: "Primarily my speaking lacks proper preparation."
"I feel that I do not give the subject about which I am to speak
enough preparation." "I do not do enough preparing before coming
to class." One student did a grave injustice to a great speaker and
humorist when he declared, "I'm a sort of Will Rogers speaker in
that I don't know what I'm going to say until I get up before the
audience." The careful preparation which went into Will Rogers'
speeches, the polishing and rephrasing of his seemingly spontaneous
jests, is one of the main reasons why this student was very far from
being "a sort of Will Rogers speaker."

It should not be forgotten that there are two basic requirements
for good speaking. Having something worth while to say is just as
essential as being able to say it well. The important difference is that
the first requirement is much more easily within the reach of every
student than is the latter. Every student can, with sufficient preparation, have something worth while to say. This does not merely involve

getting a collection of statistics to read to the audience. What it does involve is set forth in Chapter 9.

One suggestion is made here, however, because of its importance. *Begin the preparation of your speech early.* Nothing but superficiality may be expected from the student who asks for help, on the day before his speech is due, in the selection of a topic. It may be true that you cannot afford to set aside a great deal of time for the preparation of a particular speech; in that case, it is all the more important to begin the preparation early. No good speech can be suddenly extracted from the mind or fabricated from books and magazines. An effective speech must germinate and grow. The longer it stays in your mind, the more truly it becomes a part of yourself, is imbued with your own philosophy, and shapes itself into your own habitual manner of thought and expression. Until it has gone through this ripening process, the speech is not really yours. It is only a collection of facts and ideas which you have borrowed, rearranged a bit, and orally reproduced. The speech which you attempt to deliver after late or hasty preparation is only resting uneasily on the surface of your mind; it has not taken root and settled there; any little shock or jar may dislodge it; notes are necessary to remind you of it; and when it is delivered, your audience sees so little resemblance in it to *you*—to your characteristic modes of expression and real interests—that it appears to them artificial and unreal.

On the other hand, a speech which has been long in the process of preparation almost delivers itself. You find your ideas and words flowing with unaccustomed ease, and the result is pleasant and stimulating for both you and your audience. Fortunately, it is not true that this type of speech necessarily demands an unreasonably large amount of time for its preparation. Only a small portion of the actual preparation of your speech can be accomplished while you sit at a desk with books and papers spread out before you. Before this stage is reached, you should hold your subject in mind for some time, toy with it as you walk across the campus, think of it intermittently as you attend classes, chat with friends, and read the newspaper. If this is done, a cluster of ideas gathers about the subject. Something read here, heard there, observed someplace will suggest suitable material for your speech. When you come to the point of outlining your ideas on paper, your mind will have a store of ripened thoughts ready for use. This is truly the most economical, as well as the most successful, means of preparing a speech. It also prevents those feelings of doubt and insecurity which are the mainsprings of stage fright.

COMBATING THE EFFECTS OF STAGE FRIGHT

The development of favorable attitudes and adequate speech preparation will do much to reduce your stage fright, but by themselves
they cannot entirely prevent it. The bodily tensions and physiological
disturbances will still appear, though to a less extent than if these
preventive measures have been ignored. The actual methods of com-
bating stage fright after its symptoms appear may be considered in
two groups: those to be followed while awaiting your turn to speak,
and those to apply while you are speaking.

Within the first group, the most effective method is to eliminate
tension. When you feel that your muscles are tense and shaking, your
natural reaction is to try to stiffen them and hold them still. But this
only makes them more tense, and the shakiness, although it may be
eliminated for a moment, returns and is more firmly established than
before. What the muscles need above all is to be put to use. Relax in
your seat, breathe deeply and naturally to overcome the tendency
toward jerkiness of the breath, and employ each muscle normally. It
is not only the large leg, arm, and back muscles that need to be
adjusted, but also those in the throat. Let your chin sag upon your
breast. Turn your head a bit from side to side, and swallow naturally
a few times. These motions can be made inconspicuously enough to
attract little or no attention. While you are doing them, calm the
turmoil in your mind by thinking of the opening sentences of your
speech. Try to think of something said by the previous speaker or of
some element in the speech situation to which you can refer naturally
in your opening remarks.

Do not let your mind run rapidly over your whole speech; once
you have begun a well-prepared speech the remainder will come to
you with no difficulty. Try to keep out of your mind all fears and unfavorable attitudes. This can best be done by keeping your mind
actively engaged in working out the best means of opening your
speech by relating your topic to the preceding speeches given by your
classmates. It is also wise, if there is any common group activity such
as singing, laughing, or applauding, to enter into it heartily. To maintain the muscular balance which you have achieved, when the time
comes to speak, walk deliberately to the front of the platform, take
your position slowly, and do not begin to talk until you are actually
in command of the speech situation.

While you are speaking, the best way to combat stage fright is to
move about a bit; be especially free in the movement of your head

and your hands. If your muscular tension continues, walk to another part of the platform after the first sentence or two, while you are making a transition from one phase of your introduction to another. When the nature of your speech permits, hold something in your hands to show your audience—such as a picture or an object to be displayed —or write a few words on the blackboard. It is important to look confident and well poised, however you may feel. Look at and speak directly to your listeners, smile, and address them in a friendly manner. Be just as conversational and communicative as though you were talking with a friend in private. Psychologists tell us that one of the most effective techniques for overcoming fear is to act as though you were thoroughly unafraid—to impersonate someone who is utterly unafraid. This type of approach will aid you greatly in settling naturally into the speaking situation, so that you can take complete command of it.

Finally, it should be pointed out that there are some positive advantages resulting from stage fright. Some degree of emotional stimulation is necessary to keep the speaker from being lethargic and dull. When stage fright is properly controlled (not eliminated), it serves to provide desirable bodily tone. As one teacher of speech has said, "A certain amount of stage fright is like steam in the boiler." It provides the necessary energy to keep the speech moving. While eliminating the evils of stage fright, the speaker should never go so far as to become tranquil and completely assured on the eve of a speech. For even worse than stage fright is the contrary danger of not being stimulated enough. Some even go so far as to say that if you feel absolutely *no* stage fright you are not taking the job of speaking seriously enough to accomplish it effectively.

CONCLUSION

The effective speaker's personality results from a fine adjustment between maintenance of basic individuality and adaptation to the group being addressed. An audience expects, and rightly so, that a speaker will bring to it his own feelings, convictions, knowledge, and point of view; but he can bring to the audience what he has to offer only if he is able to adapt to the group his habits of thought and expression. Generally speaking, the best speech personality is one that reflects normal physical and mental health. Where personality changes are desirable, they may best be achieved by a systematic effort to amend existing habits. Two aspects of personal adjustment have been singled out as representing healthful traits that speakers should either possess or seek to develop.

Perhaps the personality problem of which beginning speech students are most sharply aware is stage fright. Actually, stage fright is merely a specialized form of social self-consciousness. Its remedies lie far from the platform, in the general attitudes of the speaker and in the kind of preparation he gives to his speeches. Its effects, however, may be lessened by relaxation before speaking and by a moderate amount of planned physical activity while on the platform. In any event, as the student is seeking to eliminate his stage fright, he should be aware of certain advantages derived from it which ought to be retained.

In a sense, a course in speech is a course in mental hygiene, and the effects will be felt in all manner of social activities. The essential consideration is that speaking is a process involving the entire normal personality of the speaker; it is not something that we "do" apart from what we "are." Our speech *is* a large part of our personality, as others sense and experience it.

EXERCISES AND BIBLIOGRAPHY

Exercises

1. Expand the list on page 62 of habits to be changed by adding others derived from observation in your speech class. Be sure to indicate the quality to be developed as a replacement for each undesirable habit.
2. Prepare to tell the class of three examples of personal maladjustment which you have observed in recent speeches. Watch for other examples in the course of your ordinary conversations. To what extent have you developed the two aspects of personal adjustment? What steps do you contemplate for establishing them more firmly?
3. Write a 300-word description of your own problem of stage fright. In it indicate what appear to be the causes, and what remedies you are undertaking.
4. Prepare a five-minute speech. While you are delivering it, make a special effort to think with your audience and to think freely about your subject. Be sure to practice the speech orally several times before delivering it.
5. The instructor will divide the class into several discussion groups. Each group will take one of the following topics—or something similar approved by the instructor—to present before the next class session:

    a. How important a factor in speech is tact?
    b. To what extent is personality judged by speech?

    c. What is an effective speech personality?

    d. Which well-known contemporary speakers have the most pleasing personalities?

6. Prepare a four-minute talk for the class on the subject "The Important Things I Hope to Achieve in My Lifetime." While each member of the class is speaking, all the other members will write on slips of paper, which can be given to him after the instructor has checked them, two types of comments: (1) "Things I Like about Your Personality" and (2) "Things I Do Not Like about Your Personality," as those factors become evident in the talk. It will help the objectivity of these appraisals if they are unsigned, for it is not so important to know the sources of these criticisms as it is to know how you are affecting your audience.

7. Write a 250-word report of a speech you have heard, answering the following questions about it:

    a. Did the speaker seem to be handicapped by stage fright? Did he appear to have any stage fright? If so, how (and how well) did he control it?

    b. Were his thought processes clear and well organized? Did he appear to be thinking his speech through with his audience or was he simply telling them the results of his own thinking on the subject, with no discernible concern for what their thoughts might be?

    c. Did he appear to be thinking easily and freely about his subject while speaking, or was he merely delivering his ideas exactly as he had formulated them during his preparation of the speech?

Bibliography

Allport, Gordon W., *Personality: A Psychological Interpretation* (Holt, Rinehart and Winston, 1937).

Barbara, Dominick A., *Your Speech Reveals Your Personality* (Charles C. Thomas, 1958).

Kluckhohn, Clyde, and Henry Murray, *Personality in Nature, Society, and Culture* (Knopf, 1954).

Lomas, Charles W., "The Psychology of Stage Fright," *Quarterly Journal of Speech,* XXIII (February, 1937), 35–44.

MacGregor, Virginia Claire, "Personality Development in Beginning Speech Training," *Quarterly Journal of Speech,* XX (February, 1934), 47–57.

Murray, Elwood, *The Speech Personality* (Lippincott, 1944).

Overstreet, Harry A., *The Mature Mind* (Norton, 1949).

Symonds, Percival M., "An Analysis of Tact," *Journal of Educational Research,* XXI (April, 1930), 241–54.

CHAPTER 4

CONTENTS

In this discussion at Syracuse University the speaker is getting excellent cooperation from interested and responsive listeners.

EVALUATIVE
LISTENING

A sales manager for a national electronics firm had his secretary keep a record of what he actually did during office hours—and
decided that 35 to 40 percent of his salary was being paid him for
listening. The Survey Research Center of the University of Michigan,
inquiring how people acquire information that affects their voting,
learned that 27 percent of that information comes from newspapers,
58 percent from radio and television, and most of the remainder from
"personal contacts." In other words, about three fourths of the political influence they experienced resulted from listening. When Dr.
Donald E. Bird, of Stephens College, asked 110 dietitians from all
parts of the nation to estimate the importance of the various forms
of communication in their work, their replies indicated reading, 4
percent; writing, 11 percent; speaking, 22 percent; listening, 63 percent.[1]

Whenever the process of communication is studied, the results
are always similar. Paul T. Rankin, studying the importance of the
communicative skills in schools, found that teachers ranked them
as follows: listening, 44.4 percent; talking, 30.3 percent; reading, 16
percent; and writing, 9.3 percent.[2] Miriam E. Wilt, who asked 1,452
Pennsylvania public school elementary teachers to rank the four communicative skills in relative order as tools for learning, received the
following judgments:[3]

Skill	First	Second	Third	Fourth
Reading	897 (61.8%)	272 (18.7%)	268 (18.5%)	15 (1%)
Speaking	318 (21.9%)	489 (33.7%)	542 (37.3%)	103 (7.1%)
Listening	232 (16%)	620 (42.7%)	413 (28.4%)	187 (12.9%)
Writing	5 (0.3%)	71 (4.9%)	229 (15.8%)	1,147 (79%)

[1] These instances are from Ralph G. Nichols and Leonard A. Stevens, *Are You Listening?* (McGraw-Hill, 1957), p. 235.

[2] Paul T. Rankin, "Listening Ability," *Chicago Schools Journal*, XII (June, 1930), 417–20.

[3] Miriam Elizabeth Wilt, "A Study of Teacher Awareness of Listening as a Factor in Elementary Education." Unpublished doctoral dissertation, The Pennsylvania State University, 1949.

To cite additional evidence would be to belabor the obvious. That listening is important may be indicated as follows: of all the communicative skills, it is the most used; along with experience, observation, and reading, it is a principal means of learning; and as an essential part of the two-way process of communication, good listening is an aid to good speaking.

What has been said about the values of listening does not, of course, diminish the importance of effectiveness in speaking. If listeners are inattentive or unresponsive, the speaker is responsible for failing to stimulate their interest. He is the dominant force in the situation. He has chosen the topic and the manner of its development. He should present and adapt his ideas so that they can be understood by his hearers. But no speaker should be held accountable for the failure of an audience to make its own effort to participate in the communicative process. One mind on the platform cannot compensate for a lack of activity in the minds in the auditorium, any more than one mind in a social situation can keep a lively conversation going without participating minds. All must think and feel and respond together if the speaker's words are to have effect.

KINDS OF LISTENING

Listening may be overt or covert, receptive or antagonistic, evaluative or passive, communicative or expressive, informed or unprepared. Your own qualities as a listener may be considerably improved by attention to the problems represented in these paired types.

Overt or Covert Listening

There is an etiquette of listening that is fully as significant as, for example, the etiquette of eating, or of dressing, or of talking. Good manners dictate that when someone is speaking to you—whether you are in a conversational twosome or in an audience—you should make it evident that you are paying attention. This means being physically alert, looking at the speaker, and responding with physical movements, including facial expressions. It is highly discouraging, even irritating, to a speaker to have his hearers slump down in their seats, eyes downcast, faces impassive. If one member of a group behaves in this manner, his manifest unconcern disturbs not only the speaker but the others. On the other hand, even a single alert listener, whose eyes sparkle with interest, whose body leans forward, and whose head is tilted to catch every word, inspires the speaker and stimulates the others to pay closer attention. It is not enough just to *be interested* in what is being said; it is also part of your social responsibility to *look interested*. In this way you help the speaker, and in turn may be helped when you speak; you also help your fellow listeners.

As you think of the conversationalists whom you most admire, it is probable that aside from the wit or wisdom or sympathetic insight of their speech, they are notable also for the stimulation they provide by their attentiveness when others are talking. Similarly, when you find yourself taking part in a discussion, or giving a speech, you draw confidence and inspiration from the lively and encouraging responsiveness of those listeners who take the trouble to hear your remarks and to show their interest in them. Overt responsiveness is a boon you enjoy when you are speaking; it is a duty you owe when you are listening. Covert listening (in which you hide your reactions behind an impassive mask) is a form of social boorishness—a way of declaring that you care so little for the speaker that you have no intention of trying to please him.

Failure to listen at all is an absolute rejection of responsibility for maintaining the two-way flow—the give-and-take—which is essential to all communication. Only a little less detrimental is the failure to listen openly, actively, even enthusiastically. A cold and impassive reception is an almost insuperable barrier to good talk.

Receptive or Antagonistic Listening

Whether or not you may believe what a speaker is saying is another matter. What we have said about listening alertly and even enthusiastically does not in any way preclude the right of judging the message that is being delivered. The point is this: unless you listen with a genuine effort to *understand,* how can you honestly decide whether to believe or to disbelieve? If your antagonism is so marked that even before the speaker opens his mouth you have already decided to reject what he says, there can be no effective communication at all.

You may have observed the behavior of extreme partisans during the course of a political campaign. When the candidate of the opposition party appears on their television screen, they may get up at once and switch channels—or may continue to watch and to "hear" what he says, but instead of "listening," they may accompany his remarks with a derogatory patter of their own. In a public situation, where such extreme partisans must sit through the speech and cannot respond to it aloud, they may nevertheless show by their facial expressions and bodily posture that they are carrying on internally a process of complete rebuttal. This attitude of total rejection is often present whenever a controversial topic, in which the members present feel deeply, is being discussed.

Obviously, there are occasions when auditors do not intend to indicate politeness toward the speaker, and when their minds are so definitely made up that they are firmly predisposed to reject what is said. For example, if a devout Christian finds himself unwillingly in an audience addressed by a blatant and notorious atheist, the unyielding refusal to listen may be expected.

By receptive listening we simply mean opening the mind to a candid and fair consideration of what is said. In other words, it means giving the speaker a chance to state his case. Even if what he says is wholly objectionable to you, perhaps it is attractive (in part, at least) to others. For the sake of your own effectiveness in maintaining your point of view, it is wise to listen to opposing views. You will want to know what arguments are adduced and what persuasive strategies are

Note how the attention is divided between the man standing to ask a question and the unseen speaker who will answer it, with two men in the background discussing strategy. (The Pennsylvania State University)

employed. Only with this knowledge can you successfully combat whatever appeal these obnoxious views may have. The mind so tightly closed by antagonism (which, when we encounter it in others, we call prejudice) that it does not even listen to contrary opinions is a mind that limits its own effectiveness.

Evaluative or Passive Listening

If your mind is receptively open, you will hear a great many things that may be completely true, completely false, or a mixture of truth and falsity. There remains the necessity of making an evaluation. Perhaps you may agree with certain facts that are cited, but disagree with the way in which they are interpreted. Or you may give greater or less emphasis than does the speaker to the significance of certain aspects of his interpretation. This is the process of evaluation—a process that is constantly demanded, whether you may be listening to a demagogue or to a professor in the classroom, to a fellow partisan or to an opponent of your views. Like a good judge at a debate, you continually keep asking yourself about the worth, the validity, the significance of what is being said.

Passive listening is represented by the student who sits in a classroom or in an audience with his mind largely inactive, but with a direct line of stimulation from his ear to his pencil—so busily scrawling down notes summarizing the talk that he never asks himself what it really means. Even in a classroom, where students are expected to learn the content of the lectures, the best learning comes through evaluative listening. In such a situation, fewer—but more discriminating—notes are taken. Furthermore, the speaker's words are on the notebook paper as well as in the mind of the evaluative listener. The good listener can summarize what he has heard, and can also evaluate its significance by his own standards of judgment and his general experience as well as in relation to his current studies.

Communicative or Expressive Listening

Since communication is a two-way process, one duty of the listener is to "signal back" to the speaker the nature of his own reactions. If you doubt what is said, let your face indicate a questioning attitude; if you enthusiastically agree, make that fact evident; if you are puzzled, or bored, or if you think you detect a contradiction in the speaker's argument, let him know your reaction as explicitly as you can. We must realize that the audience, through its physical manifestations, can "talk back" to the speaker, even without uttering a word.

Expressive listening is self-centered: the listener is not concerned with what his behavior can indicate as a guide to the speaker, but is intent solely on expressing his own reactions. An extreme example is the "smart-aleck" listener, who, bored with the speech, tries to put on a show of his own, perhaps mimicking the speaker in an effort to attract attention to himself. Less extreme, but perhaps more common, is the listener who, oblivious of the speaker, sinks into a private reverie, his facial and bodily reactions signaling that what is passing through his own mind has no reference to what the speaker may be saying. Still another kind of "expressive" listening results from a mind so skeptical that even before hearing what the speaker says, the listener begins to "fight back" with expressions of scorn, ridicule, or disbelief. Aside from its unfairness and lack of good taste, this mode of behavior is resented by the other listeners, who may truly wish to hear the speaker out. It is much better to listen with quiet attentiveness and then, if you are so minded, seek an opportunity to make a rejoinder to those views with which you disagree.

Informed or Unprepared Listening

Still another kind of listening problem results from the degree of preparation you bring to a speech or lecture. If your professor asks you to read a chapter on the economic theories of Adam Smith, in a subsequent lecture, *assuming your knowledge of these theories,* he may compare them with the theories of Karl Marx. If you have not read the assigned chapter, his lecture may be practically meaningless. Similarly, when you listen to political speeches, or talks on social conditions, or a discussion of the school segregation question, it is obvious that the speaker can be more effective for you, at least, if you have taken the trouble to find out something about the problem he is discussing.

From whatever point of view listening may be considered, we inevitably keep returning to the theme that *communication is a two-way process.* We have indicated five areas in which listeners have responsibilities that are just as real and just as meaningful as the responsibilities of the speaker. We shall now consider some of the problems which often result in ineffective or nonevaluative listening. These problems relate to the structure of the human personality and the ways in which our minds operate.

CHARACTERISTICS OF THE LISTENING MIND

Personality theories are largely speculative. "What is man?" asked the ancient Psalmist, and the answer is still elusive. Freudian psychiatry conceives of an "unconscious mind" in which the id and the super-ego contend, under the oversight of the ego, and Freud concluded: "Thought is a detour on the road to self-gratification." Social psychologists, such as George Herbert Mead, think of mind as being formed largely by social pressures and experiences. The psychologist William McDougall pictured man as being dominated by instinctive urges, such as hunger, desire for recognition, and ambition for power over others. What the listening mind is really like is a question that has widely differing answers, depending upon which school of psychology is speaking. Nevertheless, certain characteristics of the human mind are generally agreed upon and have considerable pertinence to you in guiding the development of your own listening ability.

The Difficulty of Suspending Judgment

Just as nature hates a physical vacuum, so does it hate a mental vacuum. If you should introduce into a vacuum sphere a small quantity of gas, the gas would expand to fill the entire cavity, however thinly. So, it appears, if you introduce into an "area of ignorance" a small segment of information, that information "expands" to fill the ignorance-vacuum. For instance, if you know nothing about the social life of ancient Egypt and you hear a speaker say, "The Egyptians maintained a slave society," you would be likely to form at once a generalized and stereotyped mental image of ancient Egyptian society. On the contrary, if you heard the speaker say that among all ancient civilizations, the Egyptian most notably maintained a status of equality for women, once again your notion of Egyptian civilization would tend to be all-inclusive—though this time of a very different sort. As it happens, both statements are true. For an accurate picture of ancient Egyptian social life, both of these—and many other—facts need to be taken into account. As a listener, it behooves you to make a sustained effort to "suspend judgment" as well as you can, warning yourself that, "this fact may be true, but it surely is not the whole truth." By systematic practice, you can learn to keep your thinking *tentative* and your judgment incomplete until all the relevant facts are known.

The Desire for Simplicity and Clarity

Confusion is as unsatisfactory as uncertainty or incompleteness. Hence, when we hear a statement that makes only partial sense to us, we tend to rephrase it in our own minds in terms easier to understand. To a degree this tendency is natural: it substitutes the comfort of understanding for the annoyance of confusion. Many people who like "Westerns," for example, because they can readily tell the "good guys" from the "bad guys," may find it difficult to enjoy a novel by Henry James, a writer who depicted the complexities of good and bad within each human personality. Similarly, when you hear a lecturer on South America say that certain nations on that continent are run by dictatorships, your response is likely to be undiscriminating. Yet, however bad all dictatorships may be, they are not all of equal severity, nor are they all equally impervious to public control.

General semanticists, who are concerned that language be used to depict actual meanings, call this tendency the "fallacy of all-ness." If the national administration makes an obvious mistake, the "all-ness" fallacy (the desire for simplicity and clarity of response) may lead some people to denounce it, therefore, as "all bad"; equally, it may lead partisans of the administration to deny that a mistake has been made and to insist that somehow it must be a part of a program that is generally "all good."

This desire for simplicity and clarity leads us to make comparisons and to draw analogies that may be basically unsound. Thus, when we read about the bickering in the United Nations, we say, "Like the League of Nations, it is falling apart," or, "Nations are like individuals; they need to be brought under the control of police power." Most of the problems we confront are nearly as complex and deserve thoughtful consideration. As listeners, we should resist being victimized by the speaker who yields to the temptation to reduce the complex problem to what seems to be its simple elements, and then airily dismisses it.

The Influence of Attitudes, Opinions, and Prejudices

More than we realize, our opinions on many subjects are predetermined by our attitudes and prejudices. As Walter Lippmann expressed it in his book entitled *Public Opinion,* "For the most part, we do not first see, then define; for the most part we define, then see." Any situation *means* to an individual not only what it is, but what he thinks it is. Thus, if as a child you were reared to believe that men are inherently wiser and more capable than women, you will "see" continual evidence that this is true, and will ignore contrary evidence. As Mr. Lippmann said, each of us carries about "pictures in his head" of what the world is like, and, instead of viewing reality, *projects* these pictures upon external reality.

Attitudes and prejudices, mostly acquired in very early childhood, exert a great influence on their possessors. Yet alert and sophisticated listeners can at least be aware of this distortion inevitably taking place in their own minds and can, accordingly, be on constant guard against it. A good question to pose repeatedly to ourselves is this: "Is this really true, or is it merely a projection of my own prejudices?" By such a cautious approach to the listening process, we open our minds to new knowledge and even to new attitudes—the fundamental goal of all education.

The Self-Interest of the Listener

We listen with different degrees of attentiveness and with differing attitudes, depending on who is speaking. To those in authority, who can affect our welfare directly, we listen with care; to those with whom we are disgruntled or to whom we are indifferent, we may listen carelessly if at all. Similarly, we listen most carefully when we realize that what is being said vitally affects ourselves. Thus, "Here is how you can get a ticket at half-price" will ordinarily receive a more attentive listening than "The scale of prices is adjustable in terms of the status of the purchasers." The importance of a personalization of the message naturally is of great interest to speakers; it reminds them of the value of framing their remarks in terms of the personal interests of the audience. But as a listener, too, it is helpful to make a practice of "translating" the speaker's words into terms applicable to yourself. If you do not do so, you may not realize that the second phrasing quoted a few sentences earlier means that you, too, may be eligible for reduced prices. Evaluative listening requires that, instead of merely asking, "What does the speaker mean?" we should also ask, "What does his message mean to me?"

In particular, listeners should listen evaluatively when the speaker is discussing something they will have to do. Examples are a professor making an assignment, or an employer describing a job to be performed, or someone responding to a request for directions. Poor listening results in many a failure to do what ought to have been done. "I'm sorry, Professor, I just didn't understand it that way" may really mean, "While you were speaking, I was thinking about something else."

The Effects of Social Facilitation

Ineffective listening frequently results from what we might call "crowd psychology." If others in the audience are obviously bored or resentful of what the speaker says, we feel, through the influence of "social sympathy," a tendency to react as does the majority. Sometimes this same influence may be exerted by merely a single individual —if he happens to be someone for whose opinion we especially care. Moreover, the degree of attention we give to a speaker's remarks may be strongly influenced by the "climate of opinion" toward him or toward his subject in the community. It is so easy for us to go along with the crowd that sociologists identify this influence as "social facilitation." But natural as this tendency is, it is a surrender of our own individuality, of our own freedom of thought, of our democratic right to do our own thinking. Because of the tendency for people to respond in terms of what "everyone thinks," for centuries beliefs persisted— in witchcraft, in monsters dwelling in the ocean, in the inferiority of women, and so on—which independent inquiry finally proved to be false. Evaluative listening not only broadens the mind but also sharpens its critical faculties.

FACTORS AFFECTING LISTENER EFFICIENCY

How, then, may we "open our ears" and do a better job of listening? At every railroad crossing there are three useful hints: *stop* whatever else you may be doing, thinking, or daydreaming about; *look* at the speaker, so that you may see additional clues to his meaning; and *listen* only to the speaker, disregarding other distracting sounds. Listening is a full-time job; it cannot be done well as a part-time activity. Too many words are missed, too many sounds confused, too many qualifying phrases unheard, too many meaningful gestures and facial expressions overlooked, too many significant inflections of voice unnoticed—even when we are most alert. Frequently, of course, as when we listen to the radio, we are unable to see the speaker. But when we can, we should look as well as listen. Psychological experiments have demonstrated that, when we use our eyes as well as our ears, not only do we add to our understanding what the eyes see but we hear more because the sense of sight stimulates the sense of hearing. It should hardly be necessary to note that undivided attention will increase the efficiency of the listener.

In 1948 Ralph G. Nichols presented a summary of his research on factors in listening comprehension.[4] The evidence he gathered indicated, surprisingly to some, that listening comprehension is not significantly influenced by the listener's note-taking ability or methods. But Nichols did find it influenced by the following factors:

Intelligence
Reading comprehension
Recognition of correct English usage
Size of the listener's vocabulary
Ability to make inferences
Ability to structuralize a speech (that is, to see the organizational plan and
    the connection of the main points)
Listening for main ideas, not merely for specific facts
Use of special techniques while listening to improve concentration
Real interest in the subject discussed
Emotional adjustment to the speaker's thesis
Ability to see significance in the subject discussed
Curiosity about the subject discussed
Physical fatigue of the listener
Audibility of the speaker

He also found that the following additional factors may influence listening comprehension, although the evidence concerning these is inconclusive:

Speaker effectiveness
Admiration for the speaker
Respect for listening as a method of learning
Susceptibility to distraction
Sex of the listener (males are better listeners, on the average)
Room ventilation and temperature
Use of only the English language at home
High school scholastic achievement
High school speech training
Experience in listening to difficult expository material

The conclusions from such studies of listening substantiate the belief that we may improve our listening ability. In the preceding list you will note that the listener will be helped by a thorough proficiency in the English language, including a wide vocabulary, by emotionally

[4] "Factors in Listening Comprehension," *Speech Monographs,* XV, no. 2 (1948), 161–62.

and intellectually favorable attitudes toward both the speaker and his subject, by practice in analyzing and organizing what is heard into easily remembered patterns, by being physically and mentally rested and alert, and by any techniques which improve individual powers of concentration.

Harry A. Overstreet, in his *Influencing Human Behavior,* points out that the power of an idea depends upon the quickness and clarity with which the idea is perceived and upon the ease with which it is recalled. This statement indicates two additional ways in which the listener may help himself: by compensating for a speaker's inadequacies and by doing everything possible to facilitate memory.

COMPENSATING FOR THE SPEAKER'S INADEQUACIES

If the listener finds it difficult to hear or understand, he should—if possible—move nearer the speaker. He may be able to signal the speaker to use more force or projection. He should try to sit where he can see the speaker clearly, so that his eye may assist in distinguishing between such sounds as *b* and *p*; *d* and *t*; *f* and *v*; *m* and *n*. More careful listening can compensate, at least in part, for careless and inadequate speaking.

Attempting to listen to a speaker in the midst of distracting and confusing noises is as unfair to the speaker as it is to the listener. One can hardly hope for any result other than misunderstanding. Each member of an audience has an obligation to insist upon the closing of doors and windows through which noises may be coming or to ask a speaker to stop until a train or plane passes. If a member of the audience wishes to carry on a conversation, he should do it outside, not where it is disturbing both to the speaker and to other listeners. There is a code of proper conduct for the listener as well as for the speaker. It applies in all speaking situations—over the telephone and in social conversation as well as in the speaker-audience situation. Failing to hold a telephone receiver to your ear breaks the chain of communication as completely as does daydreaming, looking out the window, preparing the next hour's lesson, or whispering to a neighbor while pretending to listen to a classroom lecturer or to a classmate's speech. Just as you wish other members of your speech class to help you by being good listeners, other speakers expect the same of you. The listener should do everything possible to compensate for the inadequacies of the speaker by alert and careful attention, by trying to eliminate distractions, and by improving to the utmost his listening efficiency.

LISTENING TO REMEMBER

The purpose of listening is not fulfilled by immediate understanding; we must be able to recall later the things we have heard. Several of the suggestions already made for improving listening efficiency are helpful also, of course, in improving the ability to recall at a later time what one has heard. The following additional and more specific suggestions will aid the listener: (1) It is easiest to recall the things in which we develop an interest. (2) It is easiest to recall details that have been fitted into the total plan or main ideas of the speaker. (3) Since the memory span of even skilled listeners is limited, we should avoid trying to remember great masses of uncoordinated and unrelated data. It is efficient to pick out the important ideas and to try to remember only those. (4) Memory is an active process requiring effort and determination. We must resolve to remember and not expect to forget. (5) We can facilitate memory by concentrating upon the ideas to be remembered and by mentally rephrasing them in simple language and in memorable patterns. (6) We can further aid recall by mentally summarizing the main points of a speech immediately after hearing them and at intervals thereafter.

JUDGMENTS OF SPEECH AND OF PERSONALITY

Your reaction to a speaker is really a composite of several reactions. You will form fairly definite opinions of most members of the class as *persons*—quite aside from your judgments of them as *speakers*. You may, for example, conclude that students A, B, and C are very poor speakers but very likable persons. You may decide that students D, E, and F are very good speakers but would not make good friends. Yet it is easy to exaggerate your ability to differentiate these judgments. Since speech is an intimate part of the total personality, whatever total impression a speaker makes undoubtedly results in large part from the audible and visual stimuli that his speaking has provided. Trying to separate the person from the speaker is probably an impossible task. In other words, your evaluation of a person depends both upon *how* he speaks and upon *what* he says.

It is reasonable to conclude, then, that the individual who is liked and respected by the group cannot be an altogether bad speaker, and that the individual who is disliked or distrusted cannot be in a real sense a good speaker. If the latter has more of the "platform graces" than the former but lacks sincerity, his speech is reduced to a mere exhibition. And if the likable individual lacks poise, fluency, or vividness, he cannot be fully effective. As the proficiencies of each student in the speech class improve, the critics will become more exacting. Thus the listeners will set the standards, determine new goals, and stimulate one another to maximum attainment.

THE LISTENER'S EVALUATION

It is evident from what we have just noted that every speech will be judged largely by the kind of relationship the speaker manages to establish with his audience. The following questions should assist us in the task of evaluation.

1. *Is what the speaker is saying true?* As Thomas Carlyle asked in his inaugural address when he became Rector of Edinburgh University, "If it is a good speaker, and if it is not the truth he is speaking, can there be a more horrible monster in creation?" Truth is not readily determined. Nonetheless, your first responsibility as a listener is to evaluate what is being said.

2. *Does the speech increase the audience's respect for the speaker?* If you do not first respect a speaker, you are not going to pay much attention to what he says. You will find yourself evaluating a speaker in terms of his attitude toward his audience, toward his subject, and toward himself. If he shows respect for his audience, he will in turn receive respect from them; if he shows a sincere interest in them, they will reciprocate. If he manifests enthusiasm about the opportunity to discuss his subject with them, his enthusiasm will be contagious. Listeners respect a speaker who obviously *believes in* his subject, who respects them enough to be well informed in his subject, and who—justifying his enthusiasm and interest—is fair and accurate in his presentation. Finally, an audience respects a speaker who, because of the thoroughness of his preparation, has confidence in himself.

3. *Is the speech audience-centered?* Is the speaker concerned with

the accuracy of his topic as well as with the needs and interests of his listeners? If the speaker has failed to prepare—and subsequently fails to deliver—his speech without regard for what it means to his listeners, members of the audience will gain little from it; moreover, they will probably be bored and inattentive. But any failure by the speaker does not entirely excuse a failure on the part of the listeners to follow him: "centering" the speech around his own individual problems is something only a listener can do. Good listening involves making a close and continuing application of the generalized remarks of the speaker to the listener's special concerns.

4. *Does the speech progress from introduction to conclusion?* Have you ever listened to a lecture in which it seemed to you that the speaker was still on the same point at the end of the talk as at its beginning? Such a speech lacks forward movement of ideas. Of course it lacks organization. Worse, it lacks purpose. The effective speech begins with the audience where it is and ends with the audience where the speaker wishes it to be. Sometimes a speaker will choose to begin by challenging some belief of his audience. He may say, for example, "I've heard many of you say that activities are more important than studies. In my judgment there is absolutely no basis for this belief, and I'm going to tell you why." More often, a speaker will wish to begin on a basis of agreement with his audience. For example, he may start a speech by saying, "We all know in a general way why we're in college. We're here to get a better start—we might even say a head start—in the race of life. The question is, How shall we go about getting this head start? And that's what I wish to discuss with you." In both of these examples, the speaker picks up the thinking of his audience at some definite point and guides it toward a definite goal. The speaker must be careful not to "lose" his listeners or to surprise them with some sudden, unexpected conclusion. Even more important, he must not leave them guessing at what he meant. The effective speech has ideas which *move forward* to a clear conclusion. When the speaker does not organize his speech well, the listeners have to compensate by unusual attentiveness to follow the thread of ideas and may even have to supply part of the pattern themselves.

5. *Are you listening to the speech or to the speaker?* When a listener says of a speaker, "What a beautiful voice! What graceful gestures!" the delivery is getting in the way of the message. Of course the speaker should learn to adapt himself and his manner of speaking so well to the situation that his delivery will be unobtrusive. A purpose of art is to conceal art. However, whether the delivery is graceful or awkward, the listener should make an effort to pierce through the

LISTENER'S RESPONSE CHART

Speaker _____ Date _____

Subject _____

Directions: For each of the qualities of effective speaking indicated below, check (√) the evaluative word which most nearly indicates the relative effectiveness of the speaker.

I saw you as:

(Approach, posture, facial expression, gestures, walking movements, personal appearance, appropriate clothes, distracting mannerisms.)

POOR	AVERAGE	EXCELLENT
FAIR	GOOD	

Comments: _____

_____

I heard you as:

(Audibility, voice quality, "pleasantness" of pitch, speaking rate, force, fluency, pronunciation, sense of communication.)

POOR	AVERAGE	EXCELLENT
FAIR	GOOD	

Comments: _____

_____

Speech composition:

(Interesting subject, introduction, proper scope of topic, clarity of purpose, supporting material, logical thinking, clarity and effectiveness of organization, definite conclusion, appropriateness of language.)

POOR	AVERAGE	EXCELLENT
FAIR	GOOD	

Comments: _____

_____

General effectiveness:

POOR	AVERAGE	EXCELLENT
FAIR	GOOD	

Comments: _____

_____

outer forms to the inner meanings. This does not mean that delivery is to be ignored; it cannot be. A mellifluous voice is no substitute for sound sense; on the other hand, ungainly posture should not distract from what the speaker is saying.

A RESPONSE CHART FOR THE LISTENER

We have seen that much of an audience's reaction to a speech is a response to the speaker's personality. This type of judgment is usually —although perhaps not properly—eliminated from the standards suggested for the specific evaluation of a particular speech. The usual warning to listeners not to allow any personal bias to influence their judgment seems to be based on the assumption that bias and judgment really are separable. Such an assumption is only partly true. However, it is possible to make a specific response to a given speech, apart, so far as possible, from the general response made to the speaker as a person. The following chart has been devised to guide you in making that response. Familiarity with it may help to clarify and order your thinking in your habitual listening to speeches, whether or not you are to make a written report on them.

The chart is divided into four parts, indicating four types of response that you as a listener ordinarily make to speeches. The first response to be recorded is the visual response: what impressions of the speaker and his speech did you receive through the eyes? The chief impact of a speaker with some noticeable peculiarity of dress, mannerism, or physique, for example, will be a visual one. Your response to the audible elements of the speech is to be set down in the second division of the chart. The third division concerns your reaction to the content and organization of the speech. Finally, because our responses in any social situation are never partial but always complete, you are asked to record your single over-all response to the general effectiveness of the speaker.

CONCLUSION

Listening is more than and different from merely "hearing." Listening is the active copartnership role in any act of oral communication. The work that a listener must do may be compared to that of a catcher on a baseball team. He "signals" to the pitcher (speaker) as well as receives the ball (or message). Evaluative listening is a part of the process of thinking. When you are in a communicative situation, you listen evaluatively in order to learn, to keep from being mis-led, to apply what is said to your own interests and needs, and to make your own considerable contribution to the effectiveness of the speech. When it is your turn to speak, you become sharply aware of how much influence the audience exerts: an alert and interested audience will bring out the best in you, whereas a dull and apathetic one will drag you down to its own level. What you as a speaker wish from your own listeners is what you should try to provide for your classmates when they speak.

EXERCISES AND BIBLIOGRAPHY

Exercises

1. One way of learning to improve your speech is to listen analytically to every speech given in class and to all the speeches you hear outside class. Apply the standards of judgment restated in this chapter. It is valuable speech training to make a practice of summarizing the point of every speech you hear and evaluating the technique of the speaker in presenting it.

2. Listen to a speech that is afterward to be printed. (The magazine *Vital Speeches of the Day* prints a collection of significant current speeches every two weeks.) Write down your impression of the speech upon *hearing* it. Answer these questions about it:

   a. What was the speaker's purpose?
   b. What were his main ideas?
   c. How well did his ideas support his purpose?
   d. By what means did the speaker adjust to his audience?
   e. Was his introduction adequate?
   f. Did his conclusion help to accomplish his purpose?

3. After you have written your analysis of the speech as heard, obtain a copy of it in printed form. From the printed copy check your reactions to each of the foregoing questions. Then write a brief statement indicating the following:

   a. What did the speaker apparently accomplish by his *presence* that is not evident in the written copy of the speech?
   b. What were you able to discern from the printed speech that you missed as a listener?

4. Write a brief evaluation of every member of your speech class, following the form suggested on page 91. As your instructor indicates, either write all the evaluations in sequence and hand them to him, or write them on separate, unsigned sheets, so that each one will go to the appropriate student. Such an exercise, honestly and thoughtfully done,

CRITICISM CHART

Speaker _____ Date _____

Subject _____

The Speech

1. Purpose
    clear 1 2 3 4 5 vague
    attained 1 2 3 4 5 not attained
2. Compelling 1 2 3 4 5 dull
3. Vivid 1 2 3 4 5 commonplace
4. Well ,illustrated 1 2 3 4 5 abstract
5. Language
    exact 1 2 3 4 5 inexact
    original 1 2 3 4 5 trite
    appropriate 1 2 3 4 5 inappropriate
6. Speech plan
    clear 1 2 3 4 5 confused
    audience-centered 1 2 3 4 5 subject-centered
7. Climactic 1 2 3 4 5 poorly organized
8. Thought content
    analytical 1 2 3 4 5 superficial
    personal 1 2 3 4 5 impersonal
9. Qualities of style
    emphasis
       good 1 2 3 4 5 poor
    repetition
       used well 1 2 3 4 5 used poorly
    contrast
       good 1 2 3 4 5 poor
    concreteness
       sufficient 1 2 3 4 5 insufficient
    factual evidence
       enlivened 1 2 3 4 5 uninteresting
10. Errors in grammar _____
    _____
    _____
11. Mispronunciations _____
    _____

The Speaker

1. First impression
    favorable 1 2 3 4 5 unfavorable
2. Manner
    communicative 1 2 3 4 5 ineffective

3. Appearance
   impressive 1 2 3 4 5 distracting

4. Posture
   poised 1 2 3 4 5 awkward

5. Movement
   natural 1 2 3 4 5 stiff
   adequate 1 2 3 4 5 inadequate
   varied 1 2 3 4 5 monotonous
   well poised 1 2 3 4 5 distracting

6. Gestures
   well timed 1 2 3 4 5 inappropriate
   purposeful 1 2 3 4 5 meaningless

7. Voice
   volume
       good 1 2 3 4 5 improperly controlled
   pleasing 1 2 3 4 5 unpleasant
   varied 1 2 3 4 5 monotonous
   relaxed 1 2 3 4 5 tense
   rate
       inappropriate 1 2 3 4 5 appropriate

8. Vocal defects
   lisp_____
   foreign accent_____
   nasality_____
   lazy articulation_____
   faulty projection_____
   high pitch_____

9. Personality
   alert 1 2 3 4 5 phlegmatic
   sincere 1 2 3 4 5 uninspired
   enthusiastic 1 2 3 4 5 uncommunicative
   confident 1 2 3 4 5 ill at ease

10. Eye contact
    good 1 2 3 4 5 poor

11. Facial expressiveness
    good 1 2 3 4 5 insufficient

The Audience

1. Responsive 1 2 3 4 5 inattentive
2. Unified in response 1 2 3 4 5 varied in response
3. Helpful to speaker 1 2 3 4 5 detrimental to speaker
4. Alert 1 2 3 4 5 phlegmatic

Critic_____

can be of great value to the members of the class in clarifying for them the kinds of relationships and impressions they have created.

5. Write an analysis of your reaction to a speech. Indicate what you brought to it as a creative listener. In what ways did the speech affect you individually—ways in which it could not have affected other listeners, because your response was caused in large part by your own experience, knowledge, or bias? If you were to converse with the speaker about the subject of his talk, what points would you want to make to him about it? Would you want to argue with him, inform him concerning further points about the subject, or question him in order to secure further information? Write a brief outline of a speech you might make on the same subject (to a different audience) after hearing his.

6. Go to hear some well-known lecturer or convocation speaker and use the criticism chart (on pages 94–95) as a basis for recording your evaluation of all the elements that go into an effective speech. The system of numbers is used to provide a scale on which you may indicate the speaker's success with each factor. Draw a circle around whatever number indicates your judgment of the degree of success. Number 1 indicates the greatest degree of success, and number 5 the lowest. The purpose of so detailed a chart is to emphasize the great range of considerations which go into one's evaluation of, and thus one's reaction to, a speech. Whether or not the listener may be fully aware of it, many of these twenty-six points contribute to his reaction.

Bibliography

Adams, H. M., "Listening," *Quarterly Journal of Speech,* XXIV (April, 1938), 209–11.

Nichols, Ralph G., "Listening: Questions and Problems," *Quarterly Journal of Speech,* XXXIII (February, 1947), 83–86.

Nichols, Ralph G., and Leonard A. Stevens, *Are You Listening?* (McGraw-Hill, 1957).

Oliver, Robert T., Dallas C. Dickey, and Harold P. Zelko, *Communicative Speech* (Holt, Rinehart and Winston, 1955), Chap. 4.

Pear, T. H., "Listening: Art and Science," in his *Voice and Personality* (Wiley, 1931), pp. 49–57; compare with Mortimer J. Adler, *How to Read a Book* (Simon and Schuster, 1940).

Rankin, P. T., "Listening Ability," *Chicago School Journal,* XII (January and June, 1930), 177–79 and 417–20.

Wiksell, Wesley, "The Problem of Listening," *Quarterly Journal of Speech,* XXXII (December, 1946), 505–8.

Zelko, Harold P., *How to Become a Successful Speaker* (National Foremen's Institute, 1950), Chap. 8.

Part Two

SPEECH IN GROUP ACTIVITIES

CHAPTER 5

CONTENTS

Spontaneous conversation is an important factor in all social relationships. Conversation helps to knit the ties of friendship and mutual understanding.

CONVERSATION AND
THE CONVERSATIONAL
QUALITY

It is in talk alone that we can learn our period and ourselves. In short, the first duty of a man is to speak; that is his chief business in this world; and talk, which is the harmonious speech of two or more, is by far the most accessible of pleasures. It costs nothing in money; it is all profit; it completes our education, founds and fosters our friendships, and can be enjoyed at any age and in almost any state of health.

—ROBERT LOUIS STEVENSON

O NE of the first textbooks on public speaking in the modern era was written by the late Professor James Albert Winans, of Cornell University, in 1915. His discussion of the relationship between conversation and public speaking has been but little improved upon in the intervening years. He used the illustration of a man, enthusiastic about some recent event, meeting a friend on the street and stopping to talk with him. One after another, others happen by and stop to listen. Before long there are a dozen, thirty, a hundred. At some point it becomes difficult for some to hear and see the speaker. They ask him to get up on a nearby cart. He does, and proceeds. Now at what precise point, Professor Winans asked, did private conversation become public speaking? The point, of course, is that the change is in degree and not in kind.

Essentially the same qualities make for effective speaking, whether the audience numbers one person or millions. Most of the distinctions commonly made between conversation and public speaking are arbitrary, easily overstated, and more imagined than real. Are the qualities of projection and loudness in the voice more important for the public speaker? Did you ever try to carry on a conversation at a noisy street intersection? In this age of microphones and amplifiers it cannot truthfully be said that public speaking differs from conversation because it requires more energy on the part of the speaker. Does public speaking require more specific and careful preparation? Perhaps generally, but not necessarily. There may be many conversations in life far more important to us than any public speaking we will ever do: with a personnel manager we hope to persuade to employ us; with a boss we are asking for a raise; with a lover we hope to have as a life mate. For any one of these we may prepare longer and with far greater care than for most public speeches. It is by conversations, too, that we hope to win new friends, as well as gain greater respect from old friends. Our most important use of speech may well be in conversation. Occasionally out of the most casual conversations come judgments and decisions vitally affecting our lives and destinies. But, you may be saying, there is one real difference: "The public speaker does all the talking; in conversation there is give-and-take." If you say that, however, you are overlooking an aspect of Professor Winans' carefully chosen illustration. The man on the street was doing most of the talking from the time the first man stopped and began to listen. Furthermore, in Chapter 2 we have noted at length that good public speaking is also two-way communication.

There is no better point at which to begin conscious improvement in our speech than in everyday conversation. If we learn to do our best at this universal art we will have perfected the basic attitudes and skills upon which all speaking depends. Our first reason for improving conversational skills, then, is the highly practical one of *high personal reward*. You will remember the description of Gratiano in Shakespeare's *The Merchant of Venice*: "Gratiano speaks an infinite deal of nothing . . . . His reasons are as two grains of wheat hid in two bushels of chaff; you shall seek all day ere you find them, and when you have them, they are not worth the search." Becoming a better conversationalist will bring rewards as large and as immediate as those of any achievement within your reach.

A second reason why the student of speech is concerned with improving his conversational skill is that *this is a helpful preliminary to becoming a good public speaker*. The average beginning speaker has very few opportunities outside the classroom to practice speaking to audiences. He does, however, have innumerable opportunities to converse. He should, then, while studying the principles of public speaking, consider how well they may apply to conversational situations; and while he is conversing he should be practicing the direct application of principles that will be invaluable when he speaks before a larger audience.

ELEMENTS OF GOOD CONVERSATION

Conversational "rules" may be found in liberal quantities in sources as remote from one another as Jonathan Swift's essays and James Boswell's *Life of Johnson* on the one hand and the fifteen-minutes-a-day correspondence courses on the other. The advice is as varied as the sources from which it comes. One writer stresses the lightness and insubstantiality of good conversation. He compares it to a balloon, which is tossed lightly from one conversationalist to another without ever being allowed to touch the ground. Another writer charges that the greatest danger in conversation is frothiness and insubstantiality. He declares that the best conversation is serious and methodical, more like a freight train loaded with ideas than like a balloon to be bandied about. One critic has condemned the general tendency of conversation to deal with personalities; another warns against the dry rot of abstractness. Frequently commentators warn against "talking shop," but just as frequently they advise talking about one's closest interests —which are apt to center around one's work. From the legion of books and articles on the art of conversation, only one conclusion is unmistakable: the futility of formulating any dogmatic list of rules for good conversation.

Here, however, are some suggestions which, if followed with discretion, should prove useful. They deal with conversational situations and subjects, with the duties of the host and hostess, with the conversational tone, and with the preparation to be made for conversation.

Conversational Situations

The principal reason for the confusion and contradiction in the various works on conversation is that there are so many different kinds of conversational situations. From fraternity-house "bull sessions" to formal receptions is a far cry, and no single set of rules can be formulated that would be appropriate for both. The conversational situation is composed of many factors, including the age, occupation, interest, sex, education, and character of the participants and the time, place, and purpose of the gathering. So many combinations are possible that there is an almost infinite variety of conversational situations. Woe to the conversationalist who tries to meet them all in the same manner! A "wise adaptability" is certainly the first characteristic to be developed. The student who tried to initiate a conversation on philosophy between halves at a football game was showing more earnestness than conversational judgment. It is excellent practice for the conversationalist deliberately to seek out as many different types of situations as possible and to observe carefully the special characteristics of each.

Wherever people gather, conversational groupings emerge. Different as these students may be in many ways, their topics of conversation and the communicative skills they must utilize are relatively similar.

Conversational Subjects

One class of conversational subjects consists of conventional symbols of friendly interest, such as the weather, the other person's health, and items of casual interest in the news of the day. These are convenient for "breaking the ice," but they are likely to become boring indeed if they are not at once superseded by other subjects. When the hostess politely inquires about the health of your family, for example, it is a serious error to commence a detailed account of the minor ailments suffered by each member. "They are all very well, thank you" or "We're having a round of spring colds" is all that the situation calls for. Such comments as these are also common when two acquaintances pass each other on the street. The words that are used in such a situation are wholly unimportant. The sole purpose in saying anything at all is to communicate the fact that you are aware of each other's presence and that you entertain mutually friendly feelings.

Another class of subjects consists of those that are really intended to be discussed. They may be as varied as the interests of the participants. There is, however, more uniformity in conversational topics than might be supposed. As a result of our living together in a single type of civilization, there is a common body of ideas that we all share. In a study of 601 conversations[1] of men to men, of women to women, and of mixed groups, occurring during intermissions of concerts, it was discovered that the leading topics of men's conversations are money and business, other men, women, sports, and other amusements. The leading topics of women's conversations are other women, men, clothes, amusements, and immediate surroundings. A questionnaire distributed among a random group of college students indicated that their conversations dealt preponderantly with such subjects as the opposite sex, studies, religion, current affairs, and prospects for jobs more frequently than with the light and frivolous aspects of college life. But on the evening before the "home-coming game," for example, the talk would almost inevitably revolve around something having to do with school spirit.

It is often considered good practice to direct the conversation into the channels of one's companion's interests, but this is a dangerous rule to follow. It is in effect to place the responsibility for maintaining the conversation upon the other members of the group, who may be indifferent, unwilling, or too tired to bear it. Unless a conversationalist is eager to talk about himself, it is discourteous for others to ask questions which force him to do so. The biographer and essayist Gamaliel Bradford reports in his journal that he used to pride himself upon his ability "to draw people out" as "the last word of conversational tact. . . . But I now come to see by long experience that it is really far more considerate and amiable to give at least a fair amount of yourself and your own experience, while probably the most entertaining and successful talkers are those who fill the whole time with the display of their own affairs and their own souls, but do it entertainingly."

Bradford's generalization is, of course, as dangerous as its opposite. The only safe rule is that no subject is satisfactory which does not challenge the interest of the entire group. The subjects listed on page 103 offer some cues as to topics that can on many occasions be introduced safely. By observation and by the application of what you know of the interests of the participants, you can formulate a fresh list for every occasion. To be generally avoided in mixed groups intent chiefly on sociability are topics that are morbid, pessimistic, antagonistic, or otherwise disagreeable. Politics and religion are perennially interesting, but when sharp differences of opinion are manifested they should

---

[1] J. Spencer Carlson, Stuart W. Cook, and Leroy L. Stromberg, "Sex Differences in Conversation," *Journal of Applied Psychology,* XX (December, 1936), 727–35.

be dropped. Gossip is alluring but dangerous. The gossipers come to distrust one another, each fearing that he will be the victim the next time he is absent from the group.

Duties of the Host and Hostess

An occasional conversation may drift along successfully with no directing influence, but as a general rule a conversation can no more steer itself than can a ship. In this respect conversation is just like any other group activity. To avoid confusion or conflict, a skillful guiding touch is essential. Providing this guidance is one of the prime duties of the host or hostess. The arrangement for a successful evening of conversation must begin with the invitation of the guests. Some people who will shine brilliantly in the proper company will be dull and morose when the other guests do not please them. A hostess who fills her parlor with eager talkers one evening and with good listeners another time will have two unsuccessful gatherings. A good conversation must begin with a group of well-assorted, congenial participants.

The host or hostess is responsible, too, for providing conversational "starters" as often as may be necessary, for lubricating the conversations with geniality and good humor whenever too strong a jarring note appears, for deftly shutting off an overly loquacious guest, and for encouraging any who might wish to talk but are too timid to begin. Sometimes a great deal depends upon the seating arrangement, by which congenial companions may be brought together and others, less congenial, kept apart. And, of course, the general comfort and agreeableness of the situation have much to do with the success of the conversation.

The Conversational Tone

Another chief duty of the host or hostess is to establish the conversational tone. The conversational tone should ordinarily be good-humored and genial, but not Pollyanna-ish. Violent disagreements are to be avoided, but so is the total lack of opinion which is usually responsible for complete accord. There is a middle ground of agreeable controversy, which has best been described by Robert Louis Stevenson, who talked as well as he wrote. "There is a certain attitude," he said, "combative at once and deferential, eager to fight yet most averse to quarrel, which marks out at once the talkable man. It is not eloquence, nor fairness, nor obstinacy, but a certain proportion of all these that I love to encounter in my amicable adversaries. They must not be pontiffs holding doctrine, but huntsmen questing after elements of truth. Neither must they be boys to be instructed, but fellow students with whom I may argue on equal terms." *Amicable adversaries* is perhaps the most suitable term with which to describe the ideal conversationalists. They keep the tone of the conversation spicy, alert, and vigorous, without being rancorous. They know how to have opinions without being opinionated, to contend without being contentious.

Equally to be avoided are unyielding obstinacy and the "yes-yes" type of affability. Talkers of the first kind are contemptuous of the opinions of everyone else; the latter have no respect for their own beliefs. Continual contradiction smothers good talk, and continual agreement never produces it in the first place. The first is irritating; the second is no more stimulating than coquetting with an echo. In typical social gatherings the best conversational tone is one of eager discussion, of good-natured controversy, of open-minded affirmation.

Preparation for Conversation

Joseph Addison, the English essayist, declared that he would no more attend a conversational gathering without careful preparation than he would risk his reputation with an unprepared speech. Many other conversational "wits" held the same view and gathered a store of witty remarks to fire into the conversational situation at appropriate intervals. The result was brilliant but artificial. Although this practice is still occasionally followed, it is not generally successful. But should we go to the opposite extreme of making no preparation whatever for a conversational gathering?

A commendable general kind of preparation was that practiced by Samuel Johnson, who attributed his great conversational ability to the fact that every time he talked, no matter what the circumstances, he always tried "to talk as well as he could both in sentiment and expression." When Boswell asked him for additional requirements for good conversation, Dr. Johnson replied with a statement of four rules: "There must in the first place be knowledge; there must be materials. In the second place there must be a command of words; in the third place there must be imagination, to place things in such views as they are not commonly seen in; and in the fourth place there must be presence of mind, and a resolution that is not to be overcome by failure." By study and by practice, most of these requirements can be met. A careful application of them would certainly bear fruit in the form of increased skill in conversation.

The best specific preparation for an immediate conversational situation is to be in good spirits, animated, alert, and determined to do your share in contributing sympathetically and sensitively to whatever kind of talk the mood of the group may require. If each of the conversationalists makes this type of preparation, the chill effects of dullness, indifference, and moroseness will not intrude to dampen the spirits of the rest.

Usually the members of a group are well enough known to one another so that unpleasant and tactless topics may be avoided. Conversationalists who are prone to use sarcasm and ridicule should be especially careful not to attack thoughtlessly some of the foibles of the other participants. It is well to abide by the old rule that it is better to lose a jest than a friend.

In sum, then, we may conclude that the good conversationalist must be exceedingly adaptable, should select his topics from fields that are of interest to all those present, should contribute his own ideas while being courteous in his reception of differing opinions, and should make a real effort to enter into the spirit of the group. In addition, the host and hostess must not forget their special responsibility for seeing to it that everyone present has an opportunity to participate —just as each guest makes sure that neither his manner nor what he says detracts from the enjoyment of the other participants.

BACKGROUND FOR CONVERSATION

It will be found that the great talkers have been wide readers. Sam Houston, the eminent Texan, spent a great deal of his youth among the Indians, but even then he devoted his leisure to the study of Greek. Winston Churchill's conversation and speeches are filled with allusions to the literature and history of all ages and many lands. Patrick Henry has been described as a backwoodsman, yet he was a finished scholar in comparison with many college graduates of today. As noted in Chapter 1, Quintilian outlined a course of study in literature, music, history, mathematics, and kindred subjects which would keep his speech students hard at work from earliest childhood until maturity. To his mind the first requisite for effective speaking was to have acquired worth-while ideas to express, based on a wide background of knowledge and careful thought. Quintilian's ideal is still an excellent one to follow.

The first step, then, in developing something worth while to say is *to increase your store of information*. It may be safely assumed that this is a step which many people have not taken and never will take. They are limited, then, as effective conversationalists, to talking among others whose background is relatively similar to their own. The more you know, the larger the number of people to whom you can talk effectively. However, college students are prone to underestimate their store of ideas. Measured against Quintilian's ideal, most of them are woefully lacking in background; but compared to the mass of people who have never attended college, they have better backgrounds than they suspect. You will do well to look with some degree of confidence upon the body of knowledge which you have already acquired; feel free to draw fully upon it in both your casual and prepared talk. But remember, meanwhile, that this body of knowledge should continually and rapidly expand. As Kipling said, "Yours is the world and everything that's in it"—but taking possession of the world of facts is an arduous and time-consuming job.

It should be added at once, however, that your background does not consist only of books you have read. A large part of it is your personal experience. Do not overlook the excellent conversational material in the experiences you have had. One trip through the slums with a social worker, an afternoon accompanying a visiting nurse on her calls, a few weeks as a summer-camp worker—all such firsthand experiences will give you understanding and feeling for certain problems which have a depth of value beyond what you can learn through reading. You will not become an authority in a few hours or a few weeks of experience—but you will thereby acquire attitudes and feelings which add life and rich meaning to your conversation. In general, you will always talk best to people whose backgrounds resemble your own. The kind of background you acquire, then, helps determine the kind of friends you will have.

The second step in developing something worth while to say is *to evolve and clarify a set of beliefs, attitudes, convictions, and interests*. It is disconcerting, when one urges college students to base their talk upon their interests and convictions, to hear them reply that they "have none." No one can be considered mature until he has some set of principles by which he seeks to govern his life. Of course, these principles should be flexible. They vary with circumstances, and it would be unfortunate if they did not grow and alter considerably with the passage of years. It is not dogmatism that is desired, but rather a thoughtful consideration of various aspects of the meaning of life.

The student who has reached this point in his development will clearly reveal the fact by his manner of assurance, the incisiveness of his thoughts, and the sense of real purpose which runs through his talk. Most of the triviality and aimlessness which we note in the conversation we hear is due to the fact that the speakers themselves are not aware of what they wish to do; they aim at nothing and hit it unerringly.

The third step consists in *discussing subjects for which you already have or can readily develop a genuine enthusiasm and deep-seated interest.* Everyone has many fleeting interests. But it is not safe to depend for conversational materials on the transient kind of interest which arises from the reading of a sprightly article in *The Reader's Digest* or a similar source. It is true that if the facts in the article are in themselves interesting, you might develop enough enthusiasm to make that interest seem genuinely your own. But the risk is great because the structure upon which you are building is thin. Superficiality, like murder, will generally out.

The ideal subject to talk about is one to which you have responded emotionally for a long time, perhaps for several years, but for which you have recently gathered fresh information. For example, during the past several years you may have cherished a deep dislike for a certain political leader. Perhaps you have engaged in heated arguments regarding him, and you have consistently turned off your radio when he spoke. As you examine your point of view critically, to see how you can best persuade others to agree with you, you note that your opinion is backed by more emotion than fact. You find it hard to name specific acts of his which you can wholeheartedly condemn and harder still to trace their ruinous effects. Hence you go to the *Readers' Guide to Periodical Literature,* look up a number of articles dealing with aspects of his political career, and begin the accumulation of specific evidence. As you do so, you may find yourself modifying your attitude a bit at some points and strengthening it at others. Finally, you are able to jot down three or four definite reasons for considering his policies harmful, with specific evidence to support each point. What you have to say about the man will now have significance and added interest.

You will find that talk drawn from this kind of background can hardly fail to be good, for two reasons. First, you will be sustained by a deep and earnest conviction which has taken firm root over a long period of time and which has grown soundly during your recent gathering of evidence; and, second, you will have a body of recently collected specific information which will be fresh in your mind and which you will be eager to share with others in order to win them to your point of view. This amounts almost to a definite formula for good conversation.

THE BASIC PRINCIPLE OF GOOD CONVERSATION

It would be easy to extend the foregoing suggestions almost interminably. Do not indulge in monologues, do not tell pointless anecdotes, be a good listener, give the other fellow a chance, do not talk about your operation, your aches and pains, or your neighbor's wife, do not mope, do not be a buffoon—all of these appear to be safe guideposts to good conversation, and so they are under most circumstances. But even these rules cannot be universally applied. Some operations are interesting, some people can make buffoonery attractive, and an occasional guest may be so fascinating that he is encouraged to monopolize the talk. Any attempt to establish a set conversational pattern to fit all situations must inevitably fail.

This does not mean, however, that no guidance is possible for improving conversational ability. What it does mean is that there is actually no such thing as *conversation*. There are only *conversations*. Every time two or more people talk, the situation is unique. Every such situation has to be met in terms of itself. *The basic principle of good conversation is to determine clearly the purpose of each particular conversational situation and to conduct onself in accord with that purpose.*

When a half-dozen friends meet for an evening of talk, a conversational tone is at once established. The host or someone else may give a cue by his manner or voice that the conversation is to be lighthearted and gay. Or, after a few minutes of conversation serving simply to establish an atmosphere of friendliness, one of the members may earnestly bring up a point of view he wants the others to consider. If the mood of the group permits, the talk settles down to a serious discussion. If the others are unwilling, someone will respond jestingly to his challenge, and the talk flows on along the line that fits best the temper of most of the participants.

The outdoor theater at the University of Colorado provides a pleasant setting for a conversational discussion.

Conversational failures occur most often when there is no clear or unified indication of what the tone of the talk should be. Two or more determined members of the group may clash. One may like very much to have the group discuss the ability of religion to deal with the problem of the latest scientific device of destruction. Another may want to indulge in an evening of gaiety. There must be a submission to what the general temper of the group favors, or the clash of purposes will persist and prevent the development of any consistent tone. In such a struggle for supremacy, everyone becomes uneasy, and when the group separates its members usually complain that the clashing conversationalists lack tact. Tact is, indeed, one of the most highly valued of all social virtues.

In conversation, as in general social living, the individual should be sensitive to the attitudes, feelings, and moods of others. This does not mean that the good conversationalist always surrenders his own desires. It does mean that he approaches each conversational situation alert to discover the mood of the other participants and that he thereupon adjusts his behavior to that mood. Having made such an adjustment, he may be able to convert the mood to one more appropriate to his own purpose.

If, for example, you are tired from a week of hard study and on

Saturday evening find yourself introduced to a group that is intent upon a serious discussion, you might react in one of three ways: You might wearily withdraw into yourself and let the conversation flow around you. You might excuse yourself and retire. Or you might enter briefly into the discussion and from that basis of solidarity with the group introduce a jesting note that may change the whole tenor of the evening's talk. How well that last alternative succeeds will depend entirely, of course, upon how intent the others are on continuing their serious thinking.

Conversation is essentially a social process. It depends upon similarity of purpose among the participants. Since no two people are likely to feel or think exactly alike at any given time, good conversation must presuppose a social willingness on the part of each member of a group to adapt to the others. The people who adapt most easily and completely are in general considered the most "agreeable." This does not mean, however, that they are the most influential or the most highly respected. Adaptation and communication are not the same thing. In some situations, you may feel that the thing to do is to adapt yourself completely to the desires of others; in other situations you may feel stubbornly determined to bring about an adaptation to your own mood and purpose. Ordinarily, the good conversationalist falls somewhere between these two extremes. He is an "amicable adversary." He goes part of the way, and he expects the others to come part of the way to him.

When matured by experiences of social living, the good conversationalist willingly becomes enough like the rest of the group in attitude, feeling, and mood to win their approval. He becomes one of them. Then, and only then, is he able to make effective headway in bringing about a change in their feelings. The successful conversationalist, in sum, is the individual sensitive enough to recognize readily the purpose of the group and able to direct the talk toward his own goal without giving the other participants the disturbing sense that his mood or manner is inappropriate to their own.

THE CONVERSATIONAL QUALITY IN OTHER FORMS OF SPEAKING

There is a carry-over from the art of good conversation to other forms of speaking. As we noted in the introduction to this chapter that the other forms of speaking differ from conversation more in degree than in kind, there are varying degrees of formality, of organized preparation, and of compliance with established and expected patterns. How informal and careless we can be even in the conversational situation is a serious question. There is no doubt, however, that unplanned "thinking out loud," slang, lack of information, poor posture, and other carelessness of voice, language, and action—if ever excusable in conversation—are not the qualities to be carried over into other forms of speaking.

There are valuable attributes of conversation which ought also to characterize most, if not all, speaking. We seek to identify and describe these in order to make their carry-over more likely. In Chapter 2, as a matter of fact, we have already stressed the first of this series of attributes of conversation which are in common with those of all effective speaking.

Genuine Communication

Communication implies two or more active participants. As has been stressed before, it is a two-way process. It requires a receiver as well as a sender. No one would think of picking up the receiver of his telephone and immediately talking into it. We all know that we must wait until a proper connection has been established and the person to whom we wish to speak is at the other end of the line. Then, after an exchange of identification and greetings, the talk can begin. This procedure should be followed in conversation, discussion, and public speaking. You should make certain that your audience is "on the line" before you start talking. Then be sure that the audience does not mentally hang up the receiver and become engrossed in other interests during the course of the talk.

One helpful device is to think of your speech as a train, by means of which you wish to transport your audience to the goal you have chosen for your talk. Naturally, you will want your train to be attractive and efficient, to start on time, and to run according to schedule. You will wish it to be admired and praised. But these things are not ends in themselves. They are all merely means of getting the people onto your train and of persuading them to stay on until the proposed destination is reached. If people merely come to the station to admire your train, but refuse to ride on it, your purpose has failed. So it is with your speech: your primary purpose is to get your audience to enter into the train of your ideas, and to stay with it until the goal of your speech has been reached.

Directness

If a man stepped up to you on a street corner, called you by name, then turned away from you and began to talk, you would naturally conclude either that he was eccentric or that you had been mistaken in thinking that he had addressed you in the first place. Yet many speakers treat their audiences in just this way. After a word of greeting they turn to look out the window, to stare at the floor, or to let their eyes wander along the wall. Some have learned the trick (a good one to forget) of fixing their eyes stonily on the back wall, some three or four feet above the heads of their audiences. Others may stare directly into the faces of their listeners, but with the blank expression you have sometimes seen on the face of a friend who is physically present but mentally miles away. Communicative speaking under these circumstances is impossible.

Two kinds of directness are demanded of the speaker: one is physical, the other is mental. Physical directness is achieved by really looking at, not merely toward, your audience. Keep your attention centered on your listeners, and they will keep theirs on you. The eyes are the "windows of the soul." When a speaker is delivering a memorized speech and struggling with his memory, his eyes turn inward to read the mental scroll which contains the speech, rather than outward to see whether the audience is with him. Physical directness is also broken if the speaker has to devote part of his attention to notes or to papers on which the entire speech is written out. It is broken completely if the speaker shows by nervous twitchings, sloppy posture, and general lack of ease that he is so completely concentrated upon himself that he has no attention left to give his audience.

It is possible, of course, for you to be physically direct and yet be miles away from mental contact with your audience. In addition to standing alertly and looking directly at your listeners, you need also to make every effort to relate your thinking to theirs. While you are preparing your speech, you should think of the needs and interests of your audience. While speaking, you should watch it for cues, and respond to its reactions. It is helpful to inject into your speech such phrases as, "You know from your own experience," "Perhaps you, too, have wondered," "As many of you will recall," and other observations that clearly indicate you are drawing your ideas from, and directing them to, the common experience of the group.

Clarence Darrow, one of the greatest courtroom pleaders in the history of the American bar, was not notable for physical directness when he delivered an address to the jurors. It was his habit to pace back and forth, his eyes on the floor, as though he were wrestling with his own mind, striving to bring forth the best he had to offer. Yet despite this seeming casualness (which he hoped would disarm suspicion of his forensic skill), he took great care to shape his arguments and illustrations in terms that would have the utmost effect upon the jurors. During the early phases of the trial, he would study every juror individually; then, in his closing argument he tried to present the evidence in a way that would be most appealing to each. Few speakers have the skill to be physically indirect yet mentally direct. Normally, it is essential to be both. Yet of the two, mental directness—the actual interweaving of mind with mind—is the more important.

Animation

The speaker who sounds tired, whose voice drags, and whose body droops had much better stop speaking and go home to rest. Good speaking is hard work; it requires a great amount of bodily energy and mental concentration. The speaker who rests himself while he is speaking is certain to tire his audience. As students of speech, we cannot be too strongly aware of "the narcotic influence of our own yawns." A speaker who is strongly charged with energy will magnetize his audience, just as a well-charged magnet draws metal to itself; but once the speaker or the magnet has "gone dead," the power of attraction is lost.

The speaker's animation, or his lack of it, is shown in a variety of ways. It manifests itself in his eyes: do they droop and shift, avoiding the audience as much as possible, or do they flash and sparkle as the speaker drives his points home as directly with his eyes as with his words? It reveals itself in his subject matter: is the substance of the speech thin, superficial, impersonal, and far removed from the experience of the speaker and the audience, or is it vivid, powerful, personal, alive, and filled with meaning? It shows itself in the speaker's style: are the sentences monotonous, plodding, dull, and drab, or are they alert, varied, intense, and concrete? And it is evident in his whole attitude toward his audience and toward his speech. Does he show a sense of responsibility not only to inform but also to stimulate and interest his listeners? Does he try to bring his subject to life, to make it so real for his audience that its full significance and meaning are clear? In brief, does he work hard enough to keep himself and his subject alive? If he does, he may rest assured that, whatever other faults he may have, there is little chance that his audience will ever find him dull. Of all the causes of poor speaking, lack of animation is the most easily remedied; and the remedy has a permanent effect. Hence the motto of the beginning speaker might well be, "Come alive, and keep alive!"

Physical and Vocal Freedom

A moving object always attracts attention. This is so in the fields, on the highway, in the water, in the sky—and no less so on the speaker's platform. It is one principle upon which the speaker can always count to help him gain and hold the audience's attention. Each time he moves his arm, his head, or his whole body, the audience's interest is to an extent renewed. Movement is a sign of life, and a speech without action is dead indeed. Movement is also valuable for punctuating the speech and for providing variety and emphasis. If you have more than average need for releasing physical energy, you will find the specific suggestions in Chapter 13 useful.

The speaker's animation, his attitude toward his audience, and the intensity of his interest in his subject are also revealed in his voice. The voice for effective, animated public speaking is vibrant, forceful, and varied in its rate and pitch. It follows the inflectional patterns of good conversational speaking, but to a greater degree. A voice that is alive is filled with the excitement and enthusiasm which the speaker feels. There are the same differences between the voice of an enthusiastic speaker and that of a plodding speaker as there are between a voice that is warmly greeting a real friend and one that is perfunctorily addressing a chance acquaintance. The tones of the speaker's voice should be so rich and warm that every member of the audience feels as though he is being addressed as a personal friend.

Personalization

"Names make news." People are interested in people. Any newspaper reporter learns that the more names he can weave into his stories, especially names of well-known people, the more interesting the stories will be. Beginning speakers need to learn the same thing. It may be laid down as a categorical rule that every speech should be made just as personal as the circumstances permit. Use the personal pronouns "you" and "we" very liberally. Refer frequently to the likes and dislikes of your audience, and use your own experiences, when they are applicable, for illustration. Whereas practiced speakers are often so well aware of the value of this principle that they may even overwork it and appear sometimes to talk more of themselves and their families than of their subjects, it seems to be a difficult principle for beginning speakers to learn to use.

A typical example of the unnecessarily impersonal speech is a talk given by a student in a speech class on the difficulties of distributing clothing to flood refugees. She selected a vivid title, "Shoe Counter on the Left," but that was the most interesting part of the speech. She gave statistics on the number of flood victims, spoke of the total destruction of their homes and the loss of their household goods, and remarked on the enormous bundles of clothes of assorted types and sizes which had to be distributed among them. The speech was rather dull and the audience remained uninterested. One wondered why the subject had been chosen. It was only when the speaker was questioned after her speech that it was discovered that she had actually served as a distributing clerk with the Red Cross in a recent flood disaster. As soon as that was known, the audience became very much interested. Question after question was fired at her, about the nature of her work, the reactions of the flood victims, the extent of the damage, the care of the refugees, and the plans for repairing the havoc. She had in her experience a great reservoir of valuable speech material which she had not used because she was sure that the audience would not want to know what *she* had done, seen, and felt.

Another example is that of a student who spoke on the process of manufacturing cans, a subject which seemed wholly inappropriate for the audience and the occasion. Only afterward was it learned that he had spent several summers working in a can factory, where he had had many experiences with which his talk might have been brightened and given point.

The beginning speaker is apt to shy away from the very type of material which will most certainly interest his audience. "I was there," "I saw it," "I had this experience," "I know from my own observation"—these are potent phrases, and they should be used as often as they reasonably can be.

Develop the intimate touch. This is a piece of advice around which many speakers have built their success. Make the members of your audience feel that you are a creature of real flesh and blood, that you are interested in them and in problems which are real for them and for you. "You and I know . . . ," "My friends . . . ," "I have studied the map of your state as carefully as any one of you . . . ,"

"I know your problems, and they have become my problems as well"
—these statements are taken from addresses made by the most successful speaker of his generation, Franklin D. Roosevelt, and they
reveal one of the basic reasons for his phenomenal success. *He was a
master of the intimate touch.* His radio addresses became "fireside
chats." He seemed to slip into the very homes of his hearers, and he
discussed the most complex governmental matters from the point of
view of the average family man. As one commentator declared, "The
New Deal is Franklin D. Roosevelt, neither more nor less." The
clash of conflicting opinions centered primarily around his personality and only secondarily around the issues and acts of his administration. He succeeded in personalizing himself and his speeches.

One need not be President in order to master this speech device.
It is open to every speaker who cares to use it.

CONCLUSION

Conversation merits serious study for its own sake as well as for
the aid which it offers in mastering public speaking. Good conversation is characterized by adaptability, interest, pertinence of subjects, skillful supervision by the host or hostess, tact in maintaining
a lively discussion without friction, and active participation by the
entire group. It depends upon a richness of background, a maturity
of conviction, and a freshness of current information. It rests basically
upon the principle that every conversation has its own mood and purpose, to which all participants should contribute.

There is no finer goal for the public speaker than attainment of
the conversational quality. Public speaking is not something artificial
and remote from the average person's everyday experience. It is only
natural that, since speech is a social process and its effectiveness is
measured in terms of the reactions of others to it, the best speech
quality is that with which we are most familiar. Any attempt to be
"oratorical" in the artificial sense results in indirectness, is noncon-
versational, and makes the speaker seem insincere to the audience.
The best public speaking is unobtrusive in its technique. The speaker's skill is not noticed as such by his audience. Yet underneath his
seeming artlessness is the most careful artistry—the adaptation to
public speaking of the principles which have proved successful in
conversation. In brief summary, this means that the effective speaker

will speak with geninue communicativeness, physical and mental directness, animation, physical and vocal freedom, variety, responsiveness to the moods and attitudes of his audience, and a mastery of the personalized and intimate touch.

EXERCISES AND BIBLIOGRAPHY

Exercises

1. The class may be divided into four groups, with a host or hostess for each. Then each group assembles in one corner of the room to engage in conversation. One student sits apart from each group as critic. At the end of fifteen minutes the groups come together and consider the reports of the four critics. These reports should discuss the kind of mood and purpose that developed, show which participants set the tone, and tell how well the participants succeeded in expressing themselves within the limits of the mood and purpose set by the conversation.

2. As you participate in various conversations, note the following problems, which, at one time or another, inevitably arise. Make it a point to solve them yourself when you can. If they are dealt with by someone else in the group, note the degree of skill with which they are handled. Be prepared to discuss each of these problems in class, with illustrations drawn from recent conversations in which you have participated:

   a. The subject being discussed (religion, politics, personalities, for example) takes a trend which makes it unpleasant for some members of the group.

   b. You are eager to discuss a topic which you feel would interest the whole group, but no ready opportunity arises for introducing it.

   c. One member of the group makes himself disagreeable to the rest by his manner, by what he says, or by his determination to do all of the talking.

   d. A member of the group who has something of real interest to contribute is too timid to break into the stream of conversation.

   e. A member of the group expresses an opinion which you believe is false and misleading.

   f. The conversation becomes strained and hesitant.

   g. The conversation gradually assumes a tone (argumentative, gossipy, irreverent, for example) which most of the members of the group consider to be in bad taste.

   h. Some member is carried away by the enthusiasm of the moment to express views which are far in excess of his real opinions on the subject.

i. Someone commences a long, rambling, disjointed, and uninteresting recital which cannot be interrupted without obviously leaving his narrative unfinished.

3. Write a report on a recent conversation in which you have participated. Describe the situation and characterize the other conversationalists. List the various subjects which were discussed. Was each one satisfactorily introduced into the flow of talk? Did any special problems arise? If so, how were they met? Did all of the members participate? Evaluate the conversation in terms of the basic principle of good conversation—that of determining the purpose of a conversational situation and conducting oneself in accord with that purpose.

4. Prepare a brief speech on one of the following topics:

   a. The best conversationalist I know.
   b. The kind of conversationalist I dislike most.
   c. My standards for evaluating conversation.
   d. The liveliest conversation in which I ever took part.
   e. The subjects my friends and I most frequently discuss.
   f. Interesting experiences in conversing with strangers.
   g. A conversation which affected the course of my life.
   h. My most embarrassing conversation.
   i. A recent book or article on conversation.
   j. Is conversation a lost art?
   k. The importance of being a good conversationalist.
   l. Can conversational ability be acquired?
   m. Characteristics of a good listener.
   n. Conversational bores I have known.

5. Discuss the implications for conversationalists of the following quotation:

   I taught him four speeches. . . .
   1. "Very well, thank you. And you?" This for an answer to casual salutations.
   2. "I am very glad you liked it."
   3. "There has been so much said, and, on the whole, so well said, that I will not occupy the time."
   4. "I agree, in general, with my friend on the other side of the room."

   —Edward Everett Hale.

6. Prepare a five- to seven-minute speech in which you try to be as conversational as possible with your audience. While you are working on your speech, consider each one of the characteristics of the conversational quality, and plan how you will make use of them all.

7. Write a 500-word general critique of all the speeches given by the

members of your class for the assignment in exercise 6, estimating how well the class succeeded in the use of the conversational quality. Cite specific examples of conspicuous success or failure in the application of the seven characteristics.

8. Like Antony in Shakespeare's *Julius Caesar,* the speaker should desire to be regarded by his listeners as "no orator."

> For I have neither wit, nor words, nor worth,
> Action, nor utterance, nor the power of speech
> To stir men's blood: . . .

asserted Antony, while he was in fact tremendously stirring their blood. Read this entire speech, from Act III, Scene 2. It is an excellent example of a speaker's entering into the mood of his auditors in order to draw them into his mood.

Bibliography

Barbara, Dominick A., "Don't Be Afraid of Silence," *Today's Speech,* VI (January, 1958), 13–15.

Goodspeed, E. J., "The Art of Being Outshone," *Atlantic Monthly,* CXLIV (December, 1929), 801–5.

Griswold, A. Whitney, "Our Tongue-Tied Democracy," *Today's Speech,* V (November, 1957), 29–30.

Haseltine, Olive, *Conversation* (Dutton, 1927).

Oliver, Egbert S., "The Art of Conversation," *Today's Speech,* VI (September, 1958), 3–6.

Oliver, Robert T., "A Working Bibliography on Conversation," *Quarterly Journal of Speech,* XX (November, 1934), 524–35.

ILLUSTRATIVE SPEECH

Read the following speech by Bruce Barton, "Which Knew Not Joseph." Does the speech read as though the speaker were conversational and direct? How did he go about the task of winning his hearers over to his point of view? Make a list of the means by which he personalized his speech. Did he use sufficient variety in his subject matter? Find instances of variety in substance, in attitude and in mood. What evidence is there in the speech that the speaker earnestly desired to communicate his meaning to the audience? Does the speech have the quality of intimacy? If so, how is it expressed?

Which Knew Not Joseph[2]

BY BRUCE BARTON

As President of the then Barton, Durstine, and Osborn Advertising Agency

There are two stories—and neither of them is new—which I desire to tell you, because they have a direct application to everyone's business. The first concerns a member of my profession, an advertising man, who was in the employ of a circus. It was his function to precede the circus into various communities, distribute tickets to the editor, put up on the barns pictures of the bearded lady and the man-eating snakes, and finally get in touch with the proprietor of some store and persuade him to purchase the space on either side of the elephant for his advertisement in the parade.

Coming one day to a crossroads town, our friend found that there was only one store. The proprietor did not receive him enthusiastically. "Why should I advertise?" he demanded. "I have been here for twenty years. There isn't a man, woman, or child around these parts that doesn't know where I am and what I sell." The advertising man answered very promptly (because in our business if we hesitate we are lost), and he said to the proprietor pointing across the street, "What is that building over there?" The proprietor answered, "That is the Methodist Episcopal Church." The advertising man said, "How long has that been there?" The proprietor said, "Oh, I don't know; seventy-five years probably." "And yet," exclaimed the advertising man, "they ring the church bell every Sunday morning."

My second story has also a religious flavor. It relates to a gentleman named Joseph, who is now deceased.

Those of you who were brought up on the Bible may have found there some account of his very remarkable business career. Those of you who have not read that book may have heard of Joseph through the works of Rudyard Kipling.

> Who shall doubt "the secret hid
> Under Cheops' pyramid"
> Was that the contractor did
>   Cheops out of several millions?
> And that Joseph's sudden rise

    [2] Delivered to the public-relations counsels of the electric utilities at a meeting of the National Electric Light Association, 1923.

> To comptroller of supplies
> Was a graft of monstrous size
> Worked on Pharaoh's swart civilians.

The account of Joseph in the Old Testament is much more complete and to his credit. It tells how he left his country under difficulties and, coming into a strange country, he arose, through his diligence, to become the principal person in the state, second only to the King. Now, gentlemen, the Biblical narrative brings us to that point—the point where Joseph had public relations with all the other ancient nations, while his private relations held all the best-paying jobs—it brings us up to the climax of his career and then it hands us an awful jolt. Without any words of preparation or explanation, it says bluntly:

"And Pharaoh died, and there arose a new king in Egypt which knew not Joseph."

I submit, gentlemen, that this is one of the most staggering lines which has ever been written in a business biography. Here was a man so famous that everybody knew him and presto, a few people die, a few new ones are born, and *nobody* knows him. The tide of human life has moved on; the king who exalted the friends of Joseph is followed by a king who makes them slaves; all the advertising that the name "Joseph" had enjoyed in one generation is futile and of no avail, because that generation has gone.

Now, what has all that to do with you? Very much indeed. When we gathered in this room this afternoon, there were in this country, in bed, sick, several thousand old men. It perhaps is indelicate for me to refer to that fact, but it is a fact, and we are grown up and we have to face these things. On those old men you gentlemen collectively have spent a considerable amount of time and a considerable amount of money. It is to be supposed that you have made some impression upon them regarding your service and your purposes and your necessities. But in this interval, while we have been sitting here, those old men have died and all your time and all your money and whatever you have built up in the way of good will in their minds—*all* your labor and investment have passed out with them.

In the same brief interval, there have been born in this country several thousand lusty boys and girls to whom you gentlemen mean no more than the Einstein theory. They do not know the difference between a Mazda Lamp and a stick of Wrigley's chewing gum. Nobody has ever told them that Ivory Soap floats or that children cry for Castoria, or what sort of soap you ought to use if you want to have a skin that people would like to touch. The whole job of giving them the information they are going to need in order to form an intelligent public opinion and to exercise an intelligent influence in the community has to be started from the beginning and done over again.

So the first very simple thing that I would say to you (and it is so simple that it seems to me it ought to be said at every convention of this kind) is that this business of public relations is a very constant business, that the fact that you told your story yesterday should not lead you into the delusion of supposing that you have ever told it. There is probably no fact in the United States that is easier to impress upon people's minds than that Ivory Soap floats, and yet the manfacturers of Ivory Soap think it is not inconsistent or wasteful to spend more than a million dollars a year in repeating that truth over and over again.

Cultivating good will is a day-by-day and hour-by-hour business, gentlemen. Every day and every hour the "king" dies and there arises a new "king" to whom you and all your works mean absolutely nothing.

Now, the second very simple thing which I might say to you is that in your dealings with the public, in what you write and say, you must be genuine.

When I came to New York a great many years ago I had a lot of trouble with banks. It was very hard to find any bank that would be willing to accept the very paltry weekly deposit that I wanted to make. Finally I discovered one which was not as closely guarded as the others, and I succeeded for a period of three years in being insulted by the teller every Saturday. At the end of three years when I came to draw out my money I had an audience with the vice-president who wanted personally to insult me. I said to myself, if I live and grow old in this town, some day I think I would like to take a crack at this situation.

And so as the years passed (as they have the habit of doing), and I lived and grew old, one day a bank official came in to us and said he would like to have us do some advertising for him. I said to this banker, "Now you go back to your office and shave off all the side-whiskers that there are in your bank and you take all the high hats and carry them out into the back yard of the bank and put them in a pile and light a match to the pile and burn them up, because I am going to advertise to people that you're human, and it may be a shock to have them come in and find you as you are."

So he went back to his bank and I wrote an advertisement which said:

There is a young man in this town who is looking for a friendly bank; a bank where the officers will remember his name and where some interest will be shown when he comes in, etc.

It was very successful. It was too successful. It was so successful that we could not control it, and all over the country there broke out a perfect epidemic, a kind of measles, of "friendly banks." Bankers who had not smiled since infancy and who never had had or needed an electric fan in their offices suddenly sat up and said, "Why, we are friendly."

Well, our bank dropped out. The competition was too keen. But it culminated, I think, in a letter which I saw and which was mailed by the president of a really very important bank in a large city. I won't attempt to quote it verbatim, but it was to this effect:

Dear Customer: As I sit here all alone in my office on Christmas Eve thinking of you and how much we love you, I really wish that you and every other customer could come in here personally so I could give you a good sound kiss.

Well, that is a trifle exaggerated, but the fact is this—if you don't feel these things you can't make other people feel them. Emerson said, as you will remember, "What you are thunders so loud I cannot hear what you say." Unless there is back of this desire for better public relations a real conviction, a real genuine feeling that you are in business as a matter of service, not merely as a matter of advertising service—unless there is that, then it is very dangerous, indeed, to attempt to talk to the public. For as sure as you live the public will find you out.

The third very simple thing, and the last thing that I suggest, is this: in dealing with the public the great thing is to deal with them simply, briefly, and in language that they can understand.

Two men delivered speeches about sixty years ago at Gettysburg. One man was the greatest orator of his day, and he spoke for two hours and a half, and probably nobody in the room can remember a single word that he said. The other man spoke for considerably less than five minutes, and every school child has at some time learned Lincoln's Gettysburg Address, and remembers it more or less all his life. Many prayers have been uttered in the world—many long, fine-sounding prayers—but the only prayer that any large majority of people have ever learned is the Lord's Prayer, and it is less than two hundred words long. The same thing is true of the Twenty-third Psalm, and there is hardly a Latin word in it. They are short, simple, easily understood words.

You electric light people have one difficulty. I was in Europe this spring, and I rode a great deal in taxicabs. In England I sat in a taxicab and watched the little clock go around in terms of shillings. Then I flew over to Amsterdam and watched it go around in terms of guilders. Then I went down to Brussels and it went around in terms of francs. Then I went to France and it went around in terms of francs of a different value.

I would sit there trying to divide fifteen into one hundred and multiply it by seven, and wonder just where I was getting off, and I have no doubt now that really I was transported in Europe at a very reasonable cost, but because those meters talked to me in terms that were unfamiliar I never stepped out of a taxicab without having a haunting suspicion that probably I had been "gypped."

In a degree you suffer like those taxicab men. You come to Mrs. Barton and you say, "Buy this washing machine and it will do your washing for just a few cents an hour." She says, "Isn't that wonderful!" She buys it, and at the end of the month she sits with your bill in her hands and she says, "We have run this five hours, and that will probably be so-and-so." Then she opens the bill and finds that she has not run it five hours; that she has run it 41 kw. and 11 amp. and 32 volts, and that the amount is not so-and-so but it is $2.67.

Well, that is a matter that I suppose you will eventually straighten out.

Asking an advertising man to talk about advertising at a convention like this is a good deal like asking a doctor to talk about health. I have listened to many such addresses and they are all about the same. The eminent physician says, "Drink plenty of water. Stay outdoors as much as you can. Eat good food. Don't worry. Get eight hours' sleep. And if you have anything the matter with you, call a doctor."

So I say to you that there is a certain technique about this matter of dealing with the public, and if you have anything seriously the matter with you—whether it be a big advertising problem or merely a bad letterhead (and some of you have wretched letterheads)— there probably is some advertising doctor in your town who has made a business of the thing, and it may be worth your while to call him in. But in the meantime, and in this very informal and necessarily general talk, I say to you, "Be genuine, be simple, be brief; talk to people in language that they understand; and finally, and most of all, be persistent." You can't expect to advertise in flush times and live on the memory of it when you are hard up. You can't expect to advertise when you are in trouble, or about to be in trouble, and expect to get anything in that direction. It is a day-by-day and hour-by-hour business. If the money that has been thrown away by people who advertised spasmodically were all gathered together it would found and endow the most wonderful home in the world for aged advertising men and their widows. Don't throw any more of that money away. If advertising is worth doing at all, it is worth doing all the time. For every day, gentlemen, the "king" dies, and there arises a new "king" who knows not Joseph.

CHAPTER 6

CONTENTS

Good preparation, leadership, close interaction, and active participation are all represented in this discussion of the United Nations.
(Bates College)

PRINCIPLES
AND METHODS OF
DISCUSSION

Men are never so likely to settle a question rightly as when they discuss it freely.

—THOMAS BABINGTON MACAULAY

I N a mid-position between conversation and public speaking, and possessing some characteristics of each, is a type of speaking which we call *discussion*. It has many of the informal, give-and-take qualities of conversation; yet its subject matter, form, and objectives are—as in public speaking—more precise.

"How shall we plan our annual house party this fall?" "How may college examinations be improved?" "What can nations do to control new weapons of war?" These and scores of other questions call for discussion. "Where shall I go to college?" may have been a question discussed in your own family not so long ago. *Group discussion is a process of cooperative thinking.* It is used when two or more individuals talk over a problem systematically, thus pooling their experiences and judgments, in order to arrive at the best possible solution.

Discussion builds upon the skills of the conversationalist. The methods of discussion evolve naturally from those of conversation. Every student is accustomed to talking informally: seated in the midst of a group, occasionally adding a word here and there—expressively, as he has the urge to say something, and cooperatively, as he follows the tenor of what others are saying and adds his own thoughts to theirs. When this process is completely informal, subject to frequent changes of topic, and without any special plan or delegated leadership, it is conversation. Add precise preparation, system, and leadership, and you have discussion. The participants remain at their places, they speak only when they have something to say, and they speak as briefly and as often as they wish. These are common characteristics of conversation and discussion. It is a natural advance in speech skills for the beginning student to learn to participate effectively in genuine group discussion.

Discussion, an essential tool of democracy, is formalized only to the extent necessary to give every idea a fair chance for expression and consideration. Every participant must be given an opportunity to help shape the final decision, and when the decision is reached

130

it should represent the best understanding of the group as a whole. In discussion, whether you can talk eloquently and easily is of less significance than whether you have something worth while to contribute. Each member of the group should express his ideas as well as he is able. If the others see merit in the ideas, they will help shape these into final form by aid of the combined abilities of the entire group.

THE NATURE AND FUNCTION OF DISCUSSION

Discussion is still a favorite technique man uses in understanding his environment and learning how to survive as well as how to live happily in it.

Discussion Is a Way of Learning

Man is a small finite being in a seemingly infinite universe. On a clear summer evening in the mountains, or in the country away from the lights of cities, if you have looked up at the innumerable stars and speculated about the immensity of space, you and your own knowledge have seemed pitifully small. If you had later consulted an astronomer he would have made you feel yet smaller. He could have told you that one tiny, tiny patch of faint light your eye had been just barely able to discern may have been the spiral galaxy of Andromeda. The faint light you could just glimpse had left that galaxy two and a half million light years ago. Because that galaxy is as large as the more easily visible Milky Way, it is composed of at least a hundred billion suns, many of them larger than the one which daily makes life possible for us. Yet this is but a very small part of outer space. Still beyond are at least a hundred million such galaxies.

How small, indeed, is man! How little each man in his lifetime can know! Find out how many volumes are in your college library. Estimate at your reading rate how long you would have to live to read them all if you had nothing else to do. Then your librarian probably could tell you that at year's end you would not even have finished reading the new volumes added, without even touching those of past years. Man has so much to learn! He must make use of every possible way to improve his speed and efficiency of learning. Discussion is such a way of learning. Thus children learn at home through discussion with parents who have preceded them through the experiences of each age of life. Thus, too, we learn in school, in church, in community, and at work. Since no one of us can know everything, we pool and exchange our knowledge with that of others. Discussion at its best may thus be defined as a process of cooperative thinking and learning together. In discussion with others who have had experiences different from our own not only do we learn new things, but the things which we already know have a new significance and more meaning as they fit into patterns of expanding understanding and knowledge.

Discussion Is a Way to Discovery of New Ideas

We do not mean to imply it is the only way. The world owes to the solitary thinking of many a great mind ideas which have made life richer and fuller. Yet it is no less true that when one man's mind is enriched by sharing and interacting with the thoughts of others it may come upon ideas which it never would have found alone. And our world needs new ideas and the fuller exchange of ideas. President Eisenhower made this point in September, 1959, when he said to a gathering of teachers from other nations at the White House:

We shall not be serving mankind well if we become obsessed with just the business of putting new satellites into orbit—so obsessed that we overlook the fact that we have some real problems left right here on earth. We need to put new ideas—and more of them—into orbit. And we must use every resource at our command to see that people everywhere achieve greater understanding of each other before it is too late.

We can send the human voice around the world with approximately the speed of light. Hardly a month passes without the setting of some new speed record in transportation. It is now more important than ever to discover and use all possible means for achieving better understanding among all men. Think of our daily failures in understanding: between parent and teen-ager, teacher and student, worker and employer, and next-door neighbors. Much more complicated is the achievement of understanding among a hundred and eighty million Americans. This number multiplied by sixteen is merely the numerical size of the problem of world understanding, without all the complexities of differing cultures, religions, histories, and economic and social states. It is easy to recognize the need for mutual understanding but difficult to achieve it on any broad scale. Yet upon your very campus are many opportunities for making progress, opportunities for discussions with those of different backgrounds, opportunities for reaching new understandings and developing new ideas.

The trend in industry, in government, in the professions, in science, and in learning generally is toward ever-greater specialization. There is a similar tendency for each comparatively small group of specialists to become separated from, and thus ignorant of, every other group. The increasing use of discussion stimulates new ideas which at best might otherwise be long delayed. Discussion is the medium used to cut across managerial levels in industry; to reach across subjects, disciplines, and colleges in the university; to find ideas and programs in religion that are world wide in scope; to exchange cultural, health, and technological information among nations through agencies of the United Nations.

Discussion Is a Way to Approach the Solution of Problems

Discussion is not the *only* approach, nor, indeed, the more common *final* approach to problem solving. Nor is the whole purpose of discussion problem solving. Its primary role concerns learning and the discovery of new ideas. All that we have said in connection with its attainment of those purposes applies also to discussion in its problem-solving role.

RELATIONSHIP OF DISCUSSION TO DEBATE

In a democratic society, the preliminary step in the orderly process leading toward action is *discussion,* during which all possible courses of action are examined and evaluated. The second step is *debate* over whether or not to adopt any of the possible courses of action. Discussion does not inevitably lead directly to action; it is often a forerunner of decision. Debate is frequently the final step preceding action. Both discussion and debate fulfill necessary and specialized functions.

The debate which takes place in a business meeting is usually called a discussion. This is inaccurate, confusing, and an example of the loose usage to which the term "discussion" has been subjected. The difference between discussion and the formalized argument termed "debate" can, as a matter of fact, be pointed out clearly by an illustration from parliamentary law. There can be no debate in a business meeting unless and until there is a motion on the floor.

Business meetings have the primary purpose of action, and all talk in them must be purposeful—must center about some proposed action, which is a motion. Yet frequently the meeting is faced with a problem concerning which no one is yet sufficiently informed to be able intelligently to formulate a motion. In this situation parliamentary law calls for resolving the meeting into a "committee of the whole." In this committee of the whole there can be full and free *discussion* without any motion having been presented. In fact, the objective is to clarify the thinking of the group sufficiently so that there emerges a debatable proposal, or motion. Then, the function of discussion having been completed, the committee of the whole reports this motion back to the business meeting, where debate precedes final action. From this illustration it should be clear that *discussion is a learning process, a process of sharing the information and experiences of a group, of analyzing a problem, of separating the more plausible from the less plausible solutions, and of determining the extent to which the group is in agreement.* Usually a discussion group refers its conclusions or recommendations to another group, where they are debated and acted upon. *Debate, as an equally distinctive process toward democratic action, provides the opportunity for presentation of the arguments for and against a proposed plan of action so that participants and listeners may make up their minds and be prepared to vote.*

Many of the shortcomings observable in the usual attempts to utilize discussion and debate arise from a confusion as to the differing functions of these two processes. For example, debate is criticized by some because it permits consideration of only one solution. That is, indeed, the purpose of debate. If you wish to consider more than one solution, you should be using discussion—or a series of debates. You will note that debate is the common process in the court of law. It comes, or should come, after discussion and all other methods of resolving conflicts and problems have done all they can. *Discussion, if resorted to early, would in many instances make it possible to avoid the necessity for debate.* This is particularly true in the field of legal matters, where many problems are discussed in the offices of lawyers and never brought up for trial (or debate) in court. Similarly, in legislative bodies, problems are discussed in committees before coming up for debate as bills, or proposed laws. Often discussion is attempted too late, after ill will has crystallized. This is true in many labor-management controversies. If discussion is to have a fair chance it must occur *before* the problem has become serious, *before* it has reached the stage of public argument and open conflict. Although there are many occasions in modern life when we should seek to avoid the necessity for debate, we should not make the error of believing that all debate is an undesirable, antisocial process, to be avoided whenever possible. What is needed is a sense of proper things in proper places—discussion in order to avoid conflict, to resolve a problem, to find common ground; then, just before action is finally taken, debate, involving full and free consideration of pros and cons in order to provide fair expression of both majority and minority views. In courts and legislative meetings of all types, debate is the essential tool by which men find their way to just and workable decisions. It is no exaggeration to say that where there is no discussion and no debate there is no freedom, no democracy, no real and lasting progress. Where these two procedures are confused, efficiency is lowered and the democratic process itself is made to seem tedious, ineffectual, and unreliable. Each procedure has its proper part to play.

THE VALUES OF DISCUSSION

All students, and especially all students of speech, will find at least three primary values in a study of the techniques of discussion.

First, *practice in discussion increases conversational skills,* because of the many characteristics which the two forms have in common.

Second, *the techniques of discussion are useful in a great many situations,* both in and out of college. Students who are even moderately active in college life will find many occasions to offer their counsel in the affairs of their dormitories, in student government, and in religious, social, and athletic activities. They will find skill in discussion of great value in many of their college courses. And when they are graduated they will discover that ability to participate in and lead fruitful discussion is highly regarded in almost every business and profession.

Because of the needs presented by a complex world and a technological society, the use of discussion has increased at a phenomenal rate. International conferences are often held in order to lay the bases for firmer international cooperation. Radio and television discussion programs have become commonplace. Management in most businesses utilizes frequent conferences or discussions among administrative staff members. The discussion method is the heart of democracy. It is a modern adaptation of the New England town meeting.

Scientific studies have demonstrated that judgments arrived at in discussion groups are, on the whole, superior to judgments arrived at in solitary thinking. Communities and industries have found discussion techniques of great assistance in determining as well as investigating the results of policies in such areas as delinquency, racial relations, and employer-employee relationships. Education has increasingly utilized group discussion as a situation psychologically more favorable to learning than the lecture method sometimes proves to be. The United States Department of Agriculture relies more and more on the panel-discussion technique in introducing to rural groups new discoveries and improved agricultural methods. New ideas which may provoke high resistance if presented by a lecturer are much more likely to be accepted and tried if suggested in a discussion group.

Since World War II, discussion has been widely used for its therapeutic value in military hospitals, for it has been found to be of great aid in the reconditioning and retraining of persons who have suffered disabilities. When we remember that there were ten times as many injuries in accidents in the United States during the time of that war as there were casualties among all our fighting forces, we realize that the therapeutic value of discussion is one for which we shall have constant need. The place of discussion may be expected to become increasingly important in a society in which man's social skills, his abilities to get along more efficiently and more pleasantly with his fellows, are highly valued.

Third, *mastery of the techniques of discussion will contribute directly to an improvement in public speaking.* Participants in discussion will become accustomed to speaking in whatever manner they find personally most effective for communicating ideas, with no thought of giving an exhibition of speech skills. They will find that they win attention and respect in terms of what they have to say and of the personality they reveal, and this will give them courage even though their manner of speaking may need much improvement. They will learn to be very attentive to the thinking and feeling of the group and to shape their remarks in terms of the group. Carried over into public speaking, this ability will be one of the very best assets that can be cultivated for success on the platform. In animated discussion, the participants find themselves naturally using vigorous gestures to add to their meaning and varying their voices for the sake of emphasis and clear expression of their ideas. In thoughtful analysis, they will participate with quiet earnestness and sincere interest. In all these respects they are preparing themselves to give speeches that are natural, unstrained, communicative, and purposeful.

REQUIREMENTS FOR GROUP DISCUSSION

In order that one may master the techniques of group discussion, it is profitable to consider (1) phrasing the question for discussion, (2) preparing for fruitful discussion, (3) organizing the discussion, (4) leading the discussion, and (5) participating in discussion.

Phrasing the Question

Discussion topics normally present themselves. Questions are discussed because they need answers. Usually, the kinds of questions you will find yourselves discussing fall into one of three categories. The first consists of *circumstances presenting difficulty to a group*. If your social restrictions are too rigid, if your living conditions are unsatisfactory, if members of your group are uncooperative because of lack of common understanding, if your group falls below the college average in its grades or in social or athletic activities, a thoughtful discussion of the problem is in order. The second consists of *new situations affecting a group*. Discussion naturally arises when any group is confronted by a new rule—such as prohibition of cars on the campus. It arises, too, when the approach of graduation raises the question of how to get a job, or when an election is to be held, or when war breaks out, or when an epidemic threatens to cancel planned activities. The third consists of *general social questions*. When a group's attention turns to religion, marriage, ethics, etiquette, racial and national conflicts, or other values and standards which interest the individuals in the group, discussion is spontaneous. When the problem of phrasing questions for discussion arises it is not necessary to originate them; merely recall the many questions which daily cause you concern.

For fruitful discussion, however, proper phrasing is important. Good phrasing directs the consideration of the group in a positive and constructive way; bad phrasing arouses needless antagonisms and leads into blind alleys of thought. A question should be so phrased as to encourage impartial and impersonal consideration. "Loaded" or question-begging words should not appear in the phrasing, because such words imply a predetermined conclusion. Consider such questions as "Should destructive and anti-American race prejudice be tolerated in the United States?" "Should sincere American Communists be denied the privileges of citizenship all the rest of us demand for ourselves?" Questions thus phrased do not invite honest consideration; they demand that the group agree with the clear intent of the phraser. Since they are patently unfair, they naturally lead to heated argument and antagonism.

Good discussion topics raise questions of *fact, value,* or *policy.* Diagnosticians, for instance, may discuss whether a patient has suffered a heart attack—clearly a question of fact. Or, having decided upon the diagnosis, they might discuss which of two possible medication programs is better—clearly a question of value. Or, they might discuss whether to hospitalize the patient—a question of policy.

Particularly for the classroom situation, four guiding rules will aid in phrasing discussion topics:

1. Topics should be in question form.
2. They should be so worded as to suggest no single answer.
3. They must not require unavailable knowledge, unusual experience, or extensive research.
4. They should be sufficiently limited to permit profitable discussion within the allotted time.

The following sample discussion topics would meet these requirements if used by a college class:

Fact Topics
1. What do we mean by true patriotism?
2. Can one be religious without believing in immortality?
3. What is school spirit?

Value Topics
4. Would a year of military training be of greater value to a boy than the first year of high school?
5. Do the values of a two-term outweigh those of a three-term college system?
6. Which offer the greater lifetime values in college, the courses or the activities?

Policy Topics
7. Should our college adopt the honor system for final examinations?
8. Should attendance be compulsory in college classes?
9. Upon what should a final grade in this course be based?

Preparing for Discussion

Although discussion offers no opportunity for set speeches, it does not follow that preparation is unnecessary. When members of the group are unprepared, the whole discussion is likely to be pointless and empty. The best the participants can do is to offer superficial observations suggested by what the others say. Hearing many such discussions may have predisposed you to believe that discussion is "just a lot of talk that gets nowhere." That this need not be so is readily observed when the participants are genuinely prepared. It is important, however, that preparation be of the right kind.

There are two requisites for efficient preparation for discussion: keeping an open mind, and gathering the pertinent facts and clarifying the reasoning upon which a decision is to be based. Perhaps the fundamental requirement for a good participant in a discussion is that he be willing and anxious to learn. You should not enter into a discussion determined to win approval for your own point of view. That would be argument or debate—and not discussion. You enter into a discussion because you do not yourself know all the answers. The essence of discussion is to find out what is true or desirable by pooling the judgments of the group. Do not begin your preparation by asking yourself what you believe about the question and marshaling evidence to support your views. Be tentative. Be scientific in your attitude. Be determined and anxious to consider all points of view *before making up your mind*.

With that caution before you, gather all the pertinent information you can. Explore the background of the question. You may find it helpful to look ahead to Chapter 9, where the process of finding sources and gathering data is fully discussed. If, for example, your question should be the first one of the nine listed in the preceding section, you would wish first to take stock of what you already know about patriotism. Recall some examples of what you regarded as commendably patriotic, and some which you may have thought questionable. See whether you can make some valid generalizations from these instances. Talk with others to profit from their information, experiences, and opinions. Do you know personally or from his writing anyone you consider as an authority on patriotism? Talk to such people who are available and study the writings of others. In an age of international cooperation and the United Nations, is it possible that nationalistic patriotism could be a dangerous force? Is it, for the same "environmental" reasons, possible that patriotism is more greatly needed than ever before? From the card catalogues and periodical indexes in the library discover as many viewpoints about patriotism as you can. Throughout this stage of preparation, as you go about learning all you can concerning the question and as you turn the facts over and over in your mind, remember to avoid drawing final conclusions. Hold your judgments tentative until you have a chance to profit from the thinking of the group.

At the first meeting of your discussion group, research tasks can be divided among the members to assure a greater depth of preliminary study into all aspects of the question and to make certain that an approach to the problem or a possible solution which has been proposed or tried will not be overlooked.

Organizing the Discussion

A discussion differs from a conversation in that it is orderly and systematic. It restrains and disciplines the random impulses of the participants. It progresses logically from a definite start to a conclusive (if tentative) stop. A discussion must go through several steps, each having its own purpose, and each making a cumulative contribution toward the desired goal.

1. *The topic must be clearly understood.* It must mean the same thing to all. Ambiguous terms need defining. You must avoid someone's saying later, "Oh, I didn't understand the question that way at all!" You cannot, for example, profitably discuss religion or belief in God so long as there exist among the group a half dozen or even two different interpretations of what is meant by religion or by God.

2. *The group should agree upon the principles or objectives in the light of which they wish to evaluate the question.* If, for example, the effort is to define school spirit, time may be saved by agreeing first upon the reason for needing the definition. Is this for inclusion in a manual to be given entering students? Or is it for a pep club meeting? Or has some disciplinary authority asked for a clear distinction between school spirit and rowdyism? Differing purposes may considerably modify the nature of the evaluation or definition sought.

3. *The question must be analyzed thoroughly.* The group must make certain that all relevant facts and points of view are given consideration. The background and history of the question, specific incidents which may have brought it to popular attention, various opinions which have been expressed concerning it, experiments and solutions which have been tried or even suggested—these are a few of the considerations which will help to ensure complete analysis.

4. *The group may gradually determine how far its agreements can be extended over the areas where differences occur.* The wise pattern of discussion is to expand areas of agreement—to see how much the entire group can agree upon.

5. *The leader of the discussion will make a summary of the extent of the agreement attained by the entire group.* Perhaps he may wish to

point out that a majority of the group was in agreement upon additional points. Sometimes it may be necessary to conclude that the group—at least for the present—has been unable to reach any general agreement.

Leading the Discussion

The function of a discussion leader is to ensure orderly, systematic, and cooperative consideration of the question. He is responsible for organizing and directing the prediscussion planning; he presides over the actual discussion; he keeps the discussion moving constructively forward—either introducing each successive stage of the discussion himself or calling on some member of the group to do so; he sees to it that all members of the group participate and that no one is permitted to monopolize the floor; he calls upon members of the group to introduce facts or testimony when necessary; he provides for summarization when it is needed to promote clearness and to further agreement; and he strives to keep the emphasis upon agreement and cooperative thinking in order to avoid conflict.

The best discussion leader is unobtrusive. He tries to direct the course of the discussion so effortlessly and naturally that the members are scarcely conscious of being directed. There must be nothing of the dictator in the discussion leader; it is not his function to maneuver the group into accepting *his* conclusion. He must serve the best interests of the group and make it possible for each member to contribute his own best thinking.

A simple functional plan for leadership includes the following steps for a problem-solving discussion:

1. Introduction of the problem by the leader
2. Presentation of the basic facts by members of the group
3. Presentation by the members of possible solutions to the problem
4. Analysis of the solutions, one by one
5. Decision by the group on the solution to be adopted, or (if this cannot be achieved) determination of the additional facts needed before an agreement upon any solution is possible

Participating in Discussion

The participant in any discussion must assume definite responsibilities if discussion is to be profitable. His attitude is of primary importance. Discussion is a method of exploration and of discovery. It is a learning process. The participant must think of himself not as one who knows but as one who desires to learn. He is not a teacher—at least not in the sense that a teacher transmits knowledge to others. And he is not a persuader; for the persuader has already made up his own mind and is attempting to bring others into agreement with him. The participant in a discussion is seeking to learn and to be assisted by the information, experiences, and thinking of others to arrive at conclusions which have not been in any way predetermined. As has already been emphasized, the participants in discussion must maintain open minds; and this means that the discussion question is one concerning which decisions have not already been made by any of the participants.

In industrial relations, for example, discussion may have valuable contributions to make; but not when men are out on strike, with their demands formulated, and when management is already on record with emphatic statements as to what it will and will not do. Any discussion in such a situation can be nothing but a debate—with each side striving to prove that it is right. Discussion could have been helpful only in an earlier period, before conflict had arisen to make the task of discussion exceedingly difficult and probably impossible. There can be profitable discussion in such a situation only while both management and labor representatives are in a mood to learn what the facts are and to consider the relative merits of possible solutions.

In addition to being in the right frame of mind, however, the participants in a discussion must know how to use that type of thinking which some describe as the "scientific method." This type of thinking proceeds from problem to solution through the steps of hypothesis, deduction, and verification. The member of a discussion group considers not merely his own or his favorite hypothesis; he carefully examines all hypotheses. He is not at all concerned with proving that his tentative conclusion is the right one, but he is wholly concerned with finding among all possible conclusions the one that really is the right one. He desires to test all tentative deductions in an effort to make up his mind; and he is quick to make certain that his deductions square with all new facts and information. If they do not, he abandons his temporary deductions for better ones which take into account the new facts. He accepts no conclusion as final until it has been fully verified not merely by himself but by the group, through the testing process of discussion.

There are in addition some mechanics to be mastered by a good participant in a discussion. We may state them as five commandments: (1) Carry your full share of the group responsibility in contributing and testing facts and ideas. (2) Introduce your opinions in order that they may be tested thoroughly by the group, and do not resent their being questioned, as though this involved personal affront to you. (3) Listen to others, not to disagree with them but to understand their ideas accurately and to see the full significance of their ideas to the discussion. (4) Speak up promptly to keep the discussion moving, to introduce new phases of the question as the group is ready for them, and particularly to steer away from a point concerning which the group has become locked in conflict. (5) Remember that the measure of the success of a discussion lies not in the brilliance of individual contributions but in the progress made by the group as a whole.

THE ROUND-TABLE DISCUSSION

What has been said about discussion in this chapter relates directly to the discussion form which is most commonly called round-table or group discussion. Its distinguishing characteristic is that all members of the group participate directly. In order to ensure full participation from all, (1) the group should be kept small—with seven or eight as the optimum number; (2) the group should be seated in a face-to-face arrangement, either in a circle of chairs or around a table; (3) the leader should be clearly designated and should perform his essential functions, but should not dominate the group or its pattern of thinking; (4) a systematic procedure should be followed, such as that recommended earlier in this chapter as a guide for the leader; and (5) all the participants should have accepted fully their responsibility for being well informed on the subject.

An important consideration other than that of full participation by all members is fairness. As was stressed in the section "Preparing for Discussion," one of the basic requisites of a good discussion is that all members keep an open mind. This does not mean that they should refrain from individual thinking about the question or that they should attempt the impossible feat of avoiding all personal convictions. It does mean, however, that group thinking is impossible unless all the members have sufficient respect for one another's opinions to be willing and eager to entertain them. The members in a round-table discussion should be well informed, eager to contribute, and equally eager to learn from their fellows. From the pooling of facts and ideas, the members of a group will normally emerge with sharper and clearer ideas than any of them had before the discussion began.

THE PANEL DISCUSSION

Sometimes a group must consider problems concerning which the members are not well informed. The *panel discussion* has been designed to meet this situation. Several experts sit upon the platform and discuss a question among themselves, with the audience listening in. Usually, each of the experts represents a definite point of view and is committed to some solution before the discussion commences. It is in this respect that the panel discussion may differ radically from the group discussion. The purpose of each member is to explain and defend his point of view and to answer objections to it as they are raised by other members of the panel. Consequently, the panel discussion is in reality an informal style of debate, and the opinions of the participants ordinarily remain unchanged. Television utilizes this technique when a panel of experts assembles to present varying views on such a question as whether Red China should be admitted to the United Nations. The discussion is often carried on before an audience in the studio.

The panel members are in reality addressing not one another— as they seem to be doing—but the audience listening to them. Each tries to influence the audience to agree with him and to reject the views of his opponents. After the panel members have used their allotted time, the audience is permitted to ask questions, to raise objections to what has been said, or to offer new points of view for consideration by the experts. The chairman, who has presided over the panel discussion, recognizes members of the audience, receives their questions or objections, and transmits them to the panel members for answer.

The panel discussion should end with either a vote by the audience upon the question originally presented to the panel for consideration or a summary by the chairman of the various points of view that have been presented.

THE LECTURE-FORUM

Similar in its basic pattern to the panel discussion is the lecture-forum. In this form, a speaker, usually an expert from outside the group, speaks on a topic and is then questioned by the audience. The questioning may develop into a regular group discussion, with free expression of opinion by members of the group and with a definite decision reached. Usually, however, out of deference to the guest speaker, the discussion is limited to questions and no vote is taken.

THE DEBATE-FORUM

The debate-forum differs from the lecture-forum only in that a debate replaces the lecture. The lecture is typically an informational one, and subsequent questions are concerned mainly with the understanding of the subject; the debate, however, presents both sides of a controversial issue, and the questions afterward may be concerned with the decision on the issue.

Many eminent thinkers, from John Stuart Mill down to the present, have held that the only way to reach a sound decision upon an issue is by means of debate in which both sides are assured of the fullest possible presentation. This is the view of Anglo-Saxon jurisprudence, which accords both sides a hearing before an impartial judge or jury. Thus the debate-forum may be one of the most effective media through which to present public issues and inform listeners.

THE SYMPOSIUM

Frequently, and particularly when controversial issues are involved, a series of short talks is presented by experts on various phases of the subject, or from different viewpoints. All of the speakers then participate in the following discussion, which may be thrown open to participation by the listeners. We then have the symposium-forum.

THE PERSONAL INTERVIEW

You are likely to find yourself making vital use of the principles of both conversation and discussion in many important personal interviews—in applying for a position or in conferring with a fellow employee, with a member of your family, or with your academic adviser. Yet the interview remains a distinctly specialized form.

The following points summarize the suggestions of several personnel directors and employment managers in commercial and industrial concerns hiring hundreds of men and women each year. They all find that a sense of humor, "so long as it is controlled and in good taste," is an asset for an applicant. They do not agree as to whether employer or applicant should take the initiative in a job-application interview; thus the applicant, instead of following a rule, might let the individual situation determine his decision. Some of the faults which employers find most often in prospective male employees are "overestimation of their own ability," "lack of poise and ability to state their case," and "lack of knowledge of their own interests and abilities, or inadequate vocational guidance previous to job hunting." Faults mentioned with respect to prospective female employees are "excessive make-up," "poor taste in dress," "careless posture," "lack of sincerity," and "too much acting."

These experienced interviewers testify that the three things about job applicants which first attract the attention of the prospective employer are *appearance, personality,* and *speech.* Remember that an interviewer or conferee who is meeting large numbers of persons must make a quick judgment on the basis of first appearances. (Note that a member of an audience makes a similar early judgment of a speaker.) Dress that is neat and in good taste aids decidedly. Ability to be "civil, pleasant, tactful, and interesting" is of course an asset, as is a clear, pleasing voice.

In brief, everything that we have noted about the good conversationalist and the good participant in a discussion applies to the interview situation. P. W. Boynton, employment supervisor for Socony-Vacuum Oil Company of New York, who in twenty-five years has interviewed some 75,000 job applicants, says: "Whether a man is hired or not depends primarily on the impression he makes in his first interview. We don't hire a man any more for a specific job, but for his capacity to grow. He shows us what abilities he has primarily by what he says and how he says it. We are much more interested in that interview than in his record of college grades and activities." This is an indication of how crucial one interview can be.

CONCLUSION

Discussion is a process of cooperative thinking. It is of increasing importance in a complex world in a technological age. It has real contributions to make to well-adjusted, up-to-date, and successful living—in the family, in school, at work, and at play. We usually remember far more of what we hear in a discussion than in a lecture, and we are more likely to act upon the suggestions brought out in a discussion. Discussion is not just a problem-solving process; it is one of the best ways of learning. It is a means by which we share and exchange with others experiences, information, and attitudes. We may increase the value of discussion by proper phrasing and definition of the question, by thorough preparation of subject matter, by careful organization of ideas, by competent leadership, and by wholehearted participation. There are helpful methods and techniques to be learned and practiced. The nature of the group, the situation, and the question confronting it will determine whether round table, panel, symposium, or one of the types of forum should be used. Perhaps the situation in which the individual more often will find the principles of discussion, as well as many of those of conversation, of most practical value is the personal interview.

EXERCISES AND BIBLIOGRAPHY

Exercises

1. Phrase a question suitable for discussion by your class. Define any of its terms that may be ambiguous. Restate the topic in other words, to be sure it is readily and generally understandable. Write a brief paragraph explaining why you think this topic should be discussed. In another paragraph, state the basic general principles which should be used as standards in discussion of the question. Analyze the question to discover how many different points of view must be considered. Finally, indicate the chief sources of current information on the topic. All of this material should be written on not more than two sheets of paper and should consist of 500 words or less. Hand in the material to your instructor.
2. By class vote, select for group discussion one of the topics described in the preceding exercise. With the framer of the topic as chairman, conduct a thirty-minute discussion of the topic. Use the remainder of the class hour for criticizing the progress of the discussion.
3. At the next class session, conduct a second group discussion, using another of the questions framed for exercise 1. Discuss in class the ways in which the second discussion was superior to the first and the ways in which it could have been improved still further.
4. At the next class session, conduct a third group discussion, upon still another of the topics phrased for exercise 1. The success of the class in conducting this discussion should determine whether these discussions

need to be continued. The discussion practice should be continued until the class shows that it has mastered the fundamental techniques.

5. Members of the debating team or other advanced students of speech may be invited to the class to conduct a panel discussion. The topic might be a question of current interest. Or it might be such a question as "What is good public speaking?" or "What are the opportunities for students of speech in extracurricular speech activities?"

6. If a good public speaker is available, he might be invited to the class for a lecture-forum. This would serve the double purpose of giving the class practice in the lecture-forum method and of illustrating good public speaking for purposes of later discussion. The speaker should, of course, be informed that his technique will later be analyzed and criticized!

7. Members of the class may interview selected members of the faculty or local businessmen in order to obtain experience in conducting the personal interview. Each student should prepare a preliminary plan, on which will be indicated (a) the purpose of the interview, (b) the response, or perhaps a list of possible responses, which may be anticipated, (c) ideas and facts which might prove useful in terms of each of the anticipated responses, and (d) questions which might be asked of the conferee. Needless to say, each student should familiarize himself with the background, special interests, and personality characteristics of the person he is to interview. After the round of interviews, the class members may engage in a group discussion, sharing experiences and pooling their ideas as to better techniques to use in future interviews.

Bibliography

Auer, J. J., and Henry L. Ewbank, *Handbook for Discussion Leaders* (Harper, 1947).

Chase, Stuart, *Guides to Straight Thinking* (Harper, 1956).

Cortright, R. L., and G. L. Hinds, *Creative Discussion* (Macmillan, 1959).

Ewbank, H. L., and J. J. Auer, *Discussion and Debate* (Appleton-Century-Crofts, 1951).

Kahn, Robert L., and Charles F. Cannell, *The Dynamics of Interviewing: Theory, Technique, and Cases* (Wiley, 1957).

McBurney, James H., and Kenneth G. Hance, *Discussion in Human Affairs* (Harper, 1950).

Sattler, William M., and N. E. Miller, *Discussion and Conference* (Prentice-Hall, 1954).

Utterback, William E., *Group Thinking: A Workbook for Use in Discussion Courses* (Holt, Rinehart and Winston, 1953).

Zelko, Harold P., "Emergence of a Rhetoric of Discussion," in *Re-establishing the Speech Profession,* Robert T. Oliver and Marvin G. Bauer, eds. (The Speech Association of the Eastern States, 1959), pp. 12–18.

Zelko, Harold P., *Successful Conference and Discussion Techniques* (McGraw-Hill, 1957).

CHAPTER 7

CONTENTS

Veteran debate director Brooks Quimby listens closely as his squad members prepare for an approaching contest. (Bates College)

PARLIAMENTARY PRACTICE AND DEBATE

> Debate, it seems to me, is one of the most useful of human inventions. It is the mother and father of all free inquiry and honest thought. It tests ideas, detects errors, and promotes clear thinking. A man cannot stand up before it without exposing his whole intellectual stock of goods.—H. L. MENCKEN

IN the preceding chapter distinctions were made between debate and discussion in nature and purpose. In practice these distinctions are not always sharply drawn. They are most often ignored in business meetings; yet keeping the distinction in most instances would contribute to greater efficiency in the conduct of the business. As the preceding chapter stressed, if only discussion is in order, or would best serve the meeting, then the session should be resolved into a committee of the whole. Otherwise no speaking is in order from the floor except as business, or a specific motion, is before the assembly. If members wish to talk, the presiding officer will rightly demand that a motion first be made so that there may be purpose and direction to the debate. Thus time-wasting in business meetings can be, and should be, stopped.

THE PURPOSE AND VALUE OF PARLIAMENTARY PROCEDURE

A group of people gathered for a fraternity or sorority meeting, for a student-council session, or for the transaction of any other kind of business quickly discovers that unless it follows rules of procedure it gets nothing done. *The purpose of parliamentary law is to provide systematic rules and principles of procedure which will give to any meeting or assembly good order, the opportunity for harmonious deliberation, the efficient use of time, and the orderly transaction of its business.* Since most of you belong, and will belong throughout life, to many groups and organizations, it is your responsibility to understand and to be able to work effectively with parliamentary law. If you happen to be made chairman or president of a group, your responsibility is of course increased. As a matter of fact, a person totally lacking in parliamentary skill is not likely to be—and certainly should not be—elected to a position of leadership in a group requiring orderly business procedure.

The value of knowledge and skill in parliamentary law is simply that it makes order possible where otherwise there would be chaos. Every rule of procedure will be found to implement one or more of the following purposes of all parliamentary law: (1) to facilitate the orderly transaction of the business of the organization; (2) to assure predominance of the will of the majority; and (3) to protect the rights of the minority.

If you will always conduct yourself, either as chairman or as a member of the assembly, in strict conformity with these three purposes, you will not go far wrong. Too many beginning students of parliamentary procedure attempt to memorize its rules and then make a nuisance of themselves by insisting, in great detail, upon their strict application. Far more important than knowing in detail a great many rules is understanding clearly the broad underlying philosophy and knowing fully the general purposes which alone give meaning to the specific rules.

The purposes and values of parliamentary procedure, it should hardly be necessary to emphasize, cannot be realized fully except by groups whose chairman and members are acquainted with the essential rules. In the following sections of this chapter those rules are set forth.

ORGANIZING A GROUP

In this age of cooperation and of expanding and increasing organization, you may be called upon at least occasionally to have a part in organizing a new group. The first meeting is called by any interested person to meet at some convenient place. At the time set for the meeting, the one who has called it steps forward and nominates or calls for the nomination of some person present to act as temporary chairman. The one who has called the meeting takes the vote, and the temporary chairman is elected and becomes the presiding officer. The first business under this presiding officer is the election of a secretary. Next, some person, perhaps the one who called the meeting, makes a statement about the reason for this meeting and the nature of the group which he wishes to see organized. A motion is then in order to organize such a group. If, after debate, it is carried, another motion is in order for the appointment or election of a committee to draft a constitution and bylaws for the proposed society. A sample constitution may be discussed. (See one of the references at the end of this chapter for sample constitutions and bylaws.) A time and place should be set for the next meeting—the time being determined by the newly selected committee's judgment as to when it can be ready with at least a progress report. Adjournment of this preliminary meeting is then in order.

At the second meeting there should be close adherence to all the rules of parliamentary procedure. Ordinarily it will be more efficient if each member has received some days in advance of the meeting a complete mimeographed copy of the proposed constitution and bylaws. Thus each member will know what questions he wishes to ask and what changes he would like to propose. At the meeting the first order of business is the report of the committee. It may well include a general statement of reasons for specific provisions about which the committee may anticipate questions. Each section of the proposed constitution and bylaws should be considered in order, permitting the consideration of amendments. After each section has been voted upon separately, a final vote should be taken upon adoption of the constitution as a whole, including all the amendments which by then have been incorporated into the original committee version. After the adoption of the constitution and bylaws, the chairman will proceed to the election of officers as provided by the constitution. As soon as the president is elected he takes over the chair from the temporary chairman, whose duties are now ended. The president presides over the remainder of the election of officers and appoints any appointive standing committees. Before adjournment, he should take any necessary steps to provide for the program and to make clear the place and time of the next meeting.

SELECTION AND DUTIES OF OFFICERS

Selection of officers is usually provided for in the constitution or the bylaws. Otherwise, a simple motion properly passed may remedy the omission. It is always advisable to have a standing provision limiting the term of office and, particularly, limiting the number of terms which any one individual may successively serve. Otherwise, later efforts to limit may be interpreted as an entirely unintended personal affront to an individual officeholder.

Many groups find that a nominating committee will present better slates of officers than are likely to emerge from spontaneous nominations from the floor. However, nominations from the floor are always in order unless specifically ruled out by the constitution or bylaws. No nomination requires a second, although seconds are frequently offered as a means of indicating support for a particular candidate. Since the object of any election procedure is to obtain the best possible officers, anything which will increase the chances of achieving that goal should not be overlooked. This suggests that the membership of a nominating committee should be known in advance by all the members of the group, so that each may forward to it all possible helpful suggestions. When the report of the nominating committee is in the hands of all members in advance, a good opportunity is afforded for the careful consideration of alternative nominations.

Rules governing voting are covered in a later section of this chapter. However, it should be noted here that *in elections the vote should be by secret ballot*. If there are more than two nominees for a given office, and no candidate receives a majority of all votes cast, it is usual to ballot again on the two highest candidates. This is the only way to be certain that a candidate is elected by an actual majority of the membership, unless the organization is large enough to warrant undertaking one of the weighted voting systems, which are beyond our limited consideration here. Tellers are usually appointed by the chair, who must be careful to select trusted members, and, in a warmly contested election, to see that both parties are represented in the teller group. The tellers announce the name of the person elected for each office and see that the count of the ballots is recorded with the secretary. An officer assumes the duties of office as soon as elected unless the constitution or bylaws provide otherwise.

The duties of officers must be understood and carried out properly if the objectives of any organization are to be realized. It is a rare organization, indeed, which can rise above the quality of its leadership.

The *president*, or *chairman*, has heavier responsibility than that of any other officer. Although entitled to respect from the group, he is its servant. He should be an able parliamentarian. He must pay close attention to all that is going on and be in command of the situation at all times. Courtesy demands that he stand while speaking. When he gives the floor to another he must see that this speaker receives the courteous attention of the entire assembly. He refers to himself as "the chair." When ruling on a point of order, for example, he never says "I rule . . ." but "the chair rules . . ." He uses his gavel with restraint and dignity. He must have the confidence of every member.

He should be impartial, tactful, and decisive when decisions are demanded of him. He must be helpful, quick to explain any matters concerning which members are not clear, and always ready to guide the pending business as rapidly as practicable to an action which fairly represents the assembly and which promotes its best interests. He should see that no minority loses its rights but should be resourceful in stopping merely obstructive tactics. His specific duties include holding the assembly to the prescribed order of business and seeing that every motion goes through all its necessary steps. (See later sections for detailed explanations of both these processes.) In brief, he sees to the proper disposal of proper business. Although we are limiting our discussion here to the chair's parliamentary duties, he may also have executive responsibilities. He never loses his full rights of membership, including the right to vote. He votes in every secret-ballot election and he votes *at any time when his vote would change the result*. This means that he may vote to create a tie as well as to break one and to keep a vote short of the required two thirds or to bring it to that requirement. The only membership right in which he may not indulge from the chair is that of participation in debate. He need not fully lose even this right, however, for he may call upon the vice-president or some member of the assembly to act as temporary chairman while he takes his place in the assembly and participates in debate. This privilege is one which no chairman will use except under unusual circumstances, as when in debate it becomes apparent that he is the only one who possesses some particularly significant information which may well influence many votes. Once the presiding officer has thus relinquished the chair he does not resume his position until the pending matter of business has been disposed of.

The *chairman pro tempore* is the member who acts as chairman "for the time being," or temporarily. We have just noted that when the presiding officer wishes to participate in debate he may appoint a chairman pro tempore, who then exercises all the rights and duties of the chairman until the pending matter of business is disposed of. He then returns the gavel to the chairman. If a chairman is for some reason called from a meeting, he may similarly appoint a chairman pro tempore, who will serve until his return or until the end of the meeting. If both the president and the vice-president are absent and no further line of succession is provided by the constitution, the assembly must elect a chairman pro tempore. He then exercises the full functions of the regular chairman for the duration of the meeting. Occasionally there will be a motion which would be embarrassing for the chair to put to a vote—for example, a motion for his re-election or a resolution of praise or censure for something he has done. The vice-president, the secretary, or the mover of the motion should step forward and, acting as chairman pro tempore, put the motion to a vote and announce the result.

The *vice-president* has the duty, from a parliamentary standpoint, of substituting for the president in the event of the latter's absence, ill health, or incapacity for any reason. He takes over the powers, duties, and responsibilities of the president.

The *secretary* must keep an accurate record of the business accomplished by the assembly. (Those who wish to know the exact nature of a secretary's minutes may consult one of the references at the end of this chapter.) He may be called upon at any time to read the wording of a motion or of any communication. The secretary keeps a record of all actions taken and of the disposition of all motions. He should record all business impersonally and without irrelevant comments and keep an accurate roll of the membership of the group and of the membership of all committees. He furnishes each appointed chairman of a committee with a list of all members of the committee and with any instructions or matters referred to it. He has available at each meeting the minute book, a copy of the group's constitution and bylaws, and the list of committees. He provides the chairman with a copy of the order of business for the meeting and a list of committees which are to report. In some organizations the secretarial duties are divided between a recording secretary and a corresponding secretary. The latter handles all correspondence, including notices of meetings.

The *treasurer* is in charge of the collection and disbursement of the organization's funds, but may pay only such bills as are properly authorized by action of the group. The usual voucher should state what the expenditure is for and its amount; it must be signed by the president. A treasurer's report is required at every meeting, and a statement as to the condition of the treasury may be demanded by a member at any time.

DETAILS OF PARLIAMENTARY PROCEDURE

A Quorum

A quorum is a sufficient number of members present to transact business legally. This number will vary greatly, depending upon the size of the total membership and the ease with which it may assemble in one place. For the average assembly it consists of a majority of the active membership. For a large, geographically separated membership the quorum requirement should be very small lest the conduct of business be rendered impossible. A quorum should be defined by the constitution or bylaws.

Types of Voting

A *viva-voce* (by the living voice) vote is taken orally, those in favor answering "aye" and those opposed answering "no" Both the "aye" and the "no" votes must be called for even when it seems that there has been a clear affirmative majority, because a member may change his vote at any time before the result is announced.

A vote by *show of hands* is taken by asking all who favor and then all who oppose to raise a hand. It is often easier to count raised hands than to determine whether the "ayes" or the "noes" have it. Whenever a two-thirds vote is required, the chairman should take a vote by show of hands or by some other visual means. Otherwise, because a call for division is almost certain, time will have been wasted.

Rising, or *division,* involves a vote taken by asking the members to stand. The secretary will assist the chair in counting, and for a large meeting the chair may appoint additional tellers. A call for division from any member is a command to the chair to take a rising vote. One member may thus compel such a vote. This call may be resorted to whenever it appears to some member that the chair has made an error in announcing the result of a viva-voce vote or a vote by show of hands.

A *roll call* vote is taken by the secretary, who reads the roll of the assembly and records each member's "aye" or "no" as his name is read. This is sometimes called a *record* vote.

A vote by *ballot* is taken when strict secrecy is desired. As previously noted, this is the proper vote for elections. The ballots are collected and counted by tellers appointed by the chair. The tellers announce the result to the chair or directly to the assembly and give the record of their count to the secretary.

There is psychological advantage to be gained from certain types of votes. When members must stand up and be counted, social pressures operate which may be absent in a viva-voce vote. The vote may actually be changed by a demand for division or for a roll call, although the intended use of these measures is to correct a miscount or to obtain a record.

It may be worth noting that a member is expected to vote upon all issues, but he cannot be required to do so. He may simply report himself as not voting. In order to be in position to move reconsideration later, one must have voted with the prevailing majority; this is one of the reasons why in any but a ballot vote a member may change his vote any time before the chair announces the result. He says, "Mr. Chairman, I change my vote to the prevailing majority, to be in position to move reconsideration later." Although this violates the intent of the regulation (which is to protect the member who really changes his mind), it enables a member to protect the rights of absent members whose votes he feels certain will later change the result.

Obtaining the Floor

No member has a right to speak or to present a motion until he has been recognized by the chair. To obtain such recognition he rises and addresses the chair as "Mr. Chairman" or "Madam Chairman." Regardless of what other titles the presiding officer may hold, this form of address is proper. Note that one never says "Miss Chairman." The chairman then indicates his recognition by a nod (in an informal meeting) or by mentioning the member's name, as "Mr. X has the floor" or "The chair recognizes Mr. X."

Steps through Which a Motion Must Pass

Except in certain special cases (significant types of which are noted in the table at the end of this chapter), every item of business must go through eight steps:

A member desiring to present a motion must address the chair. One seldom speaks in a parliamentary assembly without first addressing and being recognized by the chair.

The member is recognized by the chair. He is now said to "have the floor." That is, he has the right to speak or to present a motion.

The member presents his motion. The correct form is: "I move that the secretary be authorized to purchase a gavel for this society." Never say, "I make the motion that . . . ." "I move you . . . ." is equally incorrect. The mover, or proponent, of the motion may not discuss it or engage in any explanatory statement until after the chair calls for debate.

The motion must be seconded by some member other than the mover of the motion. Seconding is done customarily without rising or addressing the chairman. The member merely says, "I second the motion," or, even more commonly, "Second." The purpose of the second is to spare the assembly a waste of time on a motion which is not favored by at least two members. There are a few motions, including nominations, as already mentioned, which do not require seconding. If no one seconds a motion, the chair will ask, "Is there a second?" If still no one responds, the chair will say, "The motion is lost for want of a second."

Debate is opened by the chair's repeating the motion. He may say, "It has been moved and seconded that the secretary be authorized to purchase a gavel for this society. Is there any debate?" or he may say simply, "The floor is now open for debate."

Debate proceeds until terminated by a vote or otherwise. When more than one member seeks the floor at a given time, the chair is guided by certain principles:

The mover of a motion has first right to debate it. Even though others are quicker to request the floor, the chair will make certain whether the mover of the motion wishes to assert his right before he recognizes another. The wisdom of this procedure is apparent. Who can be better qualified than the mover of a motion to explain its purpose and need?

A member who has not yet been heard on a motion has precedence over a member who is asking to speak a second time.

Since the chair tries to keep the debate time fairly divided between proponents and opponents of the motion, he will recognize a member who intends to speak in opposition to the preceding speaker rather than one who will continue arguments on the same side.

Once recognized, a member is entitled to debate without interruptions (except those indicated in the table at the end of this chapter) unless he wanders from the question. The chair may warn a speaker that his remarks must be kept relevant to the motion under consideration and may deprive a speaker of the floor for wanton disregard of the warning.

Debate may be brought to a close by a motion to that effect. Such a motion requires a two-thirds vote, since it deprives members of the right to debate. The technical form of this motion is: "I move the previous question." As soon as seconded, the motion must be put to a vote. In effect, it means, "I move that debate be brought to a close and that we then vote on the pending question." The chair will say, "The previous question has been moved and seconded"; then to make sure that all understand the intent of the motion, he will add, "All

those in favor of closing debate will say 'Aye'; those opposed, 'No.' "
If not carried by a two-thirds vote, the motion has no effect and debate
is continued. If the motion is carried by a two-thirds vote, debate is
closed and the chair proceeds at once to take the vote on the motion.
If debate seems to have come to a close without the necessity for a
motion, the chair should not hesitate to say, "If there is no further
debate, we will proceed to vote on the question." If anyone still wishes
to debate the motion further, he must address the chair. Otherwise
the chair proceeds to the vote by general consent.

Perhaps it should also be noted that all subsidiary motions (see the
table at the end of this chapter) are in order during the period of
debate as ways of disposing of the main motion other than by adoption
or defeat. Subsidiary motions include the types of amendment soon to
be considered.

*The vote must be taken as soon as debate has come to a close in one
way or another.* In putting the vote the chair should again state the
motion or have the secretary read it, so that each member will be perfectly sure of just what is being voted upon. The chair must call first for
the votes in favor of the motion and then for those against it.

The chair must announce the result of the vote. He will say,
"The motion is carried [or lost]," or, "The ayes [or noes] have it."
Another motion is then in order.

The Order of Business

The order of business in an organization follows this general pattern:

The *call to order* is usually achieved by the chairman's rapping
on the speaker's table with a gavel to obtain attention and quiet,
then saying, "The meeting will please come to order."

Roll call is taken by the secretary at the request of the chair.
The ordinary meeting, especially that of a large group, will dispense with this, but at least a count should be taken to ascertain
the presence of a quorum.

The chair has the secretary *read the minutes* of the previous
meeting. The chair asks for any corrections. If there are none, he
says, "The minutes stand approved as read"; otherwise, "The minutes stand approved as corrected."

Reports of standing (permanent) committees are heard and acted
upon.

Reports of special committees are next in order.

Unfinished business is now called for by the chair. Items of un-finished business will be noted as the secretary reads the minutes. They consist of any old business left unfinished at a previous meet-ing or any motions definitely postponed to this meeting.

New business is next in order. It consists of the main motions to be presented for this meeting.

Adjournment by definite motion or at the announcement of the chair by common consent closes the meeting.

Classes of Motions and Methods of Amendment

Primary motions, or *main motions,* are the principal matters of business. Since it is a fundamental principle of parliamentary law that only one subject may be under consideration at a time, only one main motion may be allowed on the floor at a time. The mo-tions to take from the table and to reconsider are, in effect, specific forms of the main motion.

A motion to *reconsider* any action of the assembly may be made only by a member who voted with the prevailing side, as previously noted, and must be made at the same meeting at which the action was taken or not later than the next regular meeting. The mover of the motion to reconsider may interrupt a member on the floor in order to have his motion entered in the minutes; or the motion to reconsider may be made for the same purpose at any time previous to the chair's definite announcement that the meeting stands ad-journed. It requires a mere majority vote, and its effect is to bring the motion to which it refers back before the assembly.

Secondary motions are motions which arise from the parliamentary efforts to dispose of the main motion or to facilitate such disposal; they are called privileged, incidental, and subsidiary motions:

PRIVILEGED MOTIONS are those which concern the rights and privi-leges of the assembly or its members. They must be decided at once even though they have no immediate connection with the main mo-tion; hence they are designated as *privileged* motions. They are of two main types:

A *question of right and privilege* is an example of a privileged motion. For example, if a nonmember were engaging in debate, a member might rise and say, "Mr. Chairman, I rise to a question of right." The chair would ask him to state his question and after hearing it would give his decision. Such questions may concern the welfare of the assembly—a request for ventilation, for example—or the welfare of individuals—such as a protest against personal attacks and sarcasm.

A *call for the orders of the day* requires no second and is resorted to when a member feels that some matter is being taken up out of its proper order. The chair may yield to the demand of the member provided there is no objection, but if even one member objects a vote must be taken. A motion to make an item of business a *special order* for a given time requires a two-thirds vote because it deprives other matters of their right in the established order of business. The same objective may be achieved by the motion to suspend the rules, which also requires a two-thirds vote, or by general consent.

INCIDENTAL MOTIONS are those which arise out of the business being considered but are only incidental to it. They must be disposed of as they arise and have no order of precedence among themselves. Only privileged motions may take precedence over them.

An *appeal from a decision of the chair* is made when a member feels that some ruling by the chair has been in error. The chair may state the reason for his ruling, and the member states the reason for his objection. The assembly votes on the question of upholding the decision of the chair. The chair may vote and a tie vote sustains his ruling.

A member rises to a *point of order* when he notes any violation of parliamentary procedure, of the constitution, of the bylaws, or of the general rules which he believes to be sufficiently serious to need correction. The chair, after listening to the member's statement of his point, announces, "The point is [or is not] well taken."

A *request for information,* technically known as a *parliamentary inquiry,* may interrupt a speaker. Its purpose may be to obtain more specific information from the person who has the floor. In this case the member would say, "Mr. Chairman, I rise for information [or to a parliamentary inquiry]. I wish to ask the speaker . . . ." The chair asks the speaker whether he wishes to be questioned, and the speaker has the right to refuse to be questioned. Or the information requested may be of a more general nature, concerning parliamentary procedure: whether a certain motion would be in order or when some other item of business is scheduled to come up for consideration.

A motion *to withdraw a motion* may be made after a motion has been seconded and placed before the assembly for debate. It is not sufficient to have the consent merely of the mover and the second. Only unanimous consent or a majority vote of the assembly can permit withdrawal.

SUBSIDIARY MOTIONS are those which are applied to other motions in order to modify or aid in their final disposition in some way other than by adoption or rejection.

The motion *to lay on the table* aims to avoid either adoption or rejection of the pending main motion. Its effect is that of postponing indefinitely. Its proper purpose is to clear the way for more important matters or at least to free the assembly from what promises to be a long parliamentary battle.

The *previous question* is moved when a member wishes to bring debate to an end and vote immediately upon the pending business. The technical name of this motion causes its frequent misunderstanding by those inexperienced in parliamentary procedure. Therefore the chair should be careful to explain in putting it to a vote, "The previous question has been moved and seconded. All those in favor of closing debate, stand. . . . All those opposed, stand." A member could well avoid confusion by phrasing this motion simply, "I move that we close debate and vote immediately on the pending question [or on all pending questions]." A two-thirds vote brings debate to an end, and the chairman immediately takes the vote on the pending motion (or motions). If more than one third vote against the motion to close debate, of course, debate continues. There is a quick way to determine the outcome of an issue requiring a two-thirds vote: Double the number of "noes." Only if this number exceeds the number of "ayes" is the motion lost; otherwise it has passed.

The motion *to commit* (or *to refer to a committee*) is proper whenever it seems to members that the business at hand needs further study. A committee can give a matter longer and more careful study than can the whole assembly, can call in experts to advise it, can discuss much more thoroughly, and can investigate delicate and troublesome questions without running into the disadvantages of publicity as extensively as would the entire assembly. For these reasons, reference of problems to a committee is often desirable.

The motion *to amend* takes several forms. Each has its specific usefulness. Only one amendment may be on the floor at a time, but there may also be an amendment to this amendment. A list of the methods of amending follows, each method being illustrated by an example based on the motion, "I move that this club appropriate $5.00 from the treasury for the purchase of a gavel."

Adding: "I move to amend by adding the words 'for the president.' "

Inserting: "I move to amend by inserting the word 'walnut' before the word 'gavel.' "

Striking out: "I move to amend by striking out the words 'from the treasury.' "

Striking out and inserting: "I move to amend by striking out the words '$5.00' and inserting the words '$10.00.' "

Substitution: "I move to amend by substituting another motion: that this club assess each member $.50 to accumulate a fund for the purchase of a gavel." This is the type of amendment to use when there is a poorly worded motion on the floor. It permits the substituting of a completely new wording.

The order of voting is first upon an amendment to an amendment, then upon the amendment, and finally upon the main motion. If an amendment is lost, obviously the motion remains unchanged. If an amendment is adopted, the assembly then votes upon the motion as amended. Any number of amendments may be considered in succession.

PARTICIPATION IN DEBATE

We noted in the early part of this chapter that one of the primary purposes of parliamentary law is to protect the rights of a minority. These democratic rights are the right to be heard and the right to vote. The latter implies, of course, the right to have one's vote counted. Freedom of speech is one of the freedoms for which men have made great sacrifices. The right of full and free debate is the right of every member of an assembly. Every member should, therefore, know how to exercise that right efficiently and effectively.

Debate combines the formal use of argument and persuasion. The student who wishes to be thorough in his mastery of this art should refer to Chapters 19 and 20, "The Speech to Induce Belief" and "The Speech to Move to Action." Only brief suggestions are given here.

The debater's objective is to assist the assembly in reaching the

In the "Debate Days in Detroit" program at Wayne State University, debaters speak to audiences throughout the metropolitan community. Shown here is a debater from the University of Indiana, speaking with persuasive earnestness to the Kiwanis Club.

right decision. He seeks to provide complete information, to correct misinformation, to combine evidence, reasoning, and emotional appeal in order to win others to the course of action he believes right. He seeks to keep his arguments impersonal, for wise legislation will be decided upon issues, not upon personalities. This means that the debater addresses his remarks to the chair, never to another member of the assembly. He refers to officers by their titles, not by name; and to other members as "the preceding speaker" or "one of the proponents of the measure." The debater must confine his remarks to the motion immediately before the assembly. Courtesy requires that the debater's language be proper and dignified and that at all times he show proper respect to the assembly, its members, and its officers.

Some organizations, particularly those with large memberships, set time limits on debate, commonly limiting each member to ten minutes. Under such limitations no member may speak longer except by unanimous consent or by two-thirds vote of the membership. Time limits apply, however, to each motion. Each amendment, for example, is a separate motion. The experienced debater soon learns that his effectiveness is seldom proportional to the length of time he talks. Students of the United States Senate have noted that among the most effective debaters are those who seldom speak but always have a real message when they do rise.

CONCLUSION

The member of a modern democratic society must qualify himself to function in group meetings. This means that he must know the fundamental principles of parliamentary procedure and must know how to conduct himself effectively as a member and as a leader. We are not concerned here with those specialized rules which operate in such bodies as the United States Senate, the House of Representatives, a state legislature, or a city council. These organizations have unique rules, and studying each would be a major task in itself. The average citizen is concerned with those general rules which will enable him to function with reasonable confidence and success in the usual club or organization. This chapter has summarized those broad principles and the few specific applications which it is most important to know. The following table shows the order of precedence of motions and lists five essential pieces of information about each motion: whether it needs a second, whether it may be amended, whether it is debatable, what vote is required to carry it, and whether it may interrupt a speaker. This table should be helpful for class practice and for use in the organizations to which you belong now or may belong in future. A debater who has sound information at his command and a working knowledge of parliamentary procedure is doubly armed for citizenship in a democracy.

TABLE OF MOTIONS

Each motion in this column takes precedence over those numbered below it	Need a second?	Amend-able?	Debat-able?	Vote required?	May it interrupt a speaker?
A. PRIVILEGED MOTIONS					
1. To fix time of next meeting	yes	yes	no	majority	no
2. To adjourn (when unqualified)	yes	no	no	majority	no
3. To raise questions of right and privilege	no	no	no	chair	yes
4. To create special order	yes	yes	yes	⅔	no
B. INCIDENTAL MOTIONS					
5. To appeal a decision of chair	yes	no	yes	majority	yes
To make a point of order	no		no	chair	yes
To make a parliamentary inquiry	no		no		yes
To withdraw a motion	no	no	no	majority	no
To suspend a rule	yes	no	no	⅔	no
C. SUBSIDIARY MOTIONS					
6. To lay on (or take from) the table	yes	no	no	majority	no
7. To move the previous question	yes	no	no	⅔	no
8. To postpone definitely	yes	yes	yes	majority	no
9. To refer to a committee	yes	yes	yes	majority	no
10. To amend	yes	yes	yes	majority	no
11. To postpone indefinitely	yes	no	yes	majority	no
D. PRINCIPAL MOTION					
12. Any main motion	yes	yes	yes	majority	no

EXERCISES AND BIBLIOGRAPHY

Exercises

1. The class will meet as a student council (or some other body agreed upon). Each member will bring in one appropriate motion, written out, upon which he will attempt to secure as favorable action as possible during the class period. The others will endeavor to get his motion out of the way as quickly as possible in order to get a chance to present their own. The class will elect a chairman. He will assume that the meeting of the student council is at the stage of considering new business. He will call for new business, and some member will start things going by making his motion. As soon as the chair makes a parliamentary error, or permits one to be made, the instructor will stop the proceedings and point out what should have been done. Then the chair will appoint another class member as his successor. The new chairman will continue the business from that point.

2. Write out and hand in six different forms of amendment to each of the following main motions:

   a. I move that this class leave as its memorial an endowment fund of $250, the income from which shall be given each year as a prize for the student elected from the speech classes of that year as their best parliamentarian.

   b. I move that this board authorize the erection of a new educational theater building at a cost not to exceed $350,000.

3. The class will take a real parliamentary project: to decide how it will spend a day in some place other than its regular meeting room, with a special program. The class will select its own chairman. Committees may be appointed to select time, place, and program, and report back next time. A secretary will be elected and will keep minutes; a treasurer will be elected to collect any fees decided upon, pay bills, and turn in a final report.

4. Be prepared to give a three-minute talk on one of the following, mentioning all important points about the subject:

   a. The rights and obligations of a minority member
   b. The rights and obligations of a majority member
   c. Facts we should know about voting
   d. Common parliamentary blunders
   e. Delaying tactics—justified and unjustified
   f. Mistakes a chairman should not make
   g. Characteristics of an efficient chairman
   h. How a meeting may be speeded up

     i. Effectiveness in debate

     j. Three valuable subsidiary motions

     k. The duties of a secretary

     l. First steps in organizing a club

    m. The order of business in a meeting

    n. Steps through which a motion must pass

    o. Essential principles underlying parliamentary law

    p. Disposing of a motion other than by its adoption or defeat

    q. How I expect to put into practice my knowledge of parliamentary law

5. If you were presiding as chairman of a meeting, what would be the proper thing for you to do in each of the following situations?

    a. While a member has the floor another member rises to a point of order.

    b. After the "aye" vote has been taken, a member rises to discuss the question further.

    c. A member who voted "no" moves to reconsider an adopted motion.

    d. A member appeals from the decision of the chair.

    e. A member moves the previous question.

    f. A member declines to vote.

    g. On a vote by ballot the total number of votes cast exceeds the membership present.

    h. Member A has made a motion. Member B rises and requests the floor to discuss the motion. A second later, A addresses the chair.

    i. A motion obtains no second.

    j. A nomination is not seconded.

    k. A member objects to a request for general consent to suspend a rule.

    l. After a vote has been announced, a member calls for division.

    m. The motion to resolve the meeting into a committee of the whole is carried.

    n. A motion has been carried for the appointment of a committee. Whom would you appoint (ordinarily) as chairman of that committee?

    o. A member exceeds the time limit in debate.

Bibliography

Cushing, L. S., *Manual of Parliamentary Practice,* ed. A. S. Belles (Holt, Rinehart and Winston, 1935).

Hall, Alta B., and Alice F. Sturgis, *Textbook on Parliamentary Law* (Macmillan, 1955).

O'Brien, Joseph F., *Parliamentary Law for the Layman: Procedure and Strategy for Meetings* (Harper, 1952).

Robert, H. M., *Robert's Rules of Order* (75th Anniversary Edition; Scott, Foresman, 1951).

Sturgis, Alice F., *Learning Parliamentary Procedure* (McGraw-Hill, 1953).

Sturgis, Alice F., *Sturgis Standard Code of Parliamentary Procedure* (McGraw-Hill, 1950).

Part Three

PREPARING THE SPEECH

CHAPTER 8

CONTENTS

John F. Kennedy, shown speaking in Wisconsin during his campaign for the Democratic presidential nomination, used gestures and facial expression as well as voice and words to emphasize his purpose. (Wide World Photos, Inc.)

SETTING THE GOAL

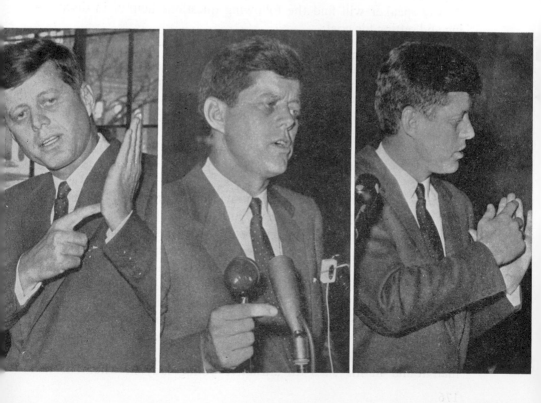

IN preceding chapters we considered the triple roles of speech: as self-expression, as communication, and as social control. It seems clear that speech has been developed by the human race in order to fulfill these needed roles. You and I when very young put forth the necessary effort—and it took long and tedious effort—to learn how to speak in order to satisfy those same age-old and universal needs. In this chapter we are concerned with defining our purpose for speaking in terms of its influence upon our listeners. We are hardly in a position to evaluate a speaker's success in a given situation until we know what his goals were. A speaker, like a rifleman, ought first to make sure of his target.

Any speaker will find the following questions helpful in discovering and setting his goal:

1. What personal purpose have I?
2. What is my general purpose?
3. What general response am I seeking from my listeners?
4. What is my specific purpose?
5. What specific response am I seeking from my listeners?

THE PERSONAL GOAL

Each of us will admit in a moment of frankness that he does his very best only when strongly motivated. The promise of some reward or high honor has stimulated many an individual to finer achievement than would otherwise have been his. Sometimes these motivations seem small to others: merely an appreciative word or a favorable response from a particular person. But their effect may be far-reaching. The fact that they may be known only to the speaker may be just as well since their value is in their motivation for him.

Some examples from classroom speeches may best make clear the range and emotional potential of personal goals. One young man found in his class an attractive young lady in whom he had an unreciprocated interest. Here, quite unknown to the class, was an impelling personal goal for him: to impress favorably that one member of the group. Another student made a speech urging everyone to be alert to the danger signs of cancer. Every listener knew that he had heard a deeply moving appeal; only a few knew the personal motivation. The speaker's closest friend had been a recent victim of cancer discovered too late. A college sophomore spoke in favor of better educational opportunities for the blind. He mentioned his personal motivation. His younger sister had been born blind. An earnest young father pled for a kindly and understanding approach to the juvenile delinquent, and revealed his strong personal motivation as he cited his own experience but a few years before as a juvenile delinquent. A freshman was in college only because of a scholarship which would be withdrawn unless he maintained a B average. Regardless of other general and specific purposes, every class speech he made was motivated by a driving personal purpose to make good scholastically.

The degree of selfishness in personal motivation may vary greatly. In many instances it will be revealed. Probably in no instance would it be considered worthy were it one's only goal. We have sought to present the personal goal in its proper and legitimate function as a power impelling the speaker to do his best in a worthy cause.

Let's consider what may happen when a personal goal is entirely lacking. "Is this what you want?" or "Do you think this will be all right?" a student may ask as he hands his instructor the outline for a speech he is preparing. If this is evidence of a lack of a real personal goal the student might better be asking, "Would you give this a passing grade?" The personal goal, well used, should help us get away from the artificiality of the educational situation. In fact, such artificiality is not confined to the classroom. Far too few speakers accept engagements, whether to address a Rotary club, a high school assembly, a literary group, or a religious convention, because they have "a burning message" to give. They may have just enough awareness of a personal goal to know that it would be advantageous for them to appear on such a program, but not enough to realize that an ineffectual and "dull" appearance might well result in more loss than gain!

An excellent illustration of the proper use of the personal goal is found in the political career of William Jennings Bryan. At thirty-four, he decided that he wanted to be President of the United States.

He did not announce his desire; instead, he started on a two-year tour of the country, speaking everywhere for the cause of currency reform. Few newspapers mentioned his name among available candidates, and no clubs were formed to promote his candidacy. Yet all over the country, as men listened to his monetary views, they said to themselves, "That young man ought to be President." As a result, when Bryan attended the Democratic party convention of 1896, merely as a delegate from the politically unimportant state of Nebraska (his right to a seat was even challenged), with no delegations pledged to support him, the stage was nonetheless set for his great "Cross of Gold" speech. He was a man with a reputation as a thinker and as a great champion of economic reform. When his powerful speech caught up the delegates in a wave of enthusiasm, they were ready and eager to tender him their nomination for the presidency, not because he had been seeking the nomination, but because he had made himself in their eyes worthy of it. It is thus, as motivation for the general and specific purposes, that the personal purpose must be used.

THE GENERAL GOAL

It is clear that when we express ourselves we do so in a variety of ways; when we communicate, the reasons are not always the same; and when we seek to control the behavior of our audiences, we do not always have the same purpose in mind. Sometimes we wish to explain some object, process, or point of view. Sometimes we wish to change the opinions of our hearers. At times we wish to induce the members of the group to take some definite action. At other times we try to inspire them with a deeper appreciation of the significance of some situation, individual, or event. And at still other times our purpose may be to provide entertainment for the group.

All these purposes are dependent upon the relationship existing between the subject matter and the audience. We explain our point of view so that it will be understood; or to induce belief in it, arouse action regarding it, inspire a deeper concept of its importance, or entertain the audience with it. It is this relationship of audience to subject matter which most definitely distinguishes the general purpose from the personal purpose. The personal purpose seeks to change or to intensify the attitudes of the audience toward the speaker himself. The general purpose seeks to affect the attitude of the audience toward the subject being discussed. The change in attitude that the speaker wishes to bring about may be any of the five that have been listed, from which are derived the five general purposes of speech: *to inform, to induce belief, to move to action, to inspire, and to entertain.*

So important are these five general goals in determining the types of materials to be used, the method of organization, and the mood and manner of the delivery of the speech, that a separate chapter will later be devoted to each. Consequently, each will be discussed here only sufficiently to clarify the nature of each purpose and to distinguish one from another.

To Inform

There are many times when a speaker's sole purpose is to give information to his audience. A classroom lecture might deal with the meaning and significance of Kant's categorical imperative. The sales manager of an insurance company might speak to his salesmen on the nature of the new policy the company has devised. A traveler just back from Europe might discuss the tourist facilities in the major European countries. A stamp collector might explain to a group of neophytes how to go about building up a collection of stamps. A football coach explains to his squad the intricacies of a new play, a fraternity treasurer makes a financial report, a housewife tells a carpenter what sort of shelves she wants put up in her kitchen. The situations which demand purely informative speeches are numerous.

There is one fact concerning informative speeches which it is vital to keep clearly in mind. Information may be distorted by the prejudice, ignorance, or deliberate intent of the speaker. When a Republican politician reveals the "facts" concerning what has happened in the Democratic administration, or vice versa; when a debater presents the "factual" background upon which his case rests; when an automobile salesman is "explaining" wherein his car differs from its competitors—the speech may be outwardly informative. The speaker so labels it, and it may indeed be composed of facts that are objectively true. But these facts are likely to be carefully selected so as to show only one side of the question, and thus in

rated as 50 percent. The minister does not usually seek to change their beliefs or to secure any definite action, but he does seek to raise their percentage of acceptance of religion as high as he can. During the week the percentage drops, and every Sunday it must again be raised.

A common example of the inspirational speech is that of a sales manager to his salesmen when he feels that they need "pepping up." We find another example on the college campus, at the "pep" meetings before athletic events. In these examples there is some fusion of two purposes—to persuade and to inspire—but the inspirational objective is predominant.

Another example of the speech to inspire is the eulogy. Most eulogies of great men are not intended to inform, convince, or persuade the audience. Their purpose is to impress the hearers anew and more deeply than before with the true significance of the virtues and ideals of the dead hero.

To Entertain

Among all the means of relaxation, recreation, and enjoyment, speaking and listening to speeches still holds an important place. Indeed, if radio and television programs and motion pictures are included, the speech designed to entertain is a leader among all the means of recreation. But even if we limit the term to include solely public speeches which have entertainment as their goal, the total audience is still varied and large. A large proportion of after-dinner speeches, public lectures, and radio and television talks are of this type. The substance of a speech to entertain is usually composed either of narrative or of humor. These two kinds of entertaining speeches differ widely from each other in method and in the sort of entertainment they provide, but they are nonetheless similar in purpose.

Whether narrative or humorous, the speech to entertain should make its purpose perfectly apparent, so that it will not engender in the audience the uneasy reaction "This is all very interesting, but where is it leading?" The audience should be made fully aware that the speech is leading to nothing but sheer enjoyment. Often a speaker will use entertainment as an element of relaxation or to divert opposition in a serious speech aimed to inform, convince, persuade, or inspire. But when the speaker's sole purpose is to entertain, the audience should be apprised of that fact by his tone, bearing, and manner of speaking. The audience should be helped to escape from all serious concerns.

GOAL AND RESPONSE

At the beginning of this chapter we noted that the speaker will be helped by asking not only, What is my general purpose? but also, What general response am I seeking from my listeners? These are really the same questions going in opposite directions, but each has its important implications. For each general goal which the speaker may have there is a general response sought from the listener:

Speaker goal	*Listener response*
To inform	To learn
To induce belief	To be convinced
To move to action	To do what is urged
To inspire	To feel inspired
To entertain	To enjoy

THE SPECIFIC GOAL

The speaker's specific goal is the particular response he wishes to secure from a given audience in a given situation. It isn't enough to talk about peace and hope that as a result your listeners will do something constructive for the cause of peace. You must tell them exactly what you expect of them. This brings a vague and general purpose into sharp focus. It helps you select purposively from the great mass of general information those facts, opinions, illustrations, and emotional appeals which are best suited to get the desired response. It helps you to exclude whatever is irrelevant or inconsequential. It not only gives purpose and concentrated direction to the organization of your speech; it helps to focus the attention of your audience precisely where you wish it to be.

You can no more plan a speech effectively before you have set your goals than you can plan a trip before you know where you are going. And it isn't enough to know which planet, or which country. You have to be much more specific than this before the tourist bureaus even know what literature to send you! Many a traveler has returned from what was to have been an enjoyable vacation overtired, disillusioned, and disappointed because he tried to see too much with too little planning and in too little time. Let's not make our listeners overtired, disillusioned, and disappointed by our lack of carefully planned goal-setting.

How these goals might be indicated for representative speaking situations is indicated in the following examples:

The Honor System

Audience: The student council of your college
General purpose: To inform
General response expected from listeners: Better understanding
Specific purpose: To explain to the council members how the honor system has worked in three representative colleges
Specific response expected from listeners: A clearer understanding of the honor system, how it works, and with what results

"Whether 'Tis Nobler—"

Audience: A convocation of freshman English classes
General purpose: To induce belief
General response expected from listeners: Belief
Specific purpose: To convince your listeners that there is more entertainment to be derived from reading one of Shakespeare's plays than from seeing a current movie
Specific response expected from listeners: At least a feeling of pleasurable anticipation for reading a play by Shakespeare

The Barren Hills

Audience: A Rotary club in an eastern industrial city
General purpose: To move to action
General response expected from listeners: Action
Specific purpose: To persuade these eastern businessmen that it is to their own advantage to pay higher taxes in order that the timberlands of the West may be restored and conserved
Specific response expected from listeners: Giving their support to the election of a congressman from their district committed to such a conservation program

"And Gladly Teach"

Audience: A class of prospective teachers
General purpose: To inspire
General response expected from listeners: New enthusiasm
Specific purpose: To inspire listeners with the high potential of their chosen field of service
Specific response expected from listeners: Deeper pride and enthusiasm for their future profession

THE FRESHMAN

Audience: A college alumni reunion banquet
General purpose: To entertain
General response expected from listeners: Enjoyment
Specific purpose: To relax and amuse these mature old grads with an inexperienced but cocksure freshman's views on current problems
Specific response expected from listeners: Hearty enjoyment of ridiculous and yet in part nostalgic idiosyncrasies of brash college freshmen

CONCLUSION

To speak with a clear goal in mind is to speak more effectively. A speaker whom the audience likes and respects has an immediate advantage, no matter what his purpose. This is why in every speech situation it is not merely proper but highly desirable that a speaker be impelled by his personal purpose, whether that be, as in this class, to get a good grade, to express an experience-strengthened conviction, or merely to be favorably regarded by his classmates. This personal goal adds life, vigor, and sincerity to a speech whether its general aim is to inform, induce belief, move to action, inspire, or entertain. And in many instances a speech combines more than one of these general goals. But the speech that stands out, that is a real masterpiece, focuses everything upon a specific purpose, concentrates upon a specific response desired from its listeners.

EXERCISES AND BIBLIOGRAPHY

Exercises

1. Listen to a speech and write a 500-word report on it. What was the speaker's general purpose? What do you believe was his specific purpose? Outline the speaker's main ideas. Were they well selected to accomplish the specific purpose? Did the speaker keep his speech aimed constantly at his goal, or did he digress at times? If you noted any digressions, do you think they were justified? Which of the three basic functions of speech did this talk serve? Do you think the speaker had any personal purpose? If so, to what extent did it influence his speech?
2. Choose a subject and phrase five different specific purposes to be accomplished concerning it, one for each of the five general purposes. List from two to four main ideas in support of each of the specific purposes. Develop fully, in outline form, at least one main idea for

each of the five groups, in order to illustrate the kinds of material with which you would construct each speech. Note carefully the different means which must be used, even though the subject is the same, for the development of the five general purposes.

3. Prepare and present a five-minute speech for some audience and occasion with which you are well acquainted. Have a specific purpose which you make clear. Hand in an outline which states in its heading the audience, the general purpose, and the specific purpose. In presenting the talk to the class, ask the students to imagine themselves the audience which you describe. Be sure to make use of all you have learned about effective use of conversational techniques.

Bibliography

Baird, A. Craig, and Franklin H. Knower, *General Speech: An Introduction* (2d ed.; McGraw-Hill, 1957).

Crocker, Lionel, *Public Speaking for College Students* (3d ed.; American Book, 1956).

Monroe, Alan H., *Principles and Types of Speech* (4th ed.; Scott, Foresman, 1949).

Sarett, Lew, William T. Foster, and Alma Johnson Sarett, *Basic Principles of Speech* (3d ed.; Houghton Mifflin, 1958).

CHAPTER 9

CONTENTS

Gathering proof and illustrative data are essential stages in preparing to speak. (Bates College)

SELECTING AND
DEVELOPING IDEAS

> I resolved that whatever should be said of my style from that time forth, there should not be any emptiness in it.—DANIEL WEBSTER, after his first speech

ALL the preceding chapters have dealt with the various ways in which influence is exerted through speech. The specific function of this chapter is to help you ensure that *what you say* will best represent your honest understanding of the facts concerning your speech topics, supported by evidence that will at once demonstrate the soundness of your ideas and make those ideas attractive to your listeners. As you can readily see, two principal problems are involved: how to *select* and how to *develop* the ideas you will present in your talks. The problems will confront you in these forms: "How do I go about finding a good subject for a talk?" and "What do I do to develop the subject after I have found it?"

Chapter 8 has indicated the first approach to both these questions. As it pointed out, you first of all determine what you want to achieve with your audience. You clarify your purpose in your own mind. It is only after you know clearly what you want to do that you can plan systematically how to do it. Just as this chapter is closely connected with the one entitled "Setting the Goal," so is it also directly related to the ones that follow: on organizing a speech, adapting to the audience, and developing a suitable speech style. More broadly, every chapter in this book is related to all the rest, for speaking is inevitably a "whole" process. Nevertheless, in mastering any complex problem, it is necessary to analyze it into parts and to deal with these one at a time. At this point, your attention is specifically invited to the questions of how to find a good subject for a speech and then what to do with it. When you sit at your desk pondering the fact that you will soon have another five-minute speech to deliver, the immediate problem is what to say.

What is the best way of solving these problems? Should you get topics from your room-mate—or instructor? Should this book supply topics for you to use? All these are possibilities. But since *you* are to be the speaker, the topics and their development should be *your own*. This chapter shows you how to solve these problems for yourself.

CONSIDER WHAT YOU ALREADY KNOW

What you talk about should, naturally, represent your own interests, experiences, beliefs, and desires. Whatever form it takes, speech is highly personal. It is a communication from yourself to your associates. In conversation your topics are chosen (however haphazardly) in terms of your own interests, the interests of your associates, and the nature of the situation. These same guideposts are the ones to follow when you are preparing a public speech. What do you really want to say? What will your audience be likely to want to hear? What seems to be demanded by the nature of the situation? The first step, then, is to take inventory of your present knowledge.

Have you a hobby—such as collecting firsthand narratives of the Civil War—which really fascinates you? If so, can you make it equally interesting to others? Have you taken a college course which has given you new insight into some field of knowledge, or one which has changed your general attitude toward life? How do you react to the political views of your parents, neighbors, or classmates? What is your purpose in acquiring a college education? Do you have any ideas about how the world might be made a better place? Mull over similar interests of your own and you will find an abundant source of good speech subjects.

Taking stock of what you already know is important, too, because it gives you clues to the interests of others. The experiences which have awakened your interest in a given subject are likely to arouse the interest of others. You will awaken the enthusiasm of your listeners to the extent to which you have analyzed accurately and re-created for them the genesis of your own interests, attitudes, and convictions.

Our search for speech subjects and ideas should not stop with an inventory of ourselves as static beings. It is not enough to take stock of what we know, what we have experienced, and what we have observed. We are constantly observing and experiencing. The speaker and the journalist have many common needs. The speaker needs to develop what the journalist calls a "nose for news." Some reporters have a genius for seeing interesting elements in the most commonplace happenings. Note, for example, the excellent use of everyday observation in Bruce Barton's speech "Which Knew Not Joseph" (at the end of Chapter 5). We must keep our eyes open, our ears alert.

For example, you may be interested in collecting stamps—in which case you probably have several stamp catalogues and you are surely a reader of the "stamp news" in the newspaper or in special magazines devoted to the subject. To many of your friends it is evident that you already know far more than they do about stamps. But this does not mean that you are content to stop with what you now know; on the contrary, your interest leads you to read broadly in history and geography, and you make special efforts to learn about the policies governing the issuance of stamps by new nations, such as Ghana.

For another example, you may be interested in international affairs. As a result, you follow in a general way the discussions concerning Red China and its relations with India. This may seem to you to be a topic suitable for a speech. But when you come to the point of preparing it, you realize that there is much you do not know. One possibility is to drop the subject; but a better procedure would be to go to the library and look up specific facts that will not only enlarge your knowledge but serve as a check on your opinions. What is required for good speaking is enthusiasm plus information. Because both are products of slow growth you should choose speech subjects out of your own experience and interests. But you will find that you need additional facts to supplement what you already know. As you gather them you add to your own education while preparing to help guide the thinking of your audience.

Your inventory of yourself is not limited, then, to the observations you have already made. It includes a quickening of your faculties for observing what is interesting and significant in your daily experience. *You, as a college student, have unusual opportunities to find speech ideas in your course of study.* The student who bemoans his lack of speech material ought to remind himself that he spends some fifteen hours a week listening to lectures or participating in discussions on a broad variety of topics. This is a tremendous advantage which few speakers outside the classroom possess. With courses in chemistry, psychology, history, sociology, literature, engineering, physics, mathematics, philosophy, art, education, government, business administration, the humanities, and other fields to draw from, college students can never plead that they are without the raw materials for speeches. Too often the student neglects or overlooks these rich storehouses of speech material with which he is constantly working. All of us are to some extent like the man who could not see the forest for the trees.

One student, for example, came to his speech class unprepared to deliver an assigned speech, because, as he said, he had had to spend the preceding days preparing for a philosophy test. But if he had selected a philosophical problem on which to speak, he could have made preparation for his examination and preparation for his speech complementary instead of conflicting tasks. Similar opportunities await you in all departments of your college work. Do not hesitate to draw upon your other courses. The speech class is a good place to begin that synthesis of the whole educational program which educational theorists have long desired. Think of the time you spend in speech preparation as a time when your knowledge of history, psychology, literature, and sociology is all brought together and fused. Gain from this union new understanding of old problems; with it you can interest and enlighten your audience.

There is a further purpose served by the speaker's taking inventory of himself as he searches for a speech subject and, later, for ideas with which to develop it. He discovers in this process his need for further information and for supporting facts and opinions. His research task is clarified and defined.

USE AVAILABLE REFERENCE SOURCES

Ordinarily, it is a mistake to go to magazines, books, and encyclopedias to find subjects for speeches; such sources should be consulted for supplementary subject matter after your topic has been selected and you have drained the resources of your own mind. This procedure is recommended primarily because it is your best guarantee of originality, your best assurance of a speech which is distinctly *yours*. The student who paraphrases an article in *The Reader's Digest* or some similar source is destroying his originality. A rehash of the ideas of another person is a poor excuse for a speech.

Just as certainly, however, as the preparation of a speech should begin with an inventory of the speaker's own knowledge, *the search for speech ideas must not end within one's self*. The search for a speech subject may be assisted by a browsing visit to the current-magazine shelves of the college or community library. A quick perusal of the tables of contents of several recent issues of magazines will give you some helpful indications as to subjects of current interest and may remind you of experiences and observations of your own which might not otherwise have occurred to you. Similarly, a visit to a bookstore may be a stimulating experience; the title of a new book or a chapter heading from the table of contents may provide just the needed stimulus to lead you to the discovery of a speech subject based on ideas of your own. You may find similarly helpful stimulation in the reviews and announcements of new books in the *Saturday Review* or the book-review section of the Sunday edition of *The New York Times*.

Your first reaction to many of the subjects which occur to you will very likely be "I don't know enough about that to make a speech on it." Doubtless you don't. That is exactly the reaction every would-be speaker should have. It is a serious responsibility to take the time of any audience. We must make certain of having things worth saying. Few indeed are those who can speak effectively on any subject without first having supplemented their previous knowledge of it. "I don't know enough . . . ." should lead inevitably to "I am going to learn more."

What to Look For

How do you test your ideas? Is it not by looking for facts which will either support or cast doubt upon them? Is it not also by checking them against the opinions and judgments of persons better informed than you are? As you continue the preparation of a speech, then, *you must look for facts and for the opinions or testimony of authorities.* As you turn to reading and research to supplement your knowledge at points where your inventory revealed it to be weak or totally lacking, you should be particularly alert for the following types of material:

Statements which clarify your own ideas
Illustrations and examples of what you have in mind
Facts and evidence which test the validity of your own experiences
Testimony and opinions of authorities concerning your views

Where to Look

The following is a minimum list of the sources for research with which everyone should be familiar:

INDEXES

Book Review Digest
Library card catalogue
The New York Times Index
Readers' Guide to Periodical Literature

STANDARD REFERENCE WORKS

An atlas
Bartlett's *Familiar Quotations*
Dictionary of American Biography
The Encyclopaedia Britannica

The Encyclopaedia of the Social Sciences
Statistical Abstract of the United States
An unabridged dictionary
Who's Who in America
The World Almanac and Book of Facts

CURRENT MAGAZINES

The Annals of the American Academy of Political and Social Science	*Look*
	National Geographic Magazine
	Nation's Business
The Atlantic	*Newsweek*
The Christian Century	*The New Yorker*
Commonweal	*Parents' Magazine*
Coronet	*The Reporter*
Current History	*The Saturday Evening Post*
Esquire	*Saturday Review*
Foreign Affairs	*Scientific American*
Fortune	*Time*
Harper's Magazine	*U.S. News & World Report*
Holiday	*Vital Speeches of the Day*
Life	*Yale Review*

These brief lists are not intended to present an imposing and comprehensive array of reference materials but to indicate some useful sources which you can find in your college library and to which you ought frequently to refer. It may take a little time to become familiar with these books and magazines, but once you have done so they will both save you time and aid you in giving body and substance to your speeches. Upon this base of minimum reference materials, you may build as large a structure of general reading as you desire. The Bible, the great literary masterpieces of all languages and all ages, a few of the current best sellers, and any books dealing with subjects that especially interest you will all prove valuable sources of materials for your speeches. So will daily newspapers, though you will do well to keep a balance in your reading so that you do not get only *one* political or socioeconomic viewpoint. As Francis Bacon wisely observed, "Reading maketh a full man."

RECORDING SPEECH MATERIALS

In preparing his speeches, every speaker should acquire and cultivate the habit of making concise, accurate notes of possible speech materials. *Write it down, label it, file it away* are three imperatives for the beginning speaker who would facilitate the preparation of his speeches. A loose-leaf notebook, preferred by some speakers, is satisfactory if it is used for only a brief time or if it does not become un-wieldy from an excessive number of notes. But it has the disadvantage of being difficult to index accurately, because the items as jotted down are not likely to be in logical order. The general preference, therefore, is for a system of filing cards 3 x 5 or 4 x 6 inches in size; alphabeti-cally arranged, they are ready for immediate reference.

In recording materials on cards, three precautions ought particularly to be observed. First, *make your reference to the source of the material exact*. Include the author's name, the title of the work quoted, the publisher, the page number, and the date of publication. The value of your reference is always determined by the source from which it comes; if the source is unknown, its value is highly questionable. Sec-ond, *record the letter or the spirit of the passage accurately*. If you copy the actual words used in your source, be sure to use quotation marks. If you paraphrase and summarize a passage, be sure that you do not distort its true meaning. If you quote a part of the passage and paraphrase the rest, be sure to distinguish between the two sections of your note by a careful use of quotation marks. Third, *make the material you record on each card a single and complete unit*. Do not put two quotations, even from the same source, on one card; if you do, you will be unable to file them accurately and will have difficulty in finding them when you want to use them. If you carry over a quotation from one card to another, the cards may become separated, causing trouble and confusion. In general, strive for brevity and com-pleteness in the references you place on cards. A quotation that is too long to be contained on a filing card is, ordinarily, too long for effec-tive use in a speech. Hence copy no more than you absolutely need, but be sure that your quotation contains that essential minimum.

The following two examples will show accepted ways of recording material from a book and from a magazine. Note that each card contains a main heading, a subheading, and an exact reference to the source from which the quotation was taken. The information contained in these sample cards should always be recorded in complete detail. If you save a moment by neglecting to write down your exact source, you may later use much more time in hunting for the missing data.

WHAT TO RECORD

In general, it is better to take notes too freely rather than not freely enough. There is a tendency to place too much trust in one's memory. When you come across anything, of any nature, which might be of

European Advisory Commission   Origin

"At the Moscow Conference attended by Secretary Hull in 1943 it
had been agreed among the three
principal Allies to establish immediately
a European Advisory Commission in
London. This body was to begin the
study of postwar political problems
of Europe and to make appropriate
recommendations to the governments."
Page 433.

Dwight D. Eisenhower, Crusade in Europe
Doubleday + Company, Garden City, N.Y., 1948

Communism   Domination by the Party

"Even the Communists themselves have
sometimes admitted that the Soviet people
are not free. Here, for example, is the
way Pravda put the matter as
recently as July 6, 1956: 'As concerns
our country, the Communist party was,
is, and will be the only sovereign
of the thoughts, spokesman of the ideas
and aspirations, director and organizer
of the people during the entire
duration of its struggle for
Communism.' "
Editorial, New York Times, July 28, 1959.

---

value to you as a speaker, the safest plan is to write it down and file
it away. Failure to do this will cause countless twinges of regret for
the host of materials that float tantalizingly on the fringes of your
memory but cannot be salvaged for use. The following are the types
of materials which you will want particularly to record:

Quotations

In your random reading or in your deliberate study of a topic, you will find statements made by authorities which you will want either to quote or to paraphrase in your speech. The effect will be somewhat as though you had actually brought the authority to the platform with you, to have him add his word in support of your point. Quotations thus can carry considerable weight, but they should be used with caution. The following rules will serve as a useful guide:

1. *The value of the authority depends upon the audience's respect for his opinions.* If your quotation is from a man who is thoroughly reliable but wholly unknown to your audience, his authority is likely to be discounted. On the other hand, the remarks of a well-known scientist, general, or politician frequently carry even more influence than his knowledge of the subject would warrant.

2. Within the limits of the preceding rule, *the worth of the authority depends upon his competency.* An authority may be said to be competent if he knows his subject thoroughly and expounds it candidly and accurately. His knowledge may be affected by his training, experience, and intelligence; his readiness to speak the exact and complete truth may depend upon how his doing so will affect his personal welfare. The audience will want to know whether the authority has reason to be prejudiced. It adds greatly to the speaker's persuasiveness when it can be shown that the authority quoted is a reluctant witness —that it would have been to his own advantage to have said the opposite of what he actually did say.

3. *The significance of your quotation must be emphasized.* Be sure the audience fully realizes the importance of the witness you have called to your aid and the significance of what he has said. If a quotation is not worth emphasizing, it is hardly worth using. A good way to make certain that it will be adequately emphasized is to prepare your audience for it by dwelling upon the importance of the problem, the need for expert advice in solving it, and the high qualifications of the expert you are about to quote. Thus you might say, "Wouldn't you like to have been at the Yalta Conference to hear what President Roosevelt really told Stalin? Well, James Byrnes was there, and this is what he said about it." After you have read the quotation, it is sometimes a good idea to repeat the substance of it in your own words.

4. *Make your quotations few and brief.* If you have many, they begin to seem commonplace. And if a quotation is long, the audience is likely to lose interest and miss the point.

Summaries of Lengthy Statements

Sometimes an entire article, a chapter of a book, or even the central point of an entire book may be summarized on a card. If something you have just read presents a fresh and stimulating point of view, jot down a summary of it. You expect to remember it, but you probably will not.

Statistics

No speech should be crowded with figures. The audience will not remember them and will find them dull. On the other hand, many speech ideas cannot be properly supported without the use of some statistics. "Automobile accidents are increasing." The only way to prove it is to cite the actual figures. "War is expensive." Present the statistics showing the cost. But, although they are necessary, statistics should not be used indiscriminately. They should be carefully selected for their *source, date,* and *representative value.* It is a truism that, though figures don't lie, liars do figure. Contradictory statistics may be found on many subjects. The reliability of a set of figures depends entirely upon its source. For this reason, statistics are all but worthless in a speech unless the source is stated. In general, the sources of statistics should meet the tests for authority that have been suggested for quotations. The date of most statistics is of importance. If your figures deal with conditions in 1951 be careful not to draw conclusions from them as to the state of affairs in 1961. Finally, make certain that your figures are truly representative. Do they mean what they profess to mean? If you assert that there are five million unemployed in the United States, make clear whether that figure refers to healthy men between the ages of eighteen and sixty who have been unable to find jobs, or rather to men and women of undetermined ages and states of health who have merely indicated that they would like to obtain jobs. If you cite figures to show that the total number of automobile accidents is increasing, point out that the ratio of automobile accidents to the number of automobiles in use and to the amount of gasoline consumed is actually decreasing. In other words, use statistics truthfully and intelligently, taking care never to distort their meanings.

The Speaker's Own Ideas

A speech should represent your own thinking. Any material from other sources should be subsidiary; it should be used merely to support and illustrate your own conclusions. You should therefore make it a habit to search your own mind thoroughly before turning elsewhere for material. Sometimes a thought worth remembering will come to you while you are engaged in something far removed from speech preparation. It is a good plan to jot the idea down and file it away for future use. Your thoughts are too valuable to waste. They are also too valuable to be underestimated. Most beginning speakers are distrustful of their own thinking. They are sure that no audience wants to know what their ideas are. Perhaps they have actually been warned against using such phrases as "I think" and "it seems to me" in a speech. Let it be said at once that no idea is any better that the support offered for it, and this support is often found in the writings, sayings, and experiences of other people. But the idea itself should be based on your own thinking and experience. You may find that your ideas are surprisingly good. Emerson noted that "our own thoughts frequently come back to us with an alienated majesty." When we hear our thoughts expressed by others, they often seem much better than they were when we harbored them ourselves. The beginning speaker must learn to find in his own mind the fountainhead for his speech materials.

Jokes

It would seem that jokes are so numerous and so readily available in books, magazines, and newspapers that the speaker could be prodigal in using them. But when he begins to search for a joke which will both amuse his audience and illustrate a point he is making, the search may be long and fruitless. Good, usable jokes are actually so scarce that when a speaker finds one he frequently uses it over and over, with different audiences, for years. The beginning speaker tends to make far too little use of humor; he fears that his attempted joke may "fall flat," that the audience will laugh at him rather than at his jest. But, since an audience welcomes and appreciates humor in a speech, the speaker who fails to take advantage of this relatively sure way of securing a favorable response is doing himself a grave injustice. When you read or hear a good joke, write it down; and when you are preparing your speech, plan to insert two or three amusing anecdotes. Sources for jokes are numerous. Among the periodicals, *Coronet, The Reader's Digest,* and *The New Yorker* are favorites. Max Eastman's *The Enjoyment of Laughter* and Bennett Cerf's *Try and Stop Me* should be read. For further guidance, the *Cumulative Book Index* contains long lists of entries under the heading "Humor."

Illustrative Stories

You should not limit yourself to humorous anecdotes. In reading the newspapers, you frequently come upon such human-interest stories as the following: an old man in California had the cornea of one of his eyes removed and grafted onto an eye of a boy who was blind; a man about to commit suicide was diverted from his purpose when he saw a dog suffering from a broken leg and stopped to care for it; during the depression 1,000 men applied in response to an advertisement for six junior engineers. Such stories are very useful indeed. With a large stock of them on file, a speaker can be sure of finding at least one item among them that will dramatize and heighten the appeal of any speech.

LIMITING AND DEFINING THE SUBJECT

Probably the most frequent error of the beginner consists in selecting speech topics that are too broad. Here are a few subjects upon which some students have vainly struggled to deliver five- to eight-minute speeches: "The Causes, Kinds, and Cure of Insanity," "Crime," "The History and Present Status of America's Foreign Policy," "The Cold War," "The World in 1975." Contrast with these general subjects the comparative narrowness of the topic upon which Edmund Burke chose to speak for five hours: "The English Parliament ought to take steps to restore the confidence of the American colonies in their mother country." The conclusion is inevitable that Burke could choose a narrow topic because he was exhaustively prepared upon it, and that the preceding broad topics were chosen at least partly to obviate the necessity for careful preparation. Surely upon such a subject as "Crime" almost anyone might gather together enough ideas to compose a five-minute speech. As one student naïvely declared, he could talk even longer than that!

In the selection of a speech subject, be certain to free your mind of any idea that you are only trying to find enough more or less closely related words to fill a specified interval of time. Approach the problem in this fashion: Granted only five minutes of time, what can you say on the proposed subject that will be both interesting and worth while to the audience? In answering that question, you might well begin by restating your tentative topic in one simple declarative sentence. Convert "Crime" to "America's criminal laws are too lax,"

"Poverty is a principal cause of crime," or "Crime has become a carefully organized business." After your selected sentence has been put in writing so that it can be thoughtfully considered, jot down the three or four substantial illustrations or hard-core ideas with which the topic is to be developed and supported. If these supporting ideas appear entirely adequate to establish the topic, and if they can be properly presented in the time allowed for the speech, then the topic may be considered sufficiently limited. Otherwise it must be further narrowed down.

The process in limiting such a topic as "Crime" is as follows:

1. Crime in America (eliminating all other countries).

2. Crime in the present day (eliminating all consideration of previous eras).

3. The causes of crime (eliminating all other aspects of the problem).

4. Poverty as a principal cause of crime (by eliminating all causes but one, a subject suitable for a brief speech is finally attained).

Any speech student will find this process essential for producing clear-cut, purposive speeches. If you have selected the subject "Crime," and have narrowed it down to the topic "Poverty is a principal cause of crime," be sure that your topic is precise and definite in your own mind. Do not be tempted to vent your wrath upon those you hold responsible for the existence of poverty or to argue that it is criminal of our government to permit the continuance of poverty. Each additional topic might become the basis for another five-minute speech; together they might profitably be combined in a speech of thirty or forty minutes. But in the brief time allowed for this particular speech there should be no straying from the single proposition that "poverty is a principal cause of crime." If that statement is adequately illustrated and supported, it will leave no time for additional random observations.

Harry Emerson Fosdick frequently began the preparation of his sermons by deciding upon a number of specific individuals in his congregation who needed his help and then casting about in his mind for the most beneficial thing he could say to them. In other words, he first selected a goal, then determined on a speech subject which would enable him to accomplish it. His practice deserves to be strongly recommended . The topic should be "pointed" in such a way that the speaker can see clearly what he must do with it. Only then will the fog roll away and the outline of the speech clearly emerge. Can one speak, for example, upon such a subject as "Woman Suffrage," or even "The History of Woman Suffrage in America"? Possibly. It has been done. But the result is likely to be a random and pointless collection of anecdotes and facts. It is much better to select so "pointed" an aspect of the subject as "Woman in a Man-Made World." Then, of course, the material to be used should be carefully selected to bear out the point of the topic.

PHRASING A TITLE

With all due deference to Shakespeare, a rose by any other name would *not* smell as sweet. Skunk cabbage has just as attractive a blossom as many flowers cultivated in our gardens, and its odor could be eliminated just as completely as that of marigolds has been; but the accident of its name is sufficient to bar it from cultivation. *Horse mackerel* could not be marketed effectively as a fish food until after it had been renamed *tuna fish*. Indeed, the value of names is so well recognized commercially that motion-picture stars carefully select professional names for their glamorous appeal and manufacturers conduct contests to discover attractive names for their products. Such names as *Kodak* and *Frigidaire* have proved invaluable in helping to sell the articles they designate. It is just as true of speeches that a good title is a valuable asset. If it is to help give point and definiteness to the speech subject it should have the following characteristics:

Brevity

"The Eventual Advantage to the United States of Having a Virtual Monopoly of Helium Gas" is not a good title; "Airships Unlimited" is better.

Suggestiveness

A good title ought to arouse curiosity, not satisfy it. "The Wheel Turns" is a title which suggests a dynamic speech without revealing what the precise subject is to be. Hence, it attracts attention. "The Barren Tree," "The Man More Stubborn than His Mules," and "Afoot in Paradise" are other examples of good suggestive titles. A normal audience is eager to discover the contents of a speech that has been so labeled. On the other hand, some titles are so literal and matter of fact as to stifle curiosity and dissipate interest. A few of this type are "Why Fraternities Should Be Abolished," "Advantages of an Elective Curriculum," "The Law as a Profession," and "How to Make Cane-Bottom Chairs." Avoid them as you would poison, for such titles *are* poison of a sort: they paralyze the audience with incipient boredom.

Vividness

"Two Years in Hell," "He Who Gets Slapped," "Twenty Thousand Leagues under the Sea," and "Around the World on One Leg" are titles which enter at once into the imagination and suggest vigorous, colorful, animated speeches. Such a title as "The Ratio of Hospitalization in an Industrial Community to the Average Length of Employment" does not meet this requirement. Such a title almost inevitably leads an audience to expect a stoop-shouldered speaker who mumbles incoherently through the dull pages of a manuscript. "Time Off for Ill Behavior" or "Steady Work—Steady Pulse" would be better. Give your topic a title that is alive!

Appropriateness

The title (as well as the tone of the speech) should be appropriate to the occasion, to the speaker, and to the subject. "The Five Greatest Thinkers in History" might be appropriate as the title for an address by a distinguished professor who is giving an evening campus lecture; but it would be pretentiously inappropriate for a five-minute classroom talk by a student. "Skating on the Brink of Hell" would be considered too sensational by most church congregations. Whenever a title might be considered "smart-alecky," in poor taste, or pretentious, it should be changed.

Accuracy

On occasion a speaker wishes to conceal his theme until the conclusion of his speech—in which case, as we have said, his title ought to be suggestive rather than literal. Nevertheless, it is highly undesirable to use an inaccurate title. If your title asserts that you will speak on "The Principal Cause of Russian-American Tension," your listeners will expect your analysis of precisely this topic—not a historical chronicle of past difficulties. If your title is announced as "Kids on Campus," the audience may not know precisely what to expect but will not be surprised by a discussion of the problems married students have in providing care for their babies while they themselves are in class.

FROM SELECTION TO DEVELOPMENT

In the preceding pages various aspects of your problem of "selection" of materials for your speeches were discussed. First there is the question of how to find a suitable subject—and our answer is that you must find it from within the range of your own interests and knowledge. However, this does not imply that you need not learn something new to talk about. Every speech is likely to be a challenge to broaden or to sharpen your knowledge of the topic selected. This will involve a search in the library, using the indexes, reference works, magazines, and books that provide the factual materials necessary for a full understanding of your subject. Suggestions were offered as to the various kinds of materials for which you should look, and a suitable method for recording them was described. Finally, as an aid to pinning down your topic, a process was suggested by which you can "limit and define" the subject in accordance with the time available, the nature of the audience, and your own convictions. When this has been done, you will find it useful to formulate a title that will dramatize your topic, bring it sharply into focus in your own mind, and arouse the interest of your prospective audience.

The remainder of this chapter will consider the means of *developing* your speech-idea, making effective use of your assembled materials. For some students, this process of development is difficult. They "say what they have to say," and do not know how (or why) to elaborate it. The *how* may best be explained by a brief description of the various "forms of support" that are available; the *why* involves a consideration of the functions your speech-idea may (or in some cases must) serve if it is to exercise influence over your listeners. In our discussion we shall consider first what it is you try to accomplish through the development of your ideas, then the means (or forms of support) by which you may develop them.

A PLAN OF DEVELOPMENT

In trying to satisfy the first requisite for good speaking—having something worth while to say—the beginning speaker's most common error is failure to develop his ideas. Many beginning speakers are content merely to state the idea and let it go at that. They wonder what more can be done with it. A frequent objection to a topic is, "Oh, but I couldn't talk for five minutes about that." Let us see. If you have had trouble in building up, analyzing, or elaborating the ideas for your speeches, you ought to find a solution for your problem in the following plan. In brief, the plan is this: Do not be content with merely stating your speech idea. Instead, do one or more of the following with it: make it clear, make it arresting, make it significant, make it familiar, make it convincing, make it attractive, make it inevitable, make it appealing.

These eight suggestions form a convenient check list by means of which the speaker can determine whether he is contributing all he should to the development of his speech-ideas. Especially if the speaker seems to "run out of ideas" or if his speeches tend to be thin and superficial, the rules here outlined ought to be rigidly followed. In other words, it may be said of this plan that it offers to all beginning speakers for many of their speeches a comprehensive view of what *can be done* in elaboration of their ideas, and it also serves as an aid to their judgment in determining just what *should be done* for an individual speech. For this purpose, you might well refer to the list as you prepare every speech you will be delivering, realizing, of course, that a speech of entertainment or exposition would not be "convincing" or "inevitable." Use only the suggestions appropriate to your purpose.

Making Your Idea Clear

You must first formulate a clear statement of your idea. You can best check this by putting it in writing. It is surprising how many speeches wander on from the introduction to the conclusion without ever telling the audience what the speaker is talking about. In a few cases, this may result from the fact that the idea is so clear to the speaker that he assumes that it is equally clear to his audience, but in most cases the idea is so hazy in the mind of the speaker that he could not express it clearly, no matter how hard he tried. Hence the first consideration is this: *be certain that your idea is clear to yourself.* Next, *phrase it clearly for your audience.* If the idea is complex or completely new to your audience, *clarify it further by definition.* This is especially necessary when you are arguing with an opponent, for it frequently happens, after strenuous and heated verbal wrangling, that the presumably opposing views are seen to be in essential agreement. For this reason debaters usually begin with a definition of their terms. There is also a sort of personal definition which speakers frequently find useful. They may say, for example, "Regardless of the dictionary meaning of the term, here is what I mean by it, and I am using it in this sense in my speech."

The use of an illustration or two is an invaluable aid in clarification. Following the statement and definition of an idea, an illustration gives it form and substance and lodges it firmly in the minds of the listeners. Whenever an audience is puzzled and uncertain as to a speaker's meaning, a "for example" will bring expressions of relief and understanding.

Finally, *the main idea of your speech should be restated,* in somewhat different words but unmistakably with the same meaning, in order that it may be nailed down and held firmly in place for the consideration of the audience. Using this device in his "fireside chat" of October 12, 1937, President Roosevelt said:

I want our great democracy to be wise enough to realize that aloofness from war is not promoted by unawareness of war. In a world of mutual suspicions, peace must be affirmatively reached for. It cannot just be wished for. It cannot just be waited for.

Making Your Idea Arresting

If you do not catch the interest and attention of the audience early in your speech, it is useless to go on. This is perhaps best illustrated in radio and television speeches, for the prospective audience easily can and freely does "tune out" speakers who do not seize and command its attention. Similarly, the prime ingredient in the success of an advertisement, a street-corner sales talk, a classroom lecture, or a public speech is its power to catch the attention of the reader, passerby, or listener. Even when your audience is physically seated before you, it can mentally "tune out" your speech and concentrate upon private thoughts. For your guidance the following devices are suggested.

1. *Your idea should be striking, different, unusual.* Sometimes an audience can be shocked into close attentiveness. This method is illustrated in a story told about Henry Ward Beecher (and denied by him) in which he is represented as beginning a sermon on a hot evening in July by pulling out a bright bandanna, mopping his brow, and stating, "It's hotter than hell!" Then, when he had the shocked attention of every member of his audience, he went on to explain that that was a remark he had heard made by a man in front of the church, but that he meant to demonstrate that hell was even hotter than New York in July. Usually the speaker will wish to be striking without being shocking, and he always should avoid being in bad taste. But he should at least devise some unusual statement of his

idea, so that it will pierce through the audience's shell of indifference and inattentiveness.

Notice how skillfully Charles Stelzle, representing the United States Department of Commerce, stated his conviction that it is the social duty of employers to pay their employees well and to treat them with consideration:

It has been estimated that it costs the state and the community, plus the expense to the individual's family, about $10,000 to raise and equip the average laborer for his life's work. And so when a man applies for a job he's offering the employer a $10,000 machine for which he pays nothing.

2. *Your idea should be personal.* Call your listeners' attention to the fact that what you have to say concerns them, individually or as a group. It may be stated as a categorical rule that no subject is suitable for a speech which does not bear a personal connection of some kind with the audience to be addressed, and that no speaker is worth listening to who cannot find and use that personal connection. This rule was well demonstrated by Rabbi Milton Steinberg in a radio sermon entitled "The Sins of Society":

We boast that our own lives are free from great wrongs. We have not murdered, we assert proudly, nor robbed, nor lied. No, we have not, most of us, regarded as individuals. And yet, to some extent at least, our fingers press the trigger of every gun fired in warfare; our sinews strike with the blow of every brutalized criminal; our hands participate in every act of oppression, and our treason is involved in every betrayal of the great ideals of men.

Aim your speech at your audience, and you will probably hit your mark; but if you merely aim your speech at a general exposition of your subject, your audience will be hit only accidentally, if at all.

3. *Your idea should be concrete.* It is enlightening to watch the immediate reaction of a bored audience when a speaker says, "Now let me tell you a story." Notice how Bruce Barton, in the opening sentence of his speech "Which Knew Not Joseph" (at the end of Chapter 5), delivered to a group of businessmen, employs simultaneously the principles of personalizing an idea and of making it concrete: "There are two stories—and neither of them is new—which I desire to tell you, because they have a direct application to everyone's business." Robert Louis Stevenson gave us very nearly the last word upon the importance of concreteness when, in "Aes Triplex," he ridiculed the philosophers' abstract definition of life:

. . . philosophy has the honor of laying before us, with modest pride, her contribution toward the subject: that life is a Permanent Possibility of Sensation. Truly a fine result! A man may very well love beef, or hunting, or a woman; but surely, surely, not a Permanent Possibility of Sensation! We may be afraid of a precipice, or a dentist, or a large enemy with a club, or even an undertaker's man; but not, certainly, of abstract death.

It may be said that abstractness *is* death for a speech, and that concreteness is the breath of life.

Making Your Idea Significant

It is necessary to show the audience that it is worth its while to listen. One common means of doing this consists in stressing the importance of your theme. Thus, Henry L. Stimson, who served both as Secretary of War and as Secretary of State, emphasized the need for world government by saying, "Lasting peace and freedom cannot be achieved until the world finds a way toward the necessary government of the whole." Sometimes this is accomplished by stylistic effect, as in the speech in the United States Senate, on August 21, 1958, in which Senator William E. Jenner of Indiana stressed the effects of dictatorial control in occupied lands, saying, "Politically, the world is covered with a blanket of silence. There is not much debate or argument. There is only stillness, and the soft sound of feet crossing the borders to freedom, or junks sailing in the winds to the land of hope."

Making Your Ideas Familiar

You must associate your idea with what your audience already knows and is interested in. You start with what is known, and go from there to what is unknown or unfamiliar. How often in describing a stranger do we say, "He is as tall as Uncle Ned, has a nose like Aunt Sally's, and is as good-natured as Cousin Tom"? Adapting this method to speech form, you might reach your audience by citing facts that are well known and at the same time arouse interest and curiosity by promising to give these familiar facts a new and fresh significance.

Another method for making your speech-idea familiar to your audience is comparison and contrast. In a speech on the English parliamentary system, for instance, you might compare and contrast it with the American congressional system. A little boy used this method when he described the taste of soda pop by saying, "It tastes like when your foot's asleep."

Making Your Idea Convincing

To convince your audience use all the resources of logic, facts, opinions of authorities, and examples. Ideally, your chief task should be to demonstrate the *truth* of your idea. For this purpose the four methods just listed are your proper tools, and they should be freely and conscientiously used. But psychologically your chief task is to make your idea *reasonable*. Sometimes this is simply a matter of showing that it is true. But, most people are like the rustic who, seeing a giraffe for the first time, exclaimed, "It's not true!" "There must be a catch in it somewhere" is a typical remark when incontrovertible evidence is presented in support of a proposition that violates the audience's sense of reasonableness. Truth and error are both rejected when they appear to be unreasonable and are both accepted when they appear to be reasonable.

Naturally, people differ in their concept of what is reasonable, but in general one may define as reasonable *that which there appears to be no reason to contradict*. The speaker who wishes his ideas to be taken as reasonable, and therefore convincing, will be careful not to run into conflict with the experiences and observations of his audience. The speaker who announces that he has just discovered facts which prove that his listeners' long-cherished beliefs are false is going to be sadly disappointed in their reaction. But the speaker who takes account of his audience's special but illogical beliefs and so phrases his ideas as to seem to supplement and complete rather than to contradict those beliefs has every prospect of success.

A further means of making your ideas appear reasonable and hence convincing is to base them on historical surveys. Show that the currents of history have culminated in the facts you are presenting. Most people still agree with Patrick Henry's dictum, "I know of no way to judge the future but by the past." If you are trying to urge a new concept upon a conservative audience, it will be fatal to present it (however logically supported) as your own discovery. The chances of success will be much greater if you find historical antecedents for it and fit it in with the beliefs and doctrines that have long been established. One characteristic of the radical that gets him his name and often makes him disliked and distrusted is his insistence that what he is presenting is a new truth, just discovered—a truth much more logical than the stupid, narrow, prejudiced beliefs upon which people have heretofore been acting. It is only natural for people to resent such an approach and to refuse to accept whatever truth might actually exist in this new view.

Making Your Idea Attractive

The audience must be made to wish to accept your idea. People desire things which are, in some way or other, to their advantage, Thus you will find your listeners eager to accept your idea if you can show that they will gain by doing so. If your speech-idea is inherently agreeable, or if it can be made to appear agreeable to the audience, its chance of acceptance is increased a hundredfold. On the other hand, unpalatable, unattractive ideas are accepted most reluctantly, if at all.

This does not mean that the speaker should present only attractive ideas. Audiences often have to be urged to do things which are not, on the surface at least, to their advantage. In such cases, the speaker's task is to find attractive features in the proposal. The educator Stringfellow Barr concluded a plea for a return to a well-rounded education by stressing the values of such an education for the student:

> You will learn to distinguish the practical from the theoretical, and you will learn in what ways the practical and the theoretical are always related. You will have received a sound basic education that will fit you to enter a professional or technical school, to embark on graduate work, or to enter directly a business or public career.

Often the speaker will find that he must take account in his speech of the costs and disadvantages of the idea he is presenting; but if he wishes to succeed in getting it adopted he should always balance this part of his discussion with a description of the advantages of accepting his idea.

Making Your Idea Inevitable

You must show that your idea is the best available solution for the problem you have described. "Something must be done—and this is the best that can be done." There are two principal methods of persuading an audience that your plan is the inevitable one. The first, used by President Wilson in his address to Congress on April 2, 1917, entails *not only a demonstration of the strong points of your plan but also the proof that no other plans are satisfactory.* Thus, after picturing the continued violation of American rights and the destruction of American lives by agents of the German government, Wilson presented three possible courses America might follow; but of these the first two were impossible, and the third was inevitable: ". . . armed neutrality, it now appears, is impracticable." And "We will not choose the path of submission and suffer the most sacred rights of our nation and our people to be ignored or violated." The challenge of war must be accepted—"The world must be made safe for democracy. Its peace must be planted upon the trusted foundations of political liberty."

Another method of showing that your idea is inevitable lies in demonstrating that *it is already fully accepted in some form or forms very similar to the one in which you are presenting it.* President Franklin D. Roosevelt used this method when he said:

> You and I have heard big manufacturers talk about control of production by the farmer as an indefensible "economy of scarcity." And yet these same manufacturers never hesitate to shut down their own huge plants, throw men out of work, and cut down the purchasing power of whole communities whenever they think they must adjust their production to an oversupply of the goods they make. When it is their baby who has the measles, they call it not "an economy of scarcity," but "sound business judgment."

Strictly speaking, no idea has been made inevitable until the audience says, "There is nothing to do but accept it." This, of course, cannot be done with all speech-ideas. Sometimes there clearly are two choices, and you can show only that in certain specific respects yours is the better of the two. But where this method can be used, it offers a valuable aid to the speaker.

Making Your Idea Appealing

You must show what positive good will be accomplished by your idea. An important element in human nature is the deep-seated desire to do what is decent, manly, and proper, even though this may involve some sacrifice. Jesus knew that even the scribes and Pharisees, the publicans and sinners possessed this ideal; and when he appealed to it, they responded. The speaker who clearly shows his listeners the *moral significance* of his ideas is likely to obtain their support. A fine example of this method of development comes from a speech, "Science and Ethics," by the noted zoologist Edwin Grant Conklin:

> As scientists we are inheritors of a noble ethical tradition; we are the successors of men who loved truth and justice and their fellowmen more than fame or fortune or life itself. The profession of the scientist, like that of the educator or the religious teacher, is essentially altruistic and should never be prostituted to unethical purposes. To us the inestimable privilege is given to add to the store of knowledge, to seek truth not only for truth's sake but also for humanity's sake, and to have a part in the greatest work of all time, namely the further progress of the human race through the advancement of both science and ethics.

FORMS OF SUPPORT

The eightfold potential for development not only has indicated what may or should be done with an idea on which you are working; it has also demonstrated many of the methods or forms of support. Here we shall present a systematic overview of the more useful of the forms of support, so that—seeing them all together—you may have a checklist of the means by which your speeches may be enriched. When you view your *subject* in relation to *yourself* and your *audience*, there are six questions that need to be answered, requiring six different forms of support:

1. What are you talking about?
   (*Identification: definition and description*)
2. What is it really like?
   (*Analysis and classification*)
3. What does it mean to you and your audience?
   (*Illustration: general and specific; real and hypothetical; literal and figurative; comparison and contrast*)
4. Why is it important?
   (*Application: challenges; questions, direct and rhetorical; restatement*)
5. Is it true?
   (*Proofs by: probability; authority; statistics; experience*)
6. What should you conclude concerning it?
   (*Synthesis: summary; evaluation; implications*)

Identification

To indicate to your audience what you are talking about, you may find either definition or description (or a combination of the two) to be helpful. Definition consists of establishing first the genus or class into which a given term falls, then the specific species, and finally the qualities which differentiate it from other species within the class. Thus, a "labor union" is an *organization* (genus) of *working men* (class) designed to *secure, protect, and improve working conditions* (differentiating it from fraternal, social, and insurance organizations). Sometimes a definition provides a sufficient identification, but it has the disadvantage of placing a heavy responsibility upon the audience to make careful note of the precise factors that are discriminated. Description is an appeal from words to facts; it is a picturization of what the term means in an actual situation or in action. This descrip-

tion may be quite extensive and offers you the opportunity to illustrate the meaning of the term with reference to an actual labor union
with which your audience is familiar.

Analysis

Analysis is a process of taking your topic apart to see what its elements are—just as a chemical analysis breaks a compound into its
elements, or as a lawyer may analyze the evidence against his client
so that he may see and evaluate each part. If you plan to make a
speech on selecting a suitable vocation, you may define what you
mean by "selecting," "suitable," and "vocation." Then you may analyze the problem to identify the difficulties that must be overcome.
Your analysis might consist of such questions as these:

Why does a problem exist?
What has brought it to a head?
Why is it worth our consideration?
In times like these do we have the opportunity of selection?
How are vocations usually chosen?
How should they be chosen?
How can we learn about available vocations?
How can we learn about our abilities and real interests?
What factors make a vocation desirable?

One result of the analysis might be to induce you to "limit your
topic" to presentation of answers to just one (or perhaps two or three)
of these questions. How vocations are chosen and how they should
be chosen, for example, are two related and partially contrasting
questions, each of which requires still further analysis before you are
ready to present satisfactory answers. The more closely you examine
the real nature of your subject, the more realistically you will be prepared to discuss it.

Classification

As a result of your analysis, you will find various parts of your
topic logically related to other parts, thus suggesting groupings that
should be made. Often it is of value to experiment with various different types of groupings in order to clarify the differing ways in
which the topic may be developed. If, for instance, you plan to speak
on "The College Student—What Is He Like?" you might make the
classifications listed below. Your speech, finally, would be based
upon whichever seems best to serve your purpose—and the separate

items within your classification would become the focal points for your main ideas:

1. *Chronological grouping:* upper division and lower division; or freshmen, sophomores, juniors, seniors, and graduate students
2. *Achievement grouping:* pundits, pluggers, and playboys
3. *Motivational grouping:* drifters, those searching for goals, and those who know what they want and go after it
4. *Evaluative grouping:* the stars (scholastic or athletic) of whom we boast, the supporting cast (average), and the liabilities (for whom we apologize)
5. *Affiliative grouping:* fraternity and sorority, independent
6. *Financial grouping:* wholly self-supporting, partially self-supporting, dependent

Illustration

When a speaker says "for instance" or "for example," his audience takes heart. It has been said that if a speech proceeds for as much as two minutes without a concrete illustration of some kind, it may be assumed that neither the speaker nor his audience knows what he is talking about. The Latin root *illustrare* means "to shed light," and illustrations rightly used are indeed enlightening. Abstractions (such as "Courage is a virtue") and generalizations (such as, "all good athletes are competitive-minded and physically well coordinated") are valuable as indicating your point of view, but they need to be made meaningful through illustrative examples. You should be acquainted with the following types of illustrations, so that you may use whichever ones (singly or in combination) will best serve your purpose in a particular speech.

1. *General* and *specific* examples. General examples, as the name implies, refer to classes or types of behavior. For instance, you might say: "Courage is a virtue. Without it, battles would be lost, the weak would be exploited by the strong, cruelty would go unchecked." Here you would have three general examples to enforce your abstract declaration. From this point you might go on to add: "For example, in the World War II Battle of the Bulge, General McAuliffe, who commanded the American soldiers in the encircled city of Bastogne, was called upon by the Germans to surrender. Regardless of the seeming hopelessness of the situation, he simply replied, 'Nuts,' and continued fighting until at last help came. This is the kind of courage with which battles are won." Here you have a specific example, reinforced by a concluding reiteration of your abstraction. A specific example always centers on a particular individual or group involved in some particular

incident. Of course an argumentative listener might reply, "Yes, and Pickett's charge in the Battle of Gettysburg was equally courageous— yet the Southern forces were defeated." Your one instance was not enough to *prove* the conclusion you seemed to have implied; but through these specific examples both you and your listener were illustrating the fact that "courage is a virtue." The concreteness ensured that you were thinking about the same idea.

2. *Real* and *hypothetical* examples. The two specific examples just cited were "real." For some speeches it is more suitable to invent an imagined example, which we call hypothetical. If you were speaking on "Interplanetary Travel," you might say, "Let us imagine what would be required on the moon. We should have to have landing facilities and a refueling station. This would require a permanent settlement, with homes, schools, and entertainment facilities. In short, we would need to establish there a real town, comparable to a village on earth." This example is "imagined" because it does not exist; you needed it to make clear one of the difficulties of interplanetary travel, so you hypothesized it. The hypothetical example is needed to complete the thought, "This is what would happen if . . . ."

3. *Literal* and *figurative* examples. Both the specific and hypothetical examples mentioned were literal, for they attempted to picture what really had or might have happened. An analogical example is based upon resemblances between items that are alike in the one essential respect cited by the speaker but are unlike in other ways. You might use an analogy in your talk on interplanetary travel by saying: "For us to establish a permanent base on the moon would be as difficult as it would be for residents of Australia to establish a steel mill in the middle of the Sahara Desert if they had only small canoes to use for transport." Or, to leave literalness even further away, you might say, "Butter is to bread what a kiss is to love-making." As is evident from these examples, an analogy might be used for emphasis or for arousing interest. Still another of its uses is to employ what is familiar to illuminate what is unfamiliar. For this purpose, you might say: "The Senate is like the Interfraternity Council, in that every member feels some responsibility to the whole group but a far greater responsibility to the special group he has been sent there to represent."

4. *Comparison* and *contrast*. Many of our judgments inevitably are based upon comparison and contrast, which is sufficient reason why these kinds of illustrations should often be used by speakers. As one student said, using comparison and contrast together in the form of analogies: "Grades are like wages paid to honest workingmen;

they are not whips to be used for punishment. They are like dividends paid in accordance with our investment of time and intelligence; they are not rewards to entice us, as carrots are dangled ahead of stubborn donkeys."

Application

The problem of how to "bring the topic home" to your audience is partly solved through use of illustrations. Other methods of value are *challenges, questions,* and *restatement.* Challenging statements are designed primarily as "interest-catchers" (such as, "The entire human population could be packed into a single box one mile square") or as a means of making listeners feel the problem being discussed is really their own—as in the statement, "I am speaking to you because you are the ones who will have to pay this suggested tax.") Restatement, as the term indicates, is merely a repetition (perhaps in different words) of what has been said before. A. T. Jersild found through experimentation that three repetitions of an idea, stated differently, and introduced into different parts of the speech, are the most effective means of impressing an idea lastingly upon the minds of listeners.[1]

Questions are used in speeches in various ways. A talk may start with several direct questions which will be, in effect, the "main ideas" to be dealt with, as did the speaker who commenced: "When we graduate from college, three questions will be uppermost in our minds: What kind of job will I have? Where will I live? And what will my future be?" Another kind of question is *rhetorical,* by which we mean a question for which the answer is obvious, asked primarily as a means of emphasis. Examples would be: "Who is willing to surrender his fundamental human rights? Wouldn't we fight rather than give up our freedom? Is liberty not worth the trouble of defending it?" A principal advantage of using questions is that they invite the audience to "think back" and indicate that you do care what is going on in their minds. Thus questions help to establish the *rapport* described in Chapter 2 as being essential to good speaking.

Proof

Earlier this chapter indicated that people tend to believe what is true, what is reasonable, what they have no reason to doubt. We have

[1] A. T. Jersild, "Modes of Emphasis in Public Speaking," *Journal of Applied Psychology,* XII (December, 1928), 611–20.

reminded you that expert testimony is sound evidence, and have stated the standard tests by which to determine whether a statement is authoritative. We have also pointed out how statistics should be used, and what tests should be applied to ensure their validity. In addition to *reasoning, authority,* and *statistics,* your assertions can and should be submitted to the test of *experience.* The experience you may cite in your speech may be your own, it may be that of the audience, or it may be the experience of other peoples or of earlier generations. In any of these instances, the practicality of your claim has met what many consider the supreme test: *it has worked.* It has been tried out, and we should now profit from the success of that trial. The effective speaker often has occasion to refer to the commonalty of the experience of himself and his listeners, as did William F. Schnitzer, Secretary-Treasurer of the AFL-CIO, when speaking on September 3, 1956, to the Swedish Confederation of Trade Unions, in Stockholm:

Yes, I might add that I note even a similarity in the negotiating techniques and tasks between our two trade-union movements. I refer particularly to your recent success in speeding up the wage payment negotiations for your Annual Central Agreement. We have been likewise much interested in the fact that your lower-paid workers have been receiving the bigger wage increases. We note that you, too, are going in for what we call fringe benefits—like employer allotments for more holiday pay and improving the lot of the government pensioners by a more effective pension system. Yes, in your country, as in ours, it is the trade-union movement which has been the sparkplug of the movement for maintaining prosperity and for improving and expanding the social security system of the land.

Synthesis

Finally, as you conclude your speech you need to draw together the strands which you originally separated in your analysis and classification. Frequently this is done through a *summary.* You may also present a final *evaluation* of the significance of your conclusions. And often it is wise to end your talk by making it clear to the audience what *implications* your conclusion has for them; in other words, what should they believe or do as a result of what you have been telling them? All three of these functions were combined in the conclusion with which W. Harold Breaton, Chairman of the National Bank of Des Moines, Iowa, ended his address to the centennial convention of Delta Tau Fraternity, speaking on "The Challenge of International Communism," in Pittsburgh, on August 21, 1958:

The side that wins this war will be the one that outthinks and outworks the other side. We cannot afford to relax each time a new synthetic olive branch is offered to us. The contest is for the allegiance of the under-privileged people of the world. We must convince them of the dependability and good motives of the United States. They must be made to understand that Communism's motives are to enslave them. With the will to do, we can compete with Russia in convincing people that private enterprise holds the greatest hope of fulfilling their aspirations—the greatest hope of their becoming their own masters. Let us work to rally to our side, not only free people, but those who live in fear behind the iron curtain. With a competitive spirit and a keen sense of justice and fairness, we can and we will win this contest.

The message that I wish to leave with you, if you forget everything else I have said, is this. Don't you for a minute think that this is someone else's problem. This is your problem and you'll be lucky if you don't have to actually fight for it, but through wisdom and attention fighting might be avoided. You happen to be an important part of a people who, during their short experience with freedom, have achieved great success, and thus accumulated great responsibilities. You, as an American, are fortunate, but the price you must pay to maintain your good fortune is attention to your government.

CONCLUSION

In this chapter we have sought to give you practical help in dealing with one of your most basic problems as a speaker: "What shall I say?" The problem requires a searching analysis of what you already know and believe, and of what you need to learn in order to extend and verify your knowledge of a topic you decide to discuss. By know-ing where to look for suitable information and what kinds to record, you can assemble the factual data that are required. Then, as you follow the eightfold plan of development, and make use of the varied forms of support, you will find that "what to say" becomes a problem well within your capacity to master.

EXERCISES AND BIBLIOGRAPHY

Exercises

1. Phrase an idea you would like to speak about in your speech class. Be prepared to show how it meets the four tests for a good topic. Which of the eight types of development will you give it? Why? How? Devise an attractive and appropriate title. Prepare to deliver the talk.

2. Suggest how each of the eight methods of development may be applied to the following ideas for speeches:

   a. Our school should not engage in the current practice of commercializing athletics.
   b. Participation in some kind of athletic contest by every able-bodied student should be encouraged.
   c. College courses should be so organized as to keep the students at work for eight hours a day, five days a week, and to leave the rest of their time free for social and extracurricular activities.
   d. Charm, etiquette, and personality development should be taught in the colleges.
   e. The way to disarm is to disarm.
   f. Excessive drinking by students on or off the campus should be strongly condemned by student opinion.
   g. The death penalty for any crime whatever should be abolished.
   h. The student who works his way through college misses many of the best educational opportunities offered by college life.
   i. Salesmanship is a vocational opportunity which college students should not overlook.
   j. College graduates shut themselves off from many worth-while vocations by insisting upon white-collar jobs.
   k. Stunt flying is an evil which the aviation industry should discourage by every available means.

3. In the following poem, E. E. Cummings, by implication at least, criticizes the typical patriotic orator for having nothing of importance to say about his subject. What would you say is the central idea the orator is trying to express? Give this idea a definite form, and then develop it according to each of the eight methods.

"NEXT TO OF COURSE GOD AMERICA I"[2]

"Next to of course god america i
love you land of the pilgrims and so forth oh
say can you see by the dawn's early my
country 'tis of centuries come and go
and are no more what of it we should worry
in every language even deafanddumb
thy sons acclaim thy glorious name by glory
by jingo by gee by gosh by gum
why talk of beauty what could be more beautiful than these heroic happy dead
who rushed like lions to the roaring slaughter

[2] From the *Collected Poems* of E. E. Cummings, published by Harcourt, Brace and Company; copyright, 1926, by Boni and Liveright, Inc., copyright, 1938, by E. E. Cummings.

> they did not stop to think they died instead
> then shall the voices of liberty be mute?"

He spoke. And drank rapidly a glass of water.

4. Listen to a speech outside the classroom and write a 250- to 300-word criticism of it, answering the following questions:

   a. Was the topic suited to the capabilities of the speaker, the interests of the audience, the nature of the occasion, and the length of the speech?
   b. Did the speaker's development of his topic indicate that he was intimately acquainted with his subject or that he had merely "read up on it" for the speech? What made you reach that conclusion?
   c. Did the speaker discuss his topic with enthusiastic interest? If so, how did he show it?
   d. Why was, or was not, the title a good one for the speech? Suggest an alternative title which you think would be just as good as or better than the one he used.

5. Write a 300-word statement indicating your judgment of the value of your experience and range of knowledge as a source of interesting speech subjects. Make this statement sufficiently autobiographical to indicate rather fully the extent of the experiences you have had and the reading you have done from which good speech subjects and material can profitably be drawn. If your self-analysis reveals a background that has little in it of value as speech material, what positive suggestions can you make for enriching your store of experience and reading?

6. Select two contemporary speakers who represent opposing points of view on some current issue (such as Republican-Democratic, labor-management, liberal versus vocational education). Choose two or three representative speeches from each—enough to give you a representative sampling of their thinking on the topic. Then analyze the speeches to determine the soundness of their thinking and the fullness of the development of their ideas. Try not to let your own convictions on the subject prejudice your analysis. After your comparative study has been completed, indicate by what means you would further develop the ideas representing the side of the controversy which you personally favor.

Bibliography

Hoffman, Randall W., and Robert Plutchick, eds., *Controversy: Readings to Stimulate Thought and Discussion* (Putnam, 1959).

King, C. Harold, "The 'Hobby' Speech," *Quarterly Journal of Speech,* XXI (June, 1935), 370–73.

CHAPTER 10

CONTENTS

Careful organization of wisely chosen speech materials is the best insurance of success in developing ideas substantial enough to merit the attention of an audience.

ORGANIZING
THE SPEECH

A FINISHED speech is more than the sum of the raw materials you have gathered, just as a successful football team is more than the sum of a few promising young athletes. A good speech is far more than a collection of good ideas. It is an organization, or ingenious pattern of well-chosen ideas and clarifying or substantiating data. An exquisite Swiss watch is more than the mere sum of its parts; it is an organization, an intricate interrelationship, a patterning of those parts into a precision timepiece. Similarly, main ideas to support the central theme of a talk are not just any two or three ideas relevant to the theme, but *the* ideas out of which the purposive pattern of the speech can best be organized.

We have considered the ways of selecting and developing ideas. The total organizational task of speech composition may now be developed as essentially one of *outlining. Introductions* and *conclusions* are of such importance that they merit special and separate consideration. Finally, the speaker must adapt his plan to the specific *type of preparation* he intends to use.

OUTLINING THE SPEECH

No builder would think of constructing a house without first having at hand a detailed plan to follow. Such a plan is prepared by a skilled architect. But the speaker is both architect and builder of his speech. We are here concerned with his role as architect, or planner.

Outlining contributes to the efficiency and effectiveness of the speaker. *First, it reveals strengths and weaknesses in the organization and development of ideas.* When the speech is thus reduced to brief structural form it is easier to visualize the whole. Misplaced ideas and illustrations as well as gaps in the evidence are now plainly noticeable. Rearrangements become obvious which will make the speech more clear. No doubt you have looked at a city map to find the most direct route to a certain location. In a similar way, looking at the outline of a speech helps one avoid dead-end ideas and circular thinking, and makes clear the most direct route to the listener's understanding. *Second, the outline reveals how well proportioned a speech is.* In outline form too long an introduction becomes immediately evident, or a disproportionate amount of time devoted to the conclusion becomes more apparent. This skeletal form of the speech also reveals clearly whether the main ideas in the body of the speech receive the correct emphasis. *Finally, the outline is an invaluable time-saver and material-organizer* in building the speech. The evidence cards which have been gathered may be sorted out rapidly and arranged in effective order. At first thought it might seem just as efficient to lay out and rearrange such evidence cards on a large table, or on the floor, until the ideas finally assume a sensible and meaningful pattern. But only a careful outline made beforehand will reveal where supporting materials are lacking, and where some materials are either irrelevant or actually distracting from the developing theme and message of the speech.

Outlining is also of great value to the listener. As a student you know the ease with which you can follow a classroom lecture that is well and clearly outlined. In this sense outlining is a helpful tool to use in studying the speeches of others. Reducing a speech to outline form makes clear its compositional strength or weakness. The ability of a listener to visualize a speech in outline form as it is being heard makes remembering its main points later much easier.

Outlines may be in topical or complete sentence form. The advantage of the complete-sentence form is that it assures clarity and completeness of thought. It may, therefore, have distinct advantages for the less experienced. However, unless the purpose or the theme of the speech is carefully worded as a complete sentence, the topical form of outline has the advantage because it is brief. The brevity of the topical form also makes it easier for the speaker to remember.

Every college student has had long acquaintance with outlining in English composition and other classes. It may nevertheless prove helpful to summarize here a few of the essential principles. The outline is the plan of the speech. It should, therefore, be complete. Yet it is the plan—not the entire speech—and so it should be as brief as is compatible with thoroughness. Clearness is aided by a threefold division of the outline: into introduction, body, and conclusion. Headings and successive subheadings are established to make clear which ideas are of paramount importance and which are subservient or supporting. Never use just one subheading. It is hardly logical to divide a thing into one part! Subheadings may constitute (1) subdivisions of the main heading, (2) amplification of a statement, (3) explanations of an assertion, or (4) proofs supporting a proposition. Numbers or letters used to label the divisions of the outline must be kept uniform. Uniform indention for ideas of parallel importance adds further to the clearness of the plan. The introduction will contain attention-getting and interest-arousing materials to prepare the listener for the theme and purpose of the speech. The body of the outline includes the full development of the speech. It may consist of two, three, or more main ideas. In the usual classroom situation, there may be time for but one main idea. Most experienced speakers will not usually expect an audience to remember more than three main points even in a much longer talk. The conclusion may be a summary or final appeal in support of the purpose of the speech.

You may wish to remind yourself of the simple mechanics of the outline:

ACCEPTABLE OUTLINE FORM

I.
  A.
    1.
    2.
      a.
      b.
        1)
        2)
          a)
          b)
  B. . . .
II. . . .

In the sample outlines which follow, the three principal parts of the outline—introduction, body, and conclusion—are labeled. Remember, however, that these are merely descriptive terms to clarify the organization in the author's mind. These terms are not properly parts of the outline as they are not topics to be developed in the plan.

The Sentence Outline

The sentence outline is a clearer form because it gives in more detail a statement of each topic, as the following outline will illustrate.

FOOTBALL: A GAME OF THRILLS

Theme: A good game of football is thrilling to the end.
General purpose: to inform
Specific purpose: to make clear the situations which made this an especially thrilling game
I want my audience to: appreciate the thrill of watching such a game as is described

INTRODUCTION

I. This year's homecoming game was a good one.

    A. The teams were evenly matched.
    B. Their morale was at top pitch.
    C. The play was brilliant and sportsmanlike.

II. The thrills and tension mounted steadily.

    A. Neither team ever gained a comfortable lead.
    B. A spectacular pass interception and 40-yard touchdown run by the visitors tied the score in the final minute of the first half.
    C. With the home team clinging insecurely to a one-point lead, the last five minutes of the thrill-packed game had every rooter on his feet alternately in consternation and exultation.

BODY

I. The play was unbelievably close.

    A. The teams were even on downs.
    B. Neither team received a misconduct penalty of any sort.
    C. Three times each team lost the ball on downs within the other's 10-yard line.
    D. The home team gained 5 yards less on the ground, and 8 yards more in the air, than the visitors.
    E. The final victory was by a one-point margin.

II. For no longer than a couple of minutes did either team hold more than a 2-point lead.

    A. The first quarter was scoreless.
    B. The last five minutes of the second quarter brought a flurry of action.

        1. The home team's try for a field goal succeeded.
        2. After a long punt return, the visitors quite quickly tied the score.
        3. A blocked kick gave the home team the opportunity to make its first touchdown, but its try for point after touchdown was blocked.
        4. Within the last minute of the half, the visitors intercepted a pass and added a 40-yard run to tie the score.
        5. The home team also blocked the kick for point after touchdown and the score remained 9 to 9 as the half ended.

C. The third quarter saw each team taking desperate chances.
   1. Until it was half over neither team could get close to the other's goal line.
   2. Then the home team recovered a fumble deep in enemy territory and followed with a long successful pass to take the lead 12 to 9. The try for two points after touchdown failed.
   3. Within two minutes the visitors had again tied the score, and then, with a successful kick, added the point after touchdown to take the lead 13 to 12.
   4. The home team fought valiantly, finally drove within range of the goal posts, and completed another field goal to grab a 2-point lead at the quarter's end.
D. The final quarter was more dramatically and almost as evenly contested, as the first.
   1. For two thirds of the quarter an inspired defense held off a desperate and varied attack.
   2. Then a long pass found its receiver; conversion point followed touchdown; and the visitors were ahead 20 to 15.
   3. One minute and fifty seconds later the home team had driven and passed the length of the field and were again ahead 21 to 20.
   4. There remained five minutes of as frantic football and as frenzied rooting as you will ever see and hear as the homecoming victory was kept safe by the narrowest of margins.

III. The fans were almost as tired as the players at game's end.
   A. They had shouted and cheered themselves hoarse.
   B. There had not been a moment's letdown in suspense from beginning to end of the game.
   C. They had spent the last five minutes of the game responding empathically with such energy to help the team that every muscle seemed tired.

CONCLUSION

A good game of football is thrilling to the end.

The Topical Outline

The topical outline uses the meaning-carrying words of what might have been a complete sentence. The topical outline can be more easily and quickly comprehended. It is more easily remembered by the speaker. It may have dangerous pitfalls, however, for the inexperienced to whom its topics are not visualized as the complete sentences (or complete thoughts) they imply.

The following example is an old one but it illustrates the fact that very brief topics may mean little or nothing to the speaker. We have, therefore, inserted explanatory sentences in parentheses. It was a plan for a sermon on the prodigal son and was credited to Dr. Charles A. Tindley, of the then East Calvary Street Church, M.E., in Philadelphia:

I. Madness
   A. Caviled   (He caviled his father)
   B. Traveled   (He traveled to a far country)
   C. Raveled   (He raveled out his character)

II. Sadness
   A. Hogs   (He fed the hogs)
   B. Togs   (He wore out his togs)
   C. Dogs   (He went to the dogs)

III. Gladness
   A. Sealed   (He was sealed by his father's ring)
   B. Vealed   (He got the fatted calf)
   C. Healed   (He was healed by his father's love)

The brevity of this outline will certainly appeal to many students. To condense the entire plan for an hour-long sermon into just twelve words is to achieve close to the ultimate in condensation. The following outline is more useful; moreover, it is understandable.

Fraternity Rushing

Theme: The rushing period should be extended
General purpose: to induce belief
Specific purpose: to win agreement that rushing rules should be changed
I want my audience to: join in support for an extension of the rushing period

Introduction

I. Vital subject
   A. Concerns most students
   B. Affects entire university

II. Timely subject
   A. Rushing just ended
   B. Effects fresh in memory

Body

I. Brief rushing period bad
   A. For the fraternities
      1. Intensifies rivalry
      2. Stirs antagonism
         a. Tug-of-war for same prospect
         b. Unfair tactics used

B. For the rushees
 1. Caught in crossfire of claims
 2. Schoolwork disrupted
    a. Rushing events time-consuming
    b. Minds distracted from work
 3. "High pressured" into unwise choice
C. Resultant poor choices inevitable
 1. Rushers can't know rushees
 2. Rushees can't know fraternities as really are

CONCLUSION

 I. A full semester of rushing will eliminate evils of haste

 II. A full semester of rushing will benefit fraternities and rushees

THE BODY OF THE SPEECH

The preceding chapter was concerned with the selection and development of ideas. Their arrangement in the outline will be discussed here. All that has been said about purpose—personal, general, and specific—applies to the development of the outline. The purpose has been listed at the top of each sample outline, for it is a factor that determines how to present your ideas. Whatever is to be the theme of your speech must be supported by certain main ideas that are actually the main headings in the body of the outline.

When the theme has been formulated, four rules will be helpful in the choice and development of the main ideas.

1. *The main ideas should be limited in number.* The necessity for this was explained earlier in this chapter, where three was suggested as a maximum number for main ideas. Let us assume, for example, that two speakers have chosen "America's Foreign Policy" as a topic and "Our foreign policy has made us a great nation" as a theme. One of them selects the following main ideas upon which to base the body of his speech:

The aims of America's foreign policy are

1. To maintain the prestige of the United States.
2. To protect American citizens and property abroad.
3. To support our allies abroad.
4. To promote trade with foreign nations.
5. To maintain a sphere of influence in the American continents.
6. To encourage the maintenance of world peace.
7. To discourage the flouting of international law, treaties, and the rights of small nations.
8. To develop the United Nations.

There is some overlapping among these ideas, but each one might legitimately be developed as a separate point. However, to do so would require a great mass of specific examples, historical surveys, quotations from recognized authorities, statistics, and other facts which would require a minimum of an hour, and probably much more time than that, for adequate development. And it would be necessary for the audience to keep eight separate points in mind in order to remember the essence of the speech. Consequently, the speech could not have much cumulative effect.

The other speaker has similar points in mind. However, being more conscious than the first speaker of how much an audience can reasonably be expected to absorb, he decides to phrase his ideas differently. Most of the points discussed by the first speaker he includes in his phrasing of the following two main ideas, which can be established in much briefer time and which will be comparatively easy for an audience to comprehend:

The aims of America's foreign policy are
1. To promote and protect the interests of American citizens in their dealings with foreign countries.
2. To exercise a bold influence for world peace and international morality.

2. *The main ideas should stand out clearly and emphatically.* The main ideas are the essential ones which, when properly ordered, will give the total impression you wish. They must not be overlapping or ambiguous lest they confuse the intended listener. Yet they must be complementary, giving strength and support to one another.

Each idea should be developed to its own climax, and each succeeding idea to a higher climax strengthened and contributed to by the preceding one. Thus the audience is made aware of a steady forward movement of ideas building up through successive lesser climaxes to one final total impression. Whether your general purpose is to teach or to move to action, there is a one best choice and order of ideas that will be most clear and emphatic.

3. *The main ideas should be adequate to support the theme.* Even if you demonstrate conclusively that each of your main ideas is true, does it inevitably follow that your theme will be accepted? And is there evidence enough to ensure the acceptance of each of the main ideas? In other words, is the gun loaded with a charge big enough to bring down the game? A speaker who advances to the platform with inadequate ammunition has lost the battle before it is begun. One basis on which the preparation of any speech must rest is an adequate supply of facts.

4. *The main ideas should be arranged in the order most effective for your audience.* Psychological as well as logical considerations must be weighed in deciding the order in which ideas are to be presented. It may mean beginning with the more acceptable ideas in order to have the audience in an agreeable, affirmative state of mind by the time the controversial portions of the speech are reached. Or the order may be climactic, building up from the less important to the more important idea. Since audiences are usually most attentive at the beginning and at the end of the speech, you may prefer to place the two more important ideas at the beginning and at the end, with matters of lesser importance in between. Because of the situation or the occasion, or because of some recent happening, you may choose as the beginning idea the one which is uppermost in the listeners' minds.

These rules may not include all of the relevant considerations affecting the arrangement of main ideas within the body of the outline. A careful re-examination of the sample outline included in this chapter for a talk on "Fraternity Rushing" will reveal that the ideas are carefully arranged in a *logical* order. In this order, each subheading is a part of the proof for its main heading. This might be considered a special application of rule 3 just given. Not only must the main headings logically establish the theme of the speech; each group of subheadings must be adequate to support their main heading.

In the outline for the speech on "Football: A Game of Thrills," you will note that the subheadings A, B, C, and D under Main Heading II of the Body are arranged in *chronological* order. This is a particularly useful and clear ordering for historical and sometimes for biographical material.

The able speaker will not rely upon any one type of pattern for organizing ideas in the body of the speech. Here is another opportunity for originality and ingenuity. Whatever order will best accomplish your specific purpose with a specific group of listeners and will at the same time evidence your artistry with ideas is the one to be used.

THE INTRODUCTION OF THE SPEECH

After you have decided upon your theme and its establishing main ideas, you face the problem of how to introduce the subject effectively. This will vary, of course, with your general purpose. Yet the tasks to be performed by your opening remarks can be listed and considered.

Repaying Audience Interest

In your speech class you have the advantage of a sympathetic group, for you are coming to know and understand one another's problems. Outside the classroom you will seldom give a speech except upon specific invitation and you may assume that the audience either wishes to hear you or wishes to hear what you have to say about a certain topic. You may also assume that your audience will be a friendly one. But you cannot assume that it will be interested in what you say, regardless of how you say it. As a general rule, start your speech by telling your listeners how your subject is of interest to them. Show how it affects them. Indicate at once that your preparation of the speech has been *audience-centered*.

In a speech in Boston commemorating the hundredth anniversary of the birth of Robert Burns, Ralph Waldo Emerson began with sincere humility:

I do not know by what untoward accident it has chanced—and I forbear to enquire—that, in this accomplished circle, it should fall to me, the worst Scotsman of all, to receive your commands, and at the latest hour, too, to respond to the sentiment just offered, and which, indeed, makes the occasion. But I am told there is no appeal, and I must trust to the inspiration of the theme to make a fitness which does not otherwise exist.

Yet, sir, I heartily feel the singular claims of the occasion. At the first announcement, from I know not whence, that the twenty-fifth of January was the hundredth anniversary of the birth of Robert Burns, a sudden consent warned the great English race, in all its kingdoms, colonies and states, all over the world, to keep the festival. We are here to hold our parliament with love and poesy, as men were wont to do in the Middle Ages. Those famous parliaments might or might not have had more stateliness, and better singers than we—though that is yet to be known—but they could not have better reason.

From his pulpit in Holy Trinity Episcopal Church in Philadelphia, on Sunday, April 23, 1865, while the body of President Lincoln lay in state at Independence Hall, one of the greatest preachers of that time, Phillips Brooks, delivered a funeral address. Note how his introductory words encompass his listeners' interest and mood:

While I speak to you today, the body of the President who ruled this people is lying, honored and loved, in our city. It is impossible with that sacred presence here for me to stand and speak of ordinary topics which occupy the pulpit. I must speak of him today; and I therefore undertake to do what I had intended to do at some future time, to invite you to

study with me the character of Abraham Lincoln, the impulses of his life
and the causes of his death. I know how hard it is to do it rightly, how
impossible it is to do it worthily. But I shall speak with confidence, because
I speak to those who love him, and whose ready love will fill out the
deficiencies in a picture which my words will weakly try to draw.

Satisfying Listener Curiosity

Your listeners will wish to know what you intend to accomplish
in the time you have at your disposal. Research has found that the
task of the listener is made easier when he is told at the outset the
speaker's goal. You know from classroom experience how much
easier it is to listen efficiently when the lecturer's introduction gives
you a sort of preview of what will be covered. Only when you are
facing a hostile audience may there be advantage in concealing for
a time your full purpose. At all other times you will arouse the interest
of your listener and enable him to follow more clearly the development of your speech if you tell him first precisely what you expect
him to get from the speech.

Note how simply one of America's greatest masters of the spoken
word, Robert Ingersoll, accomplished this as he spoke at the funeral
of his younger brother:

I am going to do that which the dead often promised he would do
for me.

Conversational directness is effectively attained by a university student beginning his speech:

I would like to talk with you this evening about American homes.
I need not speak about what home has meant to you and me; but rather
what home could mean to others. It may be as surprising to you as it was
to me to learn that to one out of every three people in this country your
and my conception of home is only a dream. A consultant to the Federal
Housing Commission tells us that there are more than ten million families
in the United States living in buildings unfit for human habitation. It is
these families—Homeless America—about which I wish to talk with you
tonight. Charles Dickens struck a fundamental truth when he wrote, "The
reform of the people's habitations must precede all other reforms; without
it all other reforms must fail."

Providing Background Information

As a speaker, presumably you have information about, or have
had experience with, your subject which is not generally possessed
by your listeners. Consequently you are familiar with certain terms,

concepts, or words which may need some explanation if they are to be understood by members of the audience. It is also necessary to supply adequate background information if only because interest follows knowledge. You will increase your listeners' interest in your subject as you make it clear to them, without, of course, being condescending as you do so. It is never wise to overestimate your audience's familiarity with your subject.

Note how carefully Brander Matthews, a distinguished professor of American literature, introduced a speech on his favorite subject to a national convention of teachers:

The history of mankind is little more than the list of the civilizations that have arisen one on the ruin of the other, the Roman supplanting the Greek, as the Assyrian had been ousted by the Babylonian. The life of each of these successive civilizations was proportioned to the vitality of the ideas by which it was animated; and we cannot estimate it or even understand it except insofar as we are able to grasp these underlying principles. What the ideas were which dominated these vanished civilizations it is for us to discover for ourselves as best we may by a study of all the records they left behind them, and especially by a reverent examination of their laws, their arts, and their writings in so far as these have been preserved to us. Of all these relics of peoples now dead and gone, none is so instructive as literature, and none is so interesting; by its aid we are enabled to reconstruct the past, as we are also helped to understand the present.

Counteracting Distractions

Your listeners will have interests that distract their attention from your speech. In the speech class, for example, the preceding speech may have made sufficient impression to keep their minds centered upon it. Some of them may have speeches to give when you are through. Others may have tests to take later in the day. Still others may have a large part of their minds occupied with wondering whether a postman will bring them an expected letter. Or their attention may be distracted by whispering in the audience, or by an approaching lunch hour, or by outside noise. It is unwise for any speaker to take for granted an eager attentiveness on the part of any audience. This is not to deny what we have just said about the general friendliness and curioisity of the audience. It is only to take into account the fact that contrary tendencies also operate. A speaker must always be ready to capture and hold the attention of his audience. There are several types of introduction with which he can do so effectively:

1. In the long run, no other method will prove so dependable as a

clear indication to the audience that what you have to say is of *vital importance* to them. For example, a student said to his classmates:

I am glad to talk with you, my fellow teen-agers, about the importance of maintaining world peace. For if war comes in the near future you and I are the ones who will be called upon to make the sacrifices of life and limb. Whatever your life is worth, that may well be the worth of peace to you!

2. The experience of many speakers has proved the value of *humor* in catching attention. Popular lecturers would hardly know how to get started without it. They find that humor quickly gathers in the attention of every listener, and puts nearly everyone in a genial mood. The ability to use humor is one of the most rewarding assets a speaker can possess. Note how Mark Twain interestingly entertained a New England audience as he responded to the toast: "The Oldest Inhabitant—The Weather of New England":

I reverently believe that the Maker who made us all, makes everything in New England—but the weather. I don't know who makes that, but I think it must be raw apprentices in the Weather Clerk's factory, who experiment and learn how in New England for board and clothes, and then are promoted to make weather for countries that require a good article and will take their custom elsewhere if they don't get it. There is a sumptuous variety about the New England weather that compels the stranger's admiration—and regret.[1]

3. A *challenge,* a *question,* or a *startling statement* will get attention and set a mood favorable to the speaker's purpose. Good-humored denunciation of an audience may serve, such as, "We college students have a lot of half-baked ideas. I'm going to talk to you about one of the worst of them."

Woodrow Wilson thus once stimulated the quick attention of a Phi Beta Kappa group at Yale University:

I must confess to you that I came here with very serious thoughts this evening, because I have been laboring under the conviction for a long time that the object of a university is to educate, and I have not seen the universities of this country achieving any remarkable or disturbing success in that direction. I have found everywhere the note which I must say I have heard sounded once or twice tonight—that apology for the intellectual side of the university. You hear it at all universities. Learning is on the defensive, is actually on the defensive, among college men, and they are being asked by way of indulgence to bring that also into the circle of their interests. Is it not time we stopped asking indulgence for learning and proclaimed its sovereignty? Is it not time we reminded the college men

[1] This speech is reproduced in full at the end of Chapter 22.

of this country that they have no right to any distinctive place in any community, unless they can show it by intellectual achievement? That if a university is a place for distinction at all it must be distinguished by the conquests of the mind? I for my part tell you plainly that that is my motto, that I have entered the field to fight for that thesis, and that for that thesis only do I care to fight.

Establishing Acceptability

Your audience will normally be uninformed about your personal qualifications for speaking on your topic. Beginning speakers often make the mistake of keeping secret the sources of their information. They neglect to mention to the audience the experience upon which the speech is based, or the books and magazine articles they have read in preparation for it. For example, a young veteran gave a speech to persuade his fellow students they should visit a nearby veterans' hospital to bring cheer to many desperately lonesome disabled men. He could have been much more persuasive had he mentioned that as a result of his own serious injury in service with the paratroopers he had spent many weeks in that hospital himself and had seen firsthand many cases of unrelieved loneliness. Personal experience must be handled with humility and good taste but it can establish one's authority to speak.

THE CONCLUSION

Fundamentally, there is but one aim for any conclusion—to bring the various threads of the speech together in one final effort to complete the speaker's purpose. It is not enough for the speaker merely to finish his discussion and stop. It is far worse for him to struggle to a weak conclusion with such a statement as, "I guess that's all I have to say, so I'll quit." The body of the speech should be definitely rounded off, so that the audience realizes it is finished. This can be done by introducing the last point with "Finally," or "Last," or in some other explicit manner. Then, with the discussion ended, the speaker should give the audience some indication that he is starting his conclusion. He may do this verbally, by saying, "In conclusion," or something similar, or he may indicate it by his manner. It is of value to the speaker to let his audience know when his conclusion is reached, for most listeners, no matter how much their interest has lagged, will give close attention to the concluding remarks. They hope that in them they will find the chief point and substance of the speech. Thus, if he has failed to do so in the body of his speech, the speaker has an excellent opportunity to achieve his purpose.

If the conclusion has but one aim, there are many means by which this aim may be accomplished. Following are some af the principal ones, briefly described and illustrated.

A Summary

A simple summary of the speaker's main ideas is often helpful. Listeners who may have held out against individual points of the speech may capitulate before the full weight of the speech. The summary has the further considerable advantage of helping the audience to remember the salient points of the speech.

An Abstract of the Speech

An epitome, or miniature reproduction, may conclude the speech. It not only contains a restatement of the main ideas, as does the summary, but it clothes them with the same sort of appeals and illustrations that the body of the speech contains. Without being an obvious recapitulation, it is a précis in which the ideas as well as their emotional color and flavoring are presented. This method was used by Field Marshal Viscount Montgomery, the British World War II commander, in concluding a speech to the English-Speaking Union at New York's Waldorf-Astoria Hotel, in November, 1949:

> The fundamental problem in the world today is not whether this nation can gain some advance over other nations in science and technology, or in the manufacture of atomic bombs. The fundamental problem is whether the Western democracies can cooperate for a common purpose and gain strength through unity: reconciling this unity with the problems of their own empires or overseas territories.
>
> Real and true cooperation between nations is not possible unless each nation concerned is prepared to suffer, if necessary, some small loss of sovereignty for the common purpose.
>
> Either the cooperation is real and true—
>
> Or it is a façade behind which nations pursue their own selfish policies. If this should happen, then our dead would indeed have died in vain.
>
> Which is it to be, real and true—or a façade?
>
> Surely there can be only one answer—it must be real and true.
>
> The worthiness of the Western democracies to survive will therefore depend:

Firstly, on their resolute and clear-headed willingness to defend all that history, and effort, and our ancestors and God have entrusted to us, and

Secondly, on our capacity for real, true, and effective cooperation in order to achieve the desired end.

The premium is not very great.

The dividend will be enormous—it will be peace and freedom.

An Illustration

Often an audience may think as it listens to a speech, "Granted that what you say is true, just how would it work if put into practice?" One way of concluding a speech is to answer this unspoken question by an illustration showing just how the speaker's proposal would work. Closely akin to this method is the use of a story which drives home the speaker's point. Such a device was used by the late clergyman and educator, W. H. P. Faunce, who in a speech in December, 1927, urged the value of an active, energizing type of education that would inspire the recipients. He closed with the following sentences:

When Theodore Roosevelt had read the book of Jacob Riis, *How the Other Half Lives,* his fighting spirit—as great in peace as in war—was aroused. He went down to lower Manhattan, climbed the creaking stair in the tenement and knocked at the door. Mr. Riis was not at home. Then the caller took out his visiting card and wrote: "Have read your book and came to help—Theodore Roosevelt." Such reading, such study, is the sort of education America needs today. . . .

An Appeal for Action

"Let us do something about it—and this is what we should do." Many speeches end on this note. It is the logical conclusion for a persuasive speech. Lincoln's conclusion to his second inaugural address, his noblest legacy to America, is of this type:

With malice toward none, with charity for all, with firmness in the right, as God gives us to see the right, let us strive on to finish the work we are in, to bind up the nation's wounds, to care for him who shall have borne the battle, and for his widow and orphans; to do all which may achieve and cherish a just and lasting peace among ourselves and with all nations.

Speeches to juries, to legislative bodies, to voters, to potential buyers, and to many other kinds of audiences almost invariably end with an appeal for the action which it is the whole purpose of the speaker to secure.

An Ethical Appeal to High Human Motives

"The right is more precious than peace," concluded President Wilson in his speech asking Congress for a declaration of war. "Spiritually and ethically we must strive to bring about clean living and right thinking," declared Theodore Roosevelt, in concluding his speech "The Man with the Muck-Rake." "We appreciate that the things of the body are important," he went on, "but we appreciate also that the things of the soul are immeasurably more important. The foundation-stone of national life is, and ever must be, the high individual character of the average citizen."

A Prophecy

What will happen if the speaker's proposal is adopted? Madame Chiang Kai-shek ended her radio address of farewell to America in January, 1950, with this ringing assertion of the triumph to be won by Chinese persistence: "Russia will never know one day of peace in China. Russia will never own China. China will remain free."

An Emphasis on the Importance of the Proposal

It is sometimes effective to remind an audience that the decision it is being asked to make is no light one. William Gladstone ended his long speech on the established church in Ireland by expatiating on this theme:

The working of our constitutional government itself is upon trial, for I do not believe there ever was a time when the whole of the legislative machinery was set in motion under the conditions of peace and order and constitutional regularity, to deal with a question graver or more profound.

Benjamin F. Fairless, president of the United States Steel Corporation, speaking in Baltimore in April, 1950, emphasized his distrust of increased power in the federal government by declaring, "In my opinion, our American economic system is in deadlier peril today than it has ever been in my lifetime."

A Question or a Problem

Sometimes the speaker deals with a problem for which he knows no solution. His aim is merely to clarify and emphasize the problem and to keep the minds of the audience open concerning it. For this kind of speech, the conclusion must often be a restatement of the problem or a question as to what might be done. This was the method used by the journalist Michael Straight in discussing what might be done by peace-hungry youth in a world threatened by war:

We cannot answer now. Possibly in thirty years, when the smoke of battle that blinds one has once more cleared away, will those of us who have survived, and are living in the new dark ages or the new millennium, be able to answer the question that holds the key to the future of our civilization.

A Strategic Retreat

After an unusually earnest, prolonged, or emphatic speech, the speaker may recognize that his audience feels he has overshot the mark. Too great enhusiasm may have aroused suspicion rather than obtained agreement. To regain the confidence of the audience, the speaker can strengthen his appeal by anticlimax rather than by climax. He feigns a retreat and then with a last thrust reiterates his appeal. Note how this method was skillfully used by Clarence Darrow in closing his final argument in defense of two youthful confessed murderers, Nathan Leopold and Richard Loeb:

I feel that I should apologize for the length of time I have taken. This case may not be as important as I think it is, and I am sure I do not need to tell this court, or to tell my friends, that I would fight just as hard for the poor as for the rich. If I should succeed in saving these boys' lives and do nothing for the progress of the law, I should feel sad, indeed. If I can succeed, my greatest reward and my greatest hope will be that I have done something for the tens of thousands of other boys, for the countless unfortunates who must tread the same road in blind childhood that these poor boys have trod—that I have done something to help human understanding, to temper justice with mercy, to overcome hate with love. . . .

Humor

Used merely for the sake of a laugh, a humorous ending is not a good one for most speeches. As a final opportunity for accomplishing the purpose of the speech, the conclusion is too important to be wasted. But when the speech is intended for entertainment, or for goodwill or good-fellowship, the humorous ending is very appropriate. For other speeches, too, humorous endings can be excellent, provided they are used for emphasis.

In the speech at Baltimore cited on page 240, Benjamin F. Fairless ended his defense of the steel industry with a combination of humor and fact, intended both to refute charges against his company and to dissipate any existing ill will:

The United States Census Bureau has recently completed its latest count of more than 400 American industries, and has reported on the degree of so-called "concentration" in each. And remember, I am speaking of entire *industries*—not individual companies.

Now how many of these industries do you think are more highly "concentrated" than the steel industry. Three? . . . Ten? . . . Fifty?

Well, guess again. The Census Bureau's own report on "steel works and rolling mills" shows that this industry is not anywhere near the top at all. It is in the great middle, along with the great body of all American industries. In fact, it stands 174th on the list. *So there are 173 entire industries which are more highly concentrated than steel.*

Now what are some of these industries where the "concentration of power" in the hands of the "big four" is so great as to menace our national welfare and to arrest the pursuit of happiness?

You'd never guess.

There is the pretzel industry for one. Honestly, that's right. I mean it.

And there are the candle-makers too.

Then there are straw hats, and streetcars, breakfast foods and chewing tobacco, wallpaper and cigar boxes, lead pencils and pianos. Then we have women's neckwear and boys' underwear. And, oh yes—window shades and garters.

Now, if every one of these—plus 159 other industries—is more highly "concentrated" than steel, and if "concentration" is really as wicked as our theorists tell us it is, I can't for the life of me understand why all these high-priced Congressional committees are wasting their time on me.

A Memorable Phrasing of the Theme

The speaker who can phrase his proposal in epigrammatic form will do well to conclude thus and leave his point in the minds of his listeners. This is the way Glenn Frank ended a speech belaboring the New Deal: "We must provide instead of prevent abundance if we are to realize the abundant life for this whole people." Alfred M. Landon was similarly epigrammatic in concluding a radio address on the state of the nation: "It is time to realize that we must apply the resources of the mind if we are to make the wishes of the heart come true." The famous orator Robert G. Ingersoll, with his tribute boiled down into one sentence, concluded his eulogy at his brother's grave: "There was, there is, no greater, stronger, manlier man."

TYPE OF PREPARATION

We add to this chapter a note on the types of preparation which a speaker may use, dependent upon the method of delivery which he uses: reading from manuscript, speaking from memory, speaking extemporaneously, and speaking impromptu.

Reading from Manuscript

There are many occasions when reading a speech from the manuscript is acceptable, and a few where it is required. The President of the United States, when making an important policy speech, cannot very well take any chance of a misstatement or an unfortunate wording. He is not likely to have the time to memorize. So he reads a carefully prepared manuscript. A scientist, a doctor, or a lawyer, or any specialist dealing with a complicated or technical subject may do the same. The art of reading from the printed page, however, needs special practice; and Chapter 12, "Improving the Style of Your Speech," will point out that our customary way of writing may be ill-suited for reading aloud. Furthermore, the practice of reading aloud does little to improve one's facility in oral use of language, one's ability to speak extemporaneously, or one's conversational directness in speaking. Too often the beginner uses the manuscript as a crutch and thereby delays his development of self-reliance. Unless your instructor requires it for a specific assignment, you are urged not to use the manuscript type of delivery at this time.

Speaking from Memory

In every age, including the present, some of the most effective speeches are delivered from memory. As with reading from manuscript, so with memorizing: it is not recommended for the person who is learning to speak more effectively. When used occasionally it may help to improve vocabulary and the fundamentals of voice and action. If, however, a speech "sounds memorized" it is not being effectively delivered, and this is a major problem of memorization. The actor learns to deliver his lines—although they are exactly memorized—in a spontaneous and impromptu manner; hence memorized delivery need not by its very nature be indirect, artificial, or stilted. Yet it will be just that when the inexperienced speaker uses this method.

Speaking Extemporaneously

For the most widely recommended type of preparation for the usual speaking situation, called the extemporaneous method, the process of preparation is thorough—or certainly should be—and may require more time than memorization does. It certainly requires far more time than does preparation for reading from a manuscript. In the extemporaneous method the outline is memorized or carried by the speaker for reference, and the exact choice of words and phrasing of ideas is left for the moment of actual delivery. Thorough preparation may call for your talking through the speech, and timing yourself, as many times as may be necessary to give you confidence. Depending upon the individual, this type of preparation may result in certain key sentences or vital phrases being practically memorized. But such memorization ought not to interfere with the conversational directness which is the goal of the extemporaneous method. The whole purpose of this type of preparation and delivery is to enable you to develop the ability to respond to the speaking situation as it develops and to compose your ideas orally with the least possible reliance upon the intermediary and time-consuming step of writing.

Speaking Impromptu

On many occasions individuals are called upon in public meetings to "say a few words" about a topic under consideration without having advance notice or time for specific preparation. Normally, this invitation occurs only when the person is known to have some special knowledge or experience relative to the topic under discussion. If the speaker really has nothing to say, the best advice is to say nothing. Even if he is well versed in the subject, an unexpected call can sometimes be momentarily confusing. One tried device is to commence by a simple statement of the problem, or by asking a question concerning it. This gives the speaker time to "cue-in" his thinking and also provides a starting point for his remarks. Furthermore, such a call almost invariably comes in the midst of a discussion—so that the impromptu remarks may and should be geared to what has been said by others. On occasion an inexperienced chairman may call on a member without notice to introduce a topic for discussion. The situation usually calls for a brief statement of what the problem is, why it is important, and what aspects of it need consideration. This is a simple outline that applies to a wide range of topics. Almost always the impromptu speaker should be careful to be concise; it is easy to ramble and to become repetitive when unprepared. Be brisk, be pointed, and be brief are three good rules to keep in mind. Better yet, when you are to attend a meeting where you are liable to be called on, do some preliminary planning. It is better to have a brief talk ready which you may not need than to need one and not have it.

CONCLUSION

When you have a purpose in mind, and when your materials are profuse, interesting, and relevant, the great need is for a careful and adequate plan. Whatever method of organization you decide upon will be determined in accordance with the method of preparation the occasion demands. A speech plan is as necessary as an architect's blueprint.

EXERCISES

1. There is no way of learning the principles of organization other than by practice. This practice should consist of analysis of as many selections as class time permits, and experimental and impromptu organization in class of several speech outlines. A good speech to analyze as a starter is "Values in a Crazy World," by John Ise (page 275). Identify the theme, the main ideas, and the introduction and conclusion. Then analyze, in writing or in class discussion, all the illustrative speeches in this book that have already been read. Your instructor may assign various additional speeches or essays for analysis, until you have demonstrated a sure ability to pick out the vital framework of a composition.
2. For each of the following theme sentences, develop two, three, or four main ideas:
   a. Character is largely formed by environment.
   b. Fraternity membership stimulates average students to better scholarship.
   c. Fraternity membership diverts superior students from their best academic work.
   d. Education enables us to profit from the mistakes of others.
   e. Success depends primarily upon having a definite goal in life.
3. Analyze the introductions presented by your classmates in a round of speeches. Identify the two best and the two worst introductions, giving your reasons. State how you would improve the two worst ones.
4. Do the same for the two best and the two worst conclusions.

5. Prepare a five-minute speech for delivery to your classroom audience. Demonstrate what you have learned from this chapter in a written outline of your speech, and in the effective form you give the speech in its delivery.
6. Listen to some major speech—a sermon or a radio talk, for example— and turn in an outline of it. Indicate the weaknesses and strengths in the organization of the speech.
7. Prepare the outline for a six-minute talk to be delivered before the student assembly of the high school from which you were graduated. Give only the one-minute introduction to the class, and then sketch, in an additional minute, what you had planned to say in the rest of your talk.

ILLUSTRATIVE SPEECH

The Heart of the American Ideal

BY RICHARD M. NIXON

At the opening of the American National Exhibition in Moscow, July 24, 1959

I am honored on behalf of President Eisenhower to open this American exhibition in Moscow.

Mrs. Nixon and I were among the many thousands of Americans who were privileged to visit the splendid Soviet exhibition in New York, and we want to take this opportunity to congratulate the people of the U.S.S.R. for the great achievements and progress so magnificently portrayed by your exhibition.

We, in turn, hope that many thousands of Soviet citizens will take advantage of this opportunity to learn about life in the United States by visiting our exhibition.

Of course, we both realize that no exhibition can portray a complete picture of all aspects of life in great nations like the U.S.S.R. and the United States.

Among the questions which some might raise with regard to our exhibition are these: To what extent does this exhibition accurately present life in the United States as it really is? Can only the wealthy people afford the things exhibited here? What about the inequality, the injustice, the other weaknesses which are supposed to be inevitable in a capitalist society?

As Mr. Khrushchev often says: "You can't leave a word out of a song." Consequently, in the limited time I have, I would like to try to answer some of those questions so that you may get an accurate picture of what America is really like.

Let us start with some of the things in this exhibit. You will see a house, a car, a television set—each the newest and most modern of its type we produce. But can only the rich in the United States afford such things? If this were the case, we would have to include in our definition of rich the millions of America's wage earners.

Let us take, for example, our 16 million factory workers. The average weekly wage of a factory worker in America is $90.54. With this income he can buy and afford to own a house, a television set and a car in the price range of those you will see in this exhibit. What is more, the great majority of American wage earners have done exactly that.

Putting it another way, there are 44 million families in the United States. Twenty-five million of these families live in houses or apartments that have as much or more floor space than the one you see in this exhibit.

Thirty-one million families own their own homes and the land on which they are built.

America's 44 million families own a total of 56 million cars, 50 million television sets and 143 million radio sets. And they buy an average of nine dresses and suits and 14 pairs of shoes per family per year.

Why do I cite these figures? Not because they indicate that the American people have more automobiles, TV sets, or houses than the people of the U.S.S.R.

In fairness we must recognize that our country industrialized sooner than the Soviet Union. And Americans are happy to note that Mr. Khrushchev has set a goal for the Soviet economy of catching up in the production of consumer goods.

We welcome this kind of competition because, when we engage in it, no one loses—everyone wins, as the living standards of people throughout the world are raised to higher levels. It also should be pointed out that, while we may be ahead of you as far as these items are concerned, you are ahead of us in other fields—for example, in the size of the rockets you have developed for the exploration of outer space.

But what these statistics do dramatically demonstrate is this: that the United States—the world's largest capitalist country—has, from the standpoint of distribution of wealth, come closest to the ideal of prosperity for all in a classless society.

As our revered Abraham Lincoln said: ". . . We do not propose any war upon capital; we do wish to allow the humblest man an equal chance to get rich with everybody else."

The 67 million American wage earners are not the downtrodden masses depicted by the critics of capitalism in the latter part of the nineteenth and early part of the twentieth centuries. They hold their heads high as they proudly enjoy the highest standard of living of any people in the world's history.

The caricature of capitalism as a predatory, monopolist-dominated society is as hopelessly out of date, as far as the United States is concerned, as a wooden plow.

This does not mean that we have solved all of our problems.

Many of you have heard about the problem of unemployment in the United States. What is not so well known is that the average period that these unemployed were out of work even during our recent recession was less than three months. And during that period the unemployed had an average income from unemployment-insurance funds of $131.49 per month.

The day has passed in the United States when the unemployed were left to shift for themselves.

The same can be said for the aged, the sick and others who are unable to earn enough to provide an adequate standard of living.

An expanded program of Social Security, combined with other Government and private programs, provides aid and assistance for those who are unable to care for themselves. For example, the average retired couple on Social Security in the United States receives an income of $116 per month apart from the additional amounts they receive from private pensions and savings accounts.

What about the strikes which take place in our economy, the latest example of which is the steel strike which is going on?

The answer is that here we have a firsthand example of how a free economy works. The workers' right to join with other workers in a union and to bargain collectively with management is recognized and protected by law. No man or woman in the United States can be forced to work for wages he considers to be inadequate or under conditions he believes are unsatisfactory.

Another problem which causes us concern is that of racial discrimination in our country. We are making great progress in solving this problem, but we shall never be satisfied until we make the American ideal of equality of opportunity a reality for every citizen regardless of his race, creed or color.

We have other problems in our society, but we are confident that for us our system of government provides the best means for solving them. But the primary reason we believe this is not because we have an economy which builds more than 1 million houses, produces 6 million cars and 6 million television sets per year.

Material progress is important, but the very heart of the American ideal is that "man does not live by bread alone." To us, progress without freedom—to use a common expression—is like "potatoes without fat."

Let me give you some examples of what freedom means to us.

President Eisenhower is one of the most popular men ever to hold that high office in our country. Yet never an hour or a day goes by in which criticism of him and his policies cannot be read in our newspapers, heard on our radio and television, or in the halls of Congress.

And he would not have it any other way. The fact that our people can and do say anything they want about a Government official; the fact that in our elections, as this voting machine in our exhibit illustrates, every voter has a free choice between those who hold public office and those who oppose them, makes ours a true people's Government.

We trust the people. We constantly submit big decisions to the people. Our history convinces us that, over the years, the people have been right much more often than they have been wrong.

As an indication of the extent of this freedom and of our faith in our own system, 40 hours of radio broadcasts from the Soviet Union can be heard without jamming in the United States each day, and over a million and a half copies of Soviet publications are purchased in our country each year.

Let us turn now to freedom of religion.

Under our Constitution, no church or religion can be supported by the state. An American can either worship in the church of his choice or choose to go to no church at all if he wishes. Acting with this complete freedom of choice, 103 million of our citizens are members of 308,000 American churches.

We also cherish the freedom to travel, both within our country and outside the United States. Within our country we live and travel where we please without travel permits, internal passports or police registration.

We also travel freely abroad. For example, 11 million Americans will travel to other countries during this year, including 10,000 to the Soviet Union. We look forward to the day when millions of Soviet citizens will travel to ours and other countries in this way.

Time will not permit me to tell you of all of the features of American life but, in summary, I think these conclusions can objectively be stated.

The great majority of Americans like our system of government. Much as we like it, however, we would not impose it on anyone else. We believe that people everywhere should have a right to choose the form of government they want.

There is another characteristic of the American people which I know impresses itself on any visitor to our country. As Mr. Mikoyan and Mr. Kozlov both pointed out after their visits to the United States, the American people are a peace-loving people. There are a number of reasons for this attitude. As this exhibition so eloquently demonstrates, we Americans enjoy an extraordinarily high standard of living.

There is nothing we want from any other people except the right to live in peace and friendship with them.

After fighting two world wars, we did not ask for or receive an acre of land from any other people. We have no desire to impose our rule on other lands today.

Our hearts go out to Mr. Khrushchev who lost a son, to Mr. Kozlov who lost two brothers, and to the millions of other Soviet mothers and fathers, brothers and sisters, sons and daughters who mourn for their loved ones lost in defending their homeland.

But, while it is generally recognized that the American people want peace, I realize that it has sometimes been charged that our Government does not share the attitude of our people. Nothing could be further from the truth.

For seven years, I have sat in the high councils of our Government and I can tell you that the primary aim of our discussions has been to find ways that we could use our strength in behalf of peace throughout the world.

Let me tell you of the background of some of those who participate in our policy discussions. The Secretary of State lost his brother in World War I. I saw boys as close to me as brothers die on barren islands 4,000 miles from home in World War II. No man in the world today has more knowledge of war and is more dedicated to peace than President Eisenhower.

Those who claim that the policies of the American Government do not represent and are not supported by the American people are engaging in a completely inaccurate and dangerous form of self-deception.

Any Administration which follows policies which do not reflect the views of our people on major issues runs the risk of defeat at the next election. When our elected officials cease to represent the people, the people have the power to replace them with others who do.

The reason the leaders of both our major political parties are united in supporting President Eisenhower's foreign policy is that they are reflecting the views of a people who are united behind these policies.

The Government and people of the United States are as one in their devotion to the cause of peace.

But dedication to peace, good will and human brotherhood should never be mistaken for weakness, softness and fear.

Much as we want peace, we will fight to defend our country and our way of life just as you have fought so courageously to defend your homeland throughout your history.

The peace we want and the peace the world needs is not the peace of surrender but the peace of justice; not peace by ultimatum but peace by negotiation.

The leaders of our two great nations have such tremendous responsibilities if peace is to be maintained in our time.

We cannot and should not gloss over the fact that we have some great and basic differences between us. What we must constantly strive to do is to see that those differences are discussed and settled at the conference table and not on the battlefield.

And until such settlements are agreed to, our leaders must exercise the greatest restraint, patience and understanding in their actions and their statements. They must do nothing which might provoke a war no one wants.

The fact that one of us may have a bigger bomb, a faster plane, or a more powerful rocket than the other at any particular time no longer adds up to an advantage. Because we have reached the point in world history where the Biblical injunction, "They that take the sword shall perish with the sword," is literally true today.

The nation which starts a war today will destroy itself. Completely apart from any retaliatory action which might be taken by a nation which is attacked, the deadly dust from radioactive bombs used in an attack will be carried by the winds back to the homeland of the aggressor.

With both of our great nations holding this terrible power in our hands, neither must ever put the other in a position where he has no choice but to fight or surrender. No nation in the world today is strong enough to issue an ultimatum to another without running the risk of self-destruction.

The Soviet exhibition in New York and the American exhibition which we open tonight are dramatic examples of what a great future lies in store for all of us if we can devote the tremendous energies of our peoples and the resources of our countries to the ways of peace rather than the ways of war.

The last half of the twentieth century can be the darkest or the brightest page in the history of civilization. The decision is in our hands to make.

The genius of the men who produced the magnificent achievements represented by these two exhibitions can be directed either to the destruction of civilization or to the creation of the best life that men have ever enjoyed on this earth.

As I have said on previous occasions, let us expand the idea of peaceful competition which Mr. Khrushchev has often enunciated. Let us extend this competition to include the spiritual as well as the material aspects of our civilization. Let us compete not in how to take lives but in how to save them. Let us work for victory not in war but for the victory of plenty over poverty, or health over disease, or understanding over ignorance wherever they exist in the world.

Above all, let us find more and more areas where we can substitute co-operation for competition in achieving our goal of a fuller, freer, richer life for every man, woman, and child on this earth.

CHAPTER 11

CONTENTS

Debaters at Wayne State University respond with enthusiasm to remarks by the speaker.

ADAPTING TO THE
AUDIENCE

> Who would succeed in the world should be wise in
> the use of his pronouns. Utter the You twenty times,
> where you once utter the I.—JOHN HAY

AN experienced speaker knows that he must respond to his audience if he expects it to respond to him. In reality, the audience is continually expressing its reaction to the speech, in terms which the speaker should recognize. Sometimes, though not often, this audience reaction takes the form of heckling. For example, when George Mason was speaking to a Virginia audience, opposing ratification of the federal Constitution, someone shouted, "Old man, the public notices that you are losing your faculties." Mason immediately shot back, "Young man, when you lose yours, nobody will notice it!" Actually, interruptions should aid a well-prepared speaker. They permit him to adapt—as he does in conversation—to his listeners' real thoughts, whether these are objections or endorsements.

Always be ready to clarify, illustrate, or emphasize your ideas to meet your audience's needs. The opportunity to do this is one of the chief advantages which the speaker has over the writer. Adolf Hitler, in *Mein Kampf,* cited this as the major factor in the speaking campaign with which he built up the Nazi party. The effectiveness of Hitler's speaking gives special value to his testimony—much as we despise the evil use to which he put his speech skill:

Our first meetings were distinguished by the fact that there were tables covered with leaflets, papers, and pamphlets of every kind. But we relied chiefly on the spoken word. And in fact the latter is the sole force capable of producing really great revolutions of sentiment, for reasons which are psychological.

An orator receives continuous guidance from his audience, enabling him to correct his lecture, since he can measure all the time on the countenances of his hearers the extent to which they are successful in following his arguments intelligently and whether his words are producing the effect he desires, whereas the writer has no acquaintance with his readers. Hence he is unable to prepare his sentences with a view to addressing a definite crowd of people, sitting in front of his eyes, but he is obliged to argue in general terms.

Supposing that an orator observes that his hearers do not understand

254

him, he will make his explanation so elementary and clear that every single one must take it in; if he feels that they are incapable of following him, he will build up his ideas carefully and slowly until the weakest member has caught up; again, once he senses that they seem not to be convinced that he is correct in his arguments, he will repeat them over and over again with fresh illustrations and himself state their unspoken objections; he will continue thus until the last group of the opposition show him by their behavior and play of expression that they have capitulated to his demonstration of the case.[1]

The advice is excellent, so far as it goes. There remains the necessity of adaptation to the moods and attitudes, as well as to the intelligence, of the audience.

ADAPTATION FROM THE LISTENER'S POINT OF VIEW

Since all speaking is aimed at influencing listeners, a good starting point is to examine the normal and proper expectations of the audience.

If you are in an auditorium waiting to hear a required lecture on "Classical Theories of Economics," you have every right to ask yourself "What has this topic to do with me?" You will doubtless have your interest heightened at once if the speaker commences by saying that he plans to discuss certain economic principles developed by Adam Smith and David Ricardo in terms of what they mean in relation to the prices *you* pay, the wages *you* receive, and the kind of standard of living *you* can expect. No matter what topic is being discussed, you have a right to expect that the speaker will relate it to your own needs and interests. You will appreciate his thoughtfulness if he uses illustrations that your experience has prepared you to understand. Your interest will be heightened if he develops his thinking around clearly stated questions that correspond to doubts or perplexities of your own. You will be delighted if, instead of being remote and technical, the discussion turns out to be vital and practical.

As a listener, you surely do not want the speaker to misrepresent his views in order to conform to your own. If he disagrees with some of your ideas, you will want to know why; you may even modify some of your own thinking, if the facts he presents justify a change. Although you may hope that he will make his explanation so simple

---

[1] From Adolf Hitler, *Mein Kampf* (*My Battle*). Reprinted by permission of Houghton Mifflin Company, publishers.

that it can be grasped easily, you will not want him to oversimplify to the extent of misrepresentation.

From your experience as a listener, you know that many speakers are so self-centered that they ignore the needs and interests of their audience. Many an excellent scholar is a poor teacher because he has forgotten how little his students really know. At the other extreme is the speaker who insults his listeners by assuming them to be far more ignorant of his topic than they actually are. It is disappointing to go away from a lecture or discussion without having learned something new.

Finally, as a listener, you expect that speakers will indicate both by what they say and by how they say it that they care about your opinions as well as their own. They will address what they have to say directly to you, not simply out into a void where you may happen to hear their remarks. They will give you a chance to "talk back"— if by no more than watching your facial expressions and bodily posture for cues to your reactions.

ADAPTATION FROM THE SPEAKER'S POINT OF VIEW

As we have seen in earlier chapters, all speaking aims at getting an appropriate response from the listeners. A teacher lectures in order to teach; his success depends not primarily upon his "output" but upon the students' "input." So it is with all speakers, under all circumstances. The effectiveness of the speech must be measured by its impact upon those who hear it, or, in some circumstances, upon those who may subsequently read it.

When you are speaking, accordingly, you cannot avoid having in mind the fact that you are speaking to specific people. Inevitably, to some extent you will be preoccupied with remembering what you are to say; with trying to be at ease and avoiding an awkward appearance; with expressing your ideas in a way that will do you credit; with shaping your remarks to suit your purpose. You will also be concerned with the exposition of your topic, or the support of your proposal: with analysis of the problem, with the explication of its parts, with interpretation of its significance. A certain amount of concentration on your purpose as well as on your subject matter is not only inevitable but highly desirable. Equally essential, however, is consideration of the audience. After all, you are speaking, and you are speaking to particular people. Unless you say what you have to say in a way that will be effective with them, your speech will be a failure.

In every speaking situation, the speaker must, in fact, have a three-way approach: through his purpose, his topic, and his hearers. In other words, he should be (1) self-centered enough to ensure that his speech aims will achieve his purpose, (2) subject-centered, in that the speech is a fair and balanced presentation of the matter being discussed, and (3) audience-centered, in such a way that the speech makes the audience understand and appreciate its purpose.

For the untrained speaker (and some speakers of considerable experience never have been *trained*), such a task seems impossible, but the kind of speech training this textbook seeks to develop makes the interweaving of these three strands so natural that the process should become almost automatic.

THE "YOU" APPROACH

Audience adaptation involves a considerable use of the personal pronouns, first and second. President Franklin D. Roosevelt, famed for his "fireside chats" delivered over the radio to millions of listeners, frequently used the phrase, "you and I know." His aim—and this is the aim of good speaking in general—was to stimulate in his listeners the feeling that they were not "being told" but being invited to "consider together" a problem of importance to them as well as to the speaker.

It would be an exaggeration to say that every speech should start with the word "you," but it is not an exaggeration to say that every talk ought to commence with a direct indication to the audience that the speaker is raising a problem of interest and value to his listeners. This principle is violated by the speaker who starts out, "For years my favorite hobby has been stamp collecting"; and by the speaker who begins, "Postage stamps are a form of taxation of relatively recent origin but now used almost universally." Much better would be the "you" approach illustrated by such an opening as, "You may complain from time to time about the cost of postage, but have you ever thought of how much you get for your money?" Or the speaker might commence by saying, "Maybe you think grown men and women who play with postage stamps are being childish. I would like to explain what it is about stamp collecting that has intrigued so many famous people, with the thought that you, too, may become interested in it."

It is perhaps in this area of audience adaptation that the study of speech makes its most important contribution to your education. Many subject areas (such as history, chemistry, engineering, litera- ture) are primarily "fields of knowledge" which the students are helped to master. Other subject areas (such as logic, languages, math- ematics, and even chemistry and physics) represent methods of dealing with subject matter, or modes of thinking about certain types of problems. Speech is especially and in a sense peculiarly devoted to thinking about specific subject areas *in relation* to the purposes of the speaker and the nature of the audience.

Aristotle, in the *Rhetoric,* one of the earliest speech textbooks, noted that ideally truth and justice should be upheld by the simple citation of relevant facts and logic. But, he continued, people have their judgment "warped" by emotion, prejudices, and self-interest.

In an address at Dartmouth College, Dr. Charles Malik, Ambassador from Lebanon to the United Nations, answers questions from the audi- ence. (Dartmouth College Photographic Bureau)

Hence, what is needed is to uphold truth and justice with arguments that take account of the emotions, special experience, and interests of the auditors. This is another way of defining the "you" approach. It means that any topic can be fruitfully discussed with other people only in terms of their own characteristics. We talk *about* subject matter; *to uphold* our own interpretation of it; but we talk *to* and *with* people. When we make our audience realize that we are discussing the topic in terms of their own needs and interests, we are using the "you" approach.

PREPARATION AND ADAPTATION

If a speech is to be adapted to its audience, the adaptation must be built into its preparation. This means, first of all, that you make your initial analysis of the subject area, formulate your purpose, gather and organize your material, and choose your illustrative and supporting points with what we have called the three-way approach: consideration of your purpose, of the facts, and of the needs and interests of your audience.

If your purpose is to inform your audience of the differences between fusion and fission in atomic explosions, you will determine what you *must* say in order to establish the essential differences, and *how* you can say these things in terms both comprehensible and interesting to your audience. Preparation, then, demands that you look into three separate areas for your subject matter: yourself—to clarify what you wish to accomplish; your resource materials—to discover and gather the essential facts; and the minds and experience of your expected audience—to guide you in phrasing your talk to accord with its level of information, its degree of interest, and its capacity to absorb technical data.

Furthermore, your preparation must be so thorough that you will know your subject well enough to be able to speak with freedom from notes or manuscript. One of the great advantages of speaking over writing is that you have your "consumers" directly before you and can adjust what you are saying to their response. If you detect doubt or uncertainty over some point in your explanation, you can support the point with an additional illustration; if you see skepticism, you can add facts or use another argument; if you see that interest is flagging, you can introduce references to your own or your audience's experiences with the subject. Such flexibility, or maneuverability,[2] is impossible without adequate preparation.

ADAPTATION IN THE DELIVERY

The test of the work involved in preparation occurs while you are actually delivering your talk: do your ideas reach your listeners? The utmost care in preparation may not anticipate all contingencies. For example, you may prepare to speak on the inadequacies of the so-called objective type of examinations—and your instructor may utilize the first part of the class hour for a surprise true-false quiz. There is no reason why you should change your own opinion (indeed, it may be strengthened); but there is every reason why you should change your planned development to rebuild your talk in such a way that you can use the quiz just completed as your primary illustration of the points you wish to make. Or, in preliminary conversation before the class assembles, you may discover that two or three of your classmates are making a special study of testing procedures for a pychology course; again, you will not wish to change your point of view, but you surely should modify your presentation, indicating to your listeners that there are members of the audience whose judgment on the topic may be better than your own.

To a high degree, adaptation is accomplished by the mode of delivery. What you say to your audience is colored considerably by whether or not your manner of speaking is realistically communicative. Do you mumble, or speak in a monotone, or rattle off your talk at a constant speed, or speak with your eyes on the windows or the floor or the ceiling? In all such instances, you are *uttering* your ideas, but are not in any real sense *talking with* your audience. Do you proceed dogmatically, with assertion following assertion; or do you interlard your presentation with questions and with references to your audience's experiences? Only in the latter instance would you be "adapting" to the fact that your audience not only hears but also thinks—that your listeners have minds of their own. Do you strain and struggle to remember what you have to say, rather than speaking confidently and easily? If so, you are "adapting" only to yourself— to your faulty preparation, or to your own stage fright, rather than to your audience.

[2] Cf. M. C. Golightly, "Maneuverability: A Skill Every Speaker Needs," *Today's Speech,* V (September, 1957), 13–14.

Adaptation to your audience, in both preparation and delivery requires that you know your audience, and that you know how to attract and keep its interest.

KNOWING THE AUDIENCE

Individuals are alike in many respects, unlike in others. The basic human urges and motives vary little from one individual to another, but the means of expressing them vary a great deal. A South Sea Islands cannibal and a California vegetarian, for example, both feel the urge of hunger, but they choose different ways of satisfying it. A food salesman would realize (1) that both could be appealed to through the hunger motive and (2) that the appeals must be shaped very differently.

Individuals who live close together and who have similar cultural, social, and occupational backgrounds tend to resemble one another not only in their basic urges but also in their means of expressing them. It follows naturally that groups of people who differ in place of residence, in cultural and intellectual attainments, and in occupation tend to emphasize their differences rather than their similarities. A number of Tennessee mountaineers are apt to resemble one another in many ways and may be appealed to in much the same manner. A number of New York City subway motormen also have a great deal in common, but as a group they are very different from the Tennessee mountaineers. Even in the same locality, the farmers, the industrial workers, the office workers, and the professional people tend to form groups which are different from one another but are internally similar. In addition to this occupational grouping, there are, of course, other groupings in the community. The church members have much in common and are different from the nonmembers; those who are "joiners" of various fraternal orders differ from the "nonjoiners"; the college graduates differ from those who have had less educational opportunity. There are still other natural groupings, based upon age, sex, nationality, avocational interest, political allegiances, and other types of interest or activity.

The speaker may gather information about his audience in a variety of ways. Some of it he may assume from the nature of the organization sponsoring his talk, from the location of the city or village in which he is to speak, and from the types of occupations represented in that territory. Additional information may be in-

In this adult class at Yankton College the speaker seems to be inviting specific responses from his intent listeners.

cluded in the invitation to make the speech, or it may be secured by questioning the person who issues the invitation. Thus the speaker can learn enough about his audience to guide his general preparation. As he travels to the town where he is to speak, enters the hall, and mingles with the audience, he receives more vivid impressions. He can then make any slight adjustments in his talk that seem necessary. Finally, while he is delivering the talk he should watch the audience closely, note the reactions to what is being said, and make any necessary adaptations as the speech progresses.

In preparing your speech you should take the measurements of your audience with respect to its intelligence, background, attitude, and knowledge of the subject.

Intelligence

A Phi Beta Kappa oration on the influence of Thomas Aquinas could probably prove most boring to the members of an off-campus audience. They would be inclined to consider it "too deep" and, after struggling for a while to understand it, would slump into inattentiveness. The speaker must be clear enough to be understood by everyone, yet thoughtful and stimulating enough to seem "empty" to none. If he underestimates the intelligence of his listeners, they will be offended; if he overestimates it, they will be confused and bored. The mind does not attend very long to anything that is too difficult to comprehend or to anything that is too simple and obvious.

The ideal solution is to formulate ideas which are stimulating and profound enough to appeal to the most intelligent members of your audience and then to state and illustrate these ideas so clearly that they will be understood and appreciated by the less intelligent members of the group. Any speaker who addresses a wide variety of audiences must have this ability if he is to be successful. Even an uneducated audience respects and appreciates profundity when it is made intelligible; and even the most educated audience welcomes simplicity of expression when the idea being expressed is worthy of its consideration. The parables of Jesus are prime examples of profound truths which were so stated as to appeal to all levels of intelligence.

There is one invariable rule to which the beginning speaker should adhere strictly if he wishes to become an effective speaker: *never condescend to your audience.* Never give it cheap and shoddy ideas on the theory that it cannot rise to anything better. Never excuse yourself for slovenly thinking on the plea that you have but sunk to the level of your audience. This practice is not fair to yourself; it dissipates and weakens your natural abilities. When Samuel Johnson was asked to explain how he had acquired his phenomenal conversational power, he replied, "Sir, I have made it a rule always to talk my best."

To feel that you must condescend to your audience is completely to miss the facts of the speaking situation. No matter what your intelligence and that of your audience may be, *every speech is a challenge to your ability to communicate your ideas.* This is especially true when you face an audience greatly your superior in intelligence: how can you make it feel the significance and worth of what you have to say? It is true when you try to get an audience of your intellectual equals to put aside their own ideas and accept yours. And it is just as true when you try to bring enlightenment to a body of your intellectual inferiors. Can you succeed in getting your own best thought accepted? That—and not whether you can succeed in finding thoughts on their low level of comprehension—is the measure of your success. This point deserves a great deal of emphasis, for we all have to listen to a great many speakers who habitually underestimate the intelligence of their audiences and insist upon aiming their speeches too low. Aim high, produce the best ideas of which you are capable, and then work carefully to develop them in such a way that they will have their maximum effectiveness with whatever the level of intelligence of the audience you are addressing.

Background

The background of the audience is the key to its knowledge, attitude, and interest. You will want to find out all you can about the kind of people you are to address. Do they have any sectional idiosyncrasies which you must take into account? Is their method of pronunciation different enough from yours so that you will have to take care not to seem "queer" or affected? What are their occupations? Is there anything in their political or religious beliefs which might have to be taken into account in phrasing your speech? Are they radical or conservative, readily responsive or dour and phlegmatic, well or poorly educated? The answers to such questions should guide you somewhat in the selection of your topic and should help a great deal in the selection of the supporting evidence and illustrative material with which you develop it. If you can draw upon the audience's own experiences for your illustrative material, your ideas have a better chance of winning acceptance.

Attitudes

An audience may have five general attitudes toward the speech subject or toward the speaker: strongly favorable, mildly favorable, neutral, mildly antagonistic, or strongly antagonistic. It is altogether possible for an audience to be strongly favorable toward a proposition and strongly antagonistic toward the speaker; the contrary may also be true. In the first instance, the speaker would have to devote most of his efforts to establishing a feeling of confidence and friendliness toward himself. Otherwise, the audience would lose its original enthusiasm for his proposition. On the other hand, if an audience strongly favors a speaker, his task of getting it to transfer that liking to his proposal ought not to be very difficult. We always tend to trust those whom we like and to follow those whom we trust. At the height of his popularity, Franklin D. Roosevelt easily persuaded the American people to approve a variety of proposals which they had formerly condemned as idealistic or socialistic. Naturally, it is of great value for a speaker to be aware of the attitude an audience has toward him and toward his subject.

Knowledge of the Subject

A highly educated audience may know nothing of the background of the subject the speaker is discussing; a less educated audience may know a great deal about the subject. You would probably find readier comprehension of a speech on the construction of Hi-Fi sets in a group of mechanics than in a group of philosophers. High intelligence or education in your audience is no guarantee that your subject will not need to be simplified and well illustrated; low intelligence does not of itself indicate that your audience will be unable to follow your discussion. If you underestimate the knowledge of your listeners, you may be embarrassed to discover that they have more knowledge of the subject than you have—or than you have demonstrated; if you overestimate it, you may find your listeners puzzled and unable to understand your ideas.

Mixed Audiences

What has been said so far applies chiefly to audiences which are homogeneous. When an audience is a mixture of young and old, educated and uneducated, experts in your subject and those who are ignorant of it, your task as a speaker is much more difficult. One solution is to follow the advice given in connection with audiences of varied intelligence: adapt the quality of your ideas to the highest common denominator; their expression to the lowest. Sometimes, for some special reason, the speaker is particularly anxious that his ideas be accepted by one segment of his audience; in this case, he shapes his remarks for this segment and largely ignores the rest of the audience. This approach is used by the best writers, advertisers, and broadcasters; but it can be used only with great care in face-to-face talk. Even if your message "selects" only a portion of your listeners, you must interest all of them.

GUIDE FOR ADAPTING TO AN AUDIENCE

While preparing your speech, you should have before you the following questions to guide you in selecting, organizing, and illustrating your materials in a way that will lead your audience most surely to accept your purpose:

1. How intelligent is this audience? Are there wide variations that must be taken into account? How can I phrase complex ideas so they will be understandable by all?

2. What kinds of social, geographical, political, religious, and academic backgrounds are represented in my audience? How can I select and phrase arguments and illustrations in a way that will appeal to special interests without offending or confusing those listeners who come from differing cultural milieux (such as Catholic-Protestant-Jewish, or liberal arts—electrical engineering)?

3. If some members of the audience are quite liberal, others quite conservative, how can I state my own position in a way that will encourage support from both points of view?

4. Am I planning to tell my listeners what they already know? Am I stating my facts in such a way as to lead the audience from the familiar to the unfamiliar? If my information is new to most of the listeners, am I making it both clear and interesting?

INTERESTING THE AUDIENCE

The speaker who cannot win and hold the interest of his audience is wasting his time. Unless the audience is interested in what you are saying, it will not absorb information, it will not be convinced or persuaded, and it certainly cannot be inspired or entertained.

You must learn how to win attention—how to be interesting. As you begin speaking, the members of the audience may be busy with their own thoughts. You must win their attention to the significance of what you have to say. You must then heighten that interest so that the audience will respond emotionally—even physically. (If the members of the audience are slumped down in their seats, is is a safe conclusion that they are giving little real attention to the speech. The words "relaxed" and "indifferent" describe responses that tend to go together.) If interest and attentiveness are to be complete, the members of your audience must be stirred into a lively and animated concern over your ideas. They must be made to see how the problem being presented affects them. Then they will "respond." There can be no audience response until interest—real interest, to the point of *personal concern* —has been achieved by the speaker. To create this concern, you must know your audience.

TYPES OF INTEREST

There are three types of interest through which the speaker can appeal to his audience. These are the *primary, secondary,* and *momentary* interests.

Primary Interests

The primary interests include the basic concerns essential to welfare. Health, financial security, affection, the approval of one's fellows, and the achievement of one's ideals and ambitions may all be considered primary interests. The speaker who deals with such topics is sure of a hearing.

Secondary Interests

Secondary interests include those which influence our thoughts and actions to a considerable extent but are not vital to our welfare. A man's golf game is merely a secondary interest compared with his job and his love for his family, yet it may be influential enough to get him up at 4:00 A.M. for an early-morning round. Stamp collecting, bridge playing, baseball, mountain climbing, and music are all secondary interests for most persons, yet they have determined and enthusiastic adherents. Secondary interests vary greatly from individual to individual, from community to community, and even from season to season. Hence the speaker must analyze his audience before framing appeals based on secondary interests.

Momentary Interests

The momentary interests are those which arise out of the happenings of the day. They may be exceedingly intense and may for a brief time seem just as important as the primary interests; but shortly they are forgotten and others take their place. A state of international tension in Central Europe can seize the attention of the world for a few days. Everyone will talk about it with as much emotional intensity as though his own well-being were at stake. But in a few days some other momentary interest—a kidnaping, a heavyweight boxing championship, a disastrous storm, or a crucial election campaign—has stolen the spotlight of public interest. A speaker who is alert to this continually shifting stream of momentary interests will always find an approach to catch the attention of his audience.

DIRECT AND DERIVED INTERESTS

Sometimes the speaker will wish to choose as his subject one of the primary, secondary, or momentary interests. He may present ideas for the improvement of his listeners' health, finances, or social standing. Or he may discover in advance what the secondary interests of his audience are and choose as the subject of his speech the one which appeals most widely. Thus he may talk to baseball fans about a plan for reorganizing the big leagues and to gardeners about a new perennial. Or, if a drought is turning a portion of the country into a "dust bowl," he may speak on the seriousness and extent of the problem and on means of meeting it. This is known as a utilization of *direct interests,* for the speaker discusses subjects in which his audience is already interested before hearing the speech.

Often the speaker selects his subject on some principle other than that of audience interest. Indeed, he may elect to speak on a certain topic precisely because his audience is not interested in it. For example, he may wish to overcome an indifference to politics, to literature, to international affairs, or to a campus problem. A speaker will often want to draw upon his own interests, special knowledge, and experience. He may wish to air his own enthusiasm or anxiety concerning a subject toward which there is little audience interest. In any of these cases the speaker's choice of subject matter does not depend upon the direct interests of the audience.

The speaker may, however, center attention upon his subject by the employment of what William James has called *derived interest:* the speaker must create interest by relating his topic to what already interests his listeners. A student speaker who gave a potentially interesting speech on his hobby of raising goldfish found his audience indifferent until, in his closing remarks, he mentioned how profitable his hobby had been. If he had begun his talk by linking his subject to the primary interest of his audience in the problem of how to earn money, he would have created an eager attentiveness.

The power of derived interest is demonstrated repeatedly in the ordinary concerns of everyday living. A boy may dislike studying physics—until he discovers that it will help him to develop his new hobby of building a Hi-Fi set. Geography ceases to be dull when it is associated with an active interest in the problems being discussed in the United Nations. When one family began to plan a trip to Mexico for the following summer, the younger members suddenly developed an unsuspected enthusiasm for the Spanish language. This same principle of transfer of interest may be employed by a speaker to influence his audience.

Although audience interest is important, it should not be considered by the speaker as the chief goal of his speech. Interest is an essential means to achieving the speaker's end, but it should never be allowed to supplant the purpose of the speech. A speaker should try not merely to keep his audience interested but continually *to direct that interest toward the accomplishment of his goal.* Many speakers fall into the trap of considering audience gratification a sure sign of success. It may, in fact, be a sign that the audience has conquered the speaker: that it has won him away from the pursuit of his object and converted him into an agent for satisfying his listeners' desire for amusement. This is what has happened when a speaker goes before an audience with a serious purpose but is beguiled by applause and the evident appreciation of his wit to use his time in a mere recital of humorous stories.

Your first question should be, "Am I holding the interest of my audience?" But your second, and no less important, question should be, "Am I holding the interest at the expense of my purpose, or am I using the interest to advance and accomplish my aim?"

In the selection of your subject, you should remember that the interest of the audience is only one of several important considerations. Choose your topic from the field of your listeners' direct interests only when you can at the same time select it in accordance with your own interests, knowledge, and purposes, with the requirements of the time limit, and with the occasion. Thus the interest of the audience plays a distinct but secondary role in the selection of your subject. However, after the subject has been selected and you have begun to plan the development of your speech, the interest of the audience should at once assume primary importance. You should not consider your speech ready for delivery until you are reasonably certain that you have devised a method for closely associating it with primary, secondary, or momentary interests held by your audience. You may be able to utilize direct interests only infrequently, but you should make it a point whenever they are lacking to use the principle of derived interest to take their place.

ELEMENTS OF INTEREST

In searching for means of making your subject interesting, you may well ask yourself, How concrete and specific are my ideas? Does my organization provide for variety? What sort of combination of the novel and familiar will the speech contain? Are the ideas vital to the audience? Do they represent conflict and provide suspense? Are there humorous possibilities to be developed? These factors may be called the *elements of interest.*

Concreteness

The five senses are our basic avenues for gaining information: "Seeing is believing." "The proof of the pudding is in the eating." "The nose knows." These common sayings reflect the trust which people have in the evidence of their senses. There is, on the other hand, a distrust of anything which is too abstract for sensory identification. When your ideas stray very far from the concrete, it is very probable that you do not know precisely what you mean, and it is almost certain that your audience does not. If you are discussing loyalty, patriotism, honesty, or any other abstraction, make your speech concrete with illustrations, examples, analogies, and particular facts. This is the first essential for attracting and holding an audience's interest.

Note how Stuart Chase, by the simple device of a vivid analogy, arouses interest in his discussion of means of controlling soil erosion:

Here is a sloping cellar door. Take a watering can and sprinkle a quart of water at its top. Measure the amount which slides off. Except for a little evaporation, the whole quart will be at the bottom almost instantly. Now tack a piece of thick carpet on the door. Again pour the quart of water on the carpet. Your measuring trough at the bottom will be lucky if it receives the merest trickle at first. Observe that the trickle continues for a long time.

The Specific and the General

Sometimes a speaker needs to use generalizations—as in the observation that "all men are mortal." Often it is more effective to use specific observations. For example, if you say "automobile," your listeners do not receive much help in visualizing the object. To say "Dodge" is more specific; to say, "A rather ramshackle 1956 Dodge stationwagon with rusty bumpers" is still more precise. Specific details are descriptive and evocative and enable the listeners to understand precisely what you mean. Generalizations, on the other hand, appeal to the intellect, and assert that a given fact has universal or at least very widespread validity. Both the specific and the general have their own kinds of usefulness.

Variety

It is a psychological fact that complete attention can be maintained for only a very few seconds. Look at a coin, and almost immediately your attention shifts from the whole object to the border, the lettering, or the design. Listen to a speaker, and if he provides variety of action, of voice, and of subject matter, you will continue to listen. Your attention will shift, but it will shift in relation to the speaker's own changes in posture, voice, and substance. However, if the speaker drones along monotonously, with no action at all, or with constant repetition of the same gesture, and if his subject matter is all of one type, your attention will shift to something that will stimulate your interest by providing variety. Otherwise, you will find yourself almost irresistibly lulled to sleep.

As has been indicated, there should be variety in voice, in action, and in the substance of the speech. No gesture is effective if used constantly. No bodily posture should be continued for long without variation. No voice, however intrinsically pleasant it may be, can hold the attention or win the admiration of an audience if it is not varied in pitch, rate, and intensity. But these changes of action and voice should not be artificial or mechanical. They can be genuine only if they correspond to changes in the speech itself. The speaker should first of all be sure that his material is varied; his voice and manner should assist his words in making his meaning clear.

Variety in the subject matter should be of several sorts. There should be some generalization, supported by a number of concrete examples. Each point should be evolved, supported, and concluded in such a way that it stands out distinctly from every other point. Thus, the speech resembles a succession of mountain peaks rather than a flat plain. The speaker may run the whole gamut of informative, argumentative, impressive, appealing, and entertaining points of view. He may vary his mood from pathos to humor, from joviality to earnestness. His serious points will stand out more impressively if contrasted at intervals with a little lightness and triviality. John Ise's speech, "Values in a Crazy World" (at the end this chapter), offers an excellent example of such varied content. With diversity in the subject matter, it will be simple and natural for the speaker's manner to change and to be in turn conversational, assertive, challenging, appealing, genial, and matter of fact.

Novelty and Familiarity

William James expressed a valuable truth when he said, "It is an odd circumstance that neither the old nor the new, by itself, is interesting: the absolutely old is insipid; the absolutely new makes no appeal at all. The old *in* the new is what claims attention—the old with a slightly new turn." There is little interest in what is already well known. It is boring, and it is condemned as "old stuff," "trite," and "platitudinous." When a speaker has nothing new to say, his audience is soon shifting about restlessly and hoping that he will stop. But attention is held no better by what is absolutely novel. In order to popularize his subject, the speaker must interpret what is new to his listeners in terms of what they already know.

The Vital

Ideas are vital when they appeal to the primary interests of the audience. Something which threatens a person's home, job, or neighborhood arouses not merely his interest but his immediate and deep concern. A speech may be interesting without being vital, but it can scarcely be vital without being interesting. That is to say, an audience may pay close attention to trival and unimportant ideas, such as may be presented in a speech intended solely to entertain, provided the other elements of interest are used. But the vital is so essential in winning attention that all experienced speakers use it frequently. An audience invariably pays attention to any speech which successfully tells how to be healthy, how to acquire more property, how to increase one's power, how to better one's reputation, how to win friends, how to avoid fear, how to protect those one loves, or how to be happier. Whenever a speaker can legitimately make use of the vital, it is to his advantage to do so.

Conflict and Suspense

"Continued next month," says the line at the end of the magazine-serial installment, and thousands of people buy the next issue to see how the story is going to come out. A million dollars in admission fees is paid by spectators of a heavyweight-championship boxing match. A hundred thousand football fans gather to watch the Rose Bowl game. Whenever conflict arises, whether it is international warfare or a dog fight on the street corner, people make it the center of their attention. "How is it going to come out?" is a universal question, applied to a thousand concerns of life.

The speaker can utilize this source of interest by picturing for his audience the conflict of attitudes which centers about his speech subject. A good example of how one speaker used this method is seen in a brief extract from a speech by Harold Fields on immigrants:

"Different periods, different prejudices," once said an eminent historian. That is particularly true today when "Lo, the poor Indian" has given way to "Lo, the poor alien." For today it is the alien who is made the target of all charges. If he is working, we say that he is taking employment away from Americans; if he is not working, we condemn him for being a charge upon relief. If he is wealthy, we criticize him for exploiting our country; if he is poor we vilify him for causing us to support him. We cause his name to be considered as synonymous with crime and illiteracy and undesirabilities and antisocial policies. He is the communist, the atheist, the anarchist, the libertine, and the instigator for everything that means license in morals, ethics, conduct of living, and standards.

Humor

Humor is an invaluable aid for the speaker. In the introduction, he can use it as a means of securing the audience's attention and creating a bond of good will between himself and his listeners. In the body of the speech, it may serve to point the interest of the audience to each of the main ideas. In the conclusion, it may be used to focus the audience's attention squarely upon the speaker's specific purpose.

In using humor, the following cautions should be observed: (1) Be sure it is appropriate to the mood of the audience and to the occasion. (2) Be sure it is pertinent to your subject and to your purpose, so that it attracts interest toward, rather than away from, your aim in speaking. (3) Introduce it naturally and easily, but do not obviously drag it in. (4) Select jokes that are brief and pointed. (5) Have your jokes so well prepared that there is no danger of your fumbling for the point. Nothing is less funny than a joke that falls flat. On the other hand, there is no easier and surer way of winning a favorable response from an audience than good, spontaneous humor. Chapter 22 contains a more detailed discussion of the use of humor.

Animation

Movement gets attention. Consider the number of electric signs at night which simulate movement. Fortunes have been made in animated cartoons. As you walk down a street you see a crowd gathered in front of a store window. What has attracted the crowd? You may be fairly sure it's action—perhaps it's a boy blowing bubbles, or monkeys playing in a cage. Your own ingenuity—plus good judgment—will guide your use of this technique in speaking. Remember ideas need to move, too.

CONCLUSION

Since the audience is the object of the speech, it is apparent that a basic requirement of the speaker is to interest the audience. Unless he gains the attention of the listeners, all his skills are in vain. Adapting to the audience requires, first, an analysis of the audience to determine its intelligence, interests, attitudes, knowledge of the subject, and general background. The speaker will also be helped by an understanding of primary, secondary, and momentary interests and how each may be utilized to gain and hold the attention of an audience. The relationship of the interests of the audience to the subject matter of the speech may be either direct or derived. Finally, in gaining and holding attention, the speaker should make full use in his speech of the elements of interest: concreteness, variety, the novel-familiar combination, the vital, conflict, suspense, humor, and animation.

EXERCISES AND BIBLIOGRAPHY

Exercises

1. Give a three-minute talk on the factors of interest you have noted in a shop window display.
2. Bring to class three full-page magazine advertisements which are excellent attention-getters. Point out to the class as briefly as possible how each utilizes the factors of interest.
3. Turn in written analyses of the adaptation to the audience of two speeches, not more than one of which may be heard on radio or television.
4. Turn in written analyses of the factors of interest found in a half-dozen commercials on radio or television programs.
5. Choose a topic in which you are interested and which you feel should be interesting to your classroom audience. Connect your subject, either directly or by derivation, with one primary, one secondary, and one momentary interest which you are confident that the members of your audience will have in common. Outline the speech, employing at least three of the elements of interest in your development of the main ideas. One of the elements of interest should be used in the introduction and one in the conclusion.
6. As you listen to the round of speeches called for in Exercise 5, select the speech which is least interesting to you and analyze the reasons for its failure to catch your interest. Develop the same subject, in outline form, in a manner which you would consider more interesting. Write

out briefly your reasons for preferring your treatment of the subject to that of your classmate. Hand one copy of your report, including the speech outline, to your instructor and one copy to the student whose speech you have revised.

7. Select from the round of speeches called for in Exercise 5 the speech which seems most interesting to you. Analyze the reasons for its success in holding your attention. To what extent was that success due to the contents of the speech? To what extent was it due to the delivery? To what extent was it due to the personality of the speaker? Was its success due in part to the mood of the audience? Write a brief report listing specific things learned from listening to and analyzing this speech which you plan to incorporate in your own future speeches.

Bibliography

Bois, J. Samuel, *Explorations in Awareness* (Harper, 1957).

Hollingworth, H. L., *The Psychology of the Audience* (American Book, 1935), particularly Chaps. III, V, VI, and XI.

Lee, Irving J., *Customs and Crises in Communication* (Harper, 1954).

Oliver, Robert T., *The Psychology of Persuasive Speech* (Rev. ed.; Longmans, Green, 1958).

Weaver, Richard M., *The Ethics of Rhetoric* (Regnery, 1953), particularly Chaps. III, IV, and VII.

ILLUSTRATIVE SPEECH

Read the following speech rapidly, to enjoy it and to get its general tone. Then go through it again, noting as many as you can find of the various types of interest and elements of interest discussed in this chapter. Note particularly how careful the speaker was to point the interest of his audience directly toward his goal. Note the growing intensity of the speech as it marches toward a conclusion.

Values in a Crazy World[3]

BY JOHN ISE

When I was asked to make a talk at this dinner, it was with specific instructions that I should try to say something that would not be too difficult for the sociologists to understand. Thus my field was rather

[3] Delivered at the annual meeting of the Mid-West Economic Association and the Mid-West Sociological Society, Des Moines, Iowa, 1937.

severely limited; but it was further restricted by the obvious desirability of confining myself to something that I could understand—not an easy task in the present state of the great science of economics. After much arduous labor, I found the limitations quite too much for me, and decided that intelligibility was not essential; that if my paper was unintelligible, the sociologists would easily recognize it was a contribution in sociological theory; the economists would assume that it was either sociology or something new in economic theory, and I would thus establish my standing as one of the new school of economic theorists—perhaps an institutionalist, or a reconstructed and stream-lined Veblen or Marx or Pareto; and I might some day serve as the subject of books and essays explaining what I really meant.

Something over two thousand years ago, a very strange people lived in southeastern Europe, on the shores of the Mediterranean Sea. Poverty-stricken, these people lived in houses without drains and without stoves, slept in beds without sheets or springs, fastened their clothes without buttons, wore no underclothes and no socks, warmed themselves over a pot of ashes, "studied poetry without books, geography without maps, and politics without newspapers"; and they had no gadgets. Yet, in their rags and hovels, they produced some of the greatest literature, philosophy, painting and sculpture of all ages. Never knowing comfort, the Greeks built what was in some respects the highest civilization ever known.

Nearly two thousand years later another race of barbarians, also without furnaces or automobiles or gadgets, began to write music. The great German musicians, Mozart, Bach, Schubert, and Beethoven, never housed comfortably, never able to travel at sixty miles an hour, without any of the advantages of rapid transit, Chambers of Commerce, Liberty Leagues, Daughters of the First American Revolution, Red Networks, moving pictures, daily tabloids of funnies or football carnivals, turned their attention to the writing of immortal music.

A century or two later, a great and highly civilized people, mostly descendants of the fifty thousand heroes who braved the dangers of the briny deep in the good ship *Mayflower,* in order to give the pagan Indians the blessings of rum and Christian civilization, found a new way of life, which was to be the efflorescence of many centuries of developing culture. They invented engines and thermostats, statistics and scientific management, advertising and salesmanship, B.O. and Halitosis, dental cripples and dishpan hands, cathedral bath rooms, calories and vitamins, cigar lighters and near beer, crooning, kidnapping and community singing, plastic surgery and schoolgirl complexions; but, alas, they knew not Plato, and they knew not Beethoven. Their unquenchable energies they devoted to the perfection of new engines with which to transport themselves quickly from places where they were bored to tears to other places where they were bored to death. Knowing the substantial joy of being comfortable, they worked themselves into hardened arteries and high blood pressure and Bright's Disease devising new ways of being still more comfortable, until they attained a level of bodily comfort quite as high as that of hogs in the shade of the old apple tree. Indifferent to the pain and tedium that they suffered in leisure time, they invented numberless gadgets to provide still more leisure time, which they devoted to such cultured activities as bridge, fan dancing, brotherly lodges and ballyhoo, flagpole sitting, stamp collecting, walkathons, endurance flying, and organizations for the uplift of the underprivileged classes that have no leisure time in which to be bored; to the invention of new gew-gaws with which to protect themselves from the boredom of their own intellectual and cultural aridity; to the task of learning to use the gadgets that they had in their cars and kitchens and bath rooms; and to the protection of American gadget civilization from insidious communists. They were so busy with all these manifold activities that they had little time for the study of any form of art, which was thought unmanly anyhow and unworthy of a great nation of rugged individualists. The study of the arts was left to the women, who had been released from domestic duties by the gadgets in the homes.

Only mechanical gadgets were welcomed by these great and highly cultured people. Political gadgets and inventions were thought highly dangerous, and those who suggested new ideas in politics and economics were listed in an ignoble register known as the Red Network. All policemen kept copies of the Red Network. The people welcomed new models of cars with great joy, but those who wanted new models of the Constitution were called damn communists and put in jail.

Perhaps all this will seem like a criticism of what is often called American civilization; but before we can offer a criticism of that hypothetical abstraction we must analyze it in the light of cold and scientific logic. Can we say that devotion to gadgets is inferior to the study of Plato or Beethoven? Can we say, categorically, that the pleasure of riding from nowhere to nowhere at eighty miles an hour is inferior in quality to the pleasure of listening to the *Eroica Symphony* or the *Götterdämmerung*? As economists we have always evaded such questions. We have assumed that whatever the people want has economic utility, whether bootleg gin or Beethoven; and from the predominance of demand for the former have assumed that American happiness was increasing day by day in every way. Economists have refused to make distinctions among different satisfactions, not because of laziness, but because they thought themselves unfitted to the task and unable to make any worth-while contribution. I share the modesty of all economists in this matter. In fact, I approach the problem of appraising consumers' choices with strong misgivings mitigated only by a comforting recollection of the fact that if I bring no heavy cargo of truth into port I am not the only economist who has ever wasted precious ink. The importance of the problem will perhaps justify even a feeble effort at its elucidation.

Perhaps much of our traditional economics is pointless and of little avail, a foundation with no super-structure, a prologue without the opera. The production of goods, more goods, more things, mountains of things—to what purpose? The assumption is that more goods mean more satisfaction, more utility—more comfort and happiness. The assumption seems to be that man has an infinite capacity for pleasurable titillations, and that titillations of all kinds are equally good for him. The truth appears to be that men are so constituted as to be capable of only a limited number of titillations; that, above a *pain* economy, the goods to which men are accustomed fade into the background and cease to have psychological importance. Only the new, unusual or unaccustomed goods stir any conscious response: and the bicycle of a generation ago brought as much satisfaction as the automobile of today. Perhaps the increased health and cleanliness of our age of wealth represent objective gains; but in other respects it is doubtful if our mountains of goods have made us any happier than the poverty-stricken pioneers of a generation or two ago. Increase in human happiness, and much more certainly improvement in the *quality* of life must be found in something else.

Consumers' goods may be classified in a great many ways, but, following Professor Hawtrey, I shall begin by dividing them into *defensive* goods—those which serve merely to prevent pain or distress, and *creative* goods—those which supply some positive, creative satisfaction. Food enables us to avoid hunger; clothing, with our furnaces and thermostats, enables us to avoid cold; knee-action cars enable us to avoid being jolted, although we may sometimes pay five dollars a day for a riding horse to give us the jolts we miss in the car; by riding to the golf club in a car we may avoid the fatigue of walking, so that we may enjoy the fatigue of playing golf; the electric eye shifts our gears and opens the door, and turns the water fountain on for us, relieving us of exhausting and fatiguing labor, so that we may take our morning setting-up exercises with more zest. Jazz, most novels, most movies, cards and puzzles and ice enable us to avoid boredom—which we may define as "an uncomfortable consciousness of cerebral innocuous desuetude." All the goods and products I have mentioned are merely defensive, as are most of the goods that litter the rooms of our homes, and the shelves of our stores. They enable us to avoid hunger, cold, discomfort, fatigue, pain or boredom. They are merely negative. Perhaps we should ask how far is distress bad? And we are in distress immediately. We are safe in saying that un-allayed hunger, cold and fatigue, characteristic of a pain economy, are bad, because they are destructive of health, or even of life—which for the present I shall assume to be good. Yet without hunger there could be no joy of eating; without cold, warmth could scarcely be felt as a good; without fatigue there could be no sweet rest. It is good to be hungry if we presently may eat, to be cold if we may warm ourselves, to be tired if we soon may rest. The want is inseparable from the satisfaction of it; and one of the faults of our age of plenty is that we seldom feel keen hunger, physical fatigue, or cold, and therefore miss in part the substantial satisfactions of a simpler and more meager economy. Pain is bad, however, because it is sympto-matic of a danger to health or life; boredom is similarly bad, indicating a lack of vigorous intellectual health. The distress that arises from dirt is bad because of its obvious relation to health, although cleanli-ness is sometimes carried beyond the needs of health, to proclaim a pecuniary capacity for conspicuous consumption, particularly when we may bathe in the cathedral bath rooms of the modern home. At any rate we look forward to Saturday night with far more joy than our pioneer ancestors did.

Many defensive products, such as thermostats and gadgets, serve merely to protect the individual from physical discomfort; but, as Professor Hawtrey says: "The whole yields no positive good; it merely brings him to the zero point, at which he is suffering from no avoidable harm"—the point that the aforesaid hogs reached with almost no trouble at all. "The man has weeded his garden, and still has to choose what he will plant in it, before he can be said to have made anything of his life." Other defensive products—machines and gadgets—increase the amount of leisure; but often to no worth-while end. The oyster and the crab likewise have leisure, the heiress and the playboy at Miami; but they build no noble lives. What does the typical man do with his leisure? "To create leisure," as Hawtrey says, "and then to occupy it by killing time is a contemptible confession of failure"; yet that is precisely what this man does. The most effective and conclusive way to kill time is of course to commit suicide. That disposes of a great amount of leisure time and eliminates all boredom at once; but few have the courage to follow this logical course. Temporary suicide and release from boredom may be achieved by getting drunk. A considerable number avail themselves of this escape. Analogous to this is the playing of certain games—bridge and poker —which enable men and women to tide over tedious afternoons or nights without undue mental strain. Many men and all women resort to cards. Automobile riding is for many a defense against boredom, which accounts for the great popularity of the automobile. To sit and think involves mental strain, to merely sit is tedious, but to sit and drive is neither straining nor tedious; and the car radio, turned to Happy Hooligan's horrible jazz, adds nothing to the demands on the mind. Most movies, newspapers—particularly the funny sections —most popular magazines, such as the *Cosmopolitan, The American* and *True Confessions,* most of the music heard over the radio, serve merely to protect people from being bored.

Here we can make out the fundamental reason for the multiplicity of organizations, societies and clubs in America, and for the over-powering anxiety of most people to join as many as possible. I know of a town of one hundred and fifty inhabitants, which has one hundred and fifty-one organizations of various kinds. It may be true, as Schopenhauer says, that it is better to be alone than with a hundred fools, but it is probably better for any one of the fools to be with the other ninety-nine. It is so much more sociable, and there is less danger of being bored.

Creative goods are goods which serve in building a richer and finer life—a life definitely above that of the hogs in the shade of the old apple tree. The hogs are not hungry, they do not suffer from cold or heat, they are comfortable, unfatigued and contented. The creative life must be something above this; and good music, good literature, artistic creations of all kinds, are competent to raise life above this physical and biological level.

A second distinction among different kinds of goods and activities we need not discuss here—the distinction based on social consequences. America stands today in a very great danger of lapsing back to some form of barbarism, because too many people are playing bridge and studying gadgets who should be reading and discussing economics, sociology, and political science. Perhaps the development of a taste for good music and the fine arts would not help much here; but good literature broadens the social outlook, perhaps quite as much as technical economics, and so is real training in intelligent citizenship.

A very important distinction, and one which the economist can use safely, is that based on the question of durability. A good sort of satisfaction, like a good coat, is one which lasts well; while a poor one, like a shoddy garment, soon wears thin. Here is a clear and objective distinction, one that does not lead us into the brambles of aesthetics.

By adopting this distinction, we avoid the pitfalls always involved in contrasting high and low wants. Many people speak of certain satisfactions as low—eating, and drinking, for instance; and of others as high—the enjoyment of literature, music and the other finer arts. The distinction is not clear and exact, however, for any of the satisfactions mentioned may be either high or low, and it may take generations to find out which. The real question is, does it wear well? If the dedication of much time and attention to the niceties of eating brings lasting happiness, it is good; if it finally palls, or if it brings gout or overweight or indigestion, it is bad. If indulgence in Bach or Beethoven proves to be a lasting and growing source of happiness, we must call it good; if it brings us to satiety and boredom, we must call it bad.

This distinction will serve not only as between different kinds of satisfaction. Good furniture is furniture that wears well, not physically but aesthetically: bad furniture seems uglier every time we look at it. We know that Chippendale and Sheraton models are good, because they have stood the test of many generations. Good literature is literature that wears well, poor literature is that which we tire of quickly, that which is soon forgotten. Let anyone read Artemus Ward or Bill Nye a few times, and note the rate at which the utility declines; then let him read Mark Twain a few times. It is easy to pick out the great literature. Mark Twain, like Walt Whitman, once regarded as vulgar, is now recognized as one of the greatest writers of all time. Like a garment of fine cloth, a service of sterling silver, a statue hewn by Praxiteles, he wears well. The English department should have a statistician to draw reputation curves for well-known writers—for

Mark Twain, Walt Whitman, and Thomas Hardy, slanting up; for Kipling, Longfellow, and Conrad, doubtless slanting downward, as we gain a perspective on them.

The same principle applies to music, and painting and all the fine arts. I recall a time when I could read a world of symphonic drama into the Spanish Fandango, when a Dudley Buck love song made me want to marry all the girls in the Sears, Roebuck catalogue. Most of us go through such a period of immaturity. Most of us test out the various grades and qualities of music, and if we have any capacity of growth, wind up with a solid appreciation of the great masters. Good music wears well. I confess that I have some difficulty with Bach—perhaps because I still enjoy romance in music and because, when I hear his fugues, I can just see those twenty children chasing each other around the table.

To make a further confession, I do not enjoy most modern music, and I find it difficult to apply my criterion of durability. To be severely frank, I never did like the stuff, so it sounds no worse the second time than the first—and usually no better. Since I cannot test it myself, I shall have to leave the test of its appraisal to my grand-children. I must say that much of it sounds the way Mid-Victorian furniture looks, and I doubt if most of it will stand the test of time; but another generation will be able to speak authoritatively.

This brings me to a final criterion for judging human recreational activities and satisfactions. What do they do to us? Do they cause us to shrink and shrivel and harden, like the meat of a stale walnut; or do they help us to grow into a broader, deeper and richer appreciation of the fine things in life? Alfred Marshall says that the fullness of life is found in the development of as *many* and as *high* faculties as possible. Mind, I do not speak of *happiness*. In the first place, I do not know what happiness is. Some philosophers say there is no such thing; others say that it is merely a matter of systematized delusions; all would have to admit that it is a matter of individual judgment. I find it is not a by-product of education; and I think education should not have the purpose of making people happy. "Its aim," as Frank Knight says, "is rather to raise problems than to solve them; the association of sadness and wisdom is proverbial, and he that increaseth knowledge increaseth sorrow." Most of my idiot friends, on the other hand, seem contented with the world as it is—with Hitler and Mussolini and Franco and American jazz and tuberculosis and hydrophobia and the Devil and all his works—happy in spite of all the world-wide grief and distress that make philosophers sad.

Pictures of complete happiness: a million Germans with their brains turned off yelling "Heil, Hitler"; twenty-five thousand students throwing their hats in the air when the home team makes a touchdown; a hundred thousand patriotic Americans at a political convention or rally, with bands and ballyhoo, saving America from God knows what! No, education does not aim to make people happy, nor does culture, nor civilization itself.

If we define happiness as comfort and satiety and contentment we may even go further and say that happiness is not always what men seek. As Frank Knight suggests, run through a list of economic wants, food, clothing, shelter, amusement, etc., and ask the candid question as to what fraction of the ordinary man's expenditure for any of them makes him "feel better," or is expected to do so. "It is a stock and conclusive objection to utopias," to quote Knight again, "that men simply will not live in a world where everything runs smoothly and life is free from care." A man who has nothing to worry about immediately busies himself in creating something, gets into some absorbing game, falls in love, prepares to conquer some enemy, or hunt lions or the North Pole, or what not. We recall also the case of Faust, that the Devil himself could not invent escapades and adventures fast enough to give his soul one moment's peace. So he died, seeking and striving, and the Angel pronounced him thereby "saved." "Wer immer strebend sich bemuht, den konnen wir erlosen." The pleasure philosophy is a false theory of life. The Hindus thought the question of happiness through to the end long ago and reached the inevitable conclusion—Nirvana—"just life enough to enjoy being dead."

Here we part with those whom Carlyle calls the "pig trough philosophers." The fullness of life is not found in the consumption of the most possible goods, the eating of the most delicately-flavored food, the wearing of the richest garments, the living in many-roomed houses. In that direction lies not life, but satiety and envy and boredom.

No, I am not talking about happiness, which I can't define, and if I could define wouldn't want badly enough to dispense with what brains I have in order to get it. I am talking about *life, the fullness of life*—the exercise of as many and high faculties as possible. I do not know whether life is good or not, but if it isn't good, we can help ourselves liberally, anyhow, while we are here, and console ourselves with the thought that we can be dead a long while. Since I must have such a large helping of being dead, I would like to be as much alive as possible while I am here. I would like to exercise as many and as high faculties as possible. I want to live with my family. I want to read much, listen to the riches of music, travel, see the beauties of nature and of great works of art, see a good show occasionally, fish a little when I have the patience, perhaps play golf, hunt antiques, dig in the ground in the springtime—I believe it was Abel who started that business, and man will never get away from it—walk through dead leaves in November, and through snow in the winter. As a good Kansas man, reared in the rarefied moral atmosphere of Kansas, I cannot of course indulge in strong drink even for the stomach's sake, but I can enjoy 3.2 beer on hot summer days, and a cigar when I have a nickel. We need not get full to have a full life, but I suppose a full life would have to include a moderate amount of wickedness.

The exercise of as many and as high faculties as possible, that is the good life, because it is *much* life. It is on this principle that man, or at any rate *some* men, may be said to be higher than the oyster. Having a somewhat larger and more deeply convoluted brain, a man *may* indeed be wiser than an oyster; but he may also be *crazier* than an oyster. Having greater resources, he can be a bigger fool than an oyster, because he can know so much more that isn't so. An investigation of political intelligence by Professor Eldridge of the University of Kansas revealed the fact that on some economic questions, men knew much less than nothing—that on some true and false questions they batted only 25 per cent. Any colony of oysters could bat 50 per cent, as could tin men or weather vanes—on the mathematical principle of probability. Man is not necessarily wiser than an oyster; but, according to Marshall, he lives a fuller life, because he exercises more faculties. Some philosophers express somewhat the same ideal in what they call the "development of personality."

Using this criterion, how shall we appraise some of the current recreational activities? Is the professional society woman a wiser, finer, nobler character because of her expensive parties? Is she learning to live more fully—"to exercise more or higher faculties"? Does the devotee of bridge grow steadily in high faculties from wondering who played the jack or who holds the ace? Man, made in the image of God, cudgeling his brains about such a question—it is blasphemy! Surely such a question is hardly worthy even of a woman—made of an ancestral rib. Does the baseball fan develop new richness of personality by listening to the radio announcer describe the game someone else is playing? Is the movie fan typically a man of many faculties, because of his devotion to such noble dramas as *Hoopla* and *Naughty Marietta?* No, these activities are merely defensive. They are resorted to by those who are trying to protect themselves from boredom. Even in our colleges, we find the students engaged mainly in activities of this sort. Nature, as the physicists say, abhors a vacuum; and some of our students would be almost complete vacua were it not for social and athletic activities. Some people accuse our students of being "Reds." Would that accusation were justified, for a red is at least full of color; but quite a few of our students are only full of vacuity.

What, by the way, do these activities do to our typical student? They leave him stranded in early middle life, a cultural wreck—or shall I say a "flat tire," or a cultural doughnut with the rim knocked off—with nothing to carry him on through the rest of his weary, stale and unprofitable journey. "Fat and forty," he can no longer dance; his favorite magazines, *The American* and *Ballyhoo,* no longer satisfy, even with the lift afforded by his Camels; athletics are hardly safe for his weak heart, even when described over the radio; jazz is warmed-over gravy. So he must protect himself from the growing weight of tedium by joining brotherly lodges, dressing himself up in a dunce cap and parading the streets, making speeches on the necessity of preserving the Constitution—which he has never read—and perhaps indulging in a glorious alcoholic release once in a while, on the occasion of a visit to his noble Alma Mater.

Yet I would not like to seem unappreciative of our students. They are the finest people in the world, the only redemption, if there is any redemption, of our educational system. Their faults are merely the faults of American life, and their virtues rise above the ordinary level of American life. I am quite out of sympathy with the cynic who described American education as the casting of false pearls before real swine. Some of our pearls are seconds, Woolworth pearls, I think; but our students, God bless them, are as fine as could be reared in a comfort-, gadget- and speed-worshipping civilization— or shall I say "barbarism"?

Building for a full life—that is what we need—the development of a taste for the *enduring* cultural values, for *good* literature and art and music, the sort of things that pile up spiritual riches within us and leave us wondering, not how we shall pass the time, but how we can find time for all the beauty that is within our reach.

In a civilization like ours, good music, literature, and the arts are needed as never before. Ours is a technological civilization, a civilization of iron and steel, of wheels and cranes and levers, of science and engineering, of roar and clatter. It is a civilization in which realism has displaced romance, in which the emotions have shrivelled in the glare of harsh reality. The man without capacity for emotional experience may be very scientific, but his life is on a dead level of monotony that smacks of spiritual death. We need emotional experience, which we can find better in music than anywhere else; in the nobility of Beethoven's *Eroica Symphony,* the pathos of Tchaikowsky's *Symphonie Pathétique,* of Schubert's *Tod und das Mädchen,* in the ecstatic grief of the *Liebestod.* As a release from the hard realities of a machine age, we need good music and the arts to keep our souls alive.

One more thought I would like to leave with you. If our economic society is not incurably sick, we may look forward to much more leisure time in the future—leisure time which we may kill by playing cards, reading the tabloids, or driving our cars rapidly past our splendid system of billboards; or may use to build up our own cultural resources. Unfortunately our business civilization provides excellent facilities for our degradation, but not much that is uplifting. The radio, which might afford us riches undreamed of, is prostituted to jazz and the advertisement of contented cows, Heel Hugger Shoes, Listerine and Odorono. Here is the greatest failure of American democracy—the greatest failure in the sense that it falls farther short of its possibilities for good than anything else I can think of. The government should broadcast over the radio, at all times during the day and evening, on different wave lengths, grand operas, symphony orchestra music, chamber music, with intermissions of oratorio, jazz of two grades—plain rotten and infernal—lectures by the greatest speakers in the country, and Amos and Andy throughout the day. You will see that I am no snob. I want the cultural proletariat to have their ham and eggs. I would gladly give them the largest and worst jazz orchestra that money will buy, and Amos and Andy on one wave length, but not on twenty.

This program would call for an expenditure of perhaps a hundred million dollars a year—one third of a cent a day, per capita, twelve per cent of the cost of our army and navy. It would give employment to thousands of competent musicians; and it would make America a decent place to live in, a decent place even for those who love good music.

Something tells me, however, that all this is not in prospect. Something tells me that if, when, and as we recover our wonted prosperity, we shall have more and worse jazz, bigger and better bridge parties, gadgets piled on gadgets, longer and faster cars and happier fools driving them faster past bigger and better billboards; and I suppose we shall always have pessimists worrying about a possible decline of such a civilization.

NOTE

This is the kind of speech which is certain to arouse controversy, since it deals vigorously with the question of values. Professor Ise was speaking in 1937, and a great many changes in American thinking have occurred since then. To what extent do you agree with his basic premise that "fullness of life" rather than "happiness" should be our goal? with his specific judgments, such as his dislike for "modern" music? Do you find any respects in which his examples seem out-of-date? Perhaps the class might find time to organize a discussion around his central theme in order to clarify the group thinking on today's campuses concerning the vital question of what values we should be pursuing. You will readily observe that Professor Ise favors a liberal arts rather than a strictly vocational education. Members of the class might profitably extend their reading in the field of educational theory and present an entire round of speeches reflecting their varying views, making references to Ise's ideas, as a means of keeping all the speeches centralized around a single focal point. From Aristotle's attempt to define happiness to the contemporary quest for learning in the "hundred best books," man has been eternally seeking a promising roadway to his own betterment.

CHAPTER 12

CONTENTS

These photographs of Prime Minister Jawaharlal Nehru of India, taken during his visit to the United States in December, 1956, show the varied aspects of "the man himself" which are reflected in his speaking style. (Wide World Photos, Inc.)

IMPROVING
THE STYLE
OF YOUR SPEECH

ARISTOTLE emphasized to his students that listeners receive from the speech their impressions of the speaker's character. Whether or not they conclude that he possesses intelligence, virtue, and good wills depends largely upon his way with words, his style. Every speaker has a style, but his problem may be whether it gives the impression he wishes. Clearness is but one dimension of meaning; other dimensions include acceptability and vividness.

The student in a beginning speech class may understandably feel that he is not personally concerned with style. "Just let me say what I have to say, honestly, clearly, straightforwardly—with no mistake as to my meaning and with a reasonable degree of effect upon my hearers," he may say. "I'm willing to let others worry about style."

Such a student cannot be blamed for his suspicion of style. The very emphasis in this book upon *extemporaneous* speech is an indication that the authors consider refinements of style less important than the spontaneous quality of genuinely direct communication between speaker and listeners. The whole tenor of our contemporary age tends to disparage stylistic ornamentation and to call instead for speed, efficiency, and vigor. The fifteen-minute program periods on television and radio demand that most broadcasted speeches be cut to bare essentials. Businessmen's luncheon clubs are designed to combine a meal and a speech into a period of time short enough to leave the afternoon free. "Stand up, speak up, and shut up!" is a popular form of the advice often given to inexperienced speakers. Style, it might appear, has been lost in the twentieth century's ceaseless rush.

However, this appearance is largely deceptive. As a matter of fact, the hypothetical student cited in the second paragraph was presenting a fairly good list of stylistic qualities in his very statement opposing the study of style. Speech style should aim to express what the speaker really wants to say, honestly, clearly, straightforwardly— with no mistake as to meaning and with a reasonable degree of effect upon the listeners. The speed, efficiency, and vigor required of speakers today are also stylistic characteristics. What has taken place is not a denial of style in speaking but the same thing that has taken place in every other age: an adaptation of style to the general temper of the period. Just as the hoop skirt and the bustle of the last century have been discarded for the comparatively trim lines of present-day feminine styles, so has speech style sought to mirror as well as to influence the kind of thinking characteristic of our time.

FUNCTIONS OF STYLE

A proper understanding of the functions of style provides the best answer to the skepticism which may greet the invitation to its study. To imagine a speech without style would be as impossible as to imagine a person without personality. Style may be obscure, inconsistent, unattractive, wordy, pretentious, or inappropriate; it may be clear, vivid, striking, forceful, inspirational, or appropriate. It may be "good" or "bad," but it cannot be absent. A dull, plodding speech, broken by hesitations, flavorless in vocabulary, incorrect in grammar, and spiritless in tempo is not a speech without style. It simply represents a kind of style no one wishes either to possess or to hear.

In contrast is a speech delivered by Winston Churchill in the English House of Commons in August, 1940—shortly after the disastrous defeat of every substantial ally the Commonwealth possessed and as the skies over London were already being pierced with what was soon to be the worst aerial attacks any modern city had to that time been forced to endure. Surely nothing could have been further from the minds of Churchill and his audience than mere stylistic excellence. Yet note how Churchill's words reflect the exalted sentiments which he felt and which the situation required:

Hitler is now sprawled over Europe. Our offensive springs are being slowly compressed, and we must resolutely and methodically prepare ourselves for the campaigns of 1941 and 1942. Two or three years are not a long time, even in our short, precarious lives. They are nothing in the history of the nation, and when we are doing the finest things in the world, and have the honor to be the sole champions of the liberties of all Europe, we must not grudge these years or weary as we toil and struggle through them.

Such words do not merely make clear an idea. They phrase a spirit. They express mounting determination which stirs the listener's understanding as well as his resolution. We could open the parliamentary addresses of Churchill almost at random and encounter such passages. They are marked by an invigorating vividness which lifts them above the plane of everyday expression. They possess a rich fullness of meaning. This is the sense in which "good style" adds something above the ordinary to words. It raises them to new heights of meaning and influence. Were we to examine more extensively the speeches of Churchill, or to listen more carefully to those of our fellow students in class, we would soon note that speech style serves more than one function.

Influencing the Immediate Audience

A primary function of style, of course, is to win the desired response from the specific audience. If it is to fulfill this function, style must adapt itself to the needs of the hearer. All considerations of listener attention, interest, and motivation are involved. To use Herbert Spencer's phrase, the speaker is striving for the "economy of the listener's attention." A style which fulfills this function is audience-centered.

Some people will object, of course, that this is not a complete measure of a good oral style. They may say that the salesman with the top sales record may have resorted to unethical methods, or that he may have drawn easier prospects than did his competitors. This is why we suggest that style is more adequately measured by a consideration of all its functions, and not just by one alone.

Expressing the Speaker's Meaning

Another function of style is to express an idea with exactness. To a scientist explaining to fellow scientists the results of an experiment this may be the only function that matters. To those who are concerned with semantics, the science of meaning, this is one of the functions of language that is least often attained. Good style ought not to be directed to creating an effect with words but to convey meaning with them. Hence you must try to use words carefully. This function is not entirely separate from the preceding one, for it also has to do with serving the listener. A speech to baseball fans could hardly convey the desired fullness of meaning without using the technical terms of the game. Yet a speech to farmers on the transportation problems of a large city should avoid technical terminology because, while it might prove the speaker's superior knowledge, it would not be instantly intelligible to the listeners. When, in discussing style, we recommend the use of imagery, rhythm, and a large vocabulary, it is not because these are impressive or attractive adornments (though we find nothing to apologize for in beauty), but because without their use the speaker's full meaning could not be expressed. How could a sermon on divine mercy fully express its message without rhythmic and figurative phraseology to suggest the emotional power of the religious concept? On the other hand, an expository speech on how to operate a computing machine would hardly be improved stylistically by heightened emotionalism or figurative language. That style best serves the listener which is at once fully meaningful to him.

Expressing the Speaker's Personality

One of the most rewarding experiences you will find in a speech course is your discovery of your real self and your ability to give it voice. For this, too, is a function of style, to express one's personality. In this sense, each speech ought to reflect your individuality. Walter Pater, the British essayist and critic, wrote of "a personal sense of fact." Buffon, the French naturalist, celebrated for his "Discourse on Style," said that style consists of the man himself; and the French critic Brunetière defined it as the speaker's manner of expressing himself. In a delightfully stimulating essay appearing in the *Saturday Review* and titled "A Sane Approach to Style," Charles W. Ferguson advises, "Not one style, but an awareness of many, so that the one best suited to the subject can be chosen—this should be the controlling principle of one who seeks to improve self-expression." He goes on to quote Schopenhauer, the German philosopher:

There is no quality of style that can be gained by reading writers who possess it; whether it be persuasiveness, imagination, the gift of drawing comparisons, boldness, bitterness, brevity, grace, ease of expression or wit, unexpected contrasts, a laconic or naïve manner, and the like. But if these qualities are already in us, exist, that is to say, potentially, we can call them forth and bring them to consciousness; we can learn the purpose to which they can be put; we can be strengthened in our inclination to use them, or get courage to do so. . . . The only way in which reading can form style is by teaching us the use to which we can put our own natural gifts.

Your style, then, is a way of so mastering the use of words that they best influence the immediate audience, most accurately convey your meaning, and do all this in that personal and individualistic way which is characteristically you. Note, as an example, in the following passage from a speech by Dwight Eisenhower, how there is revealed those qualities of simplicity and moral fervor which are widely believed to be basic in his personality:

We cannot, of course, attain perfection in human relations even within the smallest community, no matter how many laws we pass or policemen we hire. The rogue and the villain skulk on dark corners. But as we put street lamps on these corners so that decent folk may walk abroad after dark, so we can relight the lamps of brotherhood where they have been extinguished among men.

Style at its best is a revelation of the man behind the speech.

Expressing Truth So That It Will Endure

The influential pulpit speaker, Henry Ward Beecher, could say with confidence, "I have uttered some words that will never die because they are incorporated in the lives of men that will not die." Lincoln was never more mistaken than when he said at Gettysburg, "The world will little note, nor long remember what we say here." Le Bon, the discerning French student of human behavior, observed in his book, *The Crowd,* "The memorable events of history are the visible effects of the invisible changes of human thought." Your daily task is with those invisible changes of human thought. You will not do your best if you envision your task as an ordinary, assignment-fulfilling one, to be forgotten tomorrow. You will be challenged to steady improvement if you speak always of things that make a difference; if you remind yourself that something you may say in a classroom talk could be so meaningfully expressed as to have a lasting influence upon the life of some fellow-student listener. We who teach know that such experiences are not uncommon, a fact that gives to the art of speaking so much of its fascination. Your constant goal should be to express truth in words that are worthy of it—that will influence listeners now and later, that will give to truth its fullest meaning.

STYLISTIC DIFFERENCES BETWEEN WRITING AND SPEAKING

Style that is good for writing—intended for a reader—may be bad for speaking—intended for a listener. But there is no single universal standard of excellence for either. There are occasions when both readers and listeners expect formality; there are other occasions when both readers and listeners prefer the familiar, colloquial style. When the purposes of the writer and the speaker are similar, the stylistic qualities of the two may differ less; each will wish to be clear, emphatic, pleasing, and sincere. To this extent, good style for the reader is good style for the listener. Both writing and speaking are at their best when they serve effectively but unobtrusively as the medium of communication between writer or speaker and his audience. Yet, granted this basic similarity, there remain significant differences.

Directness

The speaker must be more direct and personal in the adaptation and application of his thoughts to his listeners than the writer ordinarily needs to be for his readers. This is, of course, a relative matter and, as with all generalizations, there will be exceptions. Sometimes a writer will aim just as specifically and personally at a definite reader or reader group as will the speaker at a definite listener or listener group. But more often there is a greater esthetic or mental distance between reader and writer than between speaker and listener. The listener tends to have a greater sense of the personality and physical presence of the speaker, even when hearing him over the radio or television or from a recording. Of this the speaker must be acutely aware. It means that he must shape his remarks closely to the capabilities, interests, and modes of thought of his audience. It means that he must do all he can to establish a direct and personal relationship with his audience. Specifically, it means that the speaker must make much greater use than the writer of personal pronouns, of action verbs, and of short, conversational sentences. "I," "you," and "we"; "mine," "yours," and "ours" should occur frequently in a speech.

The Use of Questions

The communicative quality of the speech will be heightened by the frequent use of questions. Questions may also be assets in writing, but they are certainly less essential. The speaker's questions may be of two types: direct and rhetorical. The direct question is the kind which in a conversational situation would call for a direct answer from a listener. Thus it tends to make the audience think with the speaker himself. Thus in a speech on education the speaker may ask, "How many qualified high school graduates are kept from a college education by rising tuition costs?" and proceed immediately to answer his own query. A rhetorical question is one which requires no answer, or, more precisely, assumes an obvious answer as mentally given by the listeners. Thus it tends to make the audience think with the speaker. When a speaker asks his audience, "Do you wish to sanction murder?" "Are you willing to see women and children slaughtered without a chance of escape?" or "Do you believe with me that the bombing of civilians in time of war should be prohibited?" he is only stating common beliefs in a form which will stir up the greatest interest and elicit the most favorable response.

The Use of Exclamations and Imperatives

The speaker will tend to use exclamatory and imperative sentences more frequently than do most writers. It has been noted earlier that the speaker tends to use shorter sentences than does the writer, since these are characteristic of conversational directness; exclamatory and imperative sentences also tend to be more typically conversational.

The Use of Connectives

One of the chief difficulties which beset the speaker more sharply than the writer is that of clarifying and unifying his ideas. Varied and meaningful connectives are useful tools for this purpose. Since most inexperienced speakers overuse "and," "but," "then," and "now," you will do well to study some of the useful connective words available in our language:

accordingly	consequently	however
admittedly	doubtless	if
after	either	incidentally
again	else	indeed
already	especially	last
also	except	meanwhile
although	finally	moreover
and	first	neither
as	for	nevertheless
because	formerly	nonetheless
before	further	nor
besides	furthermore	notwithstanding
briefly	granted	now
but	hence	only
by	here	or
concerning	hereupon	ordinarily

otherwise	then	when
previously	thereby	whenever
provided	therefore	where
second	third	whereas
since	though	wherever
so	thus	wherefore
still	too	whereupon
than	unless	whether
that	until	yet

In addition to such connecting phrases as "you may recall," "I am sure it is no news to you," "you know from your own experience," and "but perhaps its worst feature is," consider the following list:

add to this	even if	more than
and also	even so	not only . . . but also
and so	even though	now that
and then	for example	of course
and yet	for this reason	on condition that
as a result	how much more	on the contrary
as follows	if possible	on the other hand
as I have said	in addition	provided that
as if	in another sense	rather than
as though	inasmuch as	so that
at an earlier period	in brief	that is
at last	in consequence	to come to the point
at such times	in fact	to continue
at the same time	in order that	to illustrate
because of this	in other words	to recapitulate
best of all	in the first place	to repeat
by the way	it must be granted	to sum up
		with this exception

A liberal and varied use of these connectives will help to give a speech clarity and unity.

Speed of Comprehension

As a speaker you must be instantly understood. Readers can, if they wish, turn back and reread; but listeners have no such opportunity. Hence, you must be particularly careful that what you say is immediately clear. This means, specifically, that you will use simple rather than complex sentences, that you will translate abstractions into concrete expressions, that you will repeat frequently, and that you will make important sentences and ideas stand out. When the speech subject is a complex one, it is usually safe to follow the old rule: in the introduction tell the audience what you are going to say; in the body say it as clearly and emphatically as you can; and in the conclusion again point out your essential meaning.

CLARITY AND SIMPLICITY

An effective speaking style has clarity and simplicity. These closely related qualities aid instant intelligibility, but to facilitate their mastery, we shall consider them separately.

Clarity

As a speaker your first duty is to understand clearly exactly what it is that you wish to say to your audience. Your second duty is to find the means of making your ideas clear to your hearers. Clarity may be achieved by the use of definition, classification, hypothetical examples, specific examples, comparison, contrast, analogy, and statistical data. As you recall the discussion of similar types of materials in the chapter on selecting and developing ideas, you will realize how the qualities of style are woven into the very texture of the speech.

Definition is clear and precise description of an object or idea, designed to distinguish it from all other objects or ideas.

Classification is orderly and systematic grouping of materials according to one definite principle. Thus objects may be classified according to their color, size, shape, use, or essence.

A *hypothetical example* is an imaginary incident used to show how the speaker believes his idea would work in practice. "For example," he might say, "let us see how the plan of socialized medicine would affect a typical family."

A *specific example* is an actual incident showing how the speaker's plan really worked when tried. "I say a free people cannot be conquered," a speaker might say. "Look at Switzerland, for example."

Comparison and *contrast* are devices frequently used together. They are especially valuable when the speaker's subject is unfamiliar to the audience. The Security Council of the United Nations might, for example, be *compared* with the campus Interfraternity Council; the veto power exercised by the five permanent members of the Security Council might be *contrasted* with the majority vote prevailing in the Interfraternity Council meetings.

An *analogy* is the demonstration of an essential point of similarity between objects which are otherwise different. When Emerson, in speaking of the art of oratory, said, "Him we call an artist, who shall play on an assembly of men as a master on the keys of a piano," he touched upon the one aspect which these two very different artists have in common. Argument by analogy is dangerous, but analogy is a valuable tool when used strictly for the sake of clear exposition.

The presentation of *statistical data* deserves particular consideration under the heading of clarity. Originality and imagination must be employed to present statistical facts in striking and memorable ways. The problem is always one of simplification and translation into understandable and meaningful terms. A million—to say nothing of a billion—is really quite incomprehensible. Perhaps it would assist comprehensibility to point out, for example, that there are not very many more than a half million minutes in an entire year; and that there haven't been so many as a billion minutes since the birth of Christ. To present some economic data one student used the following device:

If I were to draw for you an imaginary graph for 1936 allowing an inch to represent a thousand-dollar income, I would place half of America's families within the lowest inch. I would place all but 7 percent of America's families within the first two inches—two thousand dollars. Now, in order to represent the income of the remaining few families, I would soar far upward, for the highest income on such a scale towers 350 feet above the zero line.

Simplicity

The speaker must always remember that clarity is aided by simplicity. The simple and familiar words are the tools of clearness. Short, Anglo-Saxon words are often preferable to long, classical ones. The journalist knows this well. The public speaker needs to learn it. Read again the Gettysburg Address, the Sermon on the Mount—you will not need the aid of a dictionary to understand them. Bear in mind that "syllogisms," "transcendentalism," "equations," "vectors," "synapses," and "chromosomes" are in the everyday vocabularies of relatively few people. The users of such words will be regarded by most people as unintelligible and perhaps even pretentious.

Note the clearness, and thus the power, in the use of simple language and familiar references in the following introduction to the student speech which won the Civic Intercollegiate Oratorical Contest at Ohio Wesleyan University in 1939:

Plato, in his *Republic,* tells of a prisoner chained in a dark cave with his back to the entrance. As each dawn creeps toward dusk, the shadows of the day are thrown upon the sheer walls of the cave. The manacled prisoner watches the world go by in black and white. Because he has never experienced anything but the shadows, he has never known that they are but deceitful secondhand images of the outside world.

Tragic, you say? Perhaps. Yet would you and I admit that our lives are tragic? In reality we sit in our home or little community and watch the world go by in black and white—the black and white of the newspaper page and the propaganda leaflet, the black and white of the cinema screen, the black and white of the secondhand images which the radio commentator reads. What do you think of Hitler? Mussolini? or Roosevelt? Where did you get those opinions? From shadows—shadows reflected from press, radio, and cinema. Like the man in the cave, we cannot realize that these are but deceitful secondhand images of the living world.

Do you remember when you were just a kid? How afraid you were of that awful something that lay in wait for you at the head of that dark stairway? We begin life and end it in the fear of false shadows. The shadows of prejudice and tradition are handed down from generation to generation, are perpetuated by teachers. And don't forget those unlicensed teachers: the press, the radio, the cinema—which drive the shadows of false beliefs, false loves, false hatreds into the heart of every child.

MEMORABLE PHRASING

Harry A. Overstreet contributed to an understanding of effective style when he stated that the two factors which give power to ideas are the quickness and clarity with which the ideas are received, and the ease with which they are recalled. We have already discussed the qualities of clarity and simplicity which aid in ready reception of meaning; we now turn to those which help the listener to remember the speaker's ideas.

Vividness

Some of the figures and forms of speech which contribute most to vividness are metaphors, similes, concrete terms, epigrams, alliteration, dialogue, rhythm, and freshness of phrasing. Yet neither one nor all of these together, if used mechanically, can achieve vividness. They must be used with all the imagination and originality the speaker possesses. It is useful to cultivate the habit of thinking of every speech subject in pictorial and striking terms. What the speaker has experienced personally and has felt keenly he will be able to describe most vividly.

A *metaphor* is an identification of two apparently different objects or ideas on the basis of some significant likeness common to both.

Edmund Burke used this metaphor to describe the condition of Spain in his time: "What can we expect from her?" he asked, "mighty indeed, but unwieldy: vast in bulk, but inert in spirit, a whale stranded upon the seashore of Europe." Abraham Lincoln's "A house divided against itself cannot stand" is another example.

A *simile* is a comparison between two apparently different objects or ideas on the basis of some likeness which they possess. A few examples are "Like a mighty army moves the church of God," "His eyes are like pits of burning fire," or Robert Southey's "It is with words as with sunbeams—the more they are condensed, the deeper they burn."

Specific terms carry far more vivid meanings than do generalizations. Don't talk about *athletics* when you mean *football,* and don't talk about *football* when you mean *the Army-Navy game.* If you wish to make your listeners' mouths water, don't talk about *bodily sustenance,* or even about *food,* but about *Southern-fried chicken* or *strawberry shortcake.*

Epigrams are brief, pungent, and unexpected in the turn they give to an idea. Examples are William Shakespeare's "The text is old, the orator too green"; Abraham Lincoln's "Tact is the ability to describe others as they see themselves"; Ralph Waldo Emerson's "One of the benefits of a college education is to show the boy its little avail"; Mark Twain's "A classic is something that everybody wants to have read and nobody wants to read"; and that of the British clergyman and author Sydney Smith, "He has occasional flashes of silence that make his conversation perfectly delightful."

Alliteration, when used sparingly, is believed by many to add to the ease with which listeners may recall what has been said. It consists of a repetition of sounds. Glenn Frank, former president of the University of Wisconsin, made particularly good use of alliteration. He gave his lectures such titles as "Epidemic Experimentalism," and he felt the effectiveness of such phrases as "miracle men who lead the masses," "more of Fascism than of freedom," "mass movement born of minority creation," "the decisiveness and drive of dictators," "corrective criticism," and "the press must bow to politics and the laboratories take orders from the legislature." Note also the effectiveness of this sentence from Thomas Jefferson: "When we must wait for Washington to tell us when to sow and when to reap, we shall soon want bread."

Dialogue introduced into a speech is an excellent device for dramatizing an idea—for bringing it close to everyday human experience.

The following example, from the conclusion of Henry Ward Beecher's sermon "The Love of God," shows how effective dialogue can be:

> When I come up before the eternal Judge, and say all aglow, "My Lord and my God," will he turn to me and say: "You did not come up the right road . . . go down"? I, to the face of Jehovah, will stand and say: "God! I won't go to hell; I will go to heaven: I love Thee. Now damn me if Thou canst. I love Thee." And God shall say, and the heavens flame with double and triple rainbows, and echo with joy: "Dost thou love? Enter in and be blessed forever."

Rhythm is a more important aspect of language than is readily apparent. We cannot claim to have communicated an idea fully unless we have caught and expressed its tempo and its rhythm. We know the power of music to set the mood of an occasion. The rhythm of language can perform the same service for the speaker. Perhaps Robert G. Ingersoll has been our greatest master of this art. Read aloud the following passage from Ingersoll's Decoration Day oration in 1888, noting that the rhythm of each sentence is appropriate to the mood of its description and that the vividness of the description is greatly enhanced by it:

> The past rises before me like a dream. Again we are in the great struggle for national life. We hear the sounds of preparation; the music of the boisterous drums; the silver voices of heroic bugles. We see thousands of assemblages, and hear the appeals of orators. We see the pale cheeks of women, and the flushed faces of men; and in those assemblages we see all the dead whose dust we have covered with flowers. We lose sight of them no more. We are with them when they enlist in the great army of freedom. We see them part with those they love. Some are walking for the last time in quiet, woody places with the maidens they adore. We hear the whisperings and the sweet vows of eternal love as they lingeringly part forever. Others are bending over cradles, kissing babes that are asleep. Some are receiving the blessings of old men. Some are parting with mothers who hold them and press them to their hearts again and again and say nothing. Kisses and tears, tears and kisses—divine mingling of agony and joy! And some are talking with wives and endeavoring with brave words, spoken in the old tones, to drive from their hearts the awful fear. We see them part. We see the wife standing in the door with the babe in her arms—standing in the sunlight, sobbing. At the turn of the road a hand waves—she answers by holding high in her loving arms the child. He is gone, and forever.

Freshness of phrasing is achieved by saying things differently instead of in the old, trite way. Sometimes it requires but the slightest change from the trite to make a strikingly original thought, as when

Walter Matson writes of "an easy government job in the swivel service." It is good practice to take a series of overused phrases and to give the ideas they contain fresh, striking, and original expression. See how vivid you can make the following ideas by rephrasing them:

a lame excuse	more sinned against than sinning
a long-felt need	more truth than poetry
a sadder and a wiser man	nipped in the bud
at one fell swoop	poor but honest
beat a hasty retreat	sad but true
better late than never	silence reigned
each and every one	the depths of despair
hale and hearty	the fair sex
in this day and age	the inner man
institution of higher learning	the irony of fate
last but not least	the manly art of self-defense
method in his madness	too good to be true

Force

Good style penetrates. It strikes through barriers of indifference and makes an impression on the hearers' minds. Force is commonly thought of only as a product of delivery. It is that, of course, but it must also have a basis in the style of the speech. Force is achieved largely by concentration, repetition, elements of suspense and surprise, and forward movement to a climax.

Concentration may be achieved by the use of short, simple, unamplified sentences. Patrick Henry's "liberty or death" speech is a model of forceful address. It is also an excellent example of the staccato style, with the sentences coming in successive short, sharp thrusts. The average sentence length for the entire speech is only sixteen and a half words. But this does not begin to reveal the actual extent of the staccato quality of the speech, for almost every sentence is divided into a succession of very brief, self-contained clauses. Thus one sentence runs, "We have petitioned; we have remonstrated; we have supplicated . . . ." Speech style like this has the force of a trip hammer. The speaker's ideas become blows which fall so rapidly that they can scarcely be resisted.

Repetition serves to clarify ideas and to emphasize them. An example may be noted from a speech delivered in the United States in 1925 by the Hindu poet Rabindranath Tagore: "Europe has her past. Europe's strength therefore lies in her history. We, in India, must make up our minds that we cannot borrow other people's history, and that if we stifle our own we are committing suicide. When you borrow things that do not belong to your life, they only serve to crush your life."

The strength which may be given to an idea through the use of *suspense* and *surprise* is clearly seen in a paragraph taken from William Jennings Bryan's popular lecture "The Price of a Soul." Bryan asks, How much money can a man honestly earn in a lifetime? Can he earn as much as a million dollars? Or five hundred million? Here is his answer:

Not only do I believe that a man can earn five hundred million, but I believe that men have earned it. I believe that Thomas Jefferson earned more than five hundred millions. The service that he rendered to the world was of such great value that had he collected for it five hundred millions of dollars, he would not have been overpaid. I believe that Abraham Lincoln earned more than five hundred millions, and I could go back through history, and give you the name of man after man who rendered a service so large as to entitle him to collect more than five hundred million from society, but if I presented a list containing the name of every man who, since time began, earned such an enormous sum, one thing would be true of all of them, namely: that in not a single case did the man collect the full amount. The men who have earned five hundred million dollars have been so busy earning it that they have not had time to collect it; and the men who have collected five hundred million have been so busy collecting it that they have not had time to earn it.

Climax implies a building up toward a conclusion, either through suspense or through the increasing importance of what is said. In both cases, forcefulness results from the speaker's effectiveness in drawing and holding the attention of the audience at a more and more intense pitch. Sometimes a climax can be achieved in a short space, as in the celebrated passage from Cicero's condemnation of Verres: "It is an outrage to bind a Roman citizen; to scourge him is an atrocious crime; to put him to death is almost parricide; but to crucify him—what shall I call it?"

Usually, however, the element of climax must be interwoven through the entire speech. It may result from an obvious "pointing" of everything that is said to some conclusion which is to follow. It may arise from an increasing intensity in the speech or from the emotional force which the speech gradually accumulates. One extensive study has pointed out that a very common weakness in speech style is the lack of this resolute, unwavering, forward movement of every point to one final climax. Note how carefully the following speech, written by a student speaker, builds up to its climactic conclusion. List the various methods and devices by which this result is accomplished.

THE MAN WHOM NOBODY PRAISED

Men have praised Napoleon because the gesture of his hand could move the armies of all Europe; they have raised statues to Danton and Robespierre because their fiery eloquence could break, or make, a nation; they have written epics about the wild and reckless bravery of the French peasant, who hurled himself first upon the enthroned power of the dissolute Bourbons, then at the muskets of Europe's finest armies. But I would tell you of another man of this turbulent Revolutionary period who was renowned for none of these feats. Neither was he a great scientist, nor a singer, nor entitled in any way to posterity's praise, as mankind would dole it out. In an age of heroes and supermen, he was the man whom nobody praised.

I cannot even tell you his name, for such was the life he lived that no memory of him could be preserved. If you must have a name, I ask you to walk through the ivy-grown cemetery of some quiet countryside far removed from Paris, and there, amid the mouldering headstones of graves of ancient date, choose one of simple form, and bare of ornament. Pick out the broken, almost obscured letters on that stone, and have them struck on a medal of dull bronze. Carry that medal to your home and fix it on the mantelpiece above your fireplace, that your family life may center around that name as the home life of the ancient Romans centered about the daily worship at the shrine of the household gods. For that name will represent the noblest life to which man can aspire.

Let us call it Gaston Lefarge; the man a simple peasant of the Provence countryside. Let us provide him with a wife, and children, and a small, thatched cottage, with a vine growing over its single door. Let us follow him as he goes, in simple piety, twice weekly, to the little village church, and his children as they daily go to the same priest for lessons in reading, writing, and learning the catechism. Let us imagine him quietly working his tiny field, chatting with his neighbors, joining in the regular village meetings—yet withdrawing from the increasingly sharp debates—while the storm of the Revolution gradually rises higher and higher on the horizon, and the great French Beast paws and mangles the last of the senile Bourbons.

The Terror inflames the hearts of his neighbors. The drum beat of Napoleon calls them to battle, to conquest, and to death. Austerlitz arouses them to frenzied demonstrations of patriotism; Waterloo humbles them in fear of the vengeance of the restored Bourbons. But Gaston Lefarge hears only dim echoes of the swirl of events, and continues to work his land.

History has lamented the horror of the Revolution, while admiring the genius of its promoters. Historians have decried the useless violence and slaughter of Napoleon, while praising his military and administrative genius. Mankind has leaned upon, but despised, the truer genius of the truer man, who had the courage, amid the madness of the age, to continue living his life. Had we stuff worthy of the project, we should carve from it a magnificent statue of this man who was not the greatest of the great, nor the bravest of the brave, but, much better, the sanest of the sane, Gaston Lefarge, the Man Whom Nobody Praised.

Economy

There is a great difference in the meaning which two speakers may convey in a given time. One may go directly to the point he wishes to make—explain, support, and apply it—and go on to another idea, while the other, fumbling and awkward, is trying to get his first point expressed. Repetition, elaboration, and illustration are all valuable devices, but they should be kept strictly under your control. You should not let yourself repeat and amplify merely because you have no new thought to express. That style is best which requires your hearers to expend the least effort to understand. Be economical of their time and energy. Clearly, vividly, forcefully, and *concisely* set forth your ideas. Avoid useless digressions. Avoid putting anything into your speech that does not help you to achieve your purpose. Words not readily understood, sentences unduly complex, and mannerisms of expression which distract your audience's attention from your meaning are all enemies of economy in style. The economical style is crisp, pointed, and direct, and it progresses steadily and without variation toward the conclusion that you desire to reach. Economy in style respects the attention limits of man's mind. It is good not only from the standpoint of style but also from the standpoint of psychology to avoid confusing the listener by too numerous details.

An example of economical style is found in the following paragraphs from President Truman's speech to Congress in March, 1947, in which he defended aid to Greece:

No government is perfect. One of the chief virtues of a democracy, however, is that its defects are always visible and under democratic processes can be pointed out and corrected. The Government of Greece is not perfect. Nevertheless it represents 85 percent of the members of the Greek Parliament who were chosen in an election last year. Foreign observers, including 692 Americans, considered this election to be a fair expression of the views of the Greek people.

The Greek Government has been operating in an atmosphere of chaos and extremism. It has made mistakes. The extension of aid by this country does not mean that the United States condones everything that the Greek Government has done or will do. We have condemned in the past, and we condemn now, extremist measures of the Right or the Left. We have in the past advised tolerance, and we advise tolerance now.

PLEASING DICTION

An effective speaking style is pleasing to the ear. There are many occasions when beauty of speech may not be required, but it is seldom a handicap. Pleasing style is of increasing importance as the speech occasion becomes more formal and when the purpose, or one of the purposes, of the speech is to inspire. Some aspects of stylistic beauty have been touched upon earlier and need only reiteration and amplification here. The basic elements of pleasing style are the pictorial, the rhythmic, and the musical.

The *pictorial* includes figures of speech, concreteness, illustrations, and examples, all of which have been considered previously. Pictorial language is splendidly illustrated in one of the most famous of all speeches, the Sermon on the Mount. In that speech, as in all of his teachings, Jesus was never abstract when it was possible to be concrete. Note how greatly the beauty of the following passages is enhanced by the prolific use of imagery:

Behold the fowls of the air: for they sow not, neither do they reap, nor gather into barns; yet your heavenly Father feedeth them. Are ye not much better than they? . . . And why take ye thought for raiment? Consider the lilies of the field, how they grow; they toil not, neither do they spin: and yet I say unto you, that even Solomon in all his glory was not arrayed like one of these. Wherefore, if God so clothe the grass of the field, which today is, and tomorrow is cast into the oven, shall he not much more clothe you, O ye of little faith? . . .

Therefore, whosoever heareth these sayings of mine, and doeth them, I will liken him unto a wise man, which built his house upon a rock: and the rain descended, and the floods came, and the winds blew, and beat upon that house; and it fell not: for it was founded upon a rock. And everyone that heareth these sayings of mine and doeth them not, shall be likened unto a foolish man, which built his house upon the sand: and the rain descended, and the floods came, and the winds blew, and beat upon that house; and it fell: and great was the fall of it.

The pictorial quality was used to advantage by William Jennings Bryan when, in speaking against the tariff, he warned, "You cannot send a dollar laughing down into the pocket of one man, unless you bring it up crying out of the pocket of another." It is also exemplified in the sentences with which James G. Blaine closed his eulogy on President Garfield:

With a wan, fevered face, tenderly lifted to the cooling breeze, he looked out wistfully upon the ocean's changing wonders; on its far sails;

on its restless waves, rolling shoreward to break and die beneath the noonday sun; on the red clouds of evening, arching low to the horizon; on the serene and shining pathway of the stars. Let us think that his dying eyes read a mystic meaning which only the rapt and parting soul may know. Let us believe that in the silence of the receding world he heard the great waves breaking on a farther shore and felt already upon his wasted brow the breath of the eternal morning.

Each of these quotations, although chosen to illustrate the pictorial quality, is also an example of the *rhythmical*. It should be pointed out here that, in considering speech rhythm from the standpoint of its contribution to the beauty of style, we do not mean poetic meter. Whereas meter may be defined as a regular succession of poetic feet joined into a definite pattern of sound, speech rhythm is based upon the recurrence of similar, rather than identical, sound units. Rhythm is provided by parallel construction in sentences—by balance, antithesis, and phrases in series. The passages which have just been quoted are filled with parallelisms. Their sound patterns provide a rolling splendor which is a golden mean between two extremes: the prosaic on one hand and singsong regularity on the other.

Rhythm is one of the chief elements in the musical quality of style, but it is not the only one of importance. A *musical* quality should also be sought. A speaker should avoid, when possible, all such harsh, discordant combinations of sounds as "the short, sharp sapling," and "the withered wooden whistle." Some discordant combinations, such as "the Methodist Episcopal Church" cannot, of course, be eliminated. It is also advisable to avoid rhyming words within phrases or at the end of successive word groups. Such recurring sound patterns as "the proposition of the opposition" are neither beautiful nor clear. The value of alliteration as a contribution to ease of recall has been mentioned earlier. It should also be noted that a moderate use of alliteration may give to a speech a musical quality that is pleasing. Henry Drummond's sermon "The Greatest Thing in the World" offers a good example: "To love abundantly is to live abundantly, and to love forever is to live forever."

VOCABULARY AS A FOUNDATION OF STYLE

Speech style, when reduced to the basic elements of which it is constructed, must begin with the use of individual words. It was the realization of this fact which prompted Daniel Webster to answer a friend's question as to what reading he intended to do during a recess of Congress. He replied that he intended to read the dictionary. There are no true synonyms. There is never more than one word—sometimes not even one—to convey our exact and true meaning. Each of us may at times fall into the error of Lewis Carroll's Humpty-Dumpty and think, "When I use a word it means just what I choose it to mean—neither more nor less." But the art of conveying meaning is not that simple. Words must be used with the same care that any good workman devotes to his tools: he is careful to select the right one, and he is equally careful to use it expertly. It was Coleridge who phrased for us, in his *Biographia Literaria,* "the infallible test of a blameless style: namely, its untranslatableness in words of the same language, without injury to the meaning."

The highest excellencies of style cannot be attained without a mastery of words. An improved vocabulary is, then, a foundation which beginning speakers will do well to build. Unabridged dictionaries include definitions of some 600,000 terms—an indication of the variety of meanings which our language is capable of expressing. Yet the reading vocabulary of even college seniors is variously estimated at 30,000 to 70,000 words. Of these, only a relative few are readily usable in speaking. For of our four vocabularies (reading, listening, writing, and speaking), our reading vocabulary is the largest and our speaking vocabulary is the smallest. In an investigation of words used in private correspondence, there was found to be a total of only 2,000. The New York Telephone Company recorded ordinary telephone conversations totaling 80,000 words, and found they consisted of a vocabulary of only 2,040 words. It is evident that the average speaking and writing vocabularies are very small—at least in contrast to what they might be.

THE IMPORTANCE OF WORDS

There are five very good reasons why a speaker should be eager to increase his vocabulary:

The Relationship of Words to Thought

Some psychologists believe that thoughts and words are identical. It is impossible, they say, to have the former without the latter. To increase vocabulary is tantamount to increasing thinking capacity; to be without words is, in reality, to be without thoughts. Thus Max Müller, in his *Lectures on the Science of Language,* says, "To think is to speak low. To speak is to think aloud." Edward Sapir, in *Language,* declares that "thought is nothing but language denuded of its outward garb." Whether or not this rather extreme position is correct, it is undeniable that thoughts need words for their expression. James Stephens, the Irish poet and short-story writer, spoke of it thus:

A thought is a real thing, and words are only its raiment, but a thought is as shy as a virgin: unless it is fittingly appareled, we may not look on its shadowy nakedness; it will fly from us and only return again in the darkness, crying in a thin, childish voice which we may not comprehend until, with aching minds listening and divining, we at last fashion for it those symbols which are its protection and its banner.

Whether or not we believe that thought is impossible without words, it appears that the effectiveness of any one's thinking is seriously handicapped if his vocabulary is small. Speaking before the Royal College of Surgeons, Rudyard Kipling thus described their power:

I am by calling a dealer in words, and words are, of course, the most powerful drug used by mankind. Not only do words infect, egotize, narcotize, and paralyze, but they enter into and color the minutest cells of the brain very much as madder mixed with a stag's food at the zoo colors the growth of the animal's antlers.

The Relationship of Words to Leadership

"Give me the right word and the right accent," wrote Joseph Conrad, "and I will move the world." Surely the right word is a powerful force. Political campaigns are won with catchwords; merchandise is sold with slogans; audiences are moved to action by the right combinations of words. Almost all great leaders have been great speakers. A wide vocabulary, wisely used, commands respect. A leader who cannot easily, clearly, and fluently express himself is a rarity indeed.

The Relationship of Words to Earning Capacity

After testing thousands of individuals, from millworkers to major executives, to determine the causes of variation in earning capacity, Johnson O'Connor, of the Stevens Institute of Technology, reached the conclusion that "an extensive knowledge of the exact meanings of English words accompanies outstanding success in this country more often than any other single characteristic." Words, it would appear, have a great utilitarian value—a conclusion that is not strange, when we consider how closely they are related to effective thinking and leadership.

The Relationship of Words to Social Acceptability

The easy, fluent conversationalist, who does not have to hesitate and stumble about in search of words, has an obvious advantage in social situations over his less articulate associates. Sociability and silence seldom go together. Crudeness of speech, awkwardness and hesitancy in expression, and lame attempts to carry on a sprightly conversation within the bounds of a narrow vocabulary are all social handicaps. By acquiring a ready and wide command of words, these particular handicaps can be eliminated.

The Relationship of Words to Personal Satisfaction

Most people occasionally feel thwarted and baffled by an inability to express ideas that they feel are fluttering on the verge of their consciousness. For some this is a frequent occurrence. Many students attest that the acquisition of a broad vocabulary is one of their chief goals. When increased personal satisfaction is added to the other four reasons for broadening one's command of words, the arguments in favor of doing so become overwhelming.

HOW TO USE WORDS

Words should *not* be used to demonstrate the learning of the speaker, to impress or bedazzle the audience, or to conceal any weakness in the subject matter of the speech. The true function of words— to serve as a link of communication between speaker and hearer— should not be forgotten. Their primary function should be to transmit the speaker's meaning as clearly and effectively as possible. If words attract attention to themselves and away from the basic ideas, they are poorly used. This is the essential test to which any speaking style must be submitted.

To avoid this misuse, the speaker should always endeavor to use diction that is *appropriate*: appropriate to the audience, to the occasion, to the subject, and to himself. That the language must be fitted to the capacities of the hearers is apparent: if the speaker does not make himself understood, he might better save his breath. But this principle should not be overworked. In speaking to a profane group, for example, the speaker need not use profanity. In speaking to simple, uneducated people, he should use words that they can understand, but his diction should also possess expressiveness, vigor, accuracy, and vividness. Some occasions call for an informal, colloquial type of speech, some for formality and precision. Some subjects would appear grotesque if discussed in conversational terms, whereas a "literary" style would be ruinous to others. And with his attention given to these external requirements, the speaker should not neglect the necessity of conforming his language to himself. A speaker should bring to his audience his own personality, his own intellectual and cultural attainments. It is for these that he has been asked to speak. He can remain true to himself and yet speak with enough simplicity and directness to be readily understood.

A speaker should cultivate a diction that is simple and idiomatic. He may say, "I ascended the thoroughfare to your domicile," but it would be much better to say, "I went up the street to your house."

Another important consideration in the use of words is the distinction between their *denotation,* or their exact, scientific meaning, and their *connotation,* or the cluster of associated meanings which cling to them. In the following list, for example, the two words which make up each pair are fairly similar in denotation, but very far apart in connotation:

bookish—studious
effeminate—feminine
egotistical—self-confident
elocution—oral interpretation
fanaticism—religious devotion
fiddle—violin
flighty—imaginative
foolhardy—brave
hog—pork
house—home
informer—informant
job—position
lazy—leisurely
merciless—just

militarism—preparedness
nationalist—patriot
notoriety—fame
phlegmatic—unemotional
politician—statesman
pupil—student
radical—liberal
sensational—notable
sly—clever
stingy—economical
stink—odor
stubborn—determined
timid—cautious
wages—salary

Observe, also, the difference in the following two passages. The second is the closing paragraph of Lincoln's first Inaugural Address. The first is an earlier draft of the same passage. Notice how greatly the connotative value of the second passage surpasses the first:

I close. We are not, we must not be, aliens or enemies, but fellow countrymen. Although passion has strained our bonds of affection too hardly they must not, I am sure they will not, be broken. The mystic chords which, proceeding from so many battlefields and so many patriot graves, pass through all the hearths in the broad continent of ours, will yet again harmonize in their ancient music when breathed upon by the guardian angel of the nation.

I am loathe to close. We are not enemies, but friends. We must not be enemies. Though passion may have strained, it must not break, our bonds of affection. The mystic chords of memory, stretching from every battle-field and patriot grave to every living heart and hearthstone all over this broad land, will yet swell the chorus of the Union when again touched, as surely they will be, by the better angels of our nature.

VOCABULARY BUILDING

Cultivating a love for words is the one indispensable prerequisite for developing a broad vocabulary. Collecting words has the same fascination for some people that collecting stamps or old coins has for others. Every new word represents an adventure in intellectual discovery. What does it mean? How did it get its meaning? What is the story behind its origin and development? Look up, for example, the etymology of "candidate," "ballot," "boycott," "supercilious," "gaudy," "book," and "tragedy." Each of these words has a history that is unusually picturesque; but every word, as Ralph Waldo Emerson said, is a poem in miniature. When one comes to regard the dictionary not merely as a useful handbook but as a fascinating anthology, the way to a richer vocabulary has been opened.

Out of the love for words should grow a systematic program of word mastery. The following suggestions offer a basis for such a program:

1. *Examine your reading vocabulary* to identify the words in it which you only half know, and master them sufficiently so that you can use them freely in your speech. For a start, examine the following list of words. Are any of them wholly unfamiliar? Are there any that you feel perfectly confident you can define without looking them up in a dictionary? Define each one, with the help of the dictionary if neces-sary, and keep it in mind for use whenever appropriate.

apocryphal	bituminous	coalesce
artesian	cadaver	crypt
basilisk	callow	damask
bathos	chimerical	denizen

desultory	jetty	orgies
distemper	libertine	orthodox
dog days	lucubration	rational
dormant	mausoleum	resilient
dysentery	mellifluous	salutatory
ethereal	mercurial	stultify
farce	militate	surfeit
fascist	misanthrope	theology
flexure	mitigate	unctuous
gerrymander	moratorium	virtual
glandular	neophyte	visionary

2. *Study word families,* which grow from single roots. What, for instance, do the following words have in common; host, hostage, hospital, hotel, hospitality? What is the root of the following words: loquacious, prologue, logic, logarithm, apology? Look up the common root for each of the following words: moment, remote, movie, mobilize, motif, mob; feature, difficult, artifice, faculty, official, effect, versification, facsimile; avocation, vowel, voice, advocate, vociferous; exact, manager, pedagogue, agenda, actor, actuate; and gender, gentile, gentle, genius, generous.

3. *Study the Thorndike list of 25,000 words most commonly used in English.* With his assistants, E. L. Thorndike has counted 10,000,000 consecutive words in English and American writings and upon that basis has determined the frequency with which the words occur. The 25,000 most commonly used words are found in the *Thorndike Century Junior Dictionary,* with a number after each to indicate in which thousandth it appears. Thus "crown" appears in the first thousand, "dispense" in the fifth, "coincidence" in the tenth, and "scone" in the twentieth. By a systematic study of Thorndike's list, you can be reasonably sure of learning those new words which will prove of most value in your ordinary reading and speaking.

4. *Rephrase the thoughts of someone else* as a means of enlarging your vocabulary. The rephrasing might take the form of translation from a foreign language, of précis writing, of expanding and enlarging the ideas, or of reproducing them essentially as they are found but in your own words. All of these methods require exact and discriminating knowledge of words. In précis writing, the problem is to find comprehensive words, so that the entire sense of the passage can be expressed in about one third of the original length. Expanding an idea offers an excellent opportunity to develop a fund of synonyms and parallel expressions. A rephrasing of a passage in your own words

offers you an opportunity to compare your vocabulary and effectiveness in using it with the word mastery of the original writer or speaker. As a boy, Abraham Lincoln took advantage of every opportunity to hear an itinerant preacher; he would then go into the woods, climb upon a stump, and repeat in his own words the sermon he had heard. This was the finest sort of practice.

5. *Play games with words* as a pleasant method of vocabulary building. Such word games as anagrams and acrostics have long been enjoyed. Crossword puzzles have been popular since the early 1920's. An old parlor game that has recently come into wide popularity consists of making as many words as possible out of a selected phrase (such as "fall weather"), a name (such as "General Motors Corporation"), or a group of letters (such as "lriap," "trieaml," "abetinor," or "eessly").

6. *Read widely, listen carefully, and use a dictionary for looking up all doubtful words.* This is an indispensable method of building vocabulary. A good dictionary readily available is a necessity for whatever methods of vocabulary development you choose to use.

CONCLUSION

The style of the spoken word may not be improved merely by a sense of beauty in language, by an originality and individuality of expression, by an accurate vocabulary and a command of the mechanics of grammar, by ideas expressed in wordings that will live, by phraseologies which move men to action—but by all these together.

Although there are many requirements of good style which pertain to both speaker and writer, there are some differences of which the speaker should be aware. These arise largely from the speaker's need to adapt his thought more directly and personally to his listeners and to be instantly understood. The speaker will thus make greater use than will the writer of questions, exclamatory and imperative sentences, and clarifying and unifying connectives.

An effective speaking style is clear and simple. It is also easily remembered: it has vividness, force, and economy. And it is pleasing to the ear: it has beauty and rhythm. Basic to all that the speaker may do to improve his style are the cultivation of a respect for exact diction and the development of skill in utilizing the emotional power of words.

The speaker's vocabulary is a foundation of style. Every man depends heavily upon words; they determine to a surprising extent his ability to think, his capacity for leadership, his earning capacity, his social acceptability, and his personal satisfaction.

EXERCISES AND BIBLIOGRAPHY

Exercises

1. Study the following passages, and distinguish between the good style and the bad. Some passages contain examples of both:

> Sir, you may destroy this little institution; it is weak; it is in your hands! I know it is one of the lesser lights on the literary horizon of our country: You may put it out. But if you do so you must carry through your work! You must extinguish, one after another, all those greater lights of science which for more than a century have thrown their radiance over our land. It is, sir, as I have said, a small college. And yet there are those who love it.

> I was not afraid that our curious expedition would be prevented by such apprehensions, but I doubted that it would not be possible to prevail on Dr. Johnson to relinquish for some time the felicity of a London life, which, to a man who can enjoy it with full intellectual relish, is apt to make existence in any narrower sphere seem insipid or irksome. I doubted that he would not be willing to come down from his elevated state of philosophical dignity; from a superiority of wisdom among the wise and of learning among the learned; and from flashing his wit upon minds bright enough to reflect it.

> As to the charge that he was a "trimmer," he said: "If they say to you that Borah is trimming, that he does not take a stand, ask them upon what question, upon what issue, upon what measure in Congress or this campaign he has failed to take an open and decided and positive stand. Ask them if they have any doubt as to what his position will be on all these questions in the coming Congress. What policy which touches the interest of the people of this State have I not met openly and candidly? If so, state them. What question is there tonight that touches your interest or your welfare or the welfare of the people of this State about which you entertain any possible doubt as to my position? It is because I am positive upon all these questions that the opposition is coming from certain sources to my re-election. It is because I refuse to yield my views or modify my position on certain public questions that they are dissatisfied with me. If I were more

uncertain they would be far more certain as to their support of me. If I were a little more unsteady they would be more steadfast. Do you people want a representative in the Senate who is uncertain as to policies and well hitched up to individuals—who would yield his views and modify his opinions to harmonize with the views of those whom you do not elect to represent you? A man who will not stand for what he thinks is right at home regardless of individuals or candidates at the head or tail of the ticket will not stand up for them at Washington, and God pity the miserable creature sailing upon that turbulent political sea at Washington without convictions for a compass. I have seen them and there is nothing more despicable in the world besides. Men without poise and purpose, without convictions and determination, who do not stand ready to fight for their views regardless of who opposes them upon all these great questions, are the miserable instruments by which men of sinister purposes accomplish their design. There is not a public question, not a public issue that I am not ready to discuss with men or before the people in this campaign. I am for measures, not men, and I will make my campaign on that line regardless of political consequence."

In discussing the President's proposed reorganization of the judicial system, I am told that I am to trespass a little on the Columbia Symphony Orchestra on this peaceful Sunday afternoon. I'm sorry. I wouldn't mind crashing some commercial hour. But to infringe politically on these great musical programs is like tin-canning a dog in the apse of a cathedral.

Now, listen! In spite of the yellow messengers predicting destruction that we are now receiving daily, we have the green light from the people to go ahead. And we are going.

The shadows that now lie dark upon our path will soon be dispelled and we shall walk with the light all about us if we but be true to ourselves—to ourselves as we have wished to be known in the counsels of the world and in the thought of all those who love liberty and justice and the right exalted.

It was a crisp and spicy morning in early October. The lilacs and laburnums, lit with the glory-fires of autumn, hung burning and flashing in the upper air, a fairy bridge provided by kind Nature for the wingless wild things that have their homes in the tree-tops and would visit together; the larch and the pomegranate flung their purple and yellow flames in brilliant broad splashes along the slanting sweep of the woodland; the sensuous fragrance of innumerable deciduous flowers rose upon the swooning atmosphere; far in the empty sky a solitary esophagus slept upon motionless wing; everywhere brooded stillness, serenity, and the peace of God.

2. Prepare a three-minute speech built around an idea suggested to you by some literary quotation. Pay particular attention to your use of words. The following are suggested quotations:

> Baby said
>   When she smelt the rose,
> Oh! what a pity
> I've only one nose.
> —LAURA ELIZABETH RICHARDS.

Every intellectual product must be judged from the point of view of the age and the people in which it was produced.—WALTER PATER.

Give me the young man who has brains enough to make a fool of himself.—ROBERT LOUIS STEVENSON.

Good as it is to inherit a library, it is better to collect one.—AUGUSTINE BIRRELL.

> He has married been,
> And so on earth has suffered for all sin.
> —GEORGE BIRDSEYE.

The Ancient Mariner would not have taken so well if it had been called *The Old Sailor*.—SAMUEL BUTLER.

Important principles may and must be flexible.—ABRAHAM LINCOLN.

Poverty is the parent of revolution and crime.—ARISTOTLE.

More men are killed by overwork than the importance of the world justifies.—RUDYARD KIPLING.

'Tis the fault of all art to seem antiquated and faded in the eyes of the succeeding generation.—ANDREW LANG.

Knowledge and timber shouldn't be much used till they are seasoned.—OLIVER WENDELL HOLMES.

A man's truest monument must be a man.—MINOT JUDSON SAVAGE

> This world is a difficult world, indeed,
>   And people are hard to suit. . . .
> —WALTER LEARNED.

In the life of a young man the most essential thing for happiness is the gift of friendship.—WILLIAM OSLER.

The Forgotten Man works and votes—generally he prays—but his chief business in life is to pay.—WILLIAM G. SUMNER.

The ignorant man always adores what he cannot understand.—CESARE LOMBROSO.

We must be as courteous to a man as we are to a picture, which we are willing to give the advantage of a good light.—RALPH WALDO EMERSON.

The office of government is not to confer happiness, but to give men opportunity to work out happiness for themselves.—WILLIAM ELLERY CHANNING.

It is with narrow-souled people as with narrow-necked bottles; the less they have in them the more noise they make in pouring out.—ALEXANDER POPE.

It is generally better to deal by speech than by letter.—FRANCIS BACON.

Bibliography

Brigance, William Norwood, ed., *A History and Criticism of American Public Address* (2 vols.; McGraw-Hill, 1943).

Brigance, William Norwood, *Speech Composition* (2d ed.; Appleton-Century-Crofts, 1953).

Ferguson, Charles W., *Say It with Words* (Knopf, 1959).

Fowler, Henry W., *A Dictionary of Modern English Usage* (4th ptg.; Oxford, 1950).

Hochmuth, Marie, W. N. Brigance, and Donald Bryant, *A History and Criticism of American Public Address* (Longmans, Green, 1955), Vol. III.

Strunk, William Jr., with revisions by E. B. White, *The Elements of Style* (Macmillan, 1959).

Thonssen, Lester, and A. Craig Baird, *Speech Criticism: The Development of Standards for Rhetorical Appraisal* (Ronald, 1948).

ILLUSTRATIVE SPEECH

Read the following speech to note especially its stylistic qualities. Although it was delivered on an unusually cold and snowy day, why would it have been inappropriate for the speaker to refer to this fact, or to make any other specific references to the audience situation? What qualities of style were enhanced or improved by the fact that the speech was written out in full? Find specific illustrations of as many as you can of stylistic factors discussed in this chapter.

Inaugural Address

BY JOHN F. KENNEDY

Delivered by President Kennedy at the Capitol, Washington, D.C.,
January 20, 1961.

MY FELLOW CITIZENS:

We observe today not a victory of party but a celebration of freedom—symbolizing an end as well as a beginning—signifying renewal as well as change. For I have sworn before you and Almighty God the same solemn oath our forebears prescribed nearly a century and three quarters ago.

The world is very different now. For man holds in his mortal hands the power to abolish all form of human poverty and to abolish all form of human life. And, yet, the same revolutionary beliefs for which our forebears fought are still at issue around the globe—the belief that the rights of man come not from the generosity of the state but from the hand of God.

We dare not forget today that we are the heirs of that first revolution. Let the word go forth from this time and place, to friend and foe alike, that the torch has been passed to a new generation of Americans—born in this century, tempered by war, disciplined by a cold and bitter peace, proud of our ancient heritage—and unwilling to witness or permit the slow undoing of those human rights to which this nation has always been committed, and to which we are committed today.

Let every nation know, whether it wish us well or ill, that we shall pay any price, bear any burden, meet any hardship, support any friend or oppose any foe in order to assure the survival and success of liberty.

This much we pledge—and more.

To those old Allies whose cultural and spiritual origins we share, we pledge the loyalty of faithful friends. United, there is little we cannot do in a host of new co-operative ventures. Divided, there is little we can do—for we dare not meet a powerful challenge at odds and split asunder.

To those new states whom we now welcome to the ranks of the free, we pledge our word that one form of colonial control shall not have passed merely to be replaced by a far more iron tyranny. We shall not always expect to find them supporting our every view. But we shall always hope to find them strongly supporting their own freedom—and to remember that, in the past, those who foolishly sought to find power by riding on the tiger's back inevitably ended up inside.

To those peoples in the huts and villages of half the globe struggling to break the bonds of mass misery, we pledge our best efforts to help them help themselves, for whatever period is required—not because the Communists are doing it, not because we seek their votes, but because it is right. If the free society cannot help the many who are poor, it can never save the few who are rich.

To our sister republics south of our border, we offer a special pledge —to convert our good words into good deeds—in a new alliance for progress—to assist free men and free Governments in casting off the chains of poverty. But this peaceful revolution of hope cannot become the prey of hostile powers. Let all our neighbors know that we shall join with them to oppose aggression or subversion anywhere in the Americas. And let every other power know that this Hemisphere intends to remain the master of its own house.

To that world assembly of sovereign states, the United Nations, our last best hope in an age where the instruments of war have far outpaced the instruments of peace, we renew our pledge of support—to prevent its becoming merely a forum for invective—to strengthen its shield of the new and the weak—and to enlarge the area to which its writ may run.

Finally, to those nations who would make themselves our adversary, we offer not a pledge but a request: that both sides begin anew the quest for peace, before the dark powers of destruction unleashed by science engulf all humanity in planned or accidental self-destruction.

We dare not tempt them with weakness. For only when our arms are sufficient beyond doubt can we be certain beyond doubt that they will never be employed.

But neither can two great and powerful groups of nations take comfort from their present course—both sides overburdened by the cost of modern weapons, both rightly alarmed by the steady spread of the deadly atom, yet both racing to alter that uncertain balance of terror that stays the hand of mankind's final war.

So let us begin anew—remembering on both sides that civility is not a sign of weakness and sincerity is always subject to proof. Let us never negotiate out of fear. But let us never fear to negotiate.

Let both sides explore what problems unite us instead of belaboring the problems that divide us.

Let both sides, for the first time, formulate serious and precise proposals for the inspection and control of arms—and bring the absolute power to destroy other nations under the absolute control of all nations.

Let both sides join to invoke the wonders of science instead of its terrors. Together let us explore the stars, conquer the deserts, eradicate disease, tap the ocean depths and encourage the arts and commerce.

Let both sides unite to heed in all corners of the earth the command of Isaiah—to "undo the heavy burdens . . . (and) let the oppressed go free."

And if a beachhead of co-operation can be made in the jungles of suspicion, let both sides join in the next task: creating, not a new balance of power, but a new world of law, where the strong are just and the weak secure and the peace preserved forever.

All this will not be finished in the first 100 days. Nor will it be finished in the first 1,000 days, nor in the life of this Administration, nor even perhaps in our lifetime on this planet. But let us begin.

In your hands, my fellow citizens, more than in mine, will rest the final success or failure of our course. Since this country was founded, each generation has been summoned to give testimony to its national loyalty. The graves of young Americans who answered that call encircle the globe.

Now the trumpet summons us again—not as a call to bear arms, though arms we need—not as a call to battle, though embattled we are—but a call to bear the burden of a long twilight struggle, year in and year out, "rejoicing in hope, patient in tribulation"—a struggle against the common enemies of man: tyranny, poverty, disease and war itself.

Can we forge against these enemies a grand and global alliance, north and south, east and west, that can assure a more fruitful life for all mankind? Will you join in that historic effort?

In the long history of the world, only a few generations have been granted the role of defending freedom in its hour of maximum danger. I do not shrink from this responsibility—I welcome it. I do not believe that any of us would exchange places with any other people or any other generation. The energy, the faith and the devotion which we bring to this endeavor will light our country and all who serve it— and the glow from that fire can truly light the world.

And so, my fellow Americans: Ask not what your country will do for you—ask what you can do for your country.

My fellow citizens of the world: Ask not what America will do for you, but what together we can do for the freedom of man.

Finally, whether you are citizens of America or of the world, ask of us the same high standards of strength and sacrifice that we shall ask of you. With a good conscience our only sure reward, with history the final judge of our deeds, let us go forth to lead the land we love, asking His blessing and His help, but knowing that here on earth God's work must truly be our own.

Part Four

PRESENTING THE SPEECH

CHAPTER 13

CONTENTS

These successive shots of a speaker at a political rally offer striking testimony to the expressive power of the human countenance, posture, and gestures. Note how the speaker's appearance—not merely his facial expression and his gestures but also his bodily tension—changes as he proceeds from point to point. Even without hearing the speech, listeners form impressions of the speaker's personality. (Underwood & Underwood)

IMPROVING BODILY
EXPRESSIVENESS

> When Demosthenes was asked what was the first part of oratory, he answered "Action"; and which was the second, he replied, "Action"; and which was the third, he still answered, "Action."—PLUTARCH

AN audience is influenced not only by the words that a speaker utters but by his accompanying actions, gestures, and facial expressions. For actions do speak more loudly than words. Two persons may each say "Good morning" to us, precisely the same two words, yet the accompanying facial expressions and actions (as well as the quality of voice) may make all the difference in the world to the meaning of those two words. If you wish to make a simple test to determine whether diction or action is more effective in speech, try this on a classmate: as you approach a door together, step graciously ahead and throw open the door with every physical indication that you wish your companion to precede you. But say, *"After* me, please!" Unless your companion is on guard the response will be to your action rather than to your contrary words.

THE IMPORTANCE OF BODILY ACTION

Speakers use both a *visual code* and an *auditory code*. It may not always be true that, in the words of an ancient Chinese proverb, "One picture is worth ten thousand words," but it is surely true that our understanding and our judgment are powerfully affected by what we see. "Seeing is believing." If someone should say to you, "I am tremendously excited by this," while at the same time his body drooped languidly and his hands flopped limply by his side, you would laugh with disbelief. Indeed, the television comics use disparity between their words and their actions as a primary source of humor.

During what is known as the Elocutionary Period (about 1775 to 1890) professional speakers undoubtedly overemphasized gestures. A Frenchman named Delsarte worked out an elaborate system in which specific gestures were supposed to indicate particular emotions. In the textbooks on speech of that period, drawings were inserted to show speakers exactly what gestures to use to accompany various types of expression. The result was wooden, cumbersome, and artificial. Eventually, most speech teachers revolted against formalism in the study of gestures and began to advise students to be "natural."

In conversation we all use a great many gestures and facial expressions. Students of speech have often been told to let themselves go, to relax, to do what comes naturally, on the theory that if they escape from the inhibitions of fear and self-consciousness while speaking, the gestures they use will be appropriate.

A reaction against this rather extreme laissez-faire attitude toward the use of gestures in speaking has been initiated not so much by speech teachers as by anthropologists and sociologists. These students of human societies have made extensive studies of social groups and have discovered that "group identity" is established and indicated to a considerable extent by typical gestures. For example, La Barre points out that among the Japanese a smile does not indicate amusement but simple politeness;[1] Ruesch and Kees declare that when the Germans use gestures or change bodily posture they do so merely to indicate their own internal feelings, whereas the French "desire to display style and taste in word, gesture, and action."[2] McCarthy, a specialist in child development, observes that some children develop a gesture language so effective that they feel no need for words;[3] and Schlauch, studying Russian children, has found that when there is a lack of bodily expressiveness, there is also a loss of fluency, a reduction in size of vocabulary, and a muffling of articulation.[4]

Historically, the importance of gesture in human communication is well known. Sworn to silence, the Trappist monks developed a sign vocabulary of 400 items; the Benedictine monks devised a vocabulary of 460 specific gestures. Finger talk among deaf-mutes originated at least 800 years ago; Helen Keller developed sufficient skill to "speak" with her fingers at the rate of 80 words a minute. The Cheyenne tribe of American Indians possessed a sign language with a vocabulary of 7,000 items. Secret sign languages of an elaborate nature have been

[1] Weston La Barre, "The Cultural Basis of Emotions and Gestures," *Journal of Personality,* XVI (1947), 49–68.

[2] Juergen Ruesch and Weldon Kees, *Nonverbal Communication* (University of California Press, 1956).

[3] "Language Development in Children," in Carl Murchison, *Handbook of Child Psychology* (Clark University Press, 1931).

[4] Margaret Schlauch, "Soviet Studies in Linguistics," *Science and Society,* I (1936), 152–67

developed by the Chinese Hung Society, the Sicilian Mafia, the Thugs of India, and other outlawed groups.[5] Despite all the diversity, basic sign language is sufficiently uniform so that 100 American Indian tribes, speaking 100 different languages, nonetheless could communicate on a simple plane through the use of mutually understood gestures.

Another fact noted by sociologists is that certain types of gestures indicate social position. Among these are table mannerisms, such as how the fork is grasped, and how the little finger is held while tea is being drunk. Whether or not one picks his teeth, how he uses his handkerchief, and whether and how he rubs his hands on his face are all "status symbols." An individual who shuffles his feet when he walks, and who walks or stands with drooping shoulders is likely to be regarded as "lower class." Refinement in hand gestures is often considered a sign of cultural maturity.

What can be communicated by gestures and facial and bodily movements is indicated by the estimate of Sir Richard Paget that some 700,000 distinct elementary signs can be produced by combining various gestures and movements of the upper arm, forearm, wrist, and fingers.[6] Professor Krout believes that the human hand is 20,000 times as versatile as the human mouth in producing understandable signs.[7] Anyone who has played poker knows how difficult it is to refrain from signaling meanings with the eyes, hands, or facial or postural movements. Alice Meynell, the essayist, depicted the power of gesture when she wrote: "When the Cardinal in the Vatican, with his dramatic Italian hands, bids the kneeling groups to arise, he does more than bid them. He lifts them, he gathers them up, far and near, with the gesture of both arms; he takes them to their feet with the compulsion of his expressive force."[8]

Ray L. Birdwhistell, Professor of Anthropology at the University of Buffalo, has originated the study of what he calls "kinesics," a study of bodily motions as a form of communication. The language of gestures, he believes, is just as real as spoken language—and important to understand, for it often reveals far more accurately than spoken words what the individual really means. "People, even actors," he says, "can't act well enough not to send some signals of their true feelings about what they're doing." In reporting on Dr. Birdwhistell's studies,

[5] Maurice H. Krout, *Introduction to Social Psychology* (Harper, 1942), pp. 748–803.
[6] Sir Richard Paget, *Human Speech* (Kegan, Paul, 1930).
[7] Krout, p. 323.
[8] Alice Meynell, *Collected Essays* (Burns and Oates, 1914).

Time magazine (July 15, 1957) summarizes some of his analyses of the bodily actions of various television stars:

GARRY MOORE. By limiting his gestures and movements to those he would make in conversation with people only a few feet away, he "keeps his motions congruous with the distance his audiences are from their TV sets" and comes across "as a nice guy in a chat with a neighbor."

DINAH SHORE. "Her tilted head, her feet-together position, the outward thrust of her palms and the rolling of her hands make her seem as though she's surprised at her success, that she's delighted at being listened to."

ED SULLIVAN. His reputation as "the great stone face" stems only partly from an occasional deadpan expression; his stiff body contributes the rest of the impression. Even so, the reputation is unjustified, because sharp-eyed Dr. Birdwhistell has found that, by actual count, his face motions are average for the U.S.—"less than someone from Atlanta, but more than someone from Buffalo."

NEED FOR STUDY OF BODILY ACTION

Since the evidence shows that all of us normally use a great deal of bodily action, and since the kinds we use are typical of our own personality and of our social groups, merely to advise speakers to be "natural" when they speak might seem to be enough. However, it is obvious simply from watching a series of speeches by untrained speakers (no matter how great their experience) that it is not. Moreover, when untrained speakers are told that they must "gesture"—and especially if they are taught to rehearse their gestures—the results are almost certain to be highly artificial. There is, however, a mid-position. It is possible to use gesture as a means of communication with increasing effectiveness without becoming stilted or artificial. You must realize that whenever you speak words (as well as when you do not) your body, your face, and your hands are also speaking. You cannot prevent yourself from "gesturing." However much you try to prevent it, you project meanings by the *visual code*. What you need to learn is how to manage and control these messages.

Unconscious Communication

What we utter in words is normally what we intend to say and usually to a high degree represents what we wish to say; on the other hand, our "language of action" is to a far greater degree an unconscious communication—often saying what we have no intention of expressing, and sometimes directly contradicting our spoken words.

One reason for this disparity was explained by Charles Morris, in his introduction to George Herbert Mead's *Mind, Self, and Society*: "We hear ourselves talk, as others do, but we do not see our facial expressions, nor normally watch our own actions." Consequently, we tend to "correct" any mistakes we may make in our spoken discourse, while we permit unintended messages flowing from our bodily expressiveness to go unchallenged.

Another reason why our bodily meanings are likely to be unconscious or unintended is that we are unaware how much our posture reveals. In a handbook released by the Japanese Government in the spring of 1959 as a guide for Tokyo policemen, this injunction is included: "Always stand at attention when telephoning; otherwise your slouch will show in your voice." Speakers over the radio are properly advised to gesture freely and to stand in a relaxed but erect posture, for their bearing is evident in their voice.

Prepared Gestures

The argument that rehearsing gestures necessarily makes them artificial is refuted by both common sense and observation. We must "learn" the words we use, and often they may actually be wholly or partly memorized; yet in general we manage to make our speech sound natural and spontaneous. Why cannot the same be true of gesturing—provided we give as much attention to our bodily movements as we do to our words? As a matter of fact, television and stage actors do "memorize" a great many of their actions. Elvis Presley, Groucho Marx, Bob Hope, and indeed all actors develop more or less typical patterns of facial and bodily action which identify them and help to signal to the audience the "stock emotions" with which they work. In order to be effective, they have to master their action to such a degree that, when viewed by the public, it gives "the illusion of the first time"—or, in other words, it appears to be genuinely spontaneous. Watch any skillful actor and you will confirm the fact that his acting skill expresses itself through studied use of action as well as in the way he speaks his lines.

Discursive versus Presentational Communication

Words are said to be "discursive" because they follow one another, one at a time. Thus, when you are uttering (or hearing or reading or writing) words, you produce or encounter the intended meaning only a bit at a time. This fact is a handicap to complete communication, since there is a natural tendency to guess at what is coming next—to "leap ahead" of the speaker, to jump to conclusions that may not be warranted. Similarly, by the time one sentence is spoken, you may have forgotten an important qualifying statement that was uttered some time previously. It is from such causes as these that much misunderstanding occurs.

On the other hand, the *visual code* is "presentational"—which means that what it communicates is seen "all of one piece," much as a cartoon is seen. The meanings may not be fully spelled out or carefully discriminated; but if you stand as though you are excited, if your face radiates extreme interest, and if your muscles are tense, the observer instantly gets the impression of excitement. Calmness, thoughtfulness, doubt, anger, sympathy, and many other feelings or attitudes are also signaled in a flash by bodily behavior. Moreover, since these meanings (unlike what is said in words) make their impact upon the observer all at once, their influence is powerfully felt. When the words contradict what the body says, it is likely to be the body that is believed.

THE PRINCIPLE OF EMPATHY

The student of bodily action will find it helpful to understand the principle of *empathy*. A hint as to the meaning of the word is given by its similarity to the word "sympathy." Empathy is a sort of sympathetic muscular response. If you have ever sat in an audience watching a juggler perform some difficult act and have found yourself almost reaching out as though to help him recover an object he narrowly avoids dropping, you have experienced an empathic response. You are also responding empathically when at an exciting football game you find yourself reacting physically as though to assist your favorite team as it hits the opposing line.

The same phenomenon occurs when an entire audience responds physically in sympathy with a speaker's action. This may best be illustrated by the common expression, "They were so quiet you could have heard a pin drop." This means that the breathing rate of every member of the audience is synchronized so completely with that of the speaker that all are literally holding their breath with him at a moment of climax. Such muscular response depends upon the speaker's employing a stimulating action pattern.

When you see the members of an audience clenching their fists in support of a speaker's emphatic utterances, or when you sense their physical relaxation following a moment of tenseness in the speaker's story, you know that the speaker has been getting a complete audience reaction. The speaker's action has stimulated this response.

Just what value does the empathic response have for speech, and what is its relation to bodily activity on the part of the speaker? It is clear that the speaker, in delivering a speech, is trying to stir up meanings in his hearers' minds. The term "stir up" is used advisedly, for it is impossible to *transfer* meanings from one mind to another. The speaker can merely provide stimuli which are designed to cause the kinds of response he desires. We have seen that people react with their muscles as well as with their nervous systems and that this muscular reaction is a necessary part of the perception of meaning. The listeners will not, therefore, respond as the speaker desires unless they make the proper muscular adjustments while they are listening to him. In making these muscular adjustments, they will be greatly aided if he sets up patterns for them to imitate. Therefore the speaker not only should use bodily action but should take care to use precisely the kind that will stir up the desired responses in his audience.

The principle of empathy should be considered in connection with directing the type of response desired from the audience as well as in deciding what kind of action to use. To every movement made by the speaker the audience will respond by covert imitation. If the audience is composed of people who ordinarily make considerable use of their muscles—a group of day laborers, for example—a great deal of activity on the part of the speaker is desirable. The listeners are accustomed to using their muscles; they are therefore more comfortable and will pay better attention if they are given opportunities to respond muscularly to the speech. If, on the other hand, the audience is composed of people who lead relatively inactive lives and whose muscles are soft from disuse, a great deal of action on the part of the speaker tires and hence, as they say, "disgusts" them. A soap-box orator addressing laborers on a downtown street corner must use a great deal of action to hold the interest of the crowd. A speaker addressing an academic audience or a professional group should confine his action to fine adjustments and relatively reserved movements.

VALUES OF ACTION FOR THE SPEAKER

The speaker will find that the use of a reasonable amount of overt action is of great value to him, completely apart from its effect upon the audience. As was seen in the discussion of stage fright in Chapter

3, speakers may become too tense, especially in the beginning of their speeches, to be able to control themselves effectively. The best way partly to relax the large skeletal muscles is to use them. Hence a speaker can gain control of his body and help to overcome his stage fright by moving about on the platform and by gesturing. This action will help to take his attention from himself, will increase his confidence, and will thus put him at his ease. Furthermore, if the speaker is properly keyed up, he will have a great deal of excess energy which, throughout the course of his talk, will have to be relieved in some way. Many speakers release this energy by aimless movements or by toying with a pencil or eyeglasses. This, of course, distracts the audience. In learning proper use of bodily action, the speaker must learn to perform the actions which assist him as well as the audience. The speaker should plan to use enough purposive action so that he will not have to indulge in any movement solely to drain his excess nervous energy.

VALUES OF ACTION FOR THE AUDIENCE

From the standpoint of the audience, bodily action is useful in three ways: it helps to clarify the speaker's meaning; it helps to reveal the speaker's attitudes; and it helps to indicate the relative importance of various parts of the speech.

Clarifying the Speaker's Meaning

When the speaker is indicating the size, shape, or position of an object, he can greatly help his audience to visualize his meaning by using descriptive gestures. Similarly, in indicating the twofold division of a subject, he may use his two hands. In enumerating a series of points, he may extend his fingers successively, as the points are mentioned, to make it easier for the audience to follow his outline. In describing a violent struggle, the speaker may make the situation clearer by the use of a few vigorous gestures, although he should take care not to let his speaking turn into acting. The speaker's meaning may be further clarified for the audience if he uses bodily action as punctuation—to set off one idea from another and to make transitions between main points of the speech.

Revealing the Speaker's Attitudes

The effective use of bodily action by the speaker may help to clarify his attitudes. Certain general psychological reactions are suggested by specific bodily actions. To indicate a close, intimate relation with his audience, the speaker may step toward it and, if he is on a platform, lean forward a bit. If he is denouncing something and wishes to suggest strong aversion, he may do so by pushing his hand away from him, with the palm down. The suggestion of aversion is intensified if the speaker at the same time steps back. If he is earnestly presenting a plan which he wishes to have the audience consider favorably, the speaker may step forward, with his hands outstretched, palms up, as though he were offering something to his audience. To suggest doubt or indecision, he may raise his hands somewhat, with the palms up, at the same time that his shoulders are slightly shrugged.

In general, the speaker will aim for just as much individuality in his attitude-revealing gestures as is compatible with the following likely interpretations from his audience: (1) stepping back, pushing away with the hands, and shaking the head indicate rejection, dislike, refusal, condemnation, and similar negative feelings; (2) stepping forward, raising the hands (especially with the palms up), drawing in with the arms, leaning the body forward, and nodding the head indicate acceptance, a favorable reaction, praise, recommendation of a proposal, and similar affirmative feelings.

Indicating the Relative Importance of Parts of the Speech

The attention of an audience is certain to lag at times during the course of a speech. Since this is inevitable, the speaker may well accept the fact and make up his mind that some things he says will not make much impression. When he comes to points of chief importance, however, he wants to be sure that his entire audience is alert and paying strict attention. An effective means of achieving this end is the use of suitable bodily activity, which may take the form of pounding on the lectern with a clenched fist, of slapping the hands together, of stepping directly forward with an impressive and determined air, or of pointing the index finger squarely at the audience. The chief point to observe in the use of emphatic gestures is that they must actually suggest forcefulness. A speaker who pounds on the lectern with one extended finger, who weakly slaps his palms together, or who points a slightly bent and trembling finger at his audience is sure to get a reaction, but it will be far from the one he desires. Weakness parading as force is either laughable or pitiable, but never impressive. It should also be noted that gestures must not be allowed to become habitual lest they cease to serve their purpose and become distracting instead.

If the speaker habitually pounds on the lectern the gesture will certainly lose emphasis. Another point is important: noise-making gestures, such as pounding on the lectern or clapping the hands, may attract attention to themselves rather than to the idea they seek to emphasize. The speaker should not overuse such gestures; when he does use them, he should accompany them with sharp verbal emphasis on the idea being expressed.

THE AMOUNT OF ACTION

The amount of action to be used depends upon the subject, the speaker, the occasion, and the audience. If the speaker is vital and alert, the subject fiery and controversial, the audience large and not chiefly sedentary in its occupations, and the occasion not solemn, frequent and energetic gestures may be used to advantage. With a smaller audience and a more matter-of-fact subject, the number and extent of the gestures should be reduced. In any event, the gestures should always be so appropriate that they do not attract attention to themselves. The audience should scarcely notice whether the speaker is gesturing or not, so well should the gestures be integrated with the message being delivered. The amount of action should vary somewhat with the divisions of the speech. If a speaker makes a sweeping gesture before he begins to speak, the result, ordinarily, is ludicrous. Gestures are likely to be most effective in the body of the speech and in the conclusion, when the audience has had time to be aroused to the significance of the speaker's message. Gestures will also be more effective after the audience has engaged in some external activity, such as singing together or laughing and applauding. When the audience is stirred, it likes to see the speaker aroused; when the audience is calm and unmoved, it is inclined to be critical of anything more than a bare minimum of bodily action.

IMPROVING THE VISUAL CODE

Six general principles may be used as guides for obtaining the maximum value from expressive bodily action.

1. *Free yourself from inhibitions.* Fundamentally, every speaker wants to gesture. It is second nature for him to do so. When we think of gesturing in the broad sense, as all the ways in which we convey

meaning by use of bodily action—a shrug, a tilt of the head, a wrinkle
of the nose—it is evident that gesturing is a deeply ingrained, habitual
mode of communication. But, through fear of making a mistake,
of gesturing awkwardly, or of attracting unfavorable attention, the
speaker often inhibits his impulses to gesture. Thus beginning speakers
frequently make little jerking movements of the arms or hands. They
begin a gesture but inhibit it just as it is about to get under way.
These inhibited gestures are the most awkward of all, and since the
impulse to gesture can scarcely be eliminated (and should not be)
the speaker should free himself of these inhibitions and complete his
gestures. Try descriptive gestures first, as they are easiest to use; then,
emphatic gestures; and, last of all, suggestive gestures.

2. *Use the whole body in every gesture.* Don't begin the gesture
from the wrist, from the elbow, or even from the shoulder. The result
will inevitably be wooden and mechanical. The gesture should begin
at the bottom of your feet, and even if the bodily movement is slight
the whole body should respond in unison with the extension of the
arm.

3. *Make every gesture "follow through."* The principle is the same
here as in tennis, golf, or boxing. If the gesture is cut off too abruptly,
it appears choppy and unfinished.

4. *Make your gestures lead and your words follow or accompany
them.* One of the reasons why memorized gestures are often hopelessly
ludicrous and ineffective is that the speaker usually cues himself by his
words. Thus he begins a sentence and is thereby reminded of the gesture which is to accompany it. Theatrical directors frequently ad-
monish their actors to "lead with the eye." A similar rule might be
applied to the other agents of gesturing: the hands, the body, and the
head. When a picture on the wall is to be discussed, look at it, then
mention it. If you are to gesture with the index finger as you say,
"This is the plan," begin the gesture just a trifle before you begin the
sentence.

5. *Vary your gestures.* No gesture is good enough to bear frequent
repetition. If a gesture is used frequently, it comes to be a mannerism
and is looked upon as such by the audience. Even though frequent
repetition of the same gesture may be appropriate so far as the speaker's meaning is concerned, he should utilize different gestures by which
the same idea or attitude can be conveyed.

6. *Use enough vigor to make the gestures convincing.* Do not try to
express more overt action than you really feel. If you do not feel
enough animation for the needs of your delivery, generate it. In an

interesting article in *The Saturday Evening Post,* entitled "This Magic Business," Howard Thurston, the famous magician, told how he stirred up the animation needed for his act. Just before his entrance, he related, "I am prancing around on my toes and swinging my arms like a man trying to get warm; it is my way of gathering physical pep for my entrance. I am oblivious to every other thing in the world except the vital things required of myself at this moment—that is a psychic trick I have learned through experience." Thurston's method is extreme and most speakers cannot follow it. But the speaker can at least use a portion of his abundant supply of nervous energy, which otherwise expresses itself in stage fright, to give a convincing amount of pep and energy to every gesture he makes.

PROJECTS IN BODILY ACTION

The Pantomime

If sign language is included in the general term "pantomime," then pantomime is older than speech. At any rate, it has an ancient lineage, going back at least to the theater of the Greeks of Athens. Without doubt one of the sources of our pleasure in pantomime is seeing the versatility and skill with which bodily action can be made to perform the total functions of speech. Practice in pantomime is an effective means of developing the full resources of bodily action.

Pantomimes may be divided roughly into two groups, one devoted to presenting narrative, the other to conveying a message. Naturally, the latter has to be accomplished chiefly by means of narrative, so that the two kinds are really very much alike. Both are presented without the aid of words, either spoken or written, and without special costuming and stage properties unless they are absolutely necessary. The following suggestions should assist you in the presentation of your pantomime:

1. *Select a theme or a narrative that is not too complicated.* No matter how skillful a pantomimist may be, he cannot express fine distinctions, abstractions, and complex trains of thought as effectively by gestures and bodily postures alone as he can by speech. The range of pantomime is thus somewhat narrow. Its forte is the concrete and particular rather than the abstract and the general.

2. However, *be sure that the theme or narrative is complicated*

enough to be interesting. If the pantomimist confines himself solely to what any child can do, his performance will naturally be considered childlike. There is a creative joy in trying to expand the bounds of the pantomime as far as possible and to communicate meanings which are seemingly impossible to express except in words. Here is the opportunity for the pantomimist to give full scope to his ingenuity.

3. *Plan your story or message in complete detail before you try to present it.* Then practice the presentation several times so that the whole procedure is familiar to you. An impromptu pantomime may be as disconnected and pointless as an impromptu speech.

4. *Elaborate the details;* you will find that the chief interest centers in them. You may easily, for example, go through a few general motions which the audience will readily conclude represent putting on a coat. But there will be no particular interest in the act. It is when you represent the difficulty of getting your hand into the second sleeve, perhaps catch your hand in the lining, make a mistake in buttoning the coat and rectify it, find a spot on the coat and brush it off, and otherwise build the simple act into a detailed problem that your audience becomes interested.

5. *Keep your pantomime moving.* Don't load it down with needless details, so that your audience will wonder why you don't get on to something else. Have a real plot or a real message, with complications and subdivisions. Represent struggle, and build up suspense. Keep the audience conscious that events are moving toward a climax, and end the pantomime as the climax is portrayed.

6. *Keep the audience informed as to what you are doing, but guessing as to what you will do.* This is the best answer to the question of how intelligible the pantomime should be to the audience. The pantomimist may safely keep his audience in the dark as to the meaning of his first few movements. The attempt to determine what he is portraying is part of the fun and therefore should not be made too obvious. But if the audience does not discover the basic pattern of the pantomime very soon, it becomes confused and loses interest. When you come upon a sheet of paper covered with random marks, you merely glance at it and then turn your attention to something else; but if you observe that the marks represent some sort of pattern, however complex and obscure the pattern may be, your interest is immediately engaged in trying to trace the pattern. So it is in watching a pantomime. There is no virtue in keeping the audience fooled. Any aimless series of motions would do that. Make your story or message clear enough so that it can be readily followed. But do not make it so

simple that your audience is able to tell not only what you are doing but also what you are going to do next, for there will then be no suspense, no curiosity, and hence no interest.

What are some good subjects for pantomimes? The same principle should be followed here that was suggested in regard to speech topics. Selecting the subject is a vital part of the preparation of the pantomime, and you should choose your own subject. The more individual it is, the better the chance that it will be original and different from all the others. That is, try to select a personal experience that is different from the experiences the other students have had. If, for example, you wish to represent so common a situation as eating a meal, be sure to introduce incidents which make this meal a most unusual and exciting one. In general it is best to avoid such obvious themes as fishing, changing a tire, watching a football game, and taking a bath. For one thing, they are too common; for another, they violate the principle of maintaining interest through suspense. Once the basic situation is made clear, the audience knows almost exactly what is going to happen next. A few better examples for narrative pantomimes are the following: mountain climbing, interviewing the dean, serving as waiter in a café, delivering a soap-box speech to a heckling audience, riding a bicycle through heavy traffic, and dancing with an awkward partner in a crowded ballroom. These topics and others of a similar nature offer countless opportunities for complications, surprise twists, and suspense.

The pantomime intended to convey a message should not attempt too ambitious a theme. A good source of subjects for this type of pantomime is to be found in proverbs and epigrams with which the audience is already familiar. The interest centers chiefly in how well the selected theme can be illustrated, usually by means of a narrative. The following proverbs, epigrams, and pithy sayings are suggested as suitable for pantomime representation:

1. Honesty is the best policy.
2. He who hesitates is lost.
3. A bird in the hand is worth two in the bush.
4. Faint heart ne'er won fair lady.
5. A rolling stone gathers no moss.
6. He who laughs last laughs best.
7. A little knowledge is a dangerous thing.
8. My country, right or wrong!
9. Two is company, three is a crowd.
10. Prosperity is just around the corner.
11. A loan oft loses both itself and friend.

12. Beggars can't be choosers.
13. Love will find a way.
14. Come home; all is forgiven!
15. There is no rest for the wicked.
16. If wishes were horses, beggars would ride.
17. The devil finds work for idle hands to do.
18. Man proposes, God disposes.
19. A penny saved is a penny earned.
20. Don't bite the hand that feeds you.
21. Actions speak louder than words.
22. Better late than never.
23. Beauty is more than skin deep.
24. As the twig is bent, so is the tree inclined.
25. Luck favors the well prepared.

The Speech of Demonstration

Bodily action is an integral part of the speech of demonstration. The essential feature of this speech is that it centers around some object which is displayed to the audience and which forms the center of attraction of the speech. The object should be the chief illustration by means of which the point of the speech is clarified. For example, you might explain the process of graphing. Bring with you for use in your speech large sheets of paper or pieces of cardboard on which the various types of graphs are represented, and show these graphs to the audience as you explain their nature and purpose. A similar use might be made of maps, charts, pictures, or models. Small animals, alive, stuffed, or preserved in alcohol, might be brought for a demonstration. Athletic equipment, such as golf clubs, tennis rackets, and baseballs, might be explained and their uses demonstrated. Any piece of machinery, a stamp collection, a household utensil, samples of rugs, cloth or clothing, tools used by a dentist, a doctor's kit, a collection of rare books, or any other objects which your experience, interest, and ingenuity might suggest will serve the purpose of the speech of demonstration. An interesting twist can be given to the speech by an unusual use of common objects; a speaker might, for example, use a fountain pen to demonstrate a suction pump, or a rolling pin and a bit of pie dough to show the process of rolling steel. Or the speaker might use himself as the object to be demonstrated, if he wishes to present and explain a new dance step, a sleight-of-hand trick, or some other bodily skill. Detailed consideration of this kind of speaking will be found in Chapter 16.

PLATFORM POISE AND ETIQUETTE

Speaking has a code of etiquette which is just as important as are social manners in the drawing room, at the dining table, on the dance floor, or elsewhere. The following nine points should be especially observed:

1. *Be considerate of other speakers who are on the platform with you,* A form of discourtesy which is unfortunately not at all rare may be observed when several speakers are on the platform together. Those who have spoken may be conversing in whispers or passing notes to each other. Those who are about to speak may have their notes in their hands, studying them. Or they may all be shifting about uneasily, changing their positions frequently, and otherwise distracting attention from the speaker. While you are on the platform, never forget that you are under the observation of the audience. If the audience sees you inattentive to the speaker or showing obvious signs of boredom, it will tend to follow your example, and the speaker suffers. Furthermore, the audience's sense of fair play will be outraged, and you will find it unsympathetic when it is your turn to speak. Consideration for and courtesy toward other speakers while you are on the platform is a duty both to them and to yourself.

2. *Dress appropriately.* In an intercollegiate oratorical contest in which all the speakers were dressed formally, it was observed that one of the contestants was wearing bright green socks. The glaring inappropriateness of his garb kept drawing the attention of his audience as he sat on the platform. The impression which he thus unconsciously made was a great liability to his speech. One boy in a speech class wore a turtle-neck sweater, which was entirely appropriate. But as he sat slouched down in his seat, it invariably gathered in big wrinkles around his waist, and when he arose to speak, a portion of his shirtless anatomy was revealed between his trouser top and his sweater. Not even a word of admonition after class was effective in preventing the same thing from happening again. Naturally, his speeches aroused more submerged hilarity than effective response. In general the speaker should suit his dress to the formality or informality of the occasion and should be sure that his clothing is neat. The audience reacts to a speaker's attire as evidence of the sort of person he is and of the attitude he has toward himself, his subject, and his audience.

3. *Take your position on the platform calmly and confidently.* A gen-

eral tendency of beginning speakers is to hurry to the platform and commence speaking even before they reach it. In contrast, the practiced speaker ascends the platform at a dignified pace, steps to the lectern, faces the audience, and waits for a moment to permit attention to be fully focused on him before he begins to speak. This calm and leisurely approach gives the audience confidence in the speaker and permits his own muscular tension to subside before he begins to talk.

4. *When several speakers go to the platform together, the principal speaker should go first and the chairman last,* unless it is less confusing for them to go up in the order in which they will be seated, so that no one will have to pass in front of others to get to his chair. The seating arrangement should be determined in advance, so that each speaker can go directly to his chair, without fumbling about. The speakers should take their seats with a minimum of confusion and should then give their undivided attention to the program.

5. *As you rise to speak, attend to your audience rather than to your clothes.* Many speakers have developed habits of buttoning and unbuttoning their coats, adjusting their neckties, removing or putting on their glasses—almost everything, in short, but tying their shoelaces—while they are commencing their talks. Thus, at the very time when they should be trying hardest to win the attention of the audience to their subject matter, they are distracting that attention needlessly.

6. *Turn and acknowledge the chairman, either with a slight nod or with the words "Mr. Chairman."* Then, either by your actions or by your words, acknowledge the audience. This is an act of simple courtesy, but it can be rendered ridiculous by the speaker who is so anxious to include everyone in his greeting that he names a half-dozen or more groups in his salutation before getting to his general term, "friends."

7. *While speaking, maintain an effective bodily posture.* The feet should not be held too close together, so that the speaker resembles a hitching post; on the other hand, they should not be spread too far apart, like those of a hobby horse. The speaker should neither shift his feet about continuously, as though he were standing on a hot stove, nor keep them firmly and immovably planted throughout the entire speech. He should neither teeter and sway, like a drunkard or a tree in a high breeze. nor pace back and forth, like a lion in a cage. He should not droop upon the lectern, like a wet cloth that has been dropped there. In preference to these postures, place your feet about eight or ten inches apart, at an angle of some forty-five degrees, with one foot a little in front of the other. This position balances your weight evenly, reduces the temptation to squirm and wiggle, gives you a pos-

ture that is graceful and attractive, and, when you want to move from one part of the platform to another, gives you a natural and easy starting point for your movement. At transitional points in your speech, begin to move as you finish the final words of a paragraph, keeping your eyes on your audience; begin speaking again as you bring your feet down into the new position you have selected. A ludicrous mistake often observed in oratorical or declamatory contests is that of the speaker who, when he comes to his transitional point, glances down at his feet, walks with brisk determination to another part of the platform, glances down again to be sure that he is "well planted," and then resumes his talk. If the movement is not well integrated into the speech, it had much better not be made at all. And between shifts of position, the speaker should be sure to "stay put." Vague, meaningless twitchings and shuffling of the feet are the speaker's bane and are by all means to be avoided.

Another postural problem which causes much distress is the question of what to do with one's hands. Hanging by the speaker's sides, they seem to him to be as large and unlovely as hams. He imagines everyone in the audience to be staring at them. Then he does the very things which *do* attract attention to his hands: he puts them into his pockets, then takes them out; he grasps a coat lapel, then lets it go; he folds his arms across his breast, then drops them again. Thus the continual movement goes on. Since a moving object inevitably attracts attention, the eyes of the audience follow the speaker's hands, and the thread of his speech is lost. What to do? By far the best thing to do with your hands is to let them hang quietly by your sides, where they are both inconspicuous and ready for instant use in gesturing. However, once they begin to shift nervously, it is almost impossible simply to drop them to your sides. They require more forcible restraining. Place your hands behind your back and grasp your left wrist in your right hand, thus locking your hands well enough so that you can resist the nervous impulse to shift them. After a moment, when your nerves have quieted, release your hands and let them drop back into their normal position at your sides.

8. *Distribute your remarks fairly evenly and unobtrusively over the whole audience.* Equally to be condemned are the practice of talking continuously to one small segment of the audience and the contrary practice of continually bobbing the head and the body about from one point to another. In most auditoriums, the entire audience can be observed by the speaker without his bobbing his head around. If it is necessary to vary the direction of your speaking from time to time,

do not shift from one position to another too rapidly or with machine-like regularity.

9. *When you have concluded your speech, avoid the time-worn and platitudinous "I thank you."* If the speaker has done his job conscientiously and well, he is the one to be thanked. In any event, the "thank you" ending is but a weak means of getting back into your seat. End your speech on a note of conclusiveness, with a definite tone of finality in your last words. Then give the audience a slight bow or nod of acknowledgment, and resume your seat.

CONCLUSION

It is a common mistake to regard bodily action as a mere adjunct to public speaking, which the speaker may or may not care to use. In reality, speech is action. Even the immobile speaker is judged by the eye as well as by the ear of the listener. Since a large part of all we learn comes to us through the eye, the speaker must not underrate the importance of the visual code. He should determine to use the language of action effectively. He can rely upon action to aid him for description, for emphasis, and for suggestion. He must make the principle of empathy work in his behalf, rather than against him. He must so command the language of action that it will serve both him and his audience. He must maintain a reservoir of vigor to give point and genuineness to his overt movements. He must master the various kinds of gestures, so that they will become second nature to him and will be spontaneously responsive to his needs. And he must observe the rules of platform etiquette.

Learning to use bodily action naturally and effectively is a matter of both observation and practice. One need not be in a speech class to observe animated conversationalists who are completely unconscious of any attempt to observe "rules" of bodily action—and who thus exemplify the finest natural and effective use of the visual code.

EXERCISES AND BIBLIOGRAPHY

Exercises

1. Relate a story or anecdote which takes approximately one minute and in the telling of which you use each of the three types of gesture (emphatic, descriptive, and suggestive) at least once.

2. Present a five-minute talk in which your purpose is to interest the class in purchasing some object, the use and value of which you demonstrate. Some excellent objects to use for this talk are a can opener, a multicolored-lead mechanical pencil, a slide rule, apparatus for tricks of magic, or any similar objects which you have found useful and can urge enthusiastically upon others.

3. Analyze the following self-criticisms written by students at the close of their first semester of public speaking. Do you have any problems similar to theirs? What advice could you give them for the improvement of their bodily activity? Do their comments contain any advice or suggestions useful to you?

Let us begin with my most important fault, i.e., that I do not put my real self into my speech. I am ordinarily effusive and use my hands considerably. In speech class I more or less "freeze up." Perhaps it is because my topic is not right. It is something that I have been unable to analyze.

I know that I do not use enough bodily action, but I feel this will come to me in due time.

At times, when I think about my actions, I am a little stiff or else fidgety. Otherwise my bodily action is free.

I think that one of my most severe faults is not looking directly at the audience; perhaps I am afraid doing so will throw me off my course.

I have a hard time trying to find out what to do with my hands, as they seem so lifeless just hanging at my sides. This is probably because I haven't yet acquired enough confidence and skill to properly accent my speech with those bodily gestures which we have been talking about. I start to gesture, but it is such a feeble attempt that I am certain no one watching thinks of it as such.

All my speech habits are aided by one important thing. I use my hands freely and naturally, and in coordination with the rest of my body, when I express myself. I try to make the motion, instead of outstanding, subordinate to the words, yet helpful and noticeable.

I don't mind looking into the faces of my audience just as long as they refrain from laughing at me. They never have, but if they did I would become very unbalanced.

In my last speech I was more able to think about my bodily action. Before I gave my speech I planned on what I wouldn't do when I got up there, but I did not plan what bodily movements I should use. I did plan in advance how to stand for the first minute of my speech because I knew I would be nervous. I did not plan any more because I knew that the rest would come naturally.

4. Read the following sentences aloud, with appropriate bodily activity. Practice this exercise in private so that you feel perfectly free and uninhibited, and try a variety of gestures for each sentence until you find one that seems most effective. Be prepared to demonstrate your reading to the class.

    a. There comes the messenger now!
    b. "Forward, the Light Brigade!
       Charge for the guns!" he said.
    c. What! You have no money?
    d. Oh why should the spirit of mortal be proud?
    e. Look, my lord. It comes!
    f. Out, damned spot! out, I say!
    g. Give me liberty or give me death!
    h. Breathes there the man, with soul so dead,
       Who never to himself hath said,
         This is my own, my native land!
    i. If I ever get a chance to hit that thing, I'll hit it hard.
    j. The arguments of tyranny are as contemptible as its force is dreadful.
    k. Forbid it, Almighty God!
    l. I maintain that I not only have a right to speak, but a positive and clear right to vote upon this occasion.
    m. You must either yield or take the consequences.
    n. This above all: to thine own self be true.
    o. Out of my sight, thou demon of bad news!
    p. To be, or not to be: that is the question.
    q. Rise up—for you the flag is flung—for you the bugle trills.
    r. My kingdom for a horse!
    s. Water, water, everywhere,
       Nor any drop to drink.
    t. This government cannot endure permanently half slave and half free.

5. The following selections provide further material for practice. Memorize one of them for presentation to the class with appropriate use of the visual code:

    "My other piece of advice," said Mr. Micawber, "you know. Annual income twenty pounds, annual expenditure nineteen six, result happiness. Annual income twenty pounds, annual expenditure twenty pounds ought and six, result misery. The blossom is blighted, the leaf is withered, the god of day goes down upon the dreary scene, and—in short, you are forever floored. As I am."—CHARLES DICKENS.

    There are two ways of being happy: we may either diminish our wants or augment our means. Either will do, the result is the same. And it is for each man to decide for himself, and do that which happens to be the easiest. If you are idle or sick or poor, however hard it may be for you to diminish your wants, it will be harder to augment your means. If you are active and prosperous or young or in good health, it may be easier for you to augment your means than to diminish your wants. But if you are wise, you will do both at the same time, young or old, rich or poor, sick or well. And if you are very wise, you will do both in such a way as to augment the general happiness of society.— BENJAMIN FRANKLIN.

One o' my girls had her heart set on bein' a schoolteacher, but I talked her out of it. Teachin' school is too much like bein' a preacher's wife. It's a high callin', but people expect you to give more'n they pay for.

You take the teachers here in town. The only difference between them and Christian martyrs is the date an' lack of a bonfire.

They was hired to teach an' they do it. They teach the younguns that can learn, and entertain the ones that fell on their heads when they were little. But that ain't enough. They're supposed to make obedient little angels out o' spoiled brats that never minded nobody, an' wet nurse little wildcats so their mothers can get rest, an' make geniuses out o' children that couldn't have no sense with the parents they've got.

But that ain't the worst. They've got to get up plays an' things to work the school out o' debt, an' sing in the choir, an' teach a Sunday School class, an' when they ain't doin' nothin' else they're supposed to be a good example.

Then they don't get no pay for six months an' can't pay their board and buy decent clothes an' on top of ever'thing else they can't hold hands comin' home from prayer meetin' without some pious old sister with a dirty mind startin' a scandal on 'em.

I'd just as soon be a plow mule. A mule works just as hard but it can relieve its soul by kickin' up its heels after quittin' time without startin' any talk.

—ROBERT QUILLEN.

AFTER PARTING

If, out of this sharp bitter pain, when words
Are like a knife thrust in an open wound,
You can go forward like the homing birds,
Until, with fresh compassion you have crooned
A tender lullaby to tousled heads;
Can pick up broken strands and fashion them
Into a pattern that is rich with reds,
And let no thoughts creep in that might condemn;
Why then, O mother, you may know swift growth,
And beauty will look out from troubled eyes.

For even though at parting you were loath
To go on living while your helpmeet dies,
It is through untold suffering and pain
That souls are cleansed as with a silvered rain.

—LEAH SHERMAN.

OPPORTUNITY

This I beheld, or dreamed it in a dream:—
There spread a cloud of dust along a plain;
And underneath the cloud, or in it, raged
A furious battle, and men yelled, and swords
Shocked upon swords and shields. A prince's banner
Wavered, then staggered backward, hemmed by foes.
A craven hung along the battle's edge,
And thought, "Had I a sword of keener steel—
That blue blade that the king's son bears,—but this
Blunt thing—!" he snapped and flung it from his hand,
And lowering crept away and left the field.
Then came the king's son, wounded, sore bestead,
And weaponless, and saw the broken sword,
Hilt buried in the dry and trodden sand,
And ran and snatched it, and with battle shout
Lifted afresh he hewed his enemy down,
And saved a great cause that heroic day.

—EDWARD ROWLAND SILL.

HAMLET: Speak the speech I pray you, as I pronounced it to you, trippingly on the tongue; but if you mouth it, as many of your players do, I had as lief the town-crier spoke my lines. Nor do not saw the air too much with your hand, thus, but use all gently, for in the very torrent, tempest, and, as I may say, the whirlwind of your passion, you must acquire and beget a temperance that may give it smoothness. O, it offends me to the soul to see a robustious periwig-pated fellow tear a passion to tatters, to very rags, to split the ears of the groundlings, who for the most part are capable of nothing but inexplicable dumb-shows and noise: I would have such a fellow whipped for o'erdoing Termagant; it out-herods Herod: pray you, avoid it. . . .

Be not too tame neither, but let your own discretion be your tutor; suit the action to the word, the word to the action; with this special observance, that you o'erstep not the modesty of nature: for anything so o'erdone is from the purpose of playing, whose end, both at the first and now, was and is, to hold, as 't were, the mirror up to nature; to show virtue her own feature, scorn her own image, and the very age and body of the time his form and pressure. Now this overdone, or come tardy off, though it make the unskilful laugh, cannot but make

the judicious grieve, the censure of the which one must, in your allowance, o'erweigh a whole theatre of others. O! there be players that I
have seen play, and heard others praise, and that highly, not to speak
it profanely, that, neither having th' accent of Christians nor the gait
of Christian, pagan, nor man, have so strutted and bellowed that I have
thought some of nature's journeymen had made men and not made
them well, they imitated humanity so abominably.

—WILLIAM SHAKESPEARE, *Hamlet,* Act III, Scene 2

All the world's a stage,
And all the men and women merely players:
They have their exits and their entrances,
And one man in his time plays many parts,
His acts being seven ages. At first the infant,
Mewling and puking in the nurse's arms.
Then the whining school-boy, with his satchel
And shining morning face, creeping like snail
Unwillingly to school. And then the lover,
Sighing like furnace, with a woeful ballad
Made to his mistress's eyebrow. Then a soldier,
Full of strange oaths, and bearded like the pard,
Jealous in honour, sudden, and quick in quarrel,
Seeking the bubble reputation
Even in the cannon's mouth. And then the justice,
In fair round belly with good capon lin'd,
With eyes severe, and beard of formal cut,
Full of wise saws and modern instances;
And so he plays his part. The sixth age shifts
Into the lean and slipper'd pantaloon,
With spectacles on nose and pouch on side,
His youthful hose, well sav'd, a world too wide
For his shrunk shank; and his big manly voice,
Turning again toward childish treble, pipes
And whistles in his sound. Last scene of all,
That ends this strange eventful history,
Is second childishness and mere oblivion,
Sans teeth, sans eyes, sans taste, sans everything.

—WILLIAM SHAKESPEARE, *As You Like It,* Act II, Scene 7

Bibliography

If you have time and interest for further investigation of the importance
of bodily action in speech communication, look up the various sources
cited in the footnotes of this chapter. You may also want to consult
C. Wolf, *A Psychology of Gesture* (J. Thin [Edinburgh], 1948).

CHAPTER 14

CONTENTS

A student at the University of Colorado uses the visual aid of a drawing on the blackboard to explain the vocal mechanism.

IMPROVING
THE VOICE

The human speech apparatus encompasses more physical utility, facility of adjustment, variety of tonal effect, and range of expression than any mechanical instrument known to man. It permits one to whisper and sigh, gasp and yawn, sneeze and cough, hiccough, laugh, cry, breathe, accommodate food and liquids, whistle, sing many different tones, and articulate all the speech sounds that comprise the more than 1,500 languages of mankind. Yet all these varied activities employ fundamentally the same mechanism.

—VICTOR A. FIELDS and JAMES F. BENDER

THE human voice has more variety of tonal effects and a wider range of expressiveness than any mechanical instrument ever devised. It can be pleasant to hear, or difficult to listen to. The quality of a voice suggests whether the speaker is tired or rested, enthusiastic or bored, cheerful or gloomy, confident or timid, dominant or submissive. Rightly or wrongly, people even make assumptions concerning the speaker's intelligence, range of education, family status, and vocation on the basis of vocal qualities. Everyone knows that a voice should be loud enough to be heard, without being too loud. We all realize that vocal quality is adversely affected by a head cold and by emotional strain. But in our normal, everyday speaking, most of us pay too little attention to our own voices—however sensitive we may be to those of others.

How important voice may be in our normal social relations may be indicated by a series of reports on the voice of just one man—Mark Twain. Mrs. Thomas Bailey Aldrich admitted that when her husband first brought Twain to their home, she didn't invite him to stay for dinner because she thought he was drunk—because of what seemed to her to be his "difficulty with his speech; he did not stammer exactly, but after each word he placed a period." Actually, this extreme slowness of rate was one of the characteristics that made William Dean Howells rate him as "the most consummate public performer I ever saw," adding, "it was an incomparable pleasure to hear him lecture." Rudyard Kipling said that Mark Twain had "the slowest, calmest, levelest voice in all the world." According to the novelist W.

H. Riding, "It was not a laughing voice, or a light-hearted voice, but deep and earnest like one of the graver musical instruments, rich and solemn, and in emotion vibrant and swelling with its own passionate feeling." Twain's habit of lingering over words impressed Riding very differently from the way it impressed Mrs. Aldrich: "His way of uttering them and his application of them often gave the simplest words which he habitually used a pictorial vividness, a richness of suggestion, a fullness of meaning with which genius alone could endow them." Gladys Carmen Bellamy, in her book entitled *Mark Twain as a Literary Artist*—in which all the foregoing comments are assembled —wrote that "People were most impressed, apparently, by his eyes and his voice." She noted, too, that "unpleasant human voices made him suffer, but the liquid beauty in certain rare voices was a compensation."[1] For those who wish to hear the voice of Mark Twain (who died in 1910), a recording is preserved in The Voice Library of Yale University. An excellent rendition of a typical Mark Twain lecture-recital has been made by Hal Holbrook and is available from Columbia Records ("An Evening with Mark Twain," #0L5440).

VOICE AND PERSONALITY

The reactions people had to Mark Twain's voice are more or less typical of the close attention which we all pay, consciously or unconsciously, to the voices of all with whom we associate. Very probably you are unaware of the extent to which voice influences your own judgment of others—and their judgments of you. As soon as you hear a stranger speak, you start forming opinions about him based more on his voice than even on the words he utters. You have only to hear the voice of a friend to know whether he is ill, tired, happy, or angry.

We noted in Chapter 3 that our speech personality is the sum total of our speech habits. Some persons, as a result of environmental influences or unwise schooling, have developed voices or voice habits that seem artificial and affected. The resulting lack of naturalness and spontaneity demands (in the words of Mark Twain) that their speech "be limbered up, broken up, colloquialized, and turned into the common forms of unpremeditated talk." In other words, the artificial "overcultivation" of speech makes it difficult for others to eval-

[1] Gladys Carmen Bellamy. *Mark Twain as a Literary Artist* (University of Oklahoma Press, 1950).

uate such persons as sincere and genuine. You expect the voice of
Caspar Milquetoast to bear the marks of timidity and fear. You expect the voice of a large, well-built, athletic type of person to be deep,
rich, and strong. As a matter of fact, you will find that you expect
certain types of personality to go with certain types of voice. Since
qualities of voice do tend to be identified with personality types, or
with favorable and unfavorable personality characteristics, we should
study voice with an awareness of the "pattern of expectation" to which
our voices are expected to conform—with a deep sense of the full
significance of voice as a revelation of the whole person.

VOICE IS A COMPOSITE OF HABITS

Since voice is a product of muscle movement it is evident that it
tends to become a composite of habits and habit systems. We improve
our voice by improving habits of posture and movement. For example,
correct breathing is a basic part of all voice use; and many of us will
find our breathing habits far short of ideal. What has been said in
Chapter 3 concerning habit formation and change applies, of course,
to habits of voice. When you consider the number of years during
which your present voice habits have been forming and becoming
fixed, you will realize how much long and patient practice may be
required to change these habits where they need improving. Relearning frequently is much more difficult than first learning: old habits
are persistent and highly resistant to change. But good voice habits
are necessary ingredients of effective speaking, time-consuming as
their development may be.

One of the reasons why developing better voice habits is so difficult is that a person is not conscious of precisely how each sound is
made. A given sound was first produced by trial and error in our early
experiences as a child. The degree of perfection in voice production
an individual will attain depends greatly upon his sense of hearing,
his awareness of the vocal sounds he makes, his muscular coordination, and his inner motivation, in addition to environmental influences.
Yet even when most of these factors are favorable he may not be
able to develop the most desirable vocal habits. A difficulty is that the
movements of the vocal bands, necessary to the production of sound,
are set up by involuntary muscles. Control of the vocal bands is
believed to be possible only indirectly. Even complicated principles
of air-flow dynamics may be involved. If you believe the involuntary
musculature involvement can be easily described, try telling a little

child how to make an *ah* sound. This indirect control of which we are speaking is maintained over the voice, or at least is directed by, the ear. This brings an added complication into the process because, unfortunately, the individual cannot hear his voice as others hear it. Listen to a recording of your voice and you will understand what we mean. The recording is of your voice as others hear it; but this is not the way your own ear hears it because it picks up internal resonance unheard by others. Listening to a recording of your voice habits can be of great help in improving it: when you hear your voice as it really sounds to others you will be better able to reguide the automatic indirect controls—to change the habit systems upon which your voice depends. It is a product of the accuracy and discrimination of your hearing as well as of the efficiency of your use of nerve-muscle coordinations for the correct production of the sounds of speech.

VOICE AND HEALTH ARE CLOSELY INTERRELATED

Lack of energy, disturbance of glandular secretions, disruption of metabolism, nerve injury or strain, and even worry, excessive fatigue, or extreme emotional upset are likely to have immediately discernible effects upon the voice. Biologically speaking, speech is a later-acquired responsibility of muscles and structures which have other, primary bodily functions to perform. Unless they are performing their primary functions in a normal and healthy way, we cannot expect them satisfactorily to discharge their added function of producing voice. This is why habits of bad breathing, poor posture, and excessive muscle tensions, with or without organic cause, tend to result in faulty voice. Thus the ordinary rules of mental and physical hygiene come first in any list of suggestions for voice improvement.

If you are not completely convinced that the relation between voice and mental and physical health is real rather than imaginary, listen to voices. Listen, and determine for yourself whether there is any correlation between pleasant, relaxed, clear voices, and relaxed, well-adjusted, healthy persons. Study the voices of tired, worried, excitable people, then those of rested, happy, composed people. Decide for yourself whether your voice is all that you wish it to be. You will be greatly helped in this analysis by the criticisms of your instructor, by the evaluations of your fellow students, and by recordings of your own voice.

VOICE IS A PRODUCT OF CEREBRATION

The production of voice is a mental as well as a muscular process; one cannot overstate the importance to the voice of mental attitudes and of mental ability. This is another aspect of the fact that voice is an automatic activity. Voice is, in a way, a reflection of one's whole thinking process. Even though we may find specific exercises and drills helpful, it is over-all coordination which really determines our voices. Discounting the possible results of bad habit in muscle use, or of the presence of organic defects, a good voice is an inevitable result of a precision-thinking organism. That is why good habits of thinking and general adjustment to the speaking situation have received early consideration in this book.

You will find a review of Chapters 2, 3, 9, and 10 helpful lest the following detailed analysis of voice make you forget the importance of the total process of cerebration (which is essential to coordination), of which voice is but a by-product.

QUALITIES OF THE NORMAL VOICE

In voice training, as in all other phases of speech study, it is essential to keep in mind that our goal is never a stereotyped "good pattern." We do not wish, even were it possible, for two voices to be exactly alike. Your voice is an expression of your individuality. As Amram Scheinfeld has said in the opening sentence of *You and Heredity,* "Stop and think about yourself: In all the history of the world there was never any one else exactly like you, and in all the infinity of time to come there will never be another."

It is not only difficult but dangerous to attempt to generalize very much about a "good" voice. Any voice may be more effective in some circumstances than in others. A voice which everyone admires in one person might be most inappropriate for another personality. The worst kind of voice one can imagine might be admirable if used on stage or screen to portray a certain type of character. On the other hand, you may know some voices which are mere mechanical and artificial copies of other voices—"good," in a way, but utterly lacking in genuineness and individuality.

Normal speaking situations are sufficiently similar, however, so that it is possible to indicate certain general qualities usually common to effective voices. These qualities serve as a standard by which each normal voice may be judged without in the least destroying the individuality of the voice. The objective in setting such a standard is to strengthen and refine the already fine points of the voice and to minimize the weaknesses. After all, there is no merit in being merely "different."

Audibility

Sufficient volume and force is required of the voice so that the listener may hear without undue effort. Certainly a voice that cannot be heard is inadequate—regardless of what other fine qualities it may possess. Perhaps we should note that the converse of this statement is also true. A booming, blasting voice in a small room can make the listener very uncomfortable. The effective voice will adjust to the acoustical requirements of different situations so that the listeners' task may not be made unnecessarily difficult.

Clarity

Good articulation, and thus good speech, depends upon a clear tone. It is the tone that carries. A voice that is husky, "throaty," or "breathy" interferes with the clear formulation of sounds and so limits the listeners' understanding. If listeners must ask you to repeat what you have said, there must be some lack in the clarity or distinctness of your voice, assuming the audibility of your voice and the normality of their hearing. The clarity of one's sound patterns is well tested by the telephone or the microphone. In connected speech, it is true, the listener may be able to make out the speaker's meaning even while missing a considerable number of the sounds. But every guess at what a speaker has mumbled increases the probability of misunderstanding and faulty communication. Relaxation and effortlessness of speech can be overdone. A voice that is not clear is certainly not the asset that it should and could be to its possessor.

Pleasantness

Pleasantness is a difficult quality to describe, and the standard may vary greatly from listener to listener. In general, what we are accustomed to is pleasant, and what is strange to our ears is likely to be regarded as unpleasant. Once again our guide must be the listeners' "pattern of expectation." There are some radio and television news commentators whose voices do not seem pleasant to first-time listeners, but to the ears of their accustomed following their voices are as agreeable as the feel of old shoes to one's feet. To New Englanders the nasal tone is "natural," whereas to Southerners the most acceptable speech, in addition to being musical, is somewhat drawled. British speech sounded supercilious to the American soldiers quartered in England during World War II, until they became accustomed to it, and American speech sounded slovenly and harsh to the English. When we say, then, that the voice should be pleasant, we do not mean that all voices should sound like those of Helen Hayes or Sir Laurence Olivier. Pleasantness is culturally established. Whale oil is pleasant to Eskimos, as is highly seasoned food to Mexicans. Similarly, you achieve a pleasant voice not by trying to imitate some pattern of fancied excellence but by trying to achieve the best aspects of the speech pattern of the people with whom you are communicating.

Variety

When the voice is properly used as a means of conveying ideas and feelings, it inevitably changes with every change of the speaker's mind or attitude and responds to the listeners' reactions and emotional impulses. A voice that is monotonous, or that falls into a set pattern repeated again and again, indicates a mind that is not *communicating* but is busy *remembering* what is to be said. Under stress of very strong emotion—such as extreme grief or fear—a voice may be harsh and monotonous. But in normal speaking situations the voice varies to convey the continually shifting shades of meaning intended *and felt* by the speaker. When a speaker's voice is unvaried and monotonous the fault lies with his mental and emotional attitude—perhaps even with physical indolence. When an instrument is badly used, it is not the instrument which needs change but the method of using it. Techniques for acquiring vocal variety will be discussed in detail in a later section of this chapter. Basic to these techniques, though, is the speaker's *thinking with* and *talking to* his audience, rather than *communing with himself.*

Lack of Strain

If using the voice tires the speaker, causes discomfort to his throat, or results in hoarseness, the voice is being badly used. Normally, the tones are produced easily, and even prolonged speaking should not tire the vocal organs. To be sure, the *speaker* may be tired, for effective speech requires a great deal of concentrated effort. No speaker should be surprised or perturbed if two or three hours of lecturing leaves him temporarily exhausted. But normally the weariness is general. If a speaker's throat tires and his voice becomes hoarse when he talks more loudly than usual or for a long period of time, he would profit from exercises in relaxation. Strain is the result of tension; excessive tension means that muscles are being wrongly used.

Conformity to the Speaker's Image of Himself

A confident person is likely to have a calm, steady, assured voice. A vain personality usually advertises itself in an assertive, perhaps strident, tone. A shy, timid, or uncertain person may speak in a thin quaver. One remedy for the strident voice is to try to lower the pitch and decrease the intensity. A remedy for the quavering voice is to work for a firmer control of the breath stream.

These, however, are indirect methods of attacking the problem. In time they will have a positive effect, for we revise our images of ourselves in terms of how we sound to others and to ourselves. But a much more direct approach calls for a self-examination of our personalities and a determined effort to build more socially effective images of ourselves.

The relation of voice to personality deserves repeated emphasis, for it is the key to the surest and most lasting remedy of all voice problems. It is a truism that "the voice is the mirror of the soul." We have been stressing in this chapter that the voice is the mirror of the total self. We are aware that every voice is different from every other and that we naturally associate the voices of our friends with their personalities. We are aware, too, that our voices change to conform to changes in our feelings. Anger, boredom, fear, and pleasure are accompanied by unmistakably different voices. We know how much a temporary uneasiness—such as an unwelcome disciplinary conference with the dean—may change our normal voices. Similarly, we are aware that the most discordant, harsh, or tremulous voices tend to improve materially when the speakers are among intimate friends and are relaxed and at ease.

Clearly, then, the kind of voice one has is determined in large degree by the kind of person he is. A weak, subdued voice, which lacks projection or carrying power, is the natural result of a personality that fears to assert itself. It may be observed that the possessor of such a voice will frequently speak with downcast eyes; and, however assured he may appear in many particulars, he is usually aware of a funda-mental feeling of insecurity or uncertainty. A brusque, overbearing tone may be evidence of the overcompensation of another shy person-ality, or it may indicate the assertiveness of a person accustomed to having his own way. The voice, like the face, reveals much about the nature and disposition of the speaker; it indicates, too, something of the depth and a great deal about the state of his mind.

FACTORS INFLUENCING THE NORMAL VOICE

When your vocal mechanism is normal, when you have no firmly established vocal habits that limit your effectiveness, and when your voice is not adversely affected by personality problems of one kind or another, your voice is likely to be a fairly accurate reflection of what you feel. These three qualifications must be considered with care. The first and second require a consideration of your vocal mechanism and its use. A detailed study of the complete vocal mech-anism belongs in a specialized course in voice. If you have trouble with your voice, such a course may help you to understand just what you do when you speak and may give you a basis for correcting such bad vocal habits as you may find. Here attention is centered only on the more common problems of voice, which are caused by functional maladjustments and by habits of poor modulation of the breath stream.

When the effectiveness of the voice is limited by personality traits, the remedy lies, of course, in a better adaptation of the individual to his environment. It is probable that the voices of most of the students in your class showed signs of tension in the first rounds of speeches. As we have seen, any new situation that introduces strain and uncer-tainty will reflect tension in the voice. As you and your classmates become more accustomed to speaking before the group, and as you gain confidence through increased mastery of speech skills, your voices will lose their unnatural strain. Furthermore, as training in speech helps to make your total personalities more effective—as you gain greater skill in unfolding and expressing your inner qualities—your voices will acquire additional flexibility, range, and firmness of tone.

Your voice training is not confined to the work that you do as you study this and the succeeding chapter; it is not confined even to this course. All your experiences affect the way you speak. As you improve the organization of your speeches, increase the incisiveness with which you express your ideas, add to the worth of your ideas and the interest with which you develop them, and especially as you improve your ability to adapt what you have to say to the moods and attitudes of your audience, your voice will reflect these increased communicative skills. Remember that your voice is a channel through which your ideas, feelings, and convictions are expressed. As you become more sure and more expert in their expression, your voice improves. For the sake of comparison, you may recall how tense you sounded when first introduced to a new acquaintance and how much more easily and effectively your voice did its work as you became better acquainted.

THE PROCESS OF VOICE PRODUCTION

It is customary to think of voice in terms of three essentials to its production: breathing, phonation, and resonation. Articulation, since it is primarily concerned with the phonetic consonantal sounds of the language, is a matter more largely of speech than of voice and will be considered in the following chapter.

Breathing

Without breath there would be no voice. Voice is produced by the exhalation phase of breathing; it results from certain modifications of the breath stream. Clearly, then, any disturbance of normal breathing will cause a disturbance of voice. If you have just run halfway across the campus to get to class on time, you will hope that the instructor does not call upon you to speak first. Deep emotion may similarly disturb your breathing rate and thus your speech pattern.

Those who have not yet profited fully from the suggestions in Chapter 3 for avoiding the harmful tensions of stage fright would do well at this point to reread them. Relaxation is one aid to good voice. Proper posture is another. "Bad" posture may be defined as that general carriage of the body which hinders any of the bodily functions essential to healthy living. "Good" posture is that which assists good breathing and good speaking. A military stiffness of posture is neither appropriate nor beneficial for the speaker; on the other hand, he must avoid such results of a sedentary way of life as listless slouching and a general debility of bodily tone. The speaker must give every evi-

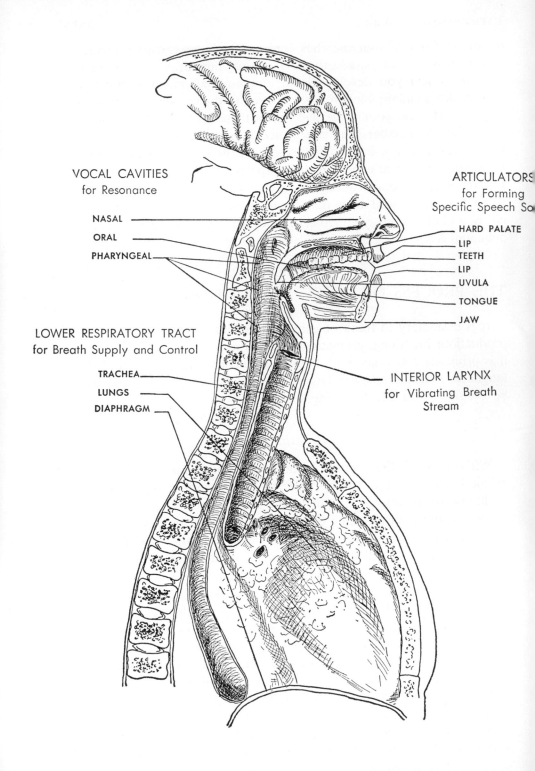

VOCAL CAVITIES
for Resonance

NASAL

ORAL

PHARYNGEAL

LOWER RESPIRATORY TRACT
for Breath Supply and Control

TRACHEA

LUNGS

DIAPHRAGM

ARTICULATORS
for Forming
Specific Speech So

HARD PALATE
LIP
TEETH
LIP
UVULA
TONGUE
JAW

INTERIOR LARYNX
for Vibrating Breath
Stream

dence of physical alertness. His posture must be sufficiently erect so that it will not hamper deep and normal breathing and so that he presents a businesslike appearance of command over the situation.

Since breathing is an automatic and largely reflex activity, our principal concern will be with freeing it from the inhibitions and restrictions which modern living habits have tended to place upon it. Natural habit, undisturbed, is amazingly likely to be healthful. When you are in a thoroughly relaxed position, just before dropping off to sleep, you will find that your breathing is slow and regular. But in the daytime we often wear restrictive clothing, let our chests cave in and walk about as though we had advanced cases of curvature of the spine, to the serious detriment of our health and our voices. Conscious attention to deep and full breathing, a definite effort to learn to speak with a large reserve of air in the lungs, and an improvement of your ability to control the rate and force of exhalation may be the main points for your general concern. If you have extensive problems in breathing, your instructor may suggest special exercises, such as exercises 7 and 8 at the end of this chapter.

Phonation

Located in the larynx along each side of the windpipe are small clusters of muscles known as the vocal bands. They act as a valve, controlling the opening, or glottis, between them. While we are speaking the glottis is successively closed and opened and little spurts of air are released, setting up sound waves. The process by which the vibrating vocal bands produce sound is known as *phonation*. The rate of the vibrations determines the pitch of the sound.

Phonation is essential to the production of all the voiced sounds of language. When the vibrations of the vocal bands are uninterrupted, we call the resultant sounds *vowel sounds;* when the vibrations are interrupted or modified by other moving muscles, we call the sounds *consonant sounds*. Serious difficulties with phonation are relatively uncommon; when they do exist, they require the attention of a speech clinician or pathologist. All students of speech should, however, practice to improve their efficiency at inhaling quickly and deeply without producing obvious gasping sounds. They should avoid shallow chest breathing by producing expansion at the waist as well as at the chest. While reading aloud or speaking, they should follow each rapid inhalation with a slow and carefully controlled exhalation. After a little practice they should be able to give meaningful expression at a reasonable rate of 70 to 100 words on one sustained exhalation. Such practice should bring about a reasonable increase in vital capacity (the amount of air drawn into the lungs), a greater degree of control of the muscles of exhalation (of waist as well as chest), and finer control of the vocal bands. Suggestions concerning matters of pitch and of force, or loudness, will be found in the next section, "Acquiring Vocal Variety."

It should be made clear that not all sounds are voiced. There are aspirate articulate noises which are not modifications of vocal tone but consist of unvocalized breath. They are considered in the next chapter, under the heading "Articulation."

Resonation

If phonation were not amplified, the human voice would not carry far and would lack richness of tones. The resonators make possible these modifications of phonation. The resonating cavities with which we are primarily concerned are those of the pharynx (that part of the throat above the larynx and opening into both nose and mouth), the mouth, and the nose, which are as important to the vibrating bands of the human voice as is the resonating cavity of a guitar or the sounding board of a piano to its vibrating wires. These resonators generate the overtones of the human voice and give it mellowness, richness, and added volume. The resonators reinforce certain frequencies and dampen out others, thus strengthening the carrying power and modifying the quality of some tones. The resonating cavities can be changed in size and shape (within the range which is possible to each person). There is also the factor of coupled resonating cavities (or the joint utilization of two or more resonators), the full importance of which is still unknown. This myriad of possible adjustments adds immeasurably to the great potentialities of the human voice as a delicately responsive instrument for expression.

Even in this brief discussion of resonance a word must be said about nasality. All but three of the sounds of our language normally are made without nasal resonance; only the consonant sounds *m, n,* and *ng* require nasal resonance. The proper production of these sounds require the passage of some of the exhaled air through the nose. Negative nasality occurs when there is a lack of nasal resonance in the true sense. It may be inflicted upon the normal voice by a head cold, which causes a stoppage in the nasal passages, by hay fever, or by sinus trouble. Some persons have developed habits of negative nasality, which may have originated during periods of temporary obstruction of the nasal passages. Relearning to use the nasal resonating cavity is all that is required to correct these habits. By humming with the mouth closed you can feel and hear the variations which can be achieved by changing the use of the nasal resonating cavity.

Many Americans use nasal resonance not only for the *m, n,* and *ng* sounds but also for vowels and nonnasal consonants. The first basic corrective step is to train your ear clearly to hear the nasal resonance. To accomplish this, you should hum the *m* sound at different pitches and with varying amounts of volume. Hum until you can hear your head buzzing with the strength of the vibration that is produced. With your forefinger held lightly against the side of your nose, you can clearly feel the vibration. As a second step, alternately produce nasal and nonnasal sounds, both listening and feeling the side of the nose to determine whether nasality is present or absent when it should be. As sample exercises, repeat aloud the following sound combinations, prolonging and accentuating the vowel and the nasal sounds:

la–le–li–lo–lu	ala–ale–ali–alo–alu
ma–me–mi–mo–mu	ama–ame–ami–amo–amu
ta–te–ti–to–tu	ata–ate–ati–ato–atu
na–ne–ni–no–nu	ana–ane–ani–ano–anu
fa–fe–fi–fo–fu	afa–afe–afi–afo–afu
nga–nge–ngi–ngo–ngu	anga–ange–angi–ango–angu
ra–re–ri–ro–ru	ara–are–ari–aro–aru

ACQUIRING VOCAL VARIETY

An interesting and effective voice is one which is lively, varied, and responsive to mood and meaning. The human voice has a great potentiality for variation and range. It should be clear from what has been said that the amount and kind of variation in a speaker's voice are often good indications of what is or is not going on in his mind. One of the speaker's chief concerns will be, then, to free himself of tensions and inhibitions so that his voice is not restrained from reflecting naturally the meaning he wishes to communicate.

The listeners' sensing of the speaker's eagerness to communicate is a sign of effective speaking. Lack of such eagerness reveals a mind too bored or too involved in its own struggles to have any real, lively interest in reaching its listeners. But a zest to communicate is not enough. Think, for example, of the many enthusiastic players of musical instruments who still require long practice with fundamentals before their listeners will hear them gladly. There are some fundamentals of voice use which must underlie an eagerness to communicate. Skill in the use of voice, like any other skill, comes from intelligently directed practice. Force, pitch, and quality are three characteristics of the voice which, although always used in combination, may be separately analyzed and practiced.

Force

The student who wishes to use his voice more efficiently will learn to regulate its force. The inexperienced speaker is all too likely to resort merely to raising the pitch of his voice and to yelling when he wishes to be heard above noise or confusion. In reality we control the force of the voice by control of the breath pressure in exhalation, by the regulation of pitch, or by both means. We shall consider force here, however, in its more limited sense—as breath pressure and as influenced by techniques for improving the projection, or "carrying," of the voice. We have noted that voice is achieved by modification or modulation of the breath stream. It should not be surprising, then, that modulating the force of the breath stream changes the force of the voice.

Greater force, or volume, may be achieved by the use of more energy. Exhale more rapidly and with greater force. To soften the voice, or diminish the force, exhale slowly and with less force.

Remember that the amount of force used by a speaker tends to be interpreted by his listeners as a clear indication of his attitude and purpose. Reserve your greatest force for your most important points. Too much force, used constantly, can become as ineffective as too little force. Variety in force is important. And force must be varied in a manner appropriate not only to the subject but also to the occasion and to the auditorium. Force, or volume, that is adequate for a small room must be greatly increased for a large auditorium. And after a speaker has become accustomed to a large auditorium he must guard against blasting the ears of his listeners in a small room.

Resonance, which has already been discussed, can greatly facilitate the speaker's use of force. It can be a great aid to projection, which is principally improved by more complete resonation, by greater accuracy and precision in the modulation of the breath stream, and by opening the mouth so that the sounds are not muffled. The student who has difficulty in getting his voice to carry will be aided by picking out and speaking directly to individuals who are seated farthest from the platform, making sure, of course, not to ignore the others.

Pitch

The first expectation we have concerning the pitch, or rate of vibration, of a speaker's voice is that it be appropriate to the speaker's age and sex. We expect the pitch of a man's voice to be lower than that of a woman's and the pitch of an adult's voice to be lower than that of a child's. Consequently, a high-pitched male voice or a deep female voice startles the listeners and erects a barrier to effective communication. Furthermore, an eccentricity of pitch helps to build an image in the minds of the audience (and perhaps in the speaker's own mind) of an ineffective or odd personality.

We also expect the speaker to use an appropriate variety of pitch. One means of varying the pitch of the speaking voice is called *inflection*; it may be defined as a change of pitch (upward, downward, or both) which is effected within the pronunciation of a word or syllable. Speech without inflection is monotonous, lifeless, and lacking in fullness of meaning. On the other hand, exaggerated, elaborate, and artificial patterns of inflection (typically used by the overeager social climber), suggest to the hearers insincerity and affectation. Between these extremes are found the genuine, normal inflections of conversational use of voice, typical of speakers who are both confident and unassuming. Pitch variations give melody to voice and thus become a part of rhythm.

Each individual should seek to determine the range of pitch within which he or she speaks most easily and naturally. For all practical purposes, the ear of the listener must be the judge of the natural pitch at which the speaker makes most pleasing use of his vocal mechanism. The speaker should also do all he can to increase his range of pitch, in order that his voice may have added variety. Voice pitch is a fairly automatic response to one's mental and emotional state. The pitch of the voice tends to respond directly to emotional change. When a speaker is excited or emotionally stirred, his voice tends to take on a pitch either higher or lower than normal. When he is calm and relaxed, his voice tends to respond in normal pitch.

Quality

Every voice has a characteristic quality which makes it distinguishable even from voices with the same force and pitch. Quality is largely determined by resonance. The presence and richness of overtones, known as timbre, is an essential part of the individuality of the voice.

The health, the mood or attitude, and, particularly, the emotional state of a speaker have much to do with determining the quality of his voice. It is relatively easy to *write* words which will conceal our feelings or emotions; but when we *speak* the words, the quality of the voice is revealing. Our feelings and emotions involve our whole beings and when unrestrained will actually influence the sizes and shapes of the resonating cavities. Anger, fright, elation, love, or worry will affect the quality of a person's voice.

There are various types of generally unpleasant vocal qualities, described respectively as guttural, hoarse, throaty, thin, pinched, falsetto, nasal, harsh, aspirate, flat, and whining. Other descriptive terms indicating types of vocal quality are mellow, deep, rich, confident, open, warm, and normal. Obviously some of these terms are based upon the impressions we receive of the speaker's personality and emotional state as we listen to the quality of his voice. This is not unnatural, since voices do respond to emotional change and since they tend to become fixed in relation to certain personality characteristics. For example, a person with a warm, buoyant, generous, optimistic nature will, as a rule, have better vocal quality than will a chronic complainer. Habitual lack of confidence is certain to reveal itself in the voice. When one whines, not only is he using an unpleasant quality of voice, he is also revealing an unpleasant personality. Similarly, a voice resonant with rich, warm overtones is a fairly dependable revelation of a confident, well-balanced temperament.

Improving the quality of the voice is a highly individual matter. It involves making the best possible use of the resonating chambers. But basic to improvement of voice quality must be the elimination of disagreeable personality habits, of emotional tensions, and of undesirable mental attitudes. An alert and critical ear is a helpful guide to the development of those fine shadings of quality which make the voice more sensitive, responsive, and meaningful.

Above all, the training of the voice requires long and patient practice. As recorded in Claude Bowers, *Beveridge and the Progressive Era,* a member of an audience hearing the great operatic soprano Lillian Nordica sing Senta's prayer from *The Flying Dutchman,* in 1892, was deeply impressed by one note and asked her afterward whether it was her "incomparable throat" which made possible "that gossamer note."

"No, no, no!" she replied, laughing, "that one note was weeks of work, work, work—over, over, over—study, study, study! You remember how the old Greek sculptors, after chiseling their marble, polished it until the human eye could not detect a roughness on the surface; then, not content with that, they would rip the nail from their thumb, and test the smoothness of the marble with the quick of the flesh underneath their nail? That is the way I obtained that note."

In such a fashion may natural ability—in use of the speaking voice as in other fields—be brought to its full fruition by devoted and intelligent endeavor.

CONCLUSION

Voice is essential, of course, to the total process of speech. Voice reveals personality. Voice and health are closely interrelated. And voice is a major communicator of intelligence. That person is fortunate whose voice can be described as audible, clear, pleasing, varied, and free of destructive tension. And because the voice mirrors the total self, its improvement involves health, personality, and intellectual ability. Voice improvement may nonetheless be aided by better understanding and more effective utilization of exhalation, phonation, and resonation. When we add to these achievements a greater mastery in the use and varying of force, pitch, and quality, we have covered the essentials for voice improvement. There remain to be considered in the following chapter those modifications of voice use so important to the communication of meaning: articulation and pronunciation.

EXERCISES AND BIBLIOGRAPHY

Exercises

1. A fruitful approach to a clearer understanding of how you may use your voice to better effect is to analyze the results you have achieved with it in various types of experience. What has happened in your home when you yelled? Or when you mumbled so that you could not be understood? Or when you talked in so subdued a voice that your family had to strain to hear you? Do you talk to your family in the same tone in which you converse with visitors? Write a brief essay describing some incidents from experiences with family or friends in which you recall the way your voice or theirs was used.
2. If your voice has been recorded as part of the course work, listen as objectively as possible to the recording and then write a brief charac-

terization of the personality you would associate with that voice if the voice were not your own. Be as analytical and honest as you can in characterizing the type of person the voice represents to you. Then ask yourself whether the effect the voice had on you is the effect you want to have on other people. When your voice is recorded again later in the course, see whether you note any significant changes in the personality pattern it represents.

3. Write a two- or three-sentence characterization of each member of the class, based wholly upon the impression each voice makes upon you. The characterizations should be handed to the instructor in order that he may read a selection of them to the class (without identifying the writers) as an object lesson of the influence exerted by the kind of voice one uses.

4. Bring to class an item from a current magazine or newspaper. As you read it aloud, the class should take notes on how well your voice conveys the precise meaning of the selection and your own attitude toward it. A general discussion should reveal a great deal about how much or how little the speakers are utilizing the communicative power of their voices.

5. Prepare a poem, a paragraph from one of your textbooks, or a scene from a play or novel for presentation to the class. Prepare a brief introduction, in which you might (a) tell why you like the selection; (b) tell why your audience will probably like it; (c) tell the theme of the selection; or (d) describe a common human problem for which the selection offers a solution. Present the selection with the same communicative directness which you used in your introductory remarks.

6. Two or more students select the same piece for exercise 5 but prepare independently. The class listens to both presentations and the members write a brief analysis and evaluation of each. The instructor may read these responses to the class, noting the relationships seen between the attitudes, moods, feelings, and vocal characteristics of the speakers.

7. Lie flat on your back and relax completely. Breathe deeply. Place your hand on your abdomen so that you can feel the expansion and contraction. Now inhale slowly to the count of five and exhale to the same count of five. Note what happens as you change the count to one for inhalation and one for exhalation. Then note what happens when you inhale to the count of one and exhale to the count of five. Note what happens when you reverse that count. Inhale to the count of five and see how high a count you can reach for the exhalation phase.

8. Practice reading aloud material in which you have in advance marked off the words in units of ten. See how many units you are able to read on each exhalation. Do not read more rapidly than is meaningful

and appropriate to the material. Practice this for at least ten minutes a day for a period of ten days. See how greatly you can increase the number of words you read rather easily per exhalation.

9. Read aloud an approved selection of at least 300 words and have the reading recorded. Then work with the selection for a time, seeking to utilize all possible vocal variety in its delivery. Make a second recording. Compare the two recordings and evaluate your progress.

10. Prepare a speech to be delivered to the class from a position that enables you to be heard but not seen. You might stand behind a screen or, if microphone and amplifier are available, even in another room. Choose a subject in which you are enthusiastically interested. Limit your talk to four minutes. Remember that the only impressions and meanings which you can give to the class in this speech must come from your words and voice, without benefit of the visual code.

11. Practice reading aloud the following selections:

Unlimited submission and obedience is due to none but God alone. He has an absolute right to command; He alone has an uncontrollable sovereignty over us, because He alone is unchangeably good. He never will nor can require of us, consistent with His nature and attributes, anything which is not fit and reasonable. His commands are all just and good. And to suppose that He has given to any particular set of men a power to require obedience to that which is unreasonable, cruel, and unjust, is robbing the Deity of His justice and goodness.— SAMUEL WEST, Massachusetts election sermon, 1776.

Tyranny brings ignorance and brutality along with it. It degrades men from their just rank into the class of brutes; it damps their spirits; it suppresses arts; it extinguishes every spark of noble ardor and generosity in the breasts of those who are enslaved by it; it makes naturally strong and great minds feeble and little, and triumphs over the ruins of virtue and humanity. This is true of tyranny in every shape: there can be nothing great and good where its influence reaches. For which reason it becomes every friend to truth and human kind, every lover of God and the Christian religion, to bear a part in opposing this hateful monster.—JONATHAN MAYHEW, preface to sermon, 1750.

The true patriot is one whose purse, as well as his heart, is open for the defense and support of his country.—NOAH WELLS, Connecticut General Assembly sermon, 1764.

True eloquence, indeed, does not consist in speech. It cannot be brought from far. Labor and learning may toil for it, but they will toil in vain. Words and phrases may be marshalled in every way, but they cannot compass it. It must exist in the man, in the subject, and in the occasion. Affected passion, intense expression, the pomp of declamation, all may aspire after it—they cannot reach it. It comes, if it come at all, like the outbreaking of a fountain from the earth, or the bursting forth of volcanic fires, with spontaneous, original, native force. The graces taught in the schools, the costly ornaments and studied contrivances of speech, shock and disgust men, when their own lives, and the fate of their wives, their children, and their country hang on the decision of the hour.—DANIEL WEBSTER, speech on Adams and Jefferson, 1826.

Shakespeare was an intellectual ocean whose waves touched all the shores of thought; within which were all the tides and waves of destiny and will; over which swept all the storms of fate, ambition, and revenge; upon which fell the gloom and darkness of despair and death, and all the sunlight of content and love, and within which was the inverted sky lit with the eternal stars—an intellectual ocean—toward which all rivers ran, and from which now the isles and continents of thought receive their dew and rain.—ROBERT G. INGERSOLL, lecture on Shakespeare, 1894.

There is no new thing to be said of Lincoln. There is no new thing to be said of the mountains, or of the sea, or of the stars. The years go their way, but the same old mountains lift their granite shoulders above the drifting clouds; the same mysterious sea beats upon the shore; and the same silent stars keep holy vigil above a tired world. But to mountains and sea and stars men turn forever in unwearied homage. And thus with Lincoln. For he was mountain in grandeur of soul, he was sea in deep undervoice of mystic loneliness, he was star in steadfast purity of purpose and of service. And he abides. —HOMER HOCH, speech in United States House of Representatives, February 12, 1923.

12. Study the implications of the following selection:

"A Word Fitly Spoken"[2]

BY JOHN T. WINTERICH

When Matthew Arnold came to this country to lecture in 1883, his New York debut was a failure. The *Herald's* account was damning in its factuality:

[2] Editorial in *Saturday Review,* March 2, 1946. Reprinted by permission of *Saturday Review*.

He only partially opened his mouth, and, consequently, could not be heard beyond the fourth row of benches. He held his manuscript in his left hand, nearly level with his face. . . . Mr. Wayne MacVeagh (who was also on the platform) penciled the word "Louder" on the back of a visiting card and sent it to Mr. Arnold, and then came several cries of "Louder" from the back seats.

The *Daily Tribune* noted that "he has the common defect of the English clergy among whom he was educated—the habit of dropping his voice at the end of a sentence, which renders it inaudible." The London *Times* correspondent cabled his paper that "Mr. Arnold's imperfect delivery was a great disappointment." It was a most inauspicious introduction to the New World.

A week or so later Arnold appeared in Boston. The *Times* reported a great improvement—and had the explanation:

He had been carefully "coached" by a professor of elocution, the result being that his voice was much louder, and that he was plainly heard. The audience, a large one, gave the lecturer a favourable reception.

The coach, Harriet R. Holman of the Duke University Library discloses in *The New England Quarterly,* was John Wesley Churchill, Jones professor of elocution at Andover Theological Seminary. Both Arnold and Churchill agree that the coaching consisted of only two brief lessons—Churchill, declared Arnold, "went twice for twenty minutes to the hall with me when it was empty, heard me read, and stopped me when I dropped my voice at the end of the sentences, which was the great trouble." Professor Churchill apparently donated his services. And more. When an articulate Arnold later lectured at Andover, he was Churchill's house guest. . . .

When Arnold returned to New York, his sponsors announced in their advertisements: "The Management beg to assure the public that Mr. Arnold will be distinctly heard in all parts of the hall." He was. Subsequently, facing an audience of 3500 in the Brooklyn Academy of Music, the Brooklyn *Eagle* reported, he "spoke slowly, deliberately, and could be heard in all parts of the house—a great improvement over his first lecture."

There is no "Elocution" entry in the telephone books of today, though "Public Speaking Instruction" is listed in the Manhattan classified telephone directory, with six practitioners, plus sixteen more or less affiliated "Radio Coaches and Critics."

Radio itself has done little enough to promote the cause of the spoken word, although it claims to set great store by "diction," by which it does not mean diction at all. The ideal radio voice, judging by frequency of occurrence, seems to be that which combines the plausibility of the insurance solicitor with the unctuousness of the undertaker.

The motion picture, for all the good it has done the cause of spoken English, might just as well have remained silent. Rarely has it been characterized by such consideration for the spoken word as in Charles Laughton's inspired interpolation of Lincoln's Gettysburg Address into the script of "Ruggles of Red Gap." In this as in so many other concerns, Hollywood is generally content with something that is a little below mediocrity rather than a little above it.

Professor Churchill, were he alive today, would find plenty of people who would benefit by his skill, but few who would avail themselves of the opportunity. A great namesake, possessed of a voice ringingly audible in all parts of the house that is the world, would certainly arouse and hold his admiration. He would find no Webster, no Everett, no Bryan, no Roosevelt. He would find plenty of audiences and plenty of speakers, but the audiences, for the most part, would have come to see rather than to listen, the speakers to be looked at rather than to be heard—what they said, how they said it, meant little.

A larger literacy is a noble goal, but we learn to speak before we learn to read, and at the other end of life our eyes are likely to give out before our voices. Between the first and the final infirmity, we could all strive with more persistence than most of us do to be heard beyond the fourth row of benches—to have something to say, be it to one man or to millions, and to have the words to say it with and the capacity to utter those words with every consideration for the power and music that are in them. Every man who talks, unless he talks only to himself, is a public speaker.

Bibliography

Gray, Giles W., and C. M. Wise, *The Bases of Speech* (3d ed.; Harper, 1959).

CHAPTER 15

CONTENTS

Students "on the air" at the University of Michigan. Since the audience can get no visual cues, carefulness of articulation and correctness of pronunciation are particularly important. (University of Michigan News Service)

IMPROVING ARTICULATION AND PRONUNCIATION

O PINIONS on articulation and pronunciation greatly differ.
Charles W. Eliot, once president of Harvard University and editor of
the famed "Harvard Classics," emphasized careful speech as his criterion of education: "I recognize but one mental acquisition as an
essential part of the education of a lady or gentleman, namely, an
accurate and refined use of the mother tongue." It is evident that
Dr. Eliot meant the way in which words are spoken as well as their
selection and use. Many discriminating persons would agree, but
other people, and they are the majority, seem to fear that such metic-
ulousness or care would produce too great uniformity in our speech.
Those who urge that there should be some set "standards" which all
others should approximate tend to overlook the many difficulties that
selecting such standards would entail. There are regional, social,
economic, and occupational differences; and even were all to agree
upon some "model," complete consistency would never be found.
It is our own opinion that good articulation or good pronunciation
is chiefly distinguished by the fact that it communicates meaning
without drawing attention to itself.

THE MEANING OF ARTICULATION

Articulation means, technically, the process by which the breath
stream is modulated, principally by movement of the articulators
—soft palate, hard palate, tongue, teeth, jaws, and lips—to form
and differentiate the consonant sounds of speech. The term *enunciation* is commonly used to designate the production of vowel
sounds. In the strict sense of this differentiation between articulation and enunciation, vowels are said to be standardized sounds produced by vibrations of the vocal bands which are uninterrupted and
are modified only by certain changes in the resonating cavities;

380

whereas the sounds we commonly describe as consonants are produced by interruptions and modifications of these vibrations by the articulators. Actually, the production of vowel sounds requires movement, or articulation, to at least as great an extent as does the production of such consonant sounds as *l, r,* and *sh*. Hence, for all practical purposes, enunciation may be regarded as simply a form of articulation. In the preceding chapter, voice was considered as the phonation and resonation of the exhaled breath stream. Articulation is considered in this chapter as the further modulation of that same exhaled breath stream to produce meaningful, understandable, and effective speech.

HOW ARTICULATION ADDS TO VOICE

Our discussion in the preceding chapter was limited to the production of voice. This was for purposes of clarity and simplification. We are now to consider another step in the process of speech production. It is not enough for the breath stream to produce voice. The breath stream must be further modulated to form the articulate sounds, words, and sentences through which we express our feelings and communicate our meanings. It is equally true that force, pitch, and quality—all discussed as essential characteristics of voice—play essential roles also in articulation. And here we shall see the importance of an additional factor: rate. We shall note also that not all sounds comprising our speech are voiced. This gives further reason for our separate analysis of voice and articulation.

Voice itself, without the aid of articulation and pronunciation, communicates primarily emotional meanings. It is the voice which reveals many personality characteristics, moods, feelings, and attitudes. The vowel sounds contribute most to the musical quality of speech. The consonants are the carriers of meaning and intelligibility. The total process of communication of meaning by speech requires the synchronized functioning of voice, articulation, and pronunciation.

The ways in which articulation adds to voice are further revealed by a consideration of the factor of force. The student of speech must not only learn to produce force in the voice but must master the art of its varying use to achieve emphasis and climax. The artificial forcefulness which we associate with insincerity is often present in changes of pitch and breath pressure—the essential mechanics of force; in fact, these only give it an appearance of being "pumped up" to meet the speaker's needs. The genuine forcefulness of sincere feeling, on the other hand, seems to pour out of an inexhaustible source, being shaped and modified in its effortless course by the articulators. Forcefulness is not an end in itself. It is a *means* to articulation, pronunciation, and effective speech.

RATE AS A FACTOR

Rate is another factor (along with pitch, force, and quality) which basically influences understandability and effectiveness of speech. It is a term used to designate a speaker's speed of utterance. Pause, duration, and rhythm are all involved in rate. They aid in the communication of fine shades of mood and emotion and, in making the factual meaning clear, they help to reveal the personality of the speaker, and they are of value in avoiding monotony and in holding and directing the attention of the listeners.

The speaking rate may be increased or decreased by varying the duration of each sound and the number and length of pauses between sounds. A speaker tends to have an individual rate of speaking. Yours may be 90 words a minute, 125 (which is average), or 160. The speaker's general rate is, however, but one of the important rate factors. If others complain that you talk too rapidly or too slowly, no doubt you should strive for a more acceptable average rate. But it is even more important that your rate should be varied to suit subject matter, mood, purpose, and audience situation.

Variety in rate will help (1) to make the speaker's meaning clear; (2) to accomplish for the listener the function which punctuation performs for the reader; (3) to mark transitions from one idea to another; (4) to emphasize important ideas; and (5) to hold attention.

Mastery of rate is achieved more easily than are basic changes in pitch or quality. The average number of words spoken per minute, as affected by duration of sounds and by pauses, can be increased or decreased through practice motivated by resolute determination and checked by accurate timing. It should be borne in mind that under stress of the actual speaking situation the rapid speaker tends to speed up and the slow speaker tends to slow down. This is but another evidence of the tenacity with which habits assert themselves when the speaker's mind is diverted from their control to the general factors of the speaking situation. The remedy is to practice the desired average rate so persistently that it dislodges the undesirable rate of speaking and becomes itself the habitual mode.

Pause

An important element of effective speaking to which beginning speakers pay far too little attention is *pause*. The experienced speaker almost always makes greater use of the pause than does the inexperienced. It is an exceedingly helpful device for emphasis and for getting an audience to think with the speaker. Every speaker should know the fundamental difference between a *pause* and a *hesitation*. A pause has a definite communicative function; during the pause the speaker, through eye contact and the confidence of his manner, maintains full command of the audience. Moreover, the pause is properly timed by the speaker for its maximum effectiveness. During a hesitation, on the other hand, the speaker loses control of his audience, of his speech, and of himself. He reveals his uncertainty by a shifting of his eyes and perhaps by other evidences of nervousness. During a pause the vibrations of the vocal bands are always stopped, so that there is no sound; but during a hesitation the speaker frequently fails to stop the vibrating vocal bands, and the disturbing "ah" or "uh" habit results. The hesitation, then, is a revelation of weakness; it should be eliminated entirely as the speaker's experience grows. The pause, however, is an evidence of strength, sureness, ease, and maturity as a speaker. It is useful for the listeners, since they will have more opportunity to think about what the speaker is saying. It is physiologically helpful to the speaker, for it gives him ample opportunity for inhalation. It frequently adds to the impressiveness of what is being said.

Duration

Duration of sound is a speech factor of which we are most conscious when we listen to the drawling speech of southern and southwestern Americans. However, you may note very readily how the duration of sounds produced by any speaker varies widely, depending upon his mood, purpose, and meaning. Duration is particularly important to the connotation of words. Solemnity, for example, is suggested in part by an elongation of the vowel sounds. Tension and excitement, on the other hand, are suggested by shortening and quickening the vowel sounds. These functions of duration may be tested very easily by reading through the familiar poem "Tam O'Shanter," in which Robert

Burns successively considers the metaphysics of witchcraft and depicts the wild terror and flight of Tam when a witch pursues him. Alexander Pope both expressed and illustrated the relation of duration of sound to meaning in the following lines from "An Essay on Criticism":

> But most by numbers judge a poet's song;
> And smooth or rough, with them is right or wrong:
> In the bright Muse though thousand charms conspire,
> Her voice is all these tuneful fools admire;
> Who haunt Parnassus but to please their ear,
> Not mend their minds, as some to church repair,
> Not for the doctrine, but the music there.
> These equal syllables alone require,
> Though oft the ear the open vowels tire;
> While expletives their feeble aid do join;
> And ten low words oft creep in one dull line.
>
> .   .   .   .   .
>
> Then, at the last and only couplet fraught
> With some unmeaning thing they call a thought,
> A needless Alexandrine ends the song
> That, like a wounded snake, drags its slow length along.

As to what the speaker should do to master duration, Pope also gives the best answer. While advising how to remedy the errors he has just described, he points out:

> True ease in writing comes from art, not chance,
> As those move easiest who have learned to dance.

Thus, the speaker should avoid the easy but false conclusion that whether his utterance of sounds is fast or slow, it at least is "natural" and therefore should be maintained. Dancing, writing—and speaking —come from "art, not chance" and those do best "who have learned" effective forms. Practice in reading selections printed in this and in the preceding chapters will make possible considerable variation in the average duration of sounds in your speech.

Rhythm

Rhythm has been discussed in the chapter on developing a speech style. Our empathic, physical (or kinesthetic) reaction to style is almost as marked as our reaction to the words used. Listeners cannot help reacting to the rhythmical quality (or to its lack) in speech. So fundamental is rhythm to good speaking that effective speech style is often described as that which "talks itself off the page"—that swings itself into the lilt of conversational talk. Rhythm involves duration and pause, variations of stress or force, and melody, or variations of pitch.

Obviously rhythm is an attribute of articulated speech, rather than of voice. It has its meaningful place in public speaking as well as in song; in prose as well as in poetry. Of course rhythm that degenerates into immature singsong or a monotonously patterned cadence is no more effective in speech that it would be in poetry. In the Psalms of the Old Testament, the masterpieces of great orators of the past, and selected passages from the speeches of Woodrow Wilson, Franklin D. Roosevelt, and Winston Churchill, effective speech rhythm is illustrated. What the beginning speaker must train above all, to improve his skill in using rhythm, is his ear. As he becomes conscious of the sound values of parallel phrasing, of balanced sentence structure, of restrained alliteration, and of language that is rhythmical without being metrical, his own ear will be his best guide to composing rhythmical speeches or to speaking with an appreciation and communication of the rhythm inherent in whatever speech he may be presenting.

Carelessness in Articulation

Slovenly articulation is a common fault which every speaker must be very careful to avoid. It destroys the charm of speech, interferes with the understanding of what is said, and limits the carrying power of the voice. Rupert Hughes, who is partly deaf, once explained why it is that deaf people may not hear remarks addressed to them but often do hear remarks which are not intended for their ears:

In ordinary conversation few people make any effort to focus their tones or articulate distinctly. We just wobble our lips and let the words spill. But when we want to convey a confidential remark to someone, we point the tone and speak with a great distinctness. That is why a stage whisper carries so far. So, when you are trying to slip a message past a deaf person, you do the very thing he has given up imploring you to do; you speak distinctly.

Faulty articulation is due in large part to lazy, immobile lips, tongue, and lower jaw; unless the organs of speech are diseased or malformed, it usually arises from an attitude of indifference toward the listener and from a lack of knowledge and training. It is a matter of the first importance for students to disabuse themselves of any notion that careful enunciation and articulation are pretentious attempts to be "elegant." They are no such thing. Dr. Lee Edward Travis in an article in *The Quarterly Journal of Speech,* stated the case very well:

. . . speech is a reflection of the personality of the speaker. With every utterance the speaker gives himself away. His speech is as a microscope directed toward his own inner self, through which others may get the most intimate glimpses. . . . Speech is a joint by which the speaker articulates with the person spoken to. The speaker's adjustments to his social situation depend upon the condition of this joint. . . . From many angles it is just as great a loss to have a speech sound missing or mutilated as it is to have a hand missing or mutilated.

Articulatory weakness may lie in the slurring or dropping of some sounds and the occasional addition or substitution of others, as in the following examples; *jist, singin, libary, goverment, jogerphy, athalete, agin, pufessor, faternity, labertory,* and *Amurica.* It may also consist in running words together, changing their form, and substituting other, simpler forms, as in the illustrative representation of one of Wordsworth's finest sonnets:

> Thee whirled a stew much widows. Latent soon
> Get in and spend din, Willie way star pars.
> Little we sea innate chew rat is sours.
> Weave give an hour arts a weigh, assorted boon.
> This seethe at bears Sir Booze hum to thumb moon,
> The win zat Will B. Howell in gat awl lowers
> Endor up gat heard an owl Ike's leaping flours,
> For this, forever wreathing weir rout of tune;
> It moves us knock. Greek hod! I'd rather be
> A pig unsuckled in a cree doubt warn
> So my tie stand in honest pleasantly
> Have glim, says Atwood, make mealless furl on,
> Have sigh to approaches rye sing from the sea
> Or Harold try to unblow his wreath adorn.

Now try reading the poem so as to convey to an audience the meaning Wordsworth sought to express:

> The world is too much with us: late and soon,
> Getting and spending, we lay waste our powers.
> Little we see in nature that is ours;
> We have given our hearts away, a sordid boon!
> This sea that bares her bosom to the moon,
> The winds that will be howling at all hours,
> And are up-gathered now like sleeping flowers;
> For this, for everything, we are out of tune;
> It moves us not.—Great God! I'd rather be
> A pagan suckled in a creed outworn;
> So might I, standing on this pleasant lea,
> Have glimpses that would make me less forlorn;
> Have sight of Proteus rising from the sea;
> Or hear old Triton blow his wreathèd horn.

CONCEPTS BASIC TO BETTER ARTICULATION

The prerequisite for remedying slovenly articulation is the adoption of a new attitude toward speech. Unless the speaker has a physical deformity of his articulatory organs, such as a harelip or a paralyzed tongue, he will be able to articulate properly if he genuinely desires to do so and if he has proper guidance and training to help him. However, perfect articulation requires as much practice and persistence as does any other physical skill, be it playing the piano or running the hundred-yard dash.

Although there are some general principles which will be useful for all, it is important to note that problems of faulty articulation are highly individual. In spelling, for example, there are some rules of general utility regarding letter combinations, but the essential consideration in improving your spelling is to pay particular attention to mastering the words which you yourself customarily misspell. Just so, there are particular types of articulatory errors, but it will make little difference to you how these may be classified unless you suffer from a major form of articulatory disorder, such as lisping, which requires clinical diagnosis and therapy. In the main, careless articulation is an individual matter, requiring advice from your instructor and conscientious remedial measures by you the speaker.

In our study of articulation, as in our concern with all other phases of speech, the principal consideration is to achieve *effective communication*. This requires both that what you say be understood and that it be interpreted in terms which will help achieve your purpose. A speaker fails to communicate if what he says is so poorly articulated that the listeners cannot understand it or, instead of reacting to what is said, think, "What slovenly speech!" We do not aim for accuracy in articulation in order to add to our social grace—although this may in fact be one of the happy consequences. Our times demand that each of us be able to make himself heard distinctly over the telephone and perhaps over the radio and the public-address system, as well as in face-to-face communication.

AVOIDING COMMON WEAKNESSES IN ARTICULATION

You will wish to make certain that you are not guilty of any of the following:

1. *Mumbling* words by speaking too far down in the throat, without projection.

2. *Slurring* words, by running them together confusingly.
3. *Muffling* words, by lazy inactivity of lips and jaws.
4. *Garbling* words, by careless substitution of wrong for right sounds.

A specific example of *mumbling* is the dropping of the final *g* in a word such as *eating,* so that the word becomes *eatin.* Certain sounds may be omitted entirely, as the *n* in *government,* so that it becomes *goverment,* and the *g* in *recognize,* so that it becomes *reconize;* or the ends of words and sometimes even the entire final word of a sentence may be permitted to fade out of hearing. This dropping of sounds may result from poor phonation as well as from poor articulation, if there is a tendency to cut off phonation before the word is completed.

Slurring takes place when entire syllables and sounds are omitted, as when one says *djeat?* for *did you eat?* or *whuzat?* for *what was that?* or *yuright* for *you are right. Probly* and *libry* are commonly heard, lazily slurred renditions of *probably* and *library.* Slurring also occurs when weak vowel sounds are omitted entirely before strong vowel sounds, as when *the ode* becomes *thode.*

Lazy lip and jaw action, resulting in *muffling,* is a very common articulatory weakness. When it is coupled with a tendency to a rather musical speech, it may produce dialects which are characteristic of certain geographical areas. It will be noted that vowels are made to predominate in musical language, whereas consonants predominate in the language of speech. Inactivity of lips and jaws makes its contribution also to the mumbling and slurring which we have already considered. It accounts for a great deal of vowel substitution, as in *constitootion;* for *constitution;* even for the insertion of surplus vowels, as in *athalete;* and for the insertion of surplus consonants. Perhaps the most frequent examples of muffled sounds are to be found in the sliding over of certain consonant combinations which are difficult to articulate. *Wheat* and *what* become *weat* and *wat; d* is substituted for *t* in a word such as *little;* the *th* is pronounced as though it were the same in *with* and *arithmetic* or as though it were a *t* in such words as *through* and *thick.* The comprehensibility of speech is thus seriously impaired.

If we define *garbling* as careless substitution of wrong for right sounds, we have already noted some illustrations. But many other specific examples may be cited. In what is known as a survival of baby talk, *w* is substituted for *r,* so that *read* becomes *wead* and *Harry* becomes *Haw'i.* A common substitution of vowels occurs in the interchange of short *i* and short *e* sounds, so that *yet* becomes *yit* and *since* becomes *sence.* There is, of course, an entire group of *affectations,* which will be considered under pronunciation. In *hunderd* for *hundred* we have an illustration of a type of error arising from careless inattention to spelling. On the other hand, spelling cannot be relied upon as a guide to proper sounds, as is shown by such words as *hiccough, breeches,* and *women.* Just as serious as the omission of sounds is the inclusion of those which should be omitted, as *a(l)mond, com(b)ing, fore(h)ead, vi(c)t(u)als,* and *of(t)en.*

AVOIDING OVERPRECISE ARTICULATION

Before turning to the exercises designed to help you with your individual problems in articulation, you would do well to consider a word of warning. Good articulation does not mean affectation or overpreciseness in speech, which attracts undesirable attention. Your primary concern is to make your speech instantly intelligible to the hearer. Overstressing of some sounds may be as serious a handicap to intelligibility of speech as understressing of others. In normal conversational speech some syllables are shortened; note, for example, the italicized letters in extra*o*rdinary and int*e*resting. We have already noted that some sounds are dropped entirely, as in mor*t*gage, thou*gh*t, Wor*ce*ster, and brou*gha*m. Similarly, within sentences certain words need to be subordinated in order that meaning-carrying words may receive emphasis.

When speech is recorded and played back, the speaker can hear himself with reasonable objectivity and is thus greatly aided in correcting mistakes of articulation or pronunciation. (Wide World Photos, Inc.)

This is frequently true of the articles *a* and *the*. Note that proper articulation does *not* require that they always be pronounced with long *a* and long *e* sounds. Before our articulation is above reproach we must learn what and how to subordinate as well as what and how to stress. Much time spent with the following exercises and in reading aloud whenever you have the opportunity will pay excellent dividends.

EXERCISES

The following exercises should be practiced once—or if possible twice—a day, for as long as is necessary to establish habits of careful articulation:

1. Read these tongue-twisters aloud, gradually increasing your speed as your articulation attains sureness and precision:

Willis wouldn't walk willingly within winding windrows.

Silly Sally sang and simpered, simpered, smiled and sang sillily, to simple Sue.

Linger longer, Lemuel Lister, lilting limitless lullabies.

She sells sea shells. Shall Sally sell sea shells?

Many a wit is not a whit wittier than Whittier.

Are our cars here?

Theophilus Thistle, the successful thistle sifter, in sifting a sieve full of unsifted thistles, thrust three thousand thistles through the thick of his thumb. Now if Theophilus Thistle, the successful thistle sifter, in sifting a sieve full of unsifted thistles, thrust three thousand thistles through the thick of his thumb, see that thou, in sifting a sieve full of unsifted thistles thrust not three thousand thistles through the thick of thy thumb. Success to the successful thistle sifter.—CHESTER POND.

THE MODERN HIAWATHA
He killed the noble Mudjokivis.
Of the skin he made him mittens,
Made them with the fur side inside,
Made them with the skin side outside,
He, to get the warm side inside,
Put the inside skin side outside;
He, to get the cold side outside,
Put the warm side fur side inside.
That's why he put the fur side inside,
Why he put the skin side outside,
Why he turned them inside outside.
—ANONYMOUS.

2. Read the following words aloud to a person standing fifty feet away, so that he will be able to distinguish readily between the paired terms:

accepted—excepted	pictures—pitchers
adapt—adopt	pleasantly—pleasantry
affect—effect	practical—practicable
amplitude—aptitude	precede—proceed
ascent—accent	scold—sold
ate—hate	secede—succeed
booths—booze	sects—sex
consolation—consultation	seminary—cemetery
different—diffident	since—sins
disillusion—dissolution	specter—scepter
exalt—exult	stirred—third
foreboding—forbidding	wandered—wondered
glacier—glazier	weather—whether
immorality—immortality	willow—mellow

3. Read the following selections aloud, with particular care in the articulation of the sounds. Strive for purity and clarity without pedantically artificial precision. Read as though to a friend seated near you. Then, by increasing the clarity and precision of the articulation but not the volume, reread the selections so that they can be heard by someone fifty feet away:

The Assyrian came down like the wolf on the fold,
And his cohorts were gleaming in purple and gold;
And the sheen of their spears was like stars on the sea,
When the blue wave rolls nightly on deep Galilee.
—GEORGE GORDON, LORD BYRON.

We are such stuff
As dreams are made on, and our little life
Is rounded with a sleep.
—WILLIAM SHAKESPEARE.

I could not love thee, dear, so much,
Lov'd I not honour more.
—RICHARD LOVELACE.

His voracity is well known, and from the circumstance that the inner angles of his lips are curved upwards, he carries an everlasting Mephistophelean grin on his face.—HERMAN MELVILLE.

Sabrina fair,
Listen where thou art sitting
Under the glassy, cool, translucent wave,
In twisted braids of lilies knitting
The loose train of thy amber-dropping hair.
—JOHN MILTON.

Come, secret sleep, with thy unuttered psalm,
Come, heavy dreamless sleep, and close and press
Upon mine eyes thy fingers dropping balm.
                              —CHRISTINA ROSSETTI.

Night's candles are burnt out, and jocund day
Stands tiptoe on the misty mountaintops.
                              —WILLIAM SHAKESPEARE.

A summer on the loftiest height, with cold fountains and blissful stillness; oh come, my friends, that the stillness may become more blissful!
                              —FRIEDRICH NIETZSCHE.

It is a beauteous evening, calm and free.
The holy time is quiet as a nun,
Breathless with adoration.
                              —WILLIAM WORDSWORTH.

Sleep is a reconciling,
A rest that peace begets;
Shall not the sun rise smiling
When fair at even it sets?
                              —ANONYMOUS.

STANDARDS OF PRONUNCIATION

Pronunciation is to speaking what spelling is to writing. It is important not only for conveying meaning but also as an index to educational
attainment. It is dangerous, however, to speak of correct pronunciation, for pronunciation is constanly changing and the standards by
which it may be judged are neither definite nor universally agreed
upon. Dictionaries, which are popularly considered to be the arbiters
of correct pronunciation, are actually only its recorders, and they sometimes disagree. The spelling of words is a very unsatisfactory indication
of their pronunciation, in English at least, as may readily be seen in
the single illustration of the diverse ways of spelling the sound *sh*: *sh*e,
*Ch*icago, *s*ure, *sch*ist, an*x*ious, con*sc*ious, o*c*ean, no*t*ion, i*ss*ue, spe*c*ial,
and mi*ss*ion. Popular usage is not a reliable guide, because, owing to
dialectal differences, foreign accents, and sheer indifference to precision in speech, there is no general agreement among the majority of
Americans as to pronunciation. Although the usage of cultivated
speakers is doubtless the best guide, it is found that they vary in
pronunciation from locality to locality and sometimes even among
themselves in a given territory.

It should not be concluded, however, that there are no standards by which the individual may govern his pronunciation. The following reasonable requirements ought to be met by every careful speaker:

1. Know the sounds of English speech, and learn to think of them in terms of their sound, rather than according to their spelling.

2. Strive to avoid eccentricity in your pronunciation. "Be not the first by whom the new are tried, Nor yet the last to put the old aside." Pronunciation varies a little with the individual. The length and emphasis given to syllables is in part an individual matter. But people expect a familiar pattern of pronunciation, and communication is hindered when you disappoint their expectations.

3. Be consistent with your own practice in the pronunciation of words having two or more acceptable pronunciations. Do not say *dāta* one time and *däta* another.

4. Decide upon your pronunciations of words on the basis of the practice of cultivated speakers of your locality and of the recommendations of a good dictionary. If you must differ from one or both of these guides to acceptable pronunciation, have some better reason than mere ignorance of what the best practice is.

THE SOUNDS OF ENGLISH

The number of vowel sounds commonly used in English speech is variously estimated at twelve to fifteen, the number of consonants at twenty-two to twenty-five, and the number of diphthongs at five or six. Obviously the twenty-six letters of the English alphabet, some of which merely repeat the sounds of others (*c* is *s* or *k; qu* is *kw; x* is *ks, gz, ksh, gzh, z* or *sh*), are not adequate for identifying these forty common speech sounds.

There are two ways of overcoming the difficulty. One is to use diacritical markings over English letters, as most dictionaries do. An excellent description of this method will be found in "A Guide to Pronunciation," in *Webster's New Collegiate Dictionary*. Every student of the English language would profit by a thorough acquaintance with the Webster guide. This method of indicating pronunciation is often preferred on the grounds of its simplicity and convenience. However, its simplicity may be doubted when we consider that sixty-six different symbols are used in the Webster dictionaries to indicate English pronunciation. The alternative is to use a phonetic alphabet to indicate sounds. This method has the advantage of employing only one symbol for each sound unit.

A detailed analysis of English speech sounds, with a consideration of American regional pronunciations and a host of practical suggestions for overcoming common errors, is presented in "Guide to Pronunciation," pages xxvi-cxxiii, in Morriss H. Needleman's *A Manual of Pronunciation*. This "Guide" will answer any questions students are likely to have concerning any sound or combination of sounds in American speech.

Study the symbols in the phonetic key, which follows, until you are able to produce and hear each one as a distinct and pure sound.

THE PHONETIC KEY[1]

CONSONANTS

[p]	as in "pen"
[b]	as in "bat"
[t]	as in "tag"
[d]	as in "dam"
[k]	as in "kin"
[g]	as in "get"
[m]	as in "may"
[n]	as in "now"
[ŋ]	as in "sing"
[f]	as in "for"
[v]	as in "vim"
[θ]	as in "thin"
[ð]	as in "then"
[s]	as in "son"
[z]	as in "zinc"
[ʃ]	as in "she"
[ʒ]	as in "azure"
[l]	as in "low"
[r]	as in "rear"
[w]	as in "will"
[j]	as in "you"
[h]	as in "hot"
[tʃ]	as in "China"
[dʒ]	as in "jury"
[hw]	as in "where"

VOWELS

[i]	as in "machine"
[ɪ]	as in "it"
[e]	as in "chaotic" (first vowel)
[ɛ]	as in "bet"
[æ]	as in "at"
[a]	as in "ask"
[ʌ]	as in "cut"
[ə]	as in "aware" (first vowel)
[ɝ]	as in "third"
[u]	as in "rule"
[ʊ]	as in "pull"
[o]	as in "hotel"
[ɔ]	as in "ought"
[ɒ]	as in "sorry"
[ɑ]	as in "father"

DIPHTHONGS

[eɪ]	as in "day"
[aɪ]	as in "ice"
[oʊ]	as in "go"
[aʊ]	as in "house"
[ɔɪ]	as in "joy"
[ju]	as in "use"

[1] Except for minor adaptations in the interest of simplicity and general usability, the authors have accepted the phonetic alphabet as used in *A Pronouncing Dictionary of American English,* by John S. Kenyon and Thomas A. Knott, published in 1944 by G. & C. Merriam Company, Springfield, Massachusetts. That the use of this alphabet has wide support by contemporary authorities in pronunciation is indicated in the article "A Symposium on Phonetics and Standards of Pronunciation," by C. K. Thomas, in *Quarterly Journal of Speech,* October, 1945, pp. 318–27.

PROBLEMS IN PRONUNCIATION

Correct pronunciation involves (1) acceptable articulation of vowels, diphthongs, and consonants; (2) proper accentuation of syllables; and (3) proper modification and combination of sounds as they are found in groups. The first two factors deal with the pronunciation of individual words, the third with the pronunciation of words in sentences. A few words change their pronunciation markedly in different contexts, and in general the problem of pronunciation is different when the speaker's attention is directed to an entire sentence than when it is centered upon a single word. Familiar examples are *a, the, wind, address, bow,* and *contract.*

Improvement in pronunciation will be continuous and permanent if the student acquires the habit of listening carefully to the pronunciation of cultivated speakers and of using the dictionary freely when in doubt.

Since pronunciation is an active physiological process involving certain patterning and coordination of muscle movements, there is a persistent biological tendency for that pronunciation to predominate which is easier to make—so long as the end product meets the test of reasonable intelligibility. We have noted that pronunciation is not static, but rather is constantly changing. Reading a few lines from Chaucer will make this apparent. If you wish, then, to choose between two acceptable pronunciations of a given word, you may be reasonably sure—other things being equal—that the pronunciation which is easier to make will have the better chance of survival. Thus *wind,* which used to rhyme with *kind,* has been rendered easier to pronounce by a shortening of the vowel sound. Countless illustrations can be given to show how dominant this principle has been in the patterns of changing pronunciations through the decades. The student who is particularly interested in the subject may compare pronunciations preferred by earlier editions of *Webster's Collegiate Dictionary* with those preferred in later editions.

EXERCISES AND BIBLIOGRAPHY

Exercises

1. Look up the preferred pronunciation of these words in a dictionary specified by your instructor:

abdomen	address (*n.*)	allies
abstract (*n.*)	address (*v.*)	alma mater
abstract (*v.*)	adept	almond
absurd	admirable	alternate (*n.*)
accent (*n.*)	adult	alternate (*v.*)
accent (*v.*)	adverse	alumni
accept	advertisement	amateur
accessories	again	ambassador
acclimate	alias	amenable
addict	allege	antisocial

2. Use the following chart as a basis for analyzing the elements of voice and articulation used in talks in the class or in materials read aloud.

COMMON SPEECH CHARACTERISTICS[2]

Factor	Desirable	Undesirable
1. Voice quality	a. Pleasant b. Resonant	a. Nasal b. Throaty c. Breathy d. Raspy e. Squeaky f. Thin g. Improper tone placement
2. Inflection and pitch variation	a. Consonant with age, sex, and physique b. Appropriate range c. Optimum pitch	a. Monotone b. Recurrent pitch pattern c. Too high d. Too low e. Unnatural inflection
3. Volume	a. Varied b. Loud enough for all to hear	a. Too weak b. Too loud c. Unchanging
4. Rate	a. Varied b. Appropriate to context and material	a. Constant b. Too few pauses c. Too many pauses d. Unsuited to context, difficulty of material, etc.
5. Force	a. Stresses (by rate, pitch, volume) important points	a. Stresses unimportant points b. Excesses of rate, pitch, volume

[2] William S. Howell collaborated with C. F. Hager in constructing this chart for use in the speech program for Instructor Training in the Army Air Corps Technical Training Command, Truax Field, Madison, Wisconsin.

COMMON SPEECH CHARACTERISTICS—(*cont.*)

Factor	*Desirable*	*Undesirable*
6. Articulation and enunciation	a. Distinct b. Audible vowels and consonants	a. Indistinct b. Omissions (of sounds and syllables) c. Vowel substitutions d. Consonant substitutions

3. Practice pronouncing the following groups of words. Your instructor may ask you to work particularly upon certain of the sounds and sound combinations:

a. beat, peat, bit, bet, pet, bean, peal, bull, pull, pebble, budge, pudge, pearly, burly, bind, pile, able, apple, bind, pined, bound, pound, boy, deploy, feeble, people, dribble, dripple, crib, cripple, bill, pill, tuber, toper, paid, bayed, hip, inhibit, rabble, grapple, rubber, upper, peep, beep, ape, Abe, jib, gyp, Paul, ball, pole, bowl, rip, rib, cup, cub.

b. some ice, some mice; free ease, freeze; heats, he eats; beater, bee eater; mostly, most lee; bringing, bring ink.

c. chip, patching, pitch, chide, butcher, search, choice, Richard, teach, choose, witch hazel, church, chalice, ancient, rich, chinks, suspension, leech, convention, match, chew, catching, torch.

d. David, darned, drained, deal, teal, kit, kid, edible, debtor, hid, hit, ridden, written, darling, rudder, did, dad, bit, bid, kitty, eddy, better, tatter, adder, addle, tattle, straddle, dab, tab, but, bud, tut, dud, Doyle, toil, coiled, halt, fouled, fault, children, bittern, burst, bird, Bert, dynamic, data, reduce, said, drain, train, brat, brad, madder, matter.

e. few, view, fail, vale, fan, van, feel, veal, many, any, philosophy, cough, effervescent, laughter, lavatory, loaf, loaves, vivacious, vaudeville, vote, evil, live, lift, different, divide, vine, fine, foul, vowel, village, filler, advantage, perversity, perceive, involved, funnel, elephant, muff, fur, rafter, half, have.

f. get, care, egged, gig, keg, crag, king, pickle, nook, gain, thicken, twig, kitten, rugged, duck, cat, gat, coat, goat, camera, glamour, castle, guzzle, gaudy, aggression, frog, queue, knuckle, meek, kin, eked, ache.

g. Emma, numb, hymn, gnu, pneumonia, enema, mate, element, jam, mill, nil, simmer, sinner, hem, hen, Amy, any, nice, mice, mule, element, whim, diaphragm, knife, noun, mound, mount, mine, mountain, monster, merchant, maim, main, imagine, immense, contamination.

h. Harry, ahoy, behold, whole, hawk, hotel, heel, anyhow, exhale, enhance, hike, halt, held, hilt, holt, hull, hale.

i. George, soldier, just, pudge, adjacent, damage, jargon, budge, pigeon, wager, jest, page, wedge, staged.

j. twelve, shelf, help, lame, silver, crawl, only, unless moonlight, penalty, vanilla, lunch, yuletide, fowl, let, island, throttle, filbert, elf, loin, oiling, oblong, troll, tranquil.

k. Russian, regime, garage, session, hiss, his, presents, measure, sur-mise, unceasingly, missing, boats, seal, zeal, action, synthetic, loose, lose, raise, race, issue, usury, pleasure, push, issue, tresses, hats, swans, seizes.

l. English, sing, sin, wrangled, bringing, blanket, thank, sting, tongue, gangrene, finger, language, lengthen, long, ring, longingly, singsong, singular, anguish, cling, along, fungus, fan, fang, sun, sung, ingredi-ent, stingy, anger, swimmingly, ink, monk, ungrateful, sponge, dis-tinguish, hung, think.

m. rover, rather, red, arrow, precept, dealer, score, reward, rooster, railroad, wrist, mirror, fruit, drink, treat, program, thrall, try, throat, true, forest, prank, farther.

n. seal, zeal, assist, Mississippi, bliss, blitz, reason, session, vice, visor, prize, wise, buys, grass, bus, Easter, ace, haze, raise, race, racer, razor.

o. the, thing, this, thistle, forth, others, thaw, saw, thought, sought, synthetic, them, width, other.

p. what, whither, meanwhile, wheat, when, whisker, freewheeling, no-where, white, beyond, yeast, bullion, union, yoke, joke, yet, canyon.

4. Practice the following tongue-twisters:

a. Fuzzy-Wuzzy was a bear; Fuzzy-Wuzzy lost his hair. Fuzzy-Wuzzy wasn't fuzzy, was he?

b. Around and round the rugged rock the ragged rascal ran.

c. How much wood would a woodchuck chuck if a woodchuck could chuck wood? A woodchuck would chuck all the wood he could chuck if a woodchuck could chuck wood.

d. The wind ceaseth and sufficeth not.

e. Neddy Noodle nipped nine neighbors' nutmegs.

f. Sam Slick sawed six slippery sticks.

g. Sister Sue sells seashells by the sea shore.

h. Betty bit a bite of bitter butter.

i. I saw Esau kissing Sue; we all three saw: I saw Esau, he saw me, and Sue saw I saw Esau.

j. The fly and the flea flew through a flaw in the flue.

k. A tree toad loved a she-toad that lived up in a tree. She was a three-toed tree-toad, but a two-toed toad was he. The two-toed tree-toad tried to win the she-toad's friendly nod. For the two-toed tree-toad loved the ground that the three-toed tree-toad trod. But vainly the two-toed tree-toad tried; he could not please her whim. In her tree-toad bower, with her V-toed power, the she-toad vetoed him.

5. Read the following selections silently, taking considerable care to note the precise and full meaning of each. Then read them aloud. Be sure that you do not limit your communication by faults of articulation or pronunciation.

Gentlemen of the Jury:—If there is a culprit here, it is not my son— it is myself—it is I!—I, who for these last twenty-five years have opposed capital punishment—have contended for the inviolability of human life—I have committed this crime, for which my son is now arraigned. Here I denounce myself, Mr. Advocate General! I have committed it under all aggravated circumstances—deliberately, repeatedly, tenaciously. Yes, this old and absurd *lex talionis*—this law of blood for blood—I have combated all my life—all my life, gentlemen of the jury! And, while I have breath, I will continue to combat it, by all my efforts as a writer, by all my words and all my votes as a legislator! I declare it before the crucifix; before that victim of the penalty of death, who sees and hears us; before that gibbet, to which, two thousand years ago, for the eternal instruction of the generations, the human law nailed the Divine.

In all that my son has written on the law of capital punishment—and for writing and publishing which he is now before you on trial—in all that he has written he has merely proclaimed the sentiments with which, from his infancy, I have inspired him. Gentlemen Jurors, the right to criticize a law, and to criticize it severely—especially a penal law—is placed beside the duty of amelioration, like a torch beside the work under the artisan's hand. This right of the journalist is as sacred, as necessary, as imprescriptible, as the right of the legislator.

What are the circumstances? A man, a convict, a sentenced wretch, is dragged on a certain morning to one of our public squares. There he finds the scaffold! He shudders, he struggles, he refuses to die. He is young yet—only twenty-nine. Ah! I know what you will say—"He is a murderer!" But hear me. Two officers seize him. His hands, his feet, are tied. He throws off the two officers. A frightful struggle ensues. His feet, bound as they are, become entangled in the ladder. He uses the scaffold against the scaffold! The struggle is prolonged. Horror seizes on the crowd. The officers—sweat and shame on their brows—pale, panting, terrified, despairing—despairing with I know not what horrible despair—shrinking under that public reprobation which ought to have visited the penalty, and spared the passive instrument, the executioner —the officers strive savagely. The victim clings to the scaffold and shrieks for pardon. His clothes are torn—his shoulders bloody—still he resists.

At length, after three quarters of an hour of this monstrous effort, of this spectacle without a name, of this agony—agony for all, be it understood—agony for the assembled spectators as well as for the condemned man—after this age of anguish, gentlemen of the jury, they take back the poor wretch to his prison. The people breathe again. The people, naturally merciful, hope that the man will be spared. But no—the guillotine, though vanquished, remains standing. There it frowns all day in the midst of a sickened population. And at night, the officers, reinforced, drag forth the wretch again, so bound that he is but an inert weight—they drag him forth, haggard, bloody, weeping, pleading, howling for life—calling upon God, calling upon his father and mother—for like a very child had this man become in the prospect of death—they drag him forth to execution. He is hoisted onto the scaffold, and his head falls! And then through every conscience runs a shudder.—VICTOR HUGO, speech in defense of his son.

> Gr-r-r—there go, my heart's abhorrence!
>   Water your damned flower-pots, do!
> If hate killed men, Brother Lawrence,
>   God's blood, would not mine kill you!
> What? yon myrtle-bush wants trimming?
>   Oh, that rose has prior claims—
> Needs its leaden vase filled brimming?
>   Hell dry you up with its flames!
>
>   .   .   .   .   .
>
> Oh, those melons! If he's able
>   We're to have a feast! So nice!
> One goes to the Abbot's table,
>   All of us get each a slice.
> How go on your flowers? None double?
>   Not one fruit-sort can you spy?
> Strange!—And I, too, at such trouble
>   Keep them close-nipped on the sly!
>   —ROBERT BROWNING.

> Hear the tolling of the bells—
>   Iron bells!
> What a world of solemn thought their monody compels!
>   In the silence of the night,
>   How we shiver with affright
> At the melancholy menace of their tone!
>   For every sound that floats
>   From the rust within their throats
>   Is a groan.

And the people—ah, the people—
They that dwell up in the steeple,
    All alone,
And who, tolling, tolling, tolling,
   In that muffled monotone,
Feel a glory in so rolling
   On the human heart a stone—
They are neither man nor woman—
They are neither brute nor human—
    They are Ghouls:—
And their king it is who tolls:—
And he rolls, rolls, rolls,
    Rolls

    A paean from the bells!
And his merry bosom swells
   With the paean of the bells!
And he dances, and he yells;
Keeping time, time, time,
In a sort of Runic rhyme,
   To the paean of the bells:—
    Of the bells:
Keeping time, time, time,
In a sort of Runic rhyme,
   To the throbbing of the bells—
Of the bells, bells, bells—
   To the sobbing of the bells:—
Keeping time, time, time,
   As he knells, knells, knells,
In a happy Runic rhyme,
   To the rolling of the bells—
Of the bells, bells, bells:—
   To the tolling of the bells—
Of the bells, bells, bells, bells,
   Bells, bells, bells—
To the moaning and the groaning of the bells.
              —EDGAR ALLAN POE.

But what is education? Of course it is not book learning. Book learning does not make five per cent of that mass of common sense that
"runs" the world, transacts its business, secures its progress, trebles
its power over nature, works out in the long run a rough average justice,
wears away the world's restraints, and lifts off its burdens. The ideal
Yankee, who "has more brains in his hands than others have in their
skulls," is not a scholar; and two-thirds of the inventions that enable

France to double the world's sunshine, and make Old and New England the workshops of the world, did not come from colleges or from minds trained in the schools of science, but struggled up, forcing their way against giant obstacles, from the irrepressible instinct of untrained natural power. Her workshops, not her colleges, made England for a while, the mistress of the world; and the hardest job her workman had was to make Oxford willing he should work his wonders.

—WENDELL PHILLIPS.

If you wish to know the difference between an orator and an elocutionist—between what is felt and what is said—between what the heart and brain can do together, and what the brain can do alone—read Lincoln's wondrous speech at Gettysburg, and then the oration of Edward Everett. The speech of Lincoln will never be forgotten. It will live until languages are dead and lips are dust. The oration of Everett will never be read.

The elocutionists believe in the virtue of voice, the sublimity of syntax, the majesty of long sentences, and the genius of gesture. The orator loves the real, the simple, the natural. He places the thought above all. He knows the greatest ideas should be expressed in the shortest words—that the greatest statues need the least drapery.

—ROBERT G. INGERSOLL.

The great triumvirate of lecture kings consisted of Gough, Beecher, and Wendell Phillips. Other men for a season, and sometimes for a few years, were as popular as any of them, but it was a calcium-light popularity, whereas the popularity of the "Big Three" endured for their entire lives.

Phillips held his place the longest, beginning lyceum work about 1845, and continuing it to his death, nearly forty years later. Gough was the most supremely popular—not the greatest of the three intellectually, but most level to the largest number of the plain people. Beecher came parallel with him and had a higher influence. Beecher touched the hearts of men; Gough held by the fear of the effects of wrong-doing; Phillips, through the intellect, reached the conscience of his generation.

—JAMES BURTON POND.

TO NIGHT

Swiftly walk o'er the western wave,
    Spirit of Night!
Out of the misty eastern cave,
Where all the long and lone daylight,
Thou wovest dreams of joy and fear,
Which make thee terrible and dear,—
    Swift be thy flight!

Wrap thy form in a mantle grey,
    Star-inwrought!
Blind with thine hair the eyes of Day;
Kiss her until she be wearied out;
Then wander o'er city, and sea, and land,
Touching all with thine opiate wand—
    Come, long-sought!

When I arose and saw the dawn,
    I sighed for thee;
When light rode high, and the dew was gone,
And noon lay heavy on flower and tree,
And the weary Day turned to his rest,
Lingering like an unloved guest,
    I sighed for thee.

Thy brother Death came, and cried,
    Wouldst thou me?
Thy sweet child Sleep, the filmy-eyed,
Murmured like a noon-tide bee,
Shall I nestle near thy side?
Wouldst thou me?—And I replied,
    No, not thee!

Death will come when thou art dead,
    Soon, too soon—
Sleep will come when thou art fled;
Of neither would I ask the boon
I ask of thee, beloved Night—
Swift be thine approaching flight,
    Come soon, soon!

          —PERCY BYSSHE SHELLEY.

Introduction, Songs of Innocence

Piping down the valleys wild,
    Piping songs of pleasant glee,
On a cloud I saw a child,
    And he laughing said to me:

"Pipe a song about a Lamb!"
    So I piped with merry cheer.
"Piper, pipe that song again";
    So I piped. He wept to hear.

"Drop thy pipe, thy happy pipe;
    Sing thy songs of happy cheer!"
So I sang the same again,
    While he wept with joy to hear.

"Piper, sit thee down and write
    In a book that all may read."
So he vanished from my sight;
    And I plucked a hollow reed,

And I made a rural pen,
    And I stained the water clear,
And I wrote my happy songs
    Every child may joy to hear.
                    —WILLIAM BLAKE.

WHY SO PALE AND WAN, FOND LOVER?

Why so pale and wan, fond lover?
    Prithee, why so pale?
Will, when looking well can't move her,
    Looking ill prevail?
    Prithee, why so pale?

Why so dull and mute, young sinner?
    Prithee, why so mute?
Will, when speaking well can't win her,
    Saying nothing do 't?
    Prithee, why so mute?

Quit, quit for shame! This will not move;
    This cannot take her.
If of herself she will not love,
    Nothing can make her.
    The devil take her!
                    —SIR JOHN SUCKLING.

THE CLOD AND THE PEBBLE

"Love seeketh not itself to please,
    Nor for itself hath any care,
But for another gives its ease,
    And builds a Heaven in Hell's despair."

So sang a little clod of clay,
    Trodden with the cattle's feet,
But a pebble of the brook
    Warbled out these metres meet:

"Love seeketh only Self to please,
    To bind another to its delight,
Joys in another's loss of ease,
    And builds a Hell in Heaven's despite."
                    —WILLIAM BLAKE.

THE TWENTY-THIRD PSALM

The Lord is my shepherd, I shall not want.
He maketh me to lie down in green pastures;
He leadeth me beside the still waters.
He restoreth my soul;
He leadeth me in the paths of righteousness for his name's sake.
Yea, though I walk through the valley of the shadow of death, I will fear
no evil;
For thou art with me; thy rod and thy staff they comfort me.
Thou preparest a table before me in the presence of mine enemies;
Thou anointest my head with oil;
My cup runneth over.
Surely goodness and mercy shall follow me all the days of my life;
And I will dwell in the house of the Lord for ever.

THE BEATITUDES

Blessed are the poor in spirit: for theirs is the kingdom of heaven.
Blessed are they that mourn: for they shall be comforted.
Blessed are the meek: for they shall inherit the earth.
Blessed are they which do hunger and thirst after righteousness:
for they shall be filled.
Blessed are the merciful: for they shall obtain mercy.
Blessed are the pure in heart: for they shall see God.
Blessed are the peacemakers: for they shall be called the children of God.
Blessed are they which are persecuted for righteousness' sake: for theirs is
the kingdom of heaven.
Blessed are ye, when men shall revile you, and persecute you, and shall say
all manner of evil against you falsely, for my sake.
Rejoice, and be exceeding glad: for great is your reward in heaven:
for so persecuted they the prophets which were before you.

Bibliography

Anderson, Virgil A., *Training the Speaking Voice* (Oxford University Press, 1942).

Brigance, W. N., and Florence Henderson, *Drill Manual for Improving Speech* (Lippincott, 1955).

Eisenson, Jon, and Mardel Ogilvie, *The Improvement of Voice and Diction* (Macmillan, 1958).

Fields, Victor A., and James F. Bender, *Voice and Diction* (Macmillan, 1949).

Needleman, Morriss H., *A Manual of Pronunciation* (Barnes and Noble, 1949).

Van Riper, Charles, and John Irwin, *Voice and Articulation* (Prentice-Hall, 1958).

CHAPTER 16

CONTENTS

For a speech to inform his listeners about the care of an infant, this speaker has brought the best possible speech materials with which to demonstrate his message.

USING VISUAL AIDS

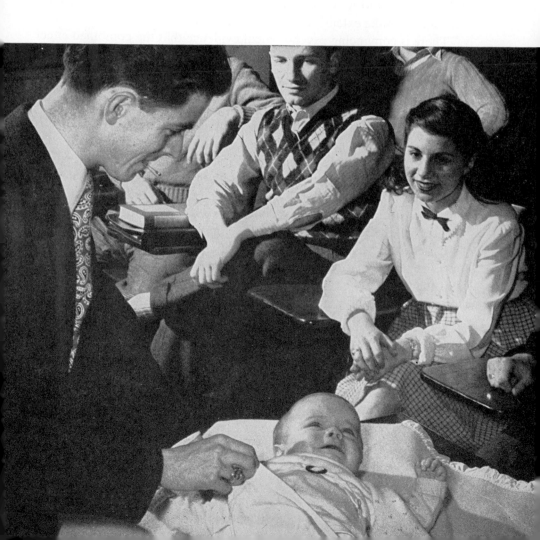

CONTINUING research is more firmly establishing principles long understood by successful speakers. What people *see* they *believe* even more unquestioningly than what they *hear*. You can confirm this from your own experience. The things you both see and hear are remembered longer and more accurately than what you merely hear. Hence you should make extensive use of visual aids.

There is convincing psychological evidence that the combined effect of seeing and hearing simultaneously is even greater than that of hearing and seeing separately. Travel lectures are illustrated; television advertising surpasses radio advertising in effectiveness; salesmen carry their demonstration kits. Chalk talks get premium results. Football coaches have always taught by diagraming plays on the blackboard; now they also use motion pictures of the season's games. Insurance salesmen carry elaborate charts and diagrams to convince prospects of the economy and protection offered by their insurance programs. In fund-raising campaigns oral appeals are reinforced by colorful brochures. All about us we find conclusive evidence that a speaker increases his effectiveness by adding eye appeal to ear appeal.

Listeners are even more understanding and impressionable as viewers. They are more eye-minded than ear-minded. You must, therefore, aim for their eyes as well as for their ears. How this is accomplished through the use of effective action was discussed in Chapter 13. This chapter will describe a variety of supplemental visual aids: photographs, models, specimens, charts, graphs, slides, motion pictures, opaque projections, and blackboard or easel drawings.

THE VALUE OF VISUAL AIDS

The complicated nature of the speaker's total task is shown by a recapitulation of his general purposes: to inform, to induce belief, to move to action, to inspire, or to entertain the listeners—or a combination of several or all of these. Research and experience indicate many ways by which visual aids may facilitate the attainment of the speaker's goals.

Visual Aids Can Increase Clarity and Understandability

Diagrams, like cartoons, not only have the value of being visible; they select and emphasize the significant, or most meaningful, aspects of a complicated concept. It is not surprising, therefore, that almost every research study comparing talks alone with talks accompanied by the showing of objects or pictures has revealed significantly greater listener comprehension when visual aids are used.

Visual Aids Can Add Attention Values of Their Own

Color, movement, design, contrast in light and dark, different shapes and sizes are but a few illustrations of specific attention values possible in the visual aid. They not only gain attention but also may help to hold it for the speaker. Hence we should not be surprised that research studies preponderantly show, first, that the speaker who makes effective use of visual aids has more attentive listeners, and, second, more enthusiastic listeners.

Visual Aids Can Make Ideas Vivid and Memorable

More than a third of a century ago, Harry A. Overstreet, in his *Influencing Human Behavior,* pointed out that the power of an idea depends upon the quickness and clarity with which it is received, and upon its ease of recall. Word pictures can be helpful, of course, but we remember much longer and far more vividly scenes from our own travels. We expect, then, the statistically significant evidence which has been reported to indicate one third better immediate recall and one half greater memory by listeners of information seen and heard as compared with information heard only.

Visual Aids Constitute an Additional Means of Emphasis

The listener's impression of a total speech can be one of confusion. The skilled speaker will make use of every means at his command to emphasize the important, the transitional, and the ultimately significant. Again, the eye can reinforce impressions gained by the ear. Visual images frequently impress themselves irresistibly upon our minds and emotions: at the very least they add another dimension to auditory images.

Visual Aids Can Help to Summarize and Give a Total Impact to Ideas

Perhaps the most effective speech is one which leaves the listener with one cumulative, overwhelming impression. A final, summarizing visual aid can greatly facilitate this. A picture which contains the speaker's message strengthens its impact on the listener-viewer. This writer will never forget the Sabbath message of a preacher who used only one visual aid: the picture of a small boy trustingly placing his hand in his father's as they start to cross a crowded avenue of life. Everyone will recall the famed poster of a young lad carrying on his shoulder a younger crippled boy, obviously too heavy for him to bear. The caption reads: "Too heavy? No Sir! He's my brother."

In short, visual aids make it possible for the speaker to accomplish his purpose in less time.

DANGERS TO BE AVOIDED

You may have noted in the preceding paragraphs how careful we have been to say that visual aids *can* be of help to the speaker. We now emphasize that they *can* be so ill chosen and so misused as to obstruct communication. Their very power to get attention, for example, makes the use of visual aids hazardous. Unless you select, prepare, and use them carefully, they may distract your audience from what you are saying. You will need to decide in each situation such questions as these: Shall I risk distracting the audience by presenting the visual aid before I refer to it in the speech? Are attention values gained or lost if the visual aids are left in place after my reference to them?

Although the average individual learns more efficiently by eye than by ear, visual learning is by no means superior in every way. On the contrary, for example, our span of attention is considerably broader auditorily than it is visually. Research shows that we can attend to no more than four or five objects visually, but may simultaneously attend to from five to eight objects auditorily. Of course, you should not tax your listeners' span of attention to its maximum, but you should bear in mind that this maximum may be only about half as great for visual as for auditory materials.

More specific dangers to be avoided will be mentioned in the remaining three sections of this chapter.

TYPES OF VISUAL AIDS

The types of visual aids used should be chosen for their suitability to the speaker's purpose and for their adaptability to the audience situation. Costliness does not necessarily coincide with effectiveness. Simplicity and clarity are the qualities that count. A complete "dress rehearsal" using the actual aids is a necessity.

Demonstration

The speaker should not overlook any opportunities for direct demonstration of experience. Thus a chemistry lecture may be accompanied by the actual performance of the experiment being explained and discussed. Certainly a lecture intended to teach persons how to tie certain knots would be greatly aided not only by the speaker's demonstrating with a piece of rope but by the listener's having a piece of rope in his own hands, so that he might learn by hearing, seeing, and doing. Demonstration is of great assistance in any talk explaining how to do things, whether it is how to serve in tennis, how to apply a tourniquet, or how to use a can opener.

When apparatus is too large to be brought before an audience or too small to be seen clearly, working models are often an effective substitute. The drama form of demonstration is sometimes both practical and extremely effective. The use of tableaux and pantomimes can add much to vividness and even to clearness. The television advertiser makes frequent use of dramatic scenes to supplement his sales talk. This type of presentation can be even more helpful to a speaker, whose audience is directly before him. A talk on folk dances, for example, would be greatly enhanced by the presence of dancers on the stage at one side of the speaker, demonstrating each dance as it is described. A talk on the art of make-up or on poise may be dramatized and made much more meaningful by a series of accompanying skits.

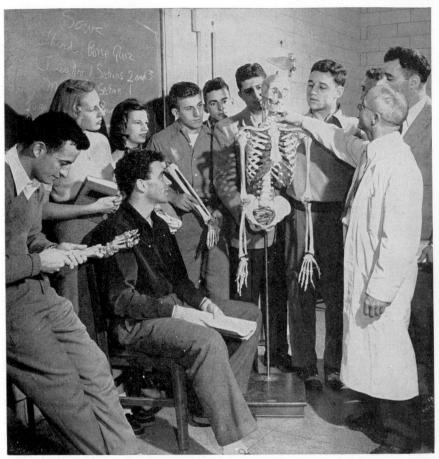

Courses in science, such as this one in zoology, could scarcely be taught without frequent and full use of visual aids.

The Blackboard

The blackboard will be the speaker's most commonly used visual aid. Though material may be put on it in advance, a more effective procedure is to put the material on the blackboard as it is referred to in the talk. The speaker or an assistant may do this. The following specific principles supplement the general suggestions which appear in the next section of this chapter:

1. Make certain that the lighting enables the entire audience to see clearly. Each listener must have a clear view of the board, with no one unable to see because of reflections on it.

2. In referring to a diagram or other material already on the board, use a pointer to direct attention where you wish it to be.

3. Stand out of the line of vision of your listeners as you are writing on the board or as you are pointing to materials already there. If you are right handed, stand to the right; if left-handed, to the left. Some practice may be required beforehand in order to write legibly while at the same time obstructing your audience's view as little as possible. Note that you should be looking at what is on the board whenever you wish your listeners to be looking there. The remainder of the time, *look at your listeners.*

4. Check beforehand so that you know how large the letters, figures, or diagrams must be for clear legibility from the most distant seat. Make a generous allowance for the nearsighted.

5. Take advantage of colored chalk whenever a color scheme will be helpful.

6. Draw the figure on the board as you explain it. This method best carries the listeners' thoughts along with your own. You may find it helpful, particularly for a large audience, to have an assistant do the blackboard work—but this will require rehearsal.

7. If the diagram is complex, or for some other reason calls for precise drawing, it may be placed on the blackboard in advance. Usually, however, it should then be kept covered until the precise moment when

Blackboard and charts communicate technical data far more clearly than can words alone. (U.S. Army)

you wish to use it in your talk. If it is thus complex, or if there is a great deal of information to be placed on the board, consider whether there might be an advantage in having the material mimeographed and placed in the hands of each listener.

8. Use the blackboard in a purposeful manner. Avoid such common mannerisms as covering the blackboard with meaningless doodling that distracts from your talk.

Charts, Graphs, Diagrams, Maps, Cartoons, and Pictures

The variety of pictures, charts, and graphs that may be used effectively is limited only by the speaker's ingenuity, resourcefulness, and imagination. A few suggestive examples are mentioned and illustrated here.

Charts are of many types.

1. Stream or tree charts clearly depict growth or development from simple beginnings to complicated later stages. You have seen such charts depicting, for example, the line of descent of a royal family. Following is an example of the tree chart (in horizontal position):

CHART OF SPEECH ACTIVITIES

Speech
- Voice and diction
  - Voice improvement
  - Phonetics
- Forensics
  - Speaker's bureau
  - Discussion
  - Debate
  - Extemporaneous speaking
  - Oratory
- Interpretive reading
  - Readers' bureau
  - Reading contests
  - Choral speaking
- Radio and television
  - Script-writing workshop
  - Announcers' workshop
  - Producers' workshop
  - Actors' workshop
- Science and correction
  - Speech-science laboratory
  - Speech-and-hearing clinic
- Theater
  - University theater
  - Community theater
  - Circular theater
  - Experimental theater

2. Data may also be presented in sequence charts, either chronological or topical. Such a chart might show, for example, the historical steps leading to World War II, or it might show in one column a list of industries and in parallel columns changes in wage rates. The following table is of this type:

AVERAGE YEARLY INCOME ACCORDING TO TRAINING

Age	Educational Level		
	GRADE SCHOOL	HIGH SCHOOL	COLLEGE
25–34	$4,000	$4,500	$5,500
35–44	4,300	5,200	7,500
45–54	4,200	5,100	8,800
55–64	3,800	4,900	7,000

Source: Bureau of Labor Statistics, United States Department of Labor. Reported in *U.S. News & World Report,* January 11, 1960. Column 1 includes those with some high school work, and column 2 those with some college work.

A simple topical chart such as the following visualizes progressive steps along the road to social and political action:

STEPS ALONG THE PATHWAY OF DEMOCRACY

Confusion → Discussion → Debate → Democratic action

3. Organizational charts may be constructed to depict the workings of businesses or governments. You will find samples of these in government or political science texts. By the use of rectangles and connecting lines, the organization of the United States government may be represented, showing the interrelationship of the three branches and the administration by the executive, through his cabinet, of the multitudinous bureaus and commissions.

4. Comparison and contrast charts are also helpful devices for summarizing and depicting relationships. Consider, for example, how difficult it would be for a speaker to make the following information clear with words alone, although the chart, too, requires explanation.

THE DIVISION OF THE ARTS*

	In time	*In space*	*In time and space*
Presentative	Music	Architecture	Dance
Representative	Literature	Painting and sculpture	Acting

* According to Robert Louis Stevenson.

A simple chart comparing the Fahrenheit and Centigrade temperature scales affords another example of how much more quickly clarity of understanding can come through the eye and the ear together than through the ear alone:

	Fahrenheit	Centigrade
Boiling point of water	212°	100°
Freezing point of water	32°	0°
Absolute zero	− 459.6°	− 273.1°

You are already familiar with *graphs* from your study of mathematics. You find them of daily help in the presentation of otherwise vague and incomprehensible data in newspapers and news magazines. Your own originality in picturing information may be stimulated by the examples given here of the more common graph forms: the pie graph, the segment-of-bar graph, the bar graph, and the line graph.

Diagrams, maps, cartoons, and *pictures* may also be found useful, provided they are large enough to be seen readily, are definite and precise helps to clearness, and are sufficiently simple to be comprehended

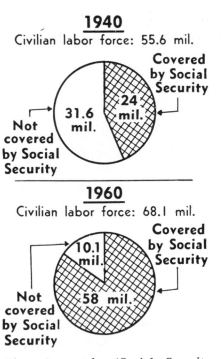

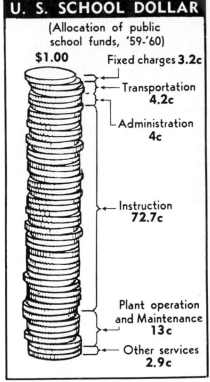

The pie graph. (Social Security Coverage for the Aged, from The New York Times, April 3, 1960)

The segment-of-bar graph. (How the U.S. Dollar Is Spent, from "The New York Times", March 27, 1960)

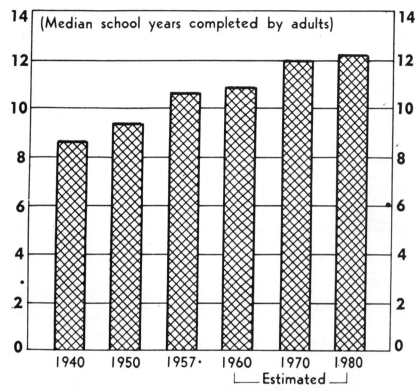

The bar graph. (Average Years of Schooling Completed by Adults in the U.S., from "The New York Times," August 9, 1959)

quickly and remembered easily. The creative and imaginative person will find ways to enliven and modify the traditional forms of charts and graphs. Proportionally sized figures, for example, can be both more interesting and more vivid than line, segment, or pie graphs.

Materials to Be Distributed

Distribution of materials to the listeners may be one of the least effective forms of visual aid. Probably its greatest asset is that it provides something which the listener may take away with him for study and review at a later time. Unless such later review is strongly motivated, however, the material is more likely merely to find its way into a wastebasket. Another serious problem encountered in placing material in the listeners' hands is that it is extremely difficult to prevent the listeners from giving their attention to the material when it should be focused upon the speaker.

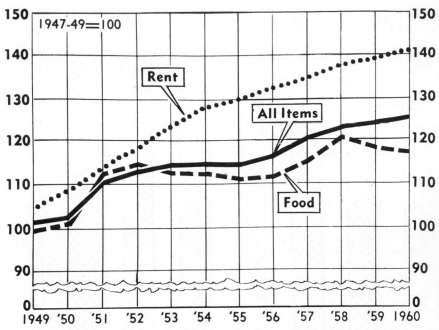

The line graph. (Trend of Consumer Prices, from "The New York Times," March 27, 1960)

But the speaker can minimize these difficulties. A working diagram or a picture in each listener's possession can be most helpful if the speaker refers to it as he explains it. An outline or instruction sheet can be of help if the speaker makes sure that the listeners follow the material as he explains it. Distributing material has the advantage that the listeners can jot down at appropriate places further explanatory notes for which they feel a need; they then have accurate material to carry away with them—material which can be a check upon the errors and frailties of memory. The time at which material is given to the listeners can be of great importance in determining its value. Remember that it will be a distraction at any time before it is actually needed and used by the speaker. It is generally advisable to have volunteer helpers pass out the material at the proper time. If the material is only supplementary and you intend to make no actual use of it during the talk, pass it out after the talk is ended.

It should be noted that printed or mimeographed materials are not the only kind that may be distributed to an audience. A speaker on plastics, for example, may pass out samples illustrating various points in his talk; a speaker on foreign money, or on old coins, may enhance his talk by passing around some bills or coins—*if the audience is suf-*

ficiently small to make this feasible. Problems of divided attention are certain to occur, however, and the speaker must weigh this disadvantage against the anticipated values. The speaker can reduce his problems if he is able to pass out enough samples of each type so that every listener can examine objects when they are being discussed, instead of long after.

As with other types of visual aid, do not overuse distributed materials. Use just enough to accomplish the aims of heightened interest and greater understanding. Remember that materials that are too numerous or too involved are certain to present a distraction.

Projected Materials

Projectors of various types are now so generally available that every speaker should be informed as to their uses. Picturization hitherto difficult or impossible is now made easy. Projected slides and motion pictures are expensive, however, and their cost must be evaluated by the speaker in terms of the effectiveness they may add to his presentation. Their use requires some modification of the usual speaking techniques. When the room is darkened, the speaker either must be prepared to get along without notes or must have a special arrangement for lighting his notes without diffusing the light. In using slides, the speaker and the operator will have to have a simple and clear signal system; they should rehearse in advance, with the operator showing the pictures, so that their timing is well worked out. Some speakers use a snap of the finger to call for the next silde. Some feel that this continual noise is more distracting and less reliable than a quick flash of a small flashlight.

Certainly the motion-picture film, when available, has tremendous value. It was demonstrated by the armed services during World War II that instructional films could considerably hasten the learning process. Colored travel films have become exceedingly popular; and nature sound films that not only show the behavior of animals and birds in their natural habitats but enable the audience to hear their calls have obvious values which are otherwise unattainable. The factors of costliness and of unavailability of films at the time and place they are needed still limit their use.

Fortunately, new types of projectors have recently been perfected which can be operated by the speaker as he faces his audience in a well-lighted room. They can project onto a screen behind and above the speaker a chart, an outline, or the page of a book which he has before him. Some of the recently developed instruments permit use of a succession of diagrams, showing progressive changes. The speaker does not have to turn to the screen. As he points with a pencil on the material before him to certain lines he may wish to emphasize, the moving point is projected onto the screen behind him. With such machines, much of the time the speaker would ordinarily spend in preparation beforehand of usable visual materials is saved; and materials which he might otherwise find it impossible to use can readily be presented directly from the page of any book or magazine.

Certain cautions with regard to the use of all types of projectors should be observed: (1) Be sure that the screen is clearly within the range of vision of all members of the audience. (2) Make certain that the image is large enough to be seen by those farthest away and that it is in focus. (3) Always make clear to the viewers the purpose of all projected material, and guide them to those points for which they are particularly to watch. (4) In using slides or other projected still materials, make sure beforehand that you have them arranged in correct order. (5) Be sure that your timing is right. Only practice and experience can tell you how rapidly you may change slides and still accomplish their purpose for a given audience and situation.

ASSURING EFFECTIVENESS

The various visual aids that have been reviewed—and the many others that might be mentioned—suggest the complexity of this addition to the usual speaker-audience situation. It is obvious that visual aids cannot and should not be used in all speeches. The following considerations may serve as guides to when and how visual aids may be used most effectively.

1. *Will visual materials really aid in the specific speaking situation?* Using pictures or other visual aids merely to fill time or to hold attention without regard to purpose is as futile and wasteful as telling a funny story which has no relation to the purpose of the speech. Check again the five purposes which visual aids may serve, as outlined on pp. 409-410. Unless the materials you have prepared will serve at least one of these purposes, you may expect them to be distractions instead of aids.

2. *Will the materials have sufficient value to justify their cost in time,*

money, and effort? You may well expect them to have some value or you would not consider using them. Value, however, is relative. Your materials should produce results that justify the expenditures you must make.

3. *Are the materials adapted to the listeners?* This problem is similar to the general one of adapting to the audience, which was discussed in Chapter 11. Your materials must be suited to the intelligence, interests, attitudes, knowledge of the subject, and general background of the listeners.

4. *Are the materials perfectly clear?* Are they large enough to be seen without difficulty? Is all lettering legible? Are color combinations the best possible for visibility? Are statistical data instantly comprehensible?

5. *Are the materials free of unnecessary and distracting details?* Materials which tell more than is necessary are wasteful of the attention of your audience and are too great a temptation to the speaker to explain more than is required. More specifically, are large numbers rounded off to the nearest hundreds, thousands, or millions? The figure 5½ million is much more quickly comprehended than 5,479,693. There are times when unnecessary exactness weakens rather than strengthens the point of the speech.

6. *Have you planned carefully to make the best possible use of the materials?* It has already been noted that the time and manner of their introduction is important. If you have charts or pictures, you must plan in advance how and where to put them so that the audience may see them clearly. You must so locate them that you will not be in the line of vision of any of the listeners. You must talk to the audience and not to the object, the blackboard, or the chart. If the materials may constitute a distraction after you have finished using them, plan for their removal. Except in unusual circumstances you cannot be making good use of the laws of attention if you have several things competing for the attention of an audience at one time.

7. *Do you follow up the advantages gained by using visual aids?* Note that visual aids often help to stimulate audience participation after a speech is concluded. As they remain before the audience, they stimulate questions and serve as reminders of points the listeners may wish to discuss or of points on which they desire further information. The visual aids, when used in this fashion, provide a valuable means of obtaining full audience participation in consideration of the subject of the speech.

8. *Have you guarded against undesirable effects?* A word should be said about the etiquette of using visual aids. If you are one of several speakers on a program, it certainly is not courteous for you to have your visual aids in distracting display while others are speaking. Second, the ethical responsibility of the speaker for the accuracy and reliability of the visual aids he uses is just as great as for the words he utters. He has an obligation to know that his materials are accurate and representative, that they are neither misleading nor deceptive. It is reassuring for a speaker to give the source of any evidence presented in charts or graphs.

A FEW SUGGESTIONS FOR PREPARING VISUAL AIDS

Ingenuity and a few inexpensive materials will make it possible to prepare many simple but effective visual aids. Any store carrying art supplies (probably your campus bookstore) can supply poster cardboard as well as poster colors and brushes. If you do not feel capable of handling the latter, get poster crayons. You will also find that many needed aids are available and will be lent to you by various departments, such as history, geography, economics, and art. If you are looking for some visual aids for a talk on insurance, you will find a local insurance agent willing to help you. For help with a travel talk, visit the nearest travel bureau. For a talk on traffic accidents, you will find your local police department of great assistance. For a talk on fire prevention, visit your fire department.

When you have to prepare your own visual aids, keep wording at a minimum. Don't try to put too much on one chart, but stick to a single, instantly intelligible point. Make instant comprehensibility the first test.

You cannot plan too meticulously for the use of whatever aids you have. Know how and where and when you are going to place them on display. If you intend to use thumb tacks, be sure they are strong enough for the material; if Scotch Tape, make certain (by trying beforehand) that it will hold. Not only bring all necessary fastening materials with you, but have someone ready and instructed to help you as needed to put up or to hold each aid as required. If an easel or a blackboard is used, make certain ahead of time that an adequate one is available. If a blackboard is to be used, make certain that you have an eraser and enough chalk.

CONCLUSION

We know that human beings learn more easily through the eye than through the ear. Moreover, the efficiency of the ear is increased when the eye has an opportunity to assist in the perceptive process. The steadily increasing variety of visual aids available to the speaker, including many splendid new mechanical facilities, challenges the speaker to make full use of them to increase his own efficiency and effectiveness.

EXERCISES AND BIBLIOGRAPHY

Exercises

1. Use the blackboard to develop some mathematical, chemical, or other type of formula.
2. Present a five-minute talk, making use of some carefully prepared visual aids, to inform the class about some little-known country, process, or product.
3. Plan a half-hour popular lecture to make extensive use of visual aids. In not more than four minutes, tell the class about your plan, about the visual aids you would use, and about the way in which you would use them.

Bibliography

Dale, Edgar, *Audio-Visual Methods in Teaching* (Holt, Rinehart and Winston, 1946).

Haas, Kenneth B., and Harry Q. Packer, *Preparation and Use of Audio-Visual Aids* (Prentice-Hall, 1955).

Hollingworth, H. L., *The Psychology of the Audience* (American Book, 1935).

Oliver, Robert T., Dallas C. Dickey, and Harold Zelko, *Communicative Speech* (Holt, Rinehart and Winston, 1955), Chap. 10.

Weaver, Gilbert Grimes, and Elroy W. Bollinger, *Visual Aids: Their Construction and Use* (Van Nostrand, 1949).

CHAPTER 17

CONTENTS

A college quiz show on the Dartmouth College radio station is on the air. (Dartmouth College Photographic Bureau) `

BEFORE MICROPHONE
AND CAMERA

THE media of mass communication have given almost limitless reach to the words of man. The motion picture, to which sound was added, the radio, and television have given to speakers not merely nation-wide but even world-wide audiences.

During the brief lifetime of today's college student not only the atomic bomb but the spoken word has exploded. From the days of Demosthenes to those of Woodrow Wilson there was little increase in the range of audience a speaker could command. Then, in the span of a single generation, camera and microphone, with their attendant instruments, brought the speaker and his voice within range of the ears and eyes of millions of people.

Only 20,000 listeners could hear Lincoln that November day at Gettysburg. Eighty-one years later, a hundred million radio listeners heard a speech by Franklin D. Roosevelt. The reach of the speaker increased five thousandfold. Indeed, the words and voices of Roosevelt and many of his contemporaries may be heard by generation after generation, in such recordings as the Columbia album, "I Can Hear It Now," prepared by Edward R. Murrow and Fred W. Friendly. News sound films, kinescope, and video tape make it certain that even personalities and voices, as well as words, of great contemporary speakers "will never die." The reach of the human voice seems almost limitless.

Earlier in this book it was pointed out that no preceding generation of college students has faced so great a demand for the spoken word as is presented by the media of mass communication of our time. Ours is not merely the age of the spoken word. It is the age of the far-reaching spoken word. It may be no more true now than it has always been

426

that the schools teach today's youth how to live in yesterday's world, but never before was yesterday's world so far behind today's needs! What the ultimate effect this vast expansion of the influence of the human voice may have upon society is not yet clear, but it is clear that training in the ablest possible utilization of these seemingly limitless media for speech should be an indispensable part of the preparation of today's speaker for tomorrow's world.

As has been stressed throughout this book, every change in the speaking situation requires some special adaptation by the speaker. Certain modifications will be required when the speaker is before a motion-picture or a television camera or when he speaks into a radio or a public-address-system microphone. The adaptation, however, is less than the uninitiated might expect. The same basic skills required for all kinds of direct public address are the ones needed by the speaker whose voice and words are carried through a microphone to thousands or millions of listeners. The audience's demand on a speaker's adequacy and preparation is, of course, compounded. An audience of only one hundred, listening for but twelve minutes, gives to a speaker twenty hours of listening time. Since that places a heavy obligation upon the speaker, consider the obligation when his listening audience numbers into the millions.

THE INFLUENCE OF THE MICROPHONE[1]

The experienced speaker and the professional actor or reader have learned to use sufficient energy, force, and projection to be heard easily by a large audience. But with the microphone the task of the speaker who reaches thousands of listeners can be made as easy as though he were speaking to but one or two in a living-room conversation. Large churches, theaters, and auditoriums would present insurmountable handicaps for the average speaker without some type of public-address system. The microphone makes it possible for huge conventions, rallies, and outdoor gatherings to be far more effective than they otherwise would be.

This increased effectiveness is achieved with an actual decrease of strain upon the speaker, because the ear of every listener is brought, in effect, almost as close as the microphone. The most delicate inflec-

---

[1] Merely for the sake of convenience the term "microphone" is used loosely in this chapter, often implying the entire set-up of microphone, amplifier, loud-speaker, and even transmitter.

tions and rich overtones of voice, which otherwise would reach only the listeners seated in the first few rows, are carried through the microphone to every listener in a large gathering. When a speaker has discovered this fact, he can devote himself to developing a vocal pattern of considerably greater variety and intimacy and of far more flexibility and directness than he could use when addressing groups of moderate size with no aid beyond his own speech power.

The speaker must know how to make the best possible use of the particular microphone situation in which he finds himself. Whether he is speaking into a public-address system, for recording, or for radio or television, the speaker needs to know how to use the facilities available. Usually he will have engineering help to adjust the amplifying equipment to his needs. He should know enough about the type of microphone he is using to respect the limitations it may impose upon his freedom of action. With a nondirectional pickup, the speaker is free to function within a complete circle described about the microphone as center. But with a unidirectional or bidirectional pickup, the speaker's area of movement is limited to one or two sides, respectively, of the microphone.

GENERAL PRINCIPLES OF MICROPHONE USE

The speaker who is going to use a microphone will find it particularly helpful to review Chapter 5, because the conversational quality is as important here as for any type of speaking. It remains for us only to point out a few specialized practical adaptations of those fundamental principles of speech that have been recommended throughout these pages.

1. *Know the directional characteristics of the microphone you are using and the amount of force you will have to use for the specific setup.* Ordinarily you will have an opportunity to check on this in advance of the actual speaking situation. As has been pointed out, you must know whether you face a nondirectional, unidirectional, or bidirectional pickup, in order that you may know what freedom of movement you have. If you have ever sat in an audience listening to a speaker who addresses half a sentence into the microphone and then turns his head away so that the other half is lost, you realize how unsatisfactory too much freedom of movement can be. If an actual test of the equipment is not possible beforehand, the chairman

or some experienced person present may be able to give you dependable information. You may learn something of the range of movement that will be permitted you by close observation of any speakers preceding you. All else failing, you may experiment as you commence your speech, watching the listeners for indications as to the distance from the microphone at which you seem to be heard most easily.

2. *Take special care to articulate clearly and distinctly.* The microphone cannot improve on the *quality* of its input. In fact, the microphone may only increase the obviousness of such faults as slurring, mumbling, and general indistinctness. Particularly over the radio, where helpful clues to meaning cannot be picked up from observable action, what is heard is all-important. If the microphone is of poor quality and low sensitivity, anything less than the best articulation will appear extremely faulty; if the microphone is of high quality and almost perfect sensitivity, it will completely reveal even the minor faults of voice and articulation. The microphone picks up and the loud-speaker reproduces *all* sounds made by the speaker. His breathiness and overstressed sibilants, which in the ordinary speaking situation might annoy only a few in the front rows, are carried with their full annoyance potential to every listener.

3. *Variations in force must be achieved within a narrower range than for direct speaking.* This should be obvious. Every change in force is amplified. The slightest change seems much greater to the listener than to the speaker. This is why even the experienced public speaker frequently causes the amplifier to "blast" the ears of his listeners when (without special training) he speaks into a microphone. He must learn to vary his force less extremely—or at least less suddenly, so that the engineer will have a chance to "ride gain" and avoid overloading.

4. *Sincerity and directness are particularly important.* Every evidence of sincerity must be made more obvious than seems necessary to the speaker, for, even at best, the microphone is between the speaker and the listeners. It is thus more difficult to make the listener *feel* the personality of the speaker. Conversational directness is more difficult to achieve through a loud-speaker. This does not mean that there are new skills to be acquired, but that what already has been said earlier in this book about ways of showing sincerity and directness take on major importance when one speaks into a microphone.

5. *Projection, so important in general public speaking, is at a minimum before the microphone.* This necessitates a major adaptation on the part of the experienced public speaker. He has become so accus-

tomed to projecting his voice in order to be easily heard by distant members of the listening audience that he has difficulty realizing that the effect of the microphone is to bring each listener within easy hearing range. It is as though each hearer were present in a small, informal conversational group.

SUGGESTIONS FOR SPEAKING OVER A PUBLIC-ADDRESS SYSTEM

In addition to observing the preceding five general principles of microphone use, if you address an audience over a public-address system you should heed four special suggestions:

1. *Use the microphone as an aid and a familiar asset.* If a public-address system has been provided, it is safe to presume that it is needed. Do not try to get along without it by disregarding it. Do not use it halfheartedly or as though you were unaccustomed to it. Make full use of it. Instead of permitting it to appear to handicap you, act as though you welcome it as a friendly aid and a further assistance to your effectiveness. The members of your audience will be grateful that they can hear you without unnecessary strain and effort.

2. *Your action and, particularly, your movement about the platform must be kept within close range of the microphone.* You will be inconsiderate of your audience if you walk so far away from the microphone or so nearly turn your back to it that your voice cannot be heard. Remember, too, that a carelessly gesturing hand striking the microphone produces a "sound effect" that is no kindness to listeners' ears.

3. *In your preliminary preparation and practice, bear in mind that the public-address system can prove distracting to your memory.* A new situation, or even new factors in a familiar situation, can be disturbing if unanticipated. What you have planned for and made yourself familiar with is not so likely to distract you from your speech.

4. *A public-address setup may tend to slow down your average rate.* The experienced speaker may anticipate this. He has found it true of a large-audience situation. In order for the voice to carry far and clearly, even with the aid of a public-address system, more time must be taken for clear and distinct utterance. When you are speaking under a definite limitation of time, it is important to take this factor

into account during preparation. Otherwise you may find yourself in the embarrassing position of talking overtime or greatly weakening the effect of your speech by having to cut out important later parts.

SUGGESTIONS FOR RADIO SPEAKING

To the general principles of microphone use presented earlier in this chapter several helpful suggestions can be added for the radio speaker. It may be worth noting that most of these suggestions have equal relevancy for a person whose speech is being recorded.

1. *The radio speaker is deprived of the visual code and must rely totally upon the auditory code.* This does not mean, however, that the radio speaker should use no action. The important contribution of almost all action to the auditory code has been sufficiently emphasized in Chapter 13. What the radio speaker must realize fully is that the only avenue of communication to his listeners is through their ears. Voice becomes all-important. His personality, his enthusiasm, his sincerity, every bit of his meaning must be carried by his voice or it will never reach his listeners.

2. *The radio speaker can use—and usually will be required to use —a manuscript.* In this sense he is often technically more a *reader* than a *speaker*. Although from the standpoint of memory and extemporaneous ability the task of the radio speaker is thus simplified, it is not easy for most persons to read in a manner as direct and conversational as the one they use when speaking. This calls for practice in reading from a manuscript in an "impromptu" manner, so that the impression of reading is not given. Incidentally, it calls for skill in handling sheets of paper so that their rustling is not heard over the air. Pages should not be clipped together. Instead of attempting to turn them without noise, experienced radio speakers usually slide each page down and off as it is read.

Timing of the radio speech is exceedingly important. An effective system is to note the timing carefully in the margin of the manuscript, after preliminary practice. That is, the place that the reader should have reached at the end of each minute can be noted. Then the reader can readily slow down or speed up to keep to this carefully rehearsed time schedule. Occasional sentences can also be marked for inclusion or omission as time may permit. This method is preferable to having to omit near the end an entire section which may be the most important part of the speech.

3. *The radio speaker seeks to have an intimate, personal, conversational manner revealed in his voice.* This is partly achieved by imagining the ear of the listener to be almost as near as the microphone is to the speaker. Thus one keeps in the voice a desirable intimacy and personal directness. As has already been stressed in the general microphone suggestions, there is a very limited use of projection. The voice has in every way the conversational manner appropriate to the living-room gathering.

4. *Radio-listener reaction to date seems to have shown a preference for lower-pitched voices.* This may be caused in part by the fact that broadcasting equipment tends to be "more kindly" in its transmission and reproduction of the lower frequencies. But whatever the cause, the radio speaker whose voice tends to be high-pitched—the tenor or soprano—should make full use of the lower range available to him or her.

5. *Ordinarily, radio listeners receive no interaudience stimulation.* The radio speaker cannot rely upon the aid of crowd psychology. He is, for example, more limited in his use of suggestion. He finds the development of emotional climax much more difficult. It may be said that it is easier to convince than to persuade a radio listener.

6. *It will assist the radio speaker to visualize his listening audience as a single individual to whom he is speaking directly.* Speaking to a radio audience, in spite of the fact that large numbers are listening, presents a problem quite different from that of addressing a large audience directly. Each radio listener is frequently alone in a room or in his automobile. At most there is a small family group together. Thus a "public-speaking manner" is inappropriate. Radio speaking is primarily direct, conversational, personal talking to individual listeners.

7. *Attention values must be kept paramount in radio speaking.* Ideally, perhaps, attention values are no more significant for radio speaking than for any other kind of speaking. But radio listeners are under no "public courtesy" compulsion to listen. They can tune out at any instant when their attention lags. That is why we say the radio speaker must be particularly alert to use all the principles of attention-getting. The student may well review at this point the principles presented in Chapter 11 for winning and holding interest and attention.

Delivery, too, must show enthusiasm. Variety and the avoidance of monotony are vitally important. These considerations are of particular significance, also, in the preparation of the manuscript of the radio speech. One must bear in mind that all that has been said in previous chapters about the necessity for instant comprehensibility has maximum application to the radio speech. All that the speaker says must be clear at first hearing. The slogan and the memorable phrase have greater effectiveness. The attention limits of the listeners must be assumed to be short. Conciseness, vividness, brevity, suspense, and climax are attributes of good radio style.

8. *The radio speech must not be "provincial" or local unless the audience is known to be limited.* Even if one is speaking to a present audience while the voice is also being broadcast to radio listeners, the speaker must keep in mind the nature and interest of the unseen listeners. Even in matters of pronunciation, "provincialisms" (such as the New England *wintah* for *winter*) are to be avoided. The radio speaker usually has the most varied audience possible. All types and ages of people may be numbered among the listeners. The speaker must interest all. His appeals must be broad and general unless he wishes to win only a select part of his audience.

9. *The so called "mike fright" can happen to anyone.* "Mike fright" is a name given to the sudden, all-alone feeling which sometimes overcomes the inexperienced speaker as he finds himself alone in a small studio with a microphone. It can and does happen to experienced speakers. It can be prevented by practice.

10. *The radio speaker should watch the producer or engineer for helpful signals.* The radio speaker should look up from his manuscript occasionally to give the engineer or producer an opportunity to signal whether to come closer to the microphone or to move farther away from it; to speed up or to slow down. These signals should be checked with him in advance.

VARIOUS KINDS OF RADIO SPEAKING

For convenience we have been discussing radio speaking as though it always consisted of a single speaker alone in a studio with his script before him. Actually, this is but one of several common varieties of radio speaking, and perhaps one of the less effective types.

While the general principles apply to all types, certain deviations should be noted.

1. For many radio speeches there is a studio audience, even if it consists only of a few friends who have come to watch. This is a help in securing the stimulation needed for real communication. Without it, the radio speaker is handicapped by the absence of stimulation or guidance from his listeners' reactions. An accustomed audience speaker who is unused to radio speaking would do well to take some friends with him for his first few speeches in order to have this help.

2. Sometimes a public speech at a banquet or in a hall is also broadcast, so that the microphone before the speaker leads out over the airways as well as into the hall's loud-speakers. This poses a variety of problems with which the beginning radio speaker may hope he will not have to contend. The timing, of course, must be as precise as if the speech were given in a studio—and sometimes the audience reaction and time taken by applause and laughter make this difficult. Another difficulty lies in the fact that the written script which is almost mandatory for radio is a handicap for the immediate audience.

3. Group discussions have become increasingly popular on the air. Some programs use as many as five participants, but three is a more manageable number. Either in their point of view or in their voices, they should be so sharply distinguished from one another that the radio audience has no doubt at any time who is speaking. Differences in age and sex also help the unseeing listener to keep distinctions clear. So does the liberal use of the names of the speakers, as one turns to ask another a question or to reply to what has been said. Although the general rules of group discussion, as presented in Chapter 6, also apply to radio speaking, at least one instruction requires special emphasis: on radio programs the speeches of individual participants in the discussion must be especially short, to provide more of a conversational tone of give-and-take.

4. Interviews are effective forms of radio speech. The roles of the interviewer, who asks the questions, and the expert, who answers them, should be clearly distinguished. Even among radio professionals there is far too great a tendency for the interviewer to dominate the program and to do too much of the talking. No doubt this is almost inevitable when the expert is totally inexperienced in this form of communication and the interviewer must "keep the ball rolling." Radio interviews are at their best when someone who really has some-

thing of interest to say not only is questioned by a skilled interlocutor who knows how, by brief and pointed questions, to elicit the most telling replies but is also himself an able communicator.

THE INFLUENCE OF THE CAMERA

The camera, in movies or in television, re-establishes the second dimension of speech. Now the listener-viewer is brought as near to the image of the speaker as auditory projection has brought him to the voice. The dimensions of seeing and hearing are again in the communication process. Before the camera, all aspects of action and visual appearance—from facial expression to poise and dress—take on new importance. We have noted how the microphone picks up and the loud-speaker reproduces *all* sounds made by the speaker. Strengths and weaknesses of articulation alike become more obvious to the listener. Similarly, the camera and film or television screen reproduce all the subtleties of facial expression and action.

The use of cameras makes possible for the listener and viewer shifting points of observation and thus of emphasis. The speaker before a battery of cameras must be alert to the possibility that at any given moment the television screen may be showing him in a close-up view of face only, in a general view taking in his whole body, or not at all, with only some visual aid or chart on the screen. And all the while, of course, the speaker is likely to be deprived of seeing any audience at all and receiving helpful stimulation from it.

It may be largely a matter of opinion whether television or radio is a more effective medium for transmitting information. The research evidence is contradictory and probably inadequate. There is, however, evidence indicating that kinescopes and films seem to be as effective as direct audience presentations for conveying information. When persuasion is the goal, there is again conflicting testimony. What is certain is that there are few lives in our nation not influenced by radio, the movies, and television. The 1961 *World Almanac* estimates there are at least 166,500,000 radio sets and more than 54,000,000 television sets in use in the United States—almost as many radios and far more television sets than in all the rest of the world. The far reach of the motion-picture industry is also well known. Commercially, radio has been with us just over forty years, the talking pictures just over thirty years, and television only twenty years. The effect of these mass media of communication upon our national economy is measured in billions of dollars. Their influence on education, religion, and recreation has not yet reached its peak, but their impact upon our social institutions is beyond measure. The speaker must learn the most effective possible utilization of every medium which gives new promise of aiding more effective human communication. The present and future expanding influence of the camera is more likely to be under- than overrated.

THE ROLE OF TELEVISION AS A TOOL OF LEARNING[2]

It seems to have been demonstrated satisfactorily that television can successfully present information, can motivate the viewer, and can teach critical thinking and motor skills. It may be too early to be certain we have eliminated the element of novelty, but presentation by television seems to have at least a slight advantage over a conventional speaking situation for the transmission of information. This is more certain to be true for a speech than for a presentation by a panel discussion unless, in the latter case, real or simulated participation by the viewers is possible. These latter advantages hold as well for delayed as for immediate recall, but any difference tends to disappear as the elapsed time lengthens. In the opinion of students in learning situations, the experience and ability of the speaker is of far more importance than whether he is being heard directly or over television.

All these general observations and experimental conclusions seem to suggest that television certainly need not hamper, and might even facilitate somewhat, the effectiveness of the speaker presenting an informational talk. There is convincing evidence that a speaker needs to learn how best to take advantage of this new medium of communication.

It is our own conclusion that extemporaneous speaking skill greatly aids the television speaker. We are certain that the greater number

[2] The authors are indebted here to relevant summary conclusions from the doctoral dissertation of Presley D. Holmes, Jr., "Television Research in the Teaching-Learning Process," completed at Wayne State University, and published with a grant from the National Educational Television and Radio Center, July 1, 1959.

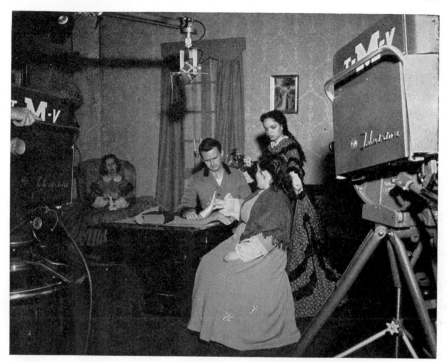

Educational television is a reality on many campuses. Students at the University of Michigan are presenting a dramatic production which may be recorded on kinescope or video tape for distribution to other stations.

of viewers enthusiastically support our condemnation of both manuscript reading and reliance upon such devices as the teleprompter. They are as distracting and as artificial and as destructive of sincerity on the television screen as they are directly before an audience.

SUGGESTIONS FOR SPEAKING BEFORE THE CAMERA

On television, or for the sound film, the voice is picked up by microphone. Suggestions already have been given for this phase of the process. There are, however, some additional suggestions which will increase effectiveness before the camera. We have emphasized that television is introducing to the speaker a means of communication vastly superior to that available in any previous generation. But as its opportunities are greater, so, too, are its requirements. Both the demands and the rewards of this medium challenge your best efforts.

1. *The visual code becomes even more important.* This means that the speaker's action, his general gracefulness, and even his facial expression all take on major importance. Close-ups will reveal details not ordinarily observable by an audience. And since the speaker can seldom be certain which camera's image is being carried to the screen at the moment, he must make certain that his appearance to any one of the cameras is satisfactory. If there are other participants, he must avoid so far as possible getting between them and the cameras. His reaction to other speakers, too, may be picked up and transmitted to the screen at any time. Fidgeting movements, nervous mannerisms, and any other distracting action habits may be emphasized on the screen at the most unexpected moment.

2. *Visual aids must be carefully considered.* One early producer of television programs asserted that what is heard is only one ninth as important as what is seen. The conclusion was that great quantities of visual aids must accompany a television talk. More recent research establishes that visual aids may be as likely to distract from a talk as to reinforce it. The student will do well at this point, therefore, to recheck what has been said in the preceding chapter concerning the general use and planning of visual aids.

3. *The speaker must be camera-conscious without making the audience aware of it.* It will require practice to work with cameras as well as with microphones and do one's best with both simultaneously. It will hardly add to an impression of directness if the speaker's image appears on the screen while he is looking away from the viewer! This means that the speaker must, in effect, be talking to the camera that is picking up his image. If notes or a manuscript is used, they will be clearly evident to those observing the telecast—most clearly evident if attempts to conceal them are suddenly revealed by a distance "shot." It will do little good for the speaker to *sound* sincere if he does not also *look* sincere.

4. *A sense of what* looks *dramatic as well as what* sounds *dramatic will be helpful.* It will be obvious that most of the suggestions made for effective radio speaking also hold for television speaking. On television one has the opportunity of adapting these to the eye as well as to the ear. Attention values are paramount. Conciseness, vividness, brevity, suspense, and climax have their visual as well as their auditory aspects. What is made dramatic is not only more clear and more vivid but also more memorable.

CONCLUSION

In this period in history, the microphone and the camera have become intimate parts of the lives of us all. As viewers and listeners, we have incorporated television, radio, and motion pictures most intimately into our everyday experiences. When we give public speeches or engage in group discussion, we are very likely to have the experience of using a microphone. And it is far from uncommon for individuals who never expect it to be called upon for radio or television appearances. The message which this chapter above all seeks to convey is that the qualities of good speech most demanded by the mass media are those needed for good conversational style in all manner of speech. The chief distinction is that the microphone and the camera demand of us more carefulness. We should do better what we should always try to do well. For this reason if for no other, training and experience in speech for radio and television is an admirable part of your general education for effective speaking.

EXERCISES AND BIBLIOGRAPHY

Exercises

1. If possible, the class should visit radio studios and have some opportunity for practice in using both directional and nondirectional microphone setups.
2. Write a speech four and a half minutes in length, suitable for radio presentation. Select a subject suitable for your own community. Take care in the composition of the speech to attract interest with the opening words, so that the listeners will stay tuned in, and to "point ahead."
3. Read the speech of exercise 2 over a radio or public-address setup so that the class may hear you over a loud-speaker. Be conversational.
4. With two or three of your classmates, plan a radio discussion of some live issue. Both in the selection of your panel members and in planning the discussion, take care to distinguish carefully among the participants, remembering that the audience will be unable to see you and must keep your identities separate by what you say and how you say it.
5. Present the discussion called for in exercise 4 behind a screen, with the class listening and participating afterward in a critical evaluation.
6. Plan and present a radio interview with another student, taking care to distinguish the "expert" from the questioner. Be sure the questions bring out the important points. Keep the interview varied and interesting.

7. Visit a television studio and watch a production. Afterward, in class discussion, evaluate the performance.

Bibliography

Abbot, Waldo, and Richard Rider, *Handbook of Broadcasting* (McGraw-Hill, 1957).

Becker, Samuel L., and H. Clay Harshbarger, *Television: Techniques for Planning and Performance* (Holt, Rinehart and Winston, 1958).

Chester, Giraud, and Garnet R. Garrison, *Television and Radio: An Introduction* (Appleton-Century-Crofts, 1956).

Henneke, Ben Graf, and Edward S. Dumit, *The Announcer's Handbook* (Holt, Rinehart and Winston, 1959).

Levenson, William B., and Edward Stasheff, *Teaching through Radio and Television* (Holt, Rinehart and Winston, 1952).

O'Meara, Carroll, *Television Program Production* (Ronald Press, 1955).

Phillips, David C., John M. Grogan, and Earl H. Ryan, *Introduction to Radio and Television* (Ronald Press, 1954).

Willis, Edgar E., *Foundations in Broadcasting: Radio and Television* (Oxford, 1950).

Part Five

TYPES OF PUBLIC SPEAKING

CHAPTER 18

CONTENTS

The speaker uses a map to help his listeners follow information that he has passed out to them. (Library of Congress)

THE SPEECH TO INFORM

K NOWLEDGE is the seedbed in which our ideas grow. The more you know about a subject, the more accurately and fruitfully you are prepared to think about it. Accumulated information, when properly integrated and interpreted, provides the safest base from which further advances in thinking may be achieved. The speaker who provides a careful statement of facts concerning a specific problem may help to mold his listeners' understanding of the subject and thus to lead them to form the proper conclusions. On the other hand, the speaker who lacks a full understanding of his subject and who therefore either willfully or ignorantly distorts the facts upon which his speech is based is a false guide to audience thinking. Modern audiences prefer speakers who can talk with calm and unpretentious confidence, based upon the certainty that they know what they are talking about.

You will find it particularly interesting to hear informative talks in your speech class from students of greatly varying vocational and professional backgrounds. The engineering student will have to make himself understood by the premedical student. The philosophy major must make his message clear to the sociology major. The future lawyer must make his field interesting and intelligible to the future teacher. The mathematically minded speaker may find it easy to make himself understood by his fellow mathematicians, but the real test of his clearness will be provided by the reaction of listeners whose chief interests lie in health education, home economics, or art. Although much of our lifetime may be spent with those who are deeply interested in our particular field, it is often necessary to meet the test of an audience whose interests are varied. And it can be a rich experience for the listener to hear competent talks on unfamiliar subjects.

VALUES OF THE SPEECH TO INFORM

One of the most common reasons for speaking is to exchange information. A stranger stops you on the street and asks you to direct him to a certain destination. A fellow student asks you to explain something in a class lecture that he did not understand. You attend

444

public lectures to hear what well-informed speakers can tell you concerning conditions in foreign countries, issues in international relations, new scientific developments, or current economic and social events. As chairman of a student-council committee you may be called upon for a factual report. Or as a major in art you may be asked to give a talk in your art class on the harmonic combination of colors in interior decoration. In one form or another, day after day, you give or listen to informative talks.

In a sense every person is a teacher, faced with constant and varying challenges to present and explain information to others. The doctor must make his instructions thoroughly comprehensible to the patient, the family, and the nurse. The coach must outline effective plays to his football, basketball, or baseball team. A large part of a lawyer's task is to offer clear statements of the facts to the judge and jury. A salesman must be able to explain the uses of his product to potential buyers. The engineer must lucidly present his findings and recommendations to a board of directors. Without question the use of speech for exchanging information ranks high among the primary needs of our practical, everyday living.

Even when the chief purpose of your speech is not to inform, you should know the methods and respect the requirements of sound informative speaking. For exposition is not only a primary type of speaking in itself but an indispensable basis for speeches to convince, to persuade, and to inspire. Your listeners will not wish to hear you unless they have confidence that you *know* what you are talking about and are helping them to understand the question being discussed.

ESSENTIALS OF THE SPEECH TO INFORM

The characteristics and requirements for all good speaking have been discussed in preceding chapters and apply, of course, to the speech to inform as well as to the other special types of speech, which will subsequently be described. There are, however, some characteristics of communicative speech that are uniquely important to the speech to inform; and there are some that have already been discussed that require particular re-emphasis here.

Presenting the Subject in Proper Perspective

No matter how obvious a fact may seem to be, it rarely can be understood rightly except in relation to other facts. If you are to give an informative talk on the American standard of living, the causes of labor trouble in Pennsylvania coal mines, or changing tendencies in modern art, you must make clear to your audience your standards of judgment and the perspective in which you have placed your subject.

1. *Make clear your own relationship to the topic.* Tell your audience the means by which you have learned about the topic—whether by experience, by reading, by research, or by casual observation. State frankly whether you are prejudiced and whether you have had opportunity to study all phases of the subject. A psychologist, for example, might say to his audience, "I cannot possibly explain to you all the different ways in which psychologists may interpret human motivation. My own training has been primarily in social psychology, and I will try to make clear to you how motives are interpreted by social psychologists."

2. *Make clear the standards of judgment you will apply.* You may discuss modern art, for example, in terms of "instant intelligibility to untrained observers" or in terms of its "complex integration of indirect symbolism." The audience should know which standard you are applying, for the first presumably would lead to condemnation of modern art and the second to its praise. Similarly, if you are analyzing the degree of democracy in a specific country, you surely must first define precisely what elements you consider essential to democracy.

3. *Keep your relationships constant.* Mapmakers are careful to draw an entire map to a precise scale, rather than to have one inch represent ten miles on one part of a map and one hundred miles— or even eleven—on another part. Speakers are not always that careful. If you are explaining the programs of the Democratic and Republican parties, you should apply the same tests of sincerity, practicality, and utility to both.

4. *Avoid disproportionate emphasis.* As a result of its presentation a subject may be accepted as either more or less important than it actually is. Similarly, it may be distorted by having certain of its elements over- or underemphasized. In a speech on juvenile delinquency, for example, you will put your subject in true perspective only by taking into consideration the normal behavior of all children, "good" as well as "bad."

Presenting the Subject Matter Clearly

You must never present so many points that your listeners find them confusing and difficult to remember. Your choice of words must be exact, and you must be certain that you say what you mean, without any vagueness or ambiguity. Such general terms as "Christianity," "democracy," "communism," or even "justice" carry no single, precise, exact meaning for all people. The instructor who assigns an "extemporaneous" speech only to find that some students think he means "impromptu" is running into a common type of misunderstanding. It has been estimated that 90 percent of all argument would be eliminated if we could avoid misunderstandings.

An outline must, of course, be clear if it is to aid the speaker, but its chief value is that it facilitates comprehension by the listener. The speaker who seeks to be understood must make clear to the listener the ending of his first main point and the beginning of the second. He must indicate the facts or authorities that substantiate a given point. He will, in other words, make it easy for the listener to construct his own outline of what he is saying.

We cannot achieve clearness without considering the listeners' knowledge. If a speaker were to deliver a talk on visible speech as developed by the Bell Telephone Laboratories to persons knowing nothing about the physics of sound and the process of representing sound by visible symbols, he would certainly have to do more defining of terms than if he were to deliver a similar talk to a group of physicists.

Using Repetition Effectively

The steps of expository development normally are *forecast, statement,* and *summary*. An old rural preacher explained his success by this formula: "First I tell them what I'm going to tell them; then I tell them; finally I tell them what I've told them." His advice has merit for us all. If your subject is sufficiently unfamiliar to your audience to justify an expository speech, you should begin with a brief preview of your theme and main points before developing your speech. Finally, in your conclusion, you should summarize, restating the essence of what you have said. Thus the essential points of the outline have been given at least three times, and repetition will have established them for your audience.

A speaker may, for example, begin his speech by saying:

In explaining the Communist program in Asia, I am first going to review the statements of the Communist leaders themselves; second, I shall examine the basic attitudes of Asian peoples toward the fundamental tenets of Communism; and third, I shall review the principal methods of attack and defense that have been used by the Communists and their opponents.

After developing these three points, he may conclude:

We see, therefore, that the Big Three Asian Communist leaders, Mao Tze-tung in China, Kyuichi Tokuda in Japan, and Ho Chih Minh in Indo-China, all agree that their economics are Marxian and that their foreign policies are dictated in Moscow. We have noted that Asian peoples, being agrarian, religious, and individualistic, are fundamentally unsympathetic to the industrial, materialistic, and totalitarian concepts of Communism. And we have seen how, nevertheless, Communism has been forced upon them by propaganda and force—against neither of which they have adequate means of defense.

Following General Statements with Specific Facts

In persuasive speaking you may often wish to set forth certain key facts before you draw the attention of your audience to the conclusion that naturally derives from them. In expository speaking, however, the deductive order of development is more easily comprehended and remembered than the inductive. This has been well demonstrated by extensive research in the field of learning. You can judge from your own experience. When a speaker presents first a general statement and then the specific facts to support it, you can fit the specific facts into a meaningful pattern in your own thinking. It is somewhat like having the counsel of a guide before you take a tour of a strange city, rather than afterward. A lecture on the thirteenth century in Europe, for example, would be clearer if it commenced, "The thirteenth century is one of the most civilized periods in human history," than if the lecturer simply proceeded to relate a series of facts about the cathedrals, religious doctrines, philosophy, literature, and socioeconomic patterns of the period, leaving his over-all judgment to be expressed at the end of the speech.

Using Concrete Data

In the chapters on selecting and developing ideas, adapting to the audience, and developing a speech style, the importance of concreteness has been emphasized repeatedly. John Ise's speech, "Values in a Crazy World" (at the end of Chapter 11), and Bruce Barton's speech "Which Knew Not Joseph" (at the end of Chapter 5), are particularly striking examples of the attention-compelling values of vivid incidents and personalized facts. The speaker must achieve a balance between concrete details and the conclusions to be drawn from them. A speech that is wholly general and abstract will be both dull and incomprehensible. On the other hand, a speech consisting of nothing but masses of concrete data will be as confusing and useless as a warehouse into which unlabeled goods have been tumbled. Concreteness consists of exact facts, whether statistics or specific illustrations. They should, of course, be used with judgment. Figures must not be so detailed that the significant fact is lost in a mass of minute details. This has been stressed in the preceding chapter, on the use of visual aids. If an expenditure of $1,978,642.35 has been made, it certainly is far more likely to be remembered by your audience if you say "just under two million dollars." However, your speech will suffer in authority, in interest, and in clarity if you neglect the research necessary to discover the true facts and substitute the lame generalization "a lot of money."

Explaining the Unfamiliar in Terms of the Familiar

People learn new things by associating them with what they already know. Unless we have some basis for association of the unfamiliar with the familiar, we cannot understand what is being discussed. Note, for example, that most foreign-language textbooks first present all directions in English, then gradually increase the amount of space devoted to the language being studied. Similarly, a speaker on the atomic bomb explains its explosive power by comparing it with that of other, better-known explosives. If you are invited to address a high school assembly on the subject of college life, you may well begin by comparing and contrasting it with what the listeners are accustomed to in high school. The process of getting an audience in a favorable mood to receive new ideas may be compared with the process of plowing and cultivating a garden before planting it.

Whatever your subject matter, going from the known to the unknown is the most effective approach. If you are explaining so common a phenomenon as anger, you will wish first to remind your audience of the obvious and well-known characteristics of anger; then you will proceed to a more detailed consideration of its psychophysiological causes, characteristics, and effects. If you are speaking on so unfamiliar a topic as "Present-day Economic Conditions among the Hopi Indians," you should freely use comparison and contrast with economic facts well known to the members of your audience—preferably, close to their own experience.

Organizing Information Meaningfully

The general principle of proceeding from the familiar to the unfamiliar is frequently insufficient as a guide for organizing the body of information you wish to present. Among the various methods of speech organization, *place order* may be best for the explanation of a factory assembly line, of layouts for an efficient kitchen, or of the structure of a rocket motor. In discussing any motor, however, the *functional order* may be a better aid to clarity, as it normally is also for such a topic as "How Tennis Is Played." In such an organization, the purpose of the motor or game is first stated, and is followed by an explanation of the processes or steps by which the purpose is achieved. A functional explanation of an automobile, as presented by a salesman, might proceed as follows:

1. *The power plant:* Compression, ignition, combustion, lubrication
2. *Control:* Steering, braking, relating speed to road conditions
3. *Comfort factors:* Roominess, springs, temperature control

The *deductive order* has already been recommended, especially for explaining ideas, systems, situations, and relationships. In a speech, for example, on the comparative intelligence of men and women, you might start with the generalization that men and women are fitted for a wide variety of functions and are inherently and culturally cast into patterns so diverse that comparisons are misleading. From this generalization you might proceed to the specific details which illustrate and support your deduction. The deductive order, like the principle of proceeding from the familiar to the unfamiliar, may often be combined with another method of organization. For example, in the speech on the automobile, which was organized functionally, you might introduce each main point in deductive form, with a generalization about the power plant, about control, and about comfort.

Time order is an obvious method of organization for presenting a biographical or historical exposition. Sometimes it is useful, but all too frequently it simply reveals a lack of ability to synthesize the subject matter and discover its real significance. A strictly chronological discussion of the life of John Milton or George Washington would probably be far less effective than a discussion based on a career order, in which Milton would be presented as (1) poet, (2) pamphleteer, and (3) politician; or Washington as (1) farmer, (2) soldier, and (3) statesman. A speaker who falls back upon encyclopedic and unimaginative time order is often revealing inexperience or lack of mature analysis. Perhaps the greatest opportunity for originality in the presentation of purely factual information is in its organization and arrangement.

However, whether you use place order, functional order, deductive order, time order, or topical order, the principal consideration is to find a logical, meaningful, and consistent manner of organizing your material so that it will be clear and significant.

Maintaining a Sense of Objectivity and Proportion

How many times have you heard a speaker, in the classroom or out, present a talk packed with detailed information, yet dull and boring? Perhaps he simply piled detail upon detail, like an almanac, without organizing them into meaningful and properly subordinated categories. An informative speech is not an occasion for display of complicated and extensive knowledge; it is, rather, a challenge to the speaker to communicate a concept adequately within the prescribed time limit. Trying to crowd an hour's material into a five-minute speech is to court failure. Learn from the cartoonist how to make your theme clear by *omitting* every detail not vital to your purpose, by *selecting* the major points indispensable to your objective, and by *emphasizing* in bold, clear strokes the factors which must be understood and remembered.

Stand away from your subject to see it in perspective. See it clearly, and see it whole. Do not view it merely as an accumulation of infinitesimal details. Look for the significance behind the facts. You know that there are definite limits to your listeners' power of attention. You know, too, how little you remember of a speech only two days after you have heard it. Learn to say less, so that the audience may remember more. Do not waste your speaking time on unimportant details. They will soon be forgotten anyway. Use the time you have to stress the vital, the essential, the memorable. Don't let overenthusiasm for your subject result in your being labeled a fanatic or a crank. Remember that you have a limited time in which to convey to your audience not only an understanding of your subject but also a sense of its true significance in relation to their other interests. Your success will depend to a considerable extent on how well you maintain your sense of proportion and objectivity.

SUBSTANCE OF THE SPEECH

The substance of the informative speech will be composed of such materials as the following:

Facts

A fact is an observable, accepted, verified, or at least verifiable, truth. It should be sharply distinguished from an *opinion*, which is an interpretation of the significance of a fact, or a judgment, or a belief. It is a fact that the United States is separated from Europe by the Atlantic Ocean. It is merely an opinion (however valid we may think it to be) that the United States should cooperate actively with the European nations in the settlement of economic problems. The distinction in this case is simple, but consider the following statements. Are they facts or opinions? "Immigrants from southern Europe make less desirable citizens than those from northern Europe." It is better to have an IQ of 120 than one of 90." "A high forehead is a sign of intelligence." "Women have contributed far less than men to the development of civilization." When such opinions as these are advanced as facts, a great many unwarranted conclusions may be reached. Whether delivering or listening to informative speeches, it is well to keep the distinction between facts and opinions clearly in mind.

Definitions

Many mistakes occur because people are confused about meanings. This is especially true when we encounter terms that are *figurative* (when you say big business is like an octopus, do you mean large, grasping, evil, complex, or something else?); *unfamiliar* (*serendipity* might be in your vocabulary but not in that of your listeners); *technical* (people may not agree in their views as to what constitutes an *introverted* personality); *abstract* (both *impressionism* and *modernism* in art are terms requiring definition); *general* (when you say *students* do you mean *scholars* or everyone enrolled in a school?); or *ambiguous* (*independent* might mean "virtuously individual" or "wilfully uncooperative"). Obviously, if communication is to occur, such terms need to be defined.

A very simple form of definition is the mere use of an accepted synonym, which may consist of one word or a phrase—such as "Serendipity is an unexpected dividend." On occasion it is helpful to define a term by referring to its etymology, as when we say, "Education is a *leading out* of the individual's innate abilities, as is indicated by its Latin root, *e-ducere*." Sometimes we define by analysis, comparison, and statement of utility or purpose, as when we say, "A llama is a South American beast of burden, resembling a camel without a hump, capable of living and working at high altitudes." Sometimes we define, at least in part, by exclusion or by negation, saying, "Unlike Hinduism, Christianity does not believe in thousands of gods, nor in earthly reincarnation."

Definitions may often be drawn from dictionaries, but frequently a speaker needs to define the special use he is making of a term. For example, you might say that "Democracy is government of, by, and for the people—and by this I mean that no action affecting our working conditions should be taken without our having a chance to discuss and vote on the question."

Description

It is clear that definition of terms is often not sufficient. If you tell your listeners that "a sycamore is a buttonwood" this may not be very helpful; nor will it add much information to define it further as "an Egyptian shade tree with a figlike fruit." It is far better to use *description*—telling your listeners about the size of the tree, the spread of its branches, how rapidly it grows, whether its wood is hard or soft, what utility it has, and whether it will grow in the climatic conditions of their locality. If you are referring to someone as being "irreligious," a definition of this term may be less helpful than a description of the kind of behavior you have in mind. For this purpose you may wish to cite examples, or to use comparisons or analogies. It may be important that the listeners understand the term in some particular context, as when you say, "A *negotiated* agreement is possible in this situation only if neither side is threatening or exerting force against the other." Whether you use definition or description (or a combination of the two) the question to be resolved is whether you can convey to the listener the understanding that you have of the term.

Classification

Classification is systematic arrangement of materials in such a way as to make their differences and their relationships apparent. Thus, students may be classified into three financial groups—the first consisting of those earning all of their expenses, the second of those earning part of their expenses, and the third of those earning none of their expenses. They may be classified on the basis of scholastic attainment, as superior, average, or inferior; or on other bases, as fraternity members or nonmembers; as freshmen, sophomores, juniors, or seniors; as candidates for the A.B., B.S., B. Mus., Ph. B., and so forth. Classification offers a useful means of organizing and comparing data.

Statistics

Statistics consist of numerical classifications. The United States Census reports, the United States *Statistical Abstract,* and the *World*

Almanac are convenient and generally reliable sources of statistical information. Statistics so easily lend themselves to misrepresentation, however, that it is well to be on one's guard against them. For example, if you say that unemployment decreases in the spring, you should make it clear that seasonal work, rather than a general economic improvement, may be the reason. If statistics show that one marriage in four ends in divorce, you may cite the additional, significant information that among married college graduates the rate is only one divorce in seventy-five marriages. In using or listening to statistics, before you base conclusions on them be sure that they include all pertinent information.

Visual Aids

With the consideration of visual aids in the preceding chapter still fresh in your mind, you will realize how helpful graphs, maps, charts, slides, films, and the blackboard can be to the task of giving information to an audience. The informative speech is perhaps the kind that is aided most by the use of visual materials.

Verbal Pictures

More readily available than some of the visual aids we have mentioned is vivid pictorial language. Analogies, illustrations, comparisons, contrasts, and specific examples will serve not only to clarify the explanation of the subject but to hold the interest of the audience. These five types of aid differ greatly from one another, but all constitute verbal pictures which contribute to the listeners' understanding. They help to make the speech specific and concrete, rather than general and abstract. Many an audience has wished that a speaker would "get down to cases," as his explanation became lost in metaphysical abstractions. Many political attacks lose effectiveness by being cast in vague generalities. Keep your ideas concrete, and neither you nor your audience will lose track of their meaning.

Abraham Lincoln related, "Among my earliest recollections I remember how, when a mere child, I used to get irritated when anybody talked to me in a way I could not understand." He determined that he would never make a statement which was not crystal clear. This is an excellent ideal for the informative speech.

TYPES

It is impossible to list all the occasions which call for the presentation of informative talks. A description of a few of the major types of situation and the particular techniques they demand should be an adequate guide for most situations.

Instructional Talks

Frequently instructions must be given to entire groups. A teacher may tell a class what to do in a fire drill. A football coach may explain to his team how to execute a complicated play. A sales manager may have some directions to present to his entire force concerning the sale of a new product. Union leaders may explain picketing and other procedures to be carried out during a strike. Announcements, too, are primarily informational talks, although they may also have a persuasive objective.

Every announcement must answer the journalistic questions what? where? when? why? and how? The order may be varied for individual and circumstantial reasons. The "how" may include how to accomplish the goal, how to get to the event, and how much the tickets will cost. It is excellent practice, after making announcements to a class, to ask if there are any questions. The questions will indicate whether the announcement has been lacking in clearness, specificity, or completeness of information.

Every instructional talk may profit from a consideration of the same five questions that the announcement is expected to answer, insofar as they are relevant. Again, an opportunity for questions from the audience afterward will afford the finest test of the speaker's thoroughness and effectiveness.

Demonstration Talks

The demonstration talk makes special demands upon the speaker. As was pointed out in Chapter 16, when the speaker brings along an object to use and demonstrate before the audience it is easier for him not only to hold interest and attention but to forget his self-consciousness and supplement his verbal messages with appropriate action messages. It is interesting to note how a speaker's own interests and vocational objectives may influence his demonstrations. A music major, for example, may bring along his violin to show how it is played;

the major in musical theory or in mathematics may take the same instrument to illustrate his talk on the development of our present system of musical notation; a physics major may use it to demonstrate his talk on the physics of sound; and another student may use it to illustrate a talk on the making of violins.

Abstract Explanations

Explanations of philosophical ideas; economic theories; types of literary style; engineering, architectural, or mathematical principles; and laws require the highest expository skills. Adequate use of illustrations and visual aids is extremely important to the effectiveness of this type of talk. Explanations frequently must be related as well as illustrated; and each step must be thoroughly understood before the next is presented.

Reports

An almost limitless variety of reports is required in the college classroom and laboratory and in almost every type of life activity. They serve both as records and as sources of new information. Whatever their nature or purpose, they place high premiums upon accuracy, proper emphasis, conciseness and thoroughness.

The primary aim of every report is to transmit information. Even though the speaker may desire to convert his hearers to some new program or policy, still the emphasis is upon facts and findings and the tone is that of unemotional exposition. More than any other kind of speaking, the report draws its chief values from accuracy and clearness. Most oral reports will also be presented in writing. Often the oral report presents merely the highlights of a more detailed written report; it is then advisable to present the material extemporaneously rather than to read certain sections, unless there are parts which should be presented with great accuracy.

A preliminary bird's-eye view of the significant results, conclusions, or recommendations of the report is essential. It should be followed by a statement of the object of the report. Then what has been done should be set forth in detail, with all description necessary to make clear the techniques, apparatus, and methods used and the scope of the report. Next there should be a discussion of data or findings. Finally, the conclusions and recommendations should end the report. Definitions are an important part of any report—definitions of the subject, the scope, the objective. The purpose of definition, as in any speech, is to set limits and to make ambiguity and misinterpretations impossible, or at least unlikely. Even in a technical report, avoid highly technical terminology wherever you can do so without endangering accuracy. Never bother to define a term which might better be avoided altogether. The speaker should be deeply conscious of the constructive contribution of *comparisons* to the clearness of any report.

In giving a report, the speaker has more than the usual need for a command of such transitional language as was discussed in Chapter 12. Too many extemporaneous speakers merely overuse "and." You must add to your vocabulary—your actual-use vocabulary—transitional phrases such as the following: to meet this need, to accomplish this, furthermore, on the other hand, nevertheless, thus, as a result, in a similar manner, of equal value, in spite of this, all these factors lead to the conclusion.

There are four types of report which deserve special consideration. The first two are usually made by officers of organizations in their line of duty; the others result from special investigations or projects.

Periodic reports may be made annually, monthly, weekly, or even daily. They must follow a set form, which is usually prescribed by precedent and which must be adhered to in essentials to permit comparison. Periodic reports seek to present an informational survey of what has happened during the period covered; they may go beyond that to include recommendations for the future. It is frequently helpful to the listeners to include in such a report a comparison with similar periods in the past.

Progress reports are presented in connection with projects which extend over a long period of time; those in charge are usually expected at certain intervals to give an accounting to a board of directors or to the public. Except that it may be highly individualistic, the progress report is similar to the periodic report. Experts in various fields are frequently called upon to devote their skills and judgments to special investigations and studies which call for reports. They may be asked to recommend an airport site to a city council, to suggest a program of curriculum revision, to examine the quality of higher education in a state, or—in more ordinary experience—to recommend a dance band for the junior hop or to examine possibilities for greater faculty-student cooperation in fraternity and sorority activities.

Examination reports require considerable detail. In a way a report upon supplementary reading done for a course is an examination report. It must indicate what has been done and give evaluations and judgments. The good examination report must indicate that the reporter has been thorough and that his conclusions were not preformed but evolved as a result of his study and investigation.

Recommendation reports must give evidence of complete study of a problem, provide a comparative evaluation of the principal possible solutions, set up standards by which a decision should be made, and apply the standards to arrive at the final recommendation.

Book Reviews

Book reviews merit consideration as a specialized type of informative speech. To be sure, it may be argued that many of them are primarily entertaining and some may even have propaganda objectives. Yet it will be found that most oral book reviews are promoted by cultural or lecture groups having educational and informative purposes.

Oral book reviews may be divided into two categories. In one, the reviewer limits himself almost entirely to reading aloud, very often with fine dramatic sense, carefully selected cuttings from the book which are intended to give the hearer a fair impression of the author's message. This is not at all a review in the usual sense of the term but is a type of interpretive reading. It is an excellent, very popular technique, requiring speech skills of a high order, but because of its nature it is more properly dealt with in a course of interpretive reading.

The aim of the other type of review is to give the audience not only a fair understanding of what the author has to present but a variety of evaluations by the speaker. When the book reviewer shows imagination, discriminating judgment, and some originality in method, his speech is highly valuable. The book review is often considered valuable because it saves people time, but a better reason for giving a book review is to provide the reader with something beyond what he would get by reading the book for himself. Your task, then, is to decide what you expect to achieve by your review. Through your knowledge of the author's life, background, and other works, can you bring out underlying motives which the ordinary reader might not discover in the book? Can you use the book as a representative of a particular literary form, and can you evaluate the book, comparing it with others of its type? Can you through this review improve the literary taste and increase the independence of judgment of your listeners? Do you wish to reveal the entire plot or only enough to motivate your hearers to read the book for themselves? Do you wish to emphasize the message of the book rather than the book itself (as might be done with Burrow's *The Dead Sea Scrolls* or Toynbee's *A Study of History*)?

Whatever your objective, set about it with originality, keeping in mind all the principles of good speechmaking. In preparing any kind of review and in deciding what kind of review to make, there are five tests which you should apply to your book.

1. How good does the book appear when it is reread? If it does not offer increasing pleasure upon successive readings you certainly will not wish to recommend it as a literary masterpiece which will survive. Probably you will not wish to urge your audience to read it. Yet it might be entirely satisfactory to review for other reasons.

2. Is it the kind of book which cannot be put down until you have finished it? This is frequently offered as an infallible test of interest in books. As a matter of fact, it tests chiefly the suspense element, the main appeal of which is to one's curiosity. A better test of the more solid, artistic qualities of a book is the inducement which it offers the reader to linger over its pages. The books which you read slowly, and whose pages you reread for the sheer delight they offer, will stand up best under close analysis; hence they offer the best subjects for reviews.

3. Does the nature of the plot keep you wondering *what* is going to happen or *how* the outcome is to be achieved? The first is a relatively cheap kind of suspense, which can readily be ended by turning to the end of the book and reading the last few pages. The latter kind is more subtle and more powerful in its effect. The climax is seen inevitably and dramatically gathering, and the interest of the reader is kept centered upon how the characters in the story will meet the threatened calamity that hovers over them. The first depends upon suspense alone; the second upon a philosophical interpretation of life. The first is very difficult to reproduce in an oral review; the second lends itself very well to thoughtful analysis and explanation.

4. Do the characters become so real to you that you think of them as actual people, wonder what they do in later life, and what they would have been like if certain incidents in the plot had not occurred? Do the characters remain essentially the same, or do the events of the plot cause them to change their personalities, attitudes, and relationships? In the best books, the characters, as Kipling said, "stand on their own feet."

5. What is the message of the book? If the book is fictional, what attitude toward life is revealed? If nonfictional, how substantial and dependable is its analysis of the problem considered? Does the author

maintain a mature and well-balanced objectivity, or is he a salesman for some particular point of view? What special significance does the message of the book have for your audience? Use your own best judgment to appraise the relative merits and demerits of the author's conclusions.

CONCLUSION

You have many occasions, often several times a day, for informative speaking. The more your education and experience provide you with knowledge and insight beyond that of your associates, the more surely will you be called upon for speeches to inform. The few special occasions mentioned in this chapter could be endlessly multiplied, for there is almost no limit to the variety of situations in which information is given and received. As a student of speech you should learn to analyze, organize, and present the information you possess, keeping in mind the following essential principles:

(1) Present your subject in its proper perspective. (2) Present your subject matter clearly. (3) Use repetition effectively. (4) Follow general statements with specific facts. (5) Hold attention and clarify meaning with concrete data. (6) Explain the unfamiliar in terms of the familiar. (7) Organize your information meaningfully. (8) Maintain your sense of objectivity and proportion.

EXERCISES AND BIBLIOGRAPHY

Exercises

1. Present to the class a four-minute informative talk in which you explain the preparation and training which are required for the profession or vocation in which you expect to be engaged ten years from now.
2. Give a five-minute explanation of an abstract theory or philosophy in which you are interested.
3. Give a three-minute digest of a long term paper you have written for another course.
4. Give an informative biographical talk about an outstanding speaker in American history, such as Edwin A. Alderman, Susan B. Anthony, Henry Ward Beecher, Albert J. Beveridge, Jeremiah S. Black, James G. Blaine, William E. Borah, Phillips Brooks, William Jennings Bryan, John C. Calhoun, Carrie Chapman Catt, Rufus Choate, Henry Clay,

Clarence Darrow, Stephen A. Douglas, Frederick Douglass, Jonathan Edwards, Charles W. Eliot, Ralph Waldo Emerson, William M. Evarts, Edward Everett, Samuel Gompers, Henry W. Grady, Patrick Henry, Robert G. Ingersoll, Robert M. La Follette, Abraham Lincoln, Theodore S. Parker, Wendell Phillips, Franklin D. Roosevelt, Charles Sumner, Booker T. Washington, Daniel Webster, Frances Willard, Woodrow Wilson, or William L. Yancey.

5. Give a talk presenting a historical theme, such as the origin of street names in your town, the history of fire fighting, how fashions have changed, or how some invention or political development changed the course of history.

6. Prepare an informative talk on a hobby of yours in which you wish to interest your listeners.

7. Give a demonstration talk, the object of which is to teach. For example, bring along a golf club and demonstrate how to use it correctly. Or show how to throw a curve ball. Or how to apply make-up.

8. Present an oral progress report describing and evaluating as you see it the progress which members of this class, or you yourself, have made in speech.

Bibliography

Harris, Robert T., and James L. Jarrett, *Language and Informal Logic* (Longmans, Green, 1956), especially Chaps. 1, "Toward a Logic for Better Communication"; 5, "Meaning and Failures of Meaning"; and 6, "Definition."

Johnson, Wendell, *Your Most Enchanted Listener* (Harper, 1956).

CHAPTER 19

CONTENTS

While he addressed a joint session of the United States Congress on December 26, 1941, Winston Churchill's stirring words were carried all over the world by radio to urge free people to unite against aggression. (Wide World Photos, Inc.)

THE SPEECH TO
INDUCE BELIEF

A T first thought it may not seem that the speech to induce belief is appreciably different from the speech to inform. Isn't it true,
you may say, that to know is to believe? Many times, of course, it is;
but many times, also, it is not. It is entirely possible that the better one
knows something (communism, for example) the more completely
one disbelieves it. It is one task to inform a Buddhist audience about
the Christian faith; it is quite another to induce Buddhist listeners to
believe in the Christian faith.

The speech to induce belief is more commonly called the speech to
convince. We believe the phrase "to induce belief" makes its purpose
clearer: to have our listeners say, "We agree with you," or "We believe
as you do."

The next chapter is concerned with the speech to move to action.
Belief may not necessarily lead to action, as every student knows who
goes home for a holiday recess *believing* he will do the work for many
standing assignments, and returns afterward with very little translated
into *action*. When we seek to induce belief we use as materials evidence and logic; but we move our listeners to action by emotional and
motivational appeals.

It is the purpose more than the subject matter which distinguishes
the speech to induce belief from that to inform. Both purpose and subject matter differentiate the speech to move to action from that to induce belief, though in many instances the speech to induce action
contains within it, and merely adds to, a basic speech to induce belief.
An illustration may clarify these distinctions. An expository speech
may *inform* listeners of Soviet Russia's past and present activities in
the Middle East. A convincing speech may *induce listeners to believe*
that Russia's policy in the Middle East is dangerous to our security.
Yet another speech may *impel action,* such as voting for national candidates committed to a policy of diminishing Russia's influence in the
Middle East. Notice that belief often occupies a position midway between understanding an idea and doing something about it. The three

464

purposes, then, which distinguish these types of speech are to inform, to induce belief (convince), and to move to action (persuade).

Often a speaker may be intent upon a long-range goal of obtaining action, but he may realize that his audience is not yet prepared for the difficult step. At such a time, a speech to induce belief may be preparatory or preliminary to later persuasion. When any crisis arises, such as an economic decline that may develop into a depression, there will be many informative speeches to bring about a better understanding of what is happening. There will then be speeches to convince people that one or another cause or one or another political party is responsible for the economic collapse. Thereafter will come the speeches to persuade, delivered by proponents of specific courses of action.

Under other circumstances, the speech to induce belief may serve an end in itself, rather than act as preparation for persuasion. An academic lecturer, for example, may seek to convince his class that the Federalist party developed the program which led to our government's financial stability; or that President Jefferson Davis's lack of political skill was a factor in the shortness of life of the Confederacy. In a course in labor problems the professor may argue that Walter Reuther is not an autocrat but an exponent of a consistent labor policy that has had generally beneficial effects. In any field of human activity or belief we must deal not only with matters of undisputed fact—which may be presented in informative speeches—but also with matters of opinion —which can be treated only as theses to be believed or disbelieved. Theorists may argue that a professor has no right to do more than merely present facts and let the class decide for itself; but when the facts require expert interpretation, or when the complexity of the subject requires that only carefully selected facts be presented, the lecturer necessarily plays the role of a molder of belief.

ESSENTIAL CONTENT OF THE SPEECH TO INDUCE BELIEF

The speech to induce belief seeks to influence permanently the opinions of its hearers—either to strengthen those opinions which the speaker considers desirable or to change those he considers undesirable. Quite probably the speaker could change opinions temporarily by the sheer power of emotional appeal, but the change would not be a permanent one. An argumentative speech will have a lasting effect

only if it is based upon information (facts, expert opinions, and reasoning based upon these) which remains just as convincing later as
when first heard by the listeners. Beliefs have to stand up under reflection and against counterarguments. A speech to induce belief
which violates the facts and the evidence may not only fail in its purpose; it is likely to arouse the suspicion of the audience and resentment
against the speaker and his cause.

The material which will prove effective both at the time of delivery
and thereafter consists of facts, opinions of experts, and the conclusions based on them. Chapter 9 presented in detail the methods of developing ideas; hence the three types of convincing materials will be
briefly noted here.

Facts

A fact, as noted in the preceding chapter, may be defined as a real
occurrence, or state of things, as distinguished from something merely
alleged or believed. A fact must be verifiable. We say that an experimental conclusion has been established as a fact when others repeating the same experiment arrive at the same conclusion. This is what
we mean by a fact's being verifiable. Facts are, of course, essential for
any speech, regardless of purpose, but they constitute a major part of
the content of speeches to inform and to induce belief because these
appeal primarily to understanding and acceptance.

Opinions of Experts

When the facts are incontrovertible and clear, almost everyone
accepts them. In other words, there is little room for difference of
opinion. In such matters the speaker needs merely to inform his audience to attain its belief. But there are innumerable conclusions which
can be reached only by circumstantial evidence. These conclusions we
should recognize as opinions rather than as definitely ascertainable
facts. Who caused World War I? Will communism outlast capitalism? Will inflation ultimately bring economic downfall? Will any
living American writer surpass Mark Twain's reputation? Have you
made the wisest possible choice of college curriculum? Answers to
such questions can be only opinions. Certain relevant facts, to be sure,
may help improve the quality of the opinion. Similarly, the opinions of
some experts may be more valuable than those of others. We go to a
lawyer for an opinion on a legal matter; to a doctor for an opinion on

our health; or to a physicist for an opinion regarding physical phe-
nomena. The more important the opinion we seek the more exacting
we will be about the qualifications of the expert upon whom we rely.
If we are told, for instance, that we must undergo serious surgery, we
may insist upon checking the opinion of more than one expert diag-
nostician.

Who is an expert? This may in itself constitute a matter of opinion.
We may decide that an expert is one who is highly regarded by others
in his field, or is qualified by training and experience. But unless our
listeners know the qualifications of those whose opinions are quoted,
these opinions may not carry weight with them. The speaker must not
only select and present the best available expert opinions, but prepare
the way for their acceptance by his listeners.

Logic

Many beliefs rest primarly upon emotion, prejudice, and personal
preference. But if you wish to establish a conviction which will long
endure and which will be proof against any later arguments and experiences to which your listeners may be subject, your appeal should
be an intellectual one. This requires that your speech be based upon
systematic thinking, or logical reasoning, inductive or deductive.

Inductive logic, as noted in the preceding chapter, consists in the
observation of specific facts and the drawing of general conclusions
from them. Sherlock Holmes used the inductive method when he observed a bit of cigar ash, a fragment of cloth, a scratch on the furniture, and from these details reconstructed the crime. A sociologist
who goes into the slums, visits a hundred homes, and formulates a
general conclusion regarding the kind of lives led by the slum dwellers
is using the inductive method. Since induction consists of the drawing
of conclusions on the basis of observed instances, it is important that
the instances cited be truly representative of the whole class involved
in the general conclusion. For example, if all the slum dwellers visited
happened to be blonds, it would not therefore be fair to assume that
blond hair is an invariable characteristic of slum dwellers. In order to
be certain that the instances upon which your induction rests are truly
representative, it is advisable to take the following precautions: be
sure they are true, see whether there are any important exceptions, take
care that your instances are all of the same kind and are drawn from
comparable circumstances, and have a sufficiently large number of in-

stances. Don't generalize concerning Mexicans from a half dozen whom you have known. The tendency to make just this kind of mistake is one of the chief weaknesses of the inductive method.

Deductive argument starts with a general tendency or "law" and draws conclusions from it regarding specific instances. The principal form of deduction is the *syllogism,* consisting of a major premise, minor premise, and conclusion, which may be illustrated with a simple example:

> All Phi Beta Kappas are intelligent. (Major premise.)
> Henry is a Phi Beta Kappa. (Minor premise.)
> Therefore Henry is intelligent. (Conclusion.)

For a syllogism to be convincing, its general statement or major premise must be generally accepted as being true. Thus it is an obvious fact which usually does not have to be stated; for this reason in most speech situations when the syllogism is used the major premise is omitted. For example, in a conversation the foregoing syllogism might run something like this: "Of course Henry is smart. He's a Phi Beta Kappa, you know." Here are some other examples of telescoped syllogisms. Can you convert them into their original syllogistic form?

1. Smith is a soldier. His bravery is unimpeachable.
2. You may believe what Jones has to say. He is a scientist.
3. Don't vote for Thomas. He is a socialist.
4. A college education is useless. Look at all the college graduates earning less money than those who never went to college.
5. The radio, which provides entertainment for millions, was a great invention.

ATTRIBUTES OF THE CONVINCING SPEAKER

A speaker who would shape the beliefs of his listeners must first win their respect. If he is known to be lacking in integrity or to be too lazy to check on the material that he presents as facts, he naturally will evoke suspicion rather than confidence. If he appears uncertain of his own beliefs and especially if he reveals a failure to understand fully the nature of the problem he is discussing, he cannot expect to convince his hearers that they should accept his conclusions. If he seems to be unfair in his attacks upon opposing views and personalities and if he shows lack of emotional restraint in expressing his opinions, the audience will not readily accept his views. It is also true, though perhaps not logical, that an audience is likely to resist the arguments of a speaker who is incompetent in his speech skills. In effect, a speech to convince asks the audience to accept the intellectual leadership of the speaker. Anything that diminishes the listeners' respect or regard for the speaker will prove an obstacle to his success.

Although it is of obvious advantage to a speaker to be an expert on the subject he discusses, he cannot always be so. If you seek to convince an audience concerning a subject with which you have had little personal experience and about which you have no special knowledge, you can and should take particular care to study the whole topic carefully and to be frank and explicit in identifying for your listeners the sources upon which you have depended in formulating the judgment you ask them to accept.

DELIVERY OF THE SPEECH TO INDUCE BELIEF

Effective delivery of speeches has been discussed in detail in Chapters 13 to 16. Aside from the general principles presented there, the chief characteristics of the delivery of the speech to convince should be judiciousness, calmness, and thoughtfulness. The speaker should always have himself and his subject well under control. Restraint is usually more convincing than passionate emotionalism. The convincing speaker should be fair in his assessment of opposing evidence and should make the audience realize that he is bringing a balanced and objective judgment to the subject. His careful analysis and the logical, factual, and authoritative support he has assembled for his conclusion should give him a confidence that will be readily sensed by the audience.

Above all, perhaps, the attitude of the convincing speaker must be fair. Readiness to admit weakness in his own case and a fair-minded admission of strong points in opposing arguments will do much to convince the audience that the speaker's final judgment has been carefully reasoned and weighed. Fanatic zeal sometimes overwhelms the judgment of an audience temporarily, but restrained fair-mindedness is much more dependable for lasting effects. The whole manner of a convincing speaker should make his audience feel, "This man knows what he is talking about and is determined to be fair."

TYPES OF THE SPEECH TO INDUCE BELIEF

What has been said concerning the substance and characteristics of the speech to induce belief obviously applies only in a general sense, with variations for each of the specialized types. It has been stated as a general principle, for example, that convincing speeches depend upon facts, logic, and authoritative opinions and are delivered in a calm and judicious manner. But many great evangelistic sermons that have depended chiefly upon a powerful current of emotional content and a vibrantly emotional delivery have brought about lasting changes of belief. It should be noted, however, that even a speech that is primarily emotional must strike deep down, affecting feelings rooted so solidly that they will not soon or easily be dislodged again. The general requirement that a speech to convince must have a *lasting effect* inevitably gives a kind of uniformity even to apparently dissimilar types.

Let us consider some familiar examples. The *good-will* speech is given by manufacturers and other businessmen to build up a lasting approval on the part of the public; such a speech may describe the public benefits offered by the firm's services, picture the leading personalities of the firm in attractive terms, and cite facts showing the fairness of the firm in dealing with its employees and the public. *Discussion of issues,* such as American foreign policy or pending tax bills, requires speeches to induce belief which set forth various points of view. *Evaluations* of college education, of religion, or fraternity membership, of political parties, of ethical codes, of fashions in clothing—of anything and everything in which the public is interested—are presented by speakers whose aim is to induce audiences to believe that the interpretations offered are correct. Widely as such types of speeches to induce belief vary, all are alike in their aim and their tendency to achieve it through citation of evidence which is logically interpreted and supported by authoritative opinion.

A type of speech to induce belief that is most familiar is the *debate.* Whether cast in the conventional form of affirmative-negative arguments taking place in legislative halls or in parliamentary sessions, the debate begins with a clearly stated proposition to be proved. The speaker points out to his audience what he is attempting to establish, draws up his best arguments and evidence to support his proposal, and then shows how the evidence leads directly to the conclusion that his proposition should be accepted as true. Such a method has the great advantage of clarity. But it has the disadvantage of being obviously argumentative. The speaker in effect announces to his audience, "I am going to convince you that I am right and that all of you who disagree with me are wrong." Sometimes, as in debate on a bill pending before Congress or in discussion of a motion introduced into the business meeting of an organization, such a frontal attack is necessary.

However, on many occasions, conviction is best approached by indirection. As Carl Van Doren once declared, "Illustration comes properly before argument, if there is to be as little as possible of reasoning in a vacuum." An audience is entitled to know why it is urged to abandon one belief and substitute another. It is for this reason that the principal attention of this chapter is devoted to inducing belief inductively, or by degrees.

THE PROBLEM-SOLVING APPROACH

The speech to induce belief may be organized either *logically* or *analytically*. Using the former method the speaker begins by telling his audience what he is advocating and then proceeds to give reasons why they should accept his conclusion. This method has the virtue of complete clarity. When the problem is well understood by your audience and when your belief concerning it is already well known, the logical method is ordinarily the one to be used. However, you may often find that the audience is not aware that there is a serious problem and has no inkling of your own views regarding it. It is then usually best to begin your speech where the audience is, rather than at the point your own thinking has reached. For many speeches to induce belief, in other words, it is psychologically sound to begin by showing your audience that *a problem exists for which some solution must be found.* Show them how serious the problem is and how it affects them personally. Then analyze the various ways in which the problem might be solved, evaluate them, and, finally, present the one solution that seems to you to be superior. This kind of speech organization may be called *the problem-solving technique.*

John Dewey, in a little book entitled *How We Think,* explained five stages through which the mind progresses in solving any kind of problem. First, there must be a recognition that a problem exists; second, the problem must be localized and defined; third, various solutions are sought; fourth, the solutions are evaluated; and, finally, one of the solutions is, at least tentatively, accepted. This, according to Dewey, is the normal and typical operation of the human mind when confronted with any kind of problem. Let us see how this problem-solving technique applies to the talk intended to induce belief.

1. There is a feeling of dissatisfaction, a "felt difficulty." Something is wrong. The *status quo* is no longer acceptable. Prior to the French Revolution, for example, a feeling of restlessness pervaded France. In the United States in 1931–32, dissatisfaction was widely evident. This feeling may be confined to a single individual, as when his own business or health is affected, or it may involve an entire community or a nation. When the dissatisfaction is present in a group of people, it almost inevitably leads to discussion in public speeches. This results in a second stage of development.

2. The situation is analyzed to discover what is wrong. This step is analogous to the doctor's diagnosis of his patient's illness. It is a process invariably followed in political campaign speeches, especially by the party out of power. "The state of the nation" is found to be unsatisfactory—step 1. Analysis (in this case obviously neither scientific nor disinterested) shows that the situation is caused by the type of political control that is being exercised—step 2. When this analysis has been made, the general dissatisfaction can be turned specifically against the "cause" which the analysis has uncovered. In this sense the old political maxim is true: "He who can phrase it can lead it." He who can tell those who are dissatisfied precisely what to be dissatisfied *with* becomes their spokesman and leader. In 1932, for example, Franklin D. Roosevelt convinced the depression-weary masses that they should be dissatisfied with their treatment under the old regime. In a speech, if the analysis has been persuasively conducted, the audience turns toward the analyst for further guidance; but his continued leadership depends upon his skill in conducting his speech through the next three steps.

3. All reasonable proposals for solving the difficulty should be presented. This is the stage at which the speaker may ask tentatively, "What is to be done?" In answering this question it is essential to give consideration to every proposal which may be favored by any considerable number of the listeners. If the speaker lists five possible solutions to the problem but does not include a sixth, which may be favored by large portions of the audience, obviously he will not satisfy his hearers as to the fairness of his analysis. The speaker should be able to list the proposals he intends to discuss and then say that the

solution to the problem must be one of these plans, since there is no other which deserves serious consideration.

4. The evidence for and against each one of these proposals should be examined in turn. In political speaking it is customary to ridicule and belittle the proposals of the opposing candidates, but it is better speech ethics and better insurance of success (at least with an intelligent, dispassionate audience) to give fair and candid consideration to every plan that is being considered. The plan which the speaker has previously determined to favor should be reserved for the final position on the list.

5. After a consideration of these plans, the speaker should discard them one by one as being incapable of really solving the problem, until he comes to his own plan—the last one on the list. In considering it, he shows its superiority to the others and points out how well it will meet the needs of the situation. With the problem carefully analyzed, all practicable plans fairly considered, and the evidence weighed, the speaker's plan should emerge as the inevitable solution. The audience not only feels that it must accept the speaker's conclusions, but it is glad to do so, as a means of escape from the unpleasant situation described in the beginning of his speech.

CONCLUSION

The speech to induce belief is informative, of course, but it has the additional purpose of establishing agreement and conviction in the listener's mind. It seeks to strengthen or to change each listener's opinions, attitudes, and beliefs permanently. It is necessary, therefore, for the speaker accurately to analyze both his audience and his subject, in order that he may take utmost advantage of his listeners' inclinations to belief and of the potentialities within his subject most likely to arouse and strengthen belief. The conquest of the mind is not by any type of force, but by its own voluntary acceptance of facts and expert or respected opinions leading to reasoned conclusions. The facts, the expert opinions, and the logic utilized by the speaker not only must secure and hold the attention and command the respect of the listeners during the presentation of the speech, but must be adequate to withstand the tests of later experience and possible attack.

In organizing the material for a speech to induce belief, the speaker may use either the strictly logical or the analytical (problem-solving) approach. Whichever approach he uses, the speaker should be fair-minded and judicious, giving adequate consideration to alternative points of view and to the limitations of his own position. It is seldom, indeed, that the truth is entirely on any one side, and the speaker risks failure if he tries to make his audience believe that it is. But the final weight of the evidence, all things considered, should lead to one conclusion—the proposal that the speaker recommends.

EXERCISES AND BIBLIOGRAPHY

Exercises

1. Select any subject you wish (such as subsidization of athletics, federal aid for education, or international union) and phrase theme sentences for it leading to (a) a speech to induce belief; (b) a speech to inform; and (c) a speech to persuade. What is the *essential* requirement of the speech to induce belief?
2. Read a speech that has inducing belief as its purpose. Report on its *organization,* telling whether it is logical or analytical and indicating the reasons why you think it should be either one or the other. Report on its *content,* showing how well or poorly it uses facts, logic, and expert testimony. Cite evidences from the text of the speaker's using either his own prestige as an expert or other factors for impressiveness. Cite evidence indicating either judiciousness or bias in attitude.
3. Prepare a five-minute speech to induce belief on any subject you can cover adequately in so brief a time. Phrase your general and specific purposes. First, outline the speech by the logical method; second, outline it by the analytical, or problem-solving, technique; finally, decide which of the two methods is better for this particular speech. Explain to the class the reasons for your choice of method of organization. If class time permits, your instructor may ask you to deliver the speech again, this time using the other method of organization.
4. Select a topic and choose three authorities whom you might cite in presenting it. Explain to the class in a three-minute speech why these men are competent to offer expert testimony upon this topic.
5. Analyze the speeches to induce belief delivered by your classmates, judging them by the single standard of their objectivity. Cite examples of this quality—and of its absence—from some of the speeches. Indicate how your evaluation of the speaker's conclusion may have been affected by the apparent fairness (or lack of fairness) in his presentation.
6. Participate in a class discussion on the differences in kinds of speech material and in manner of presentation when the speaker aims at (a) an immediate effect and (b) a lasting effect.

Bibliography

Bogoslovsky, Boris B., *The Technique of Controversy* (Harcourt, Brace, 1928).

Chase, Stuart, *Guides to Straight Thinking* (Harper, 1956).

Dewey, John, *How We Think* (Heath, 1933).

Ewbank, H. L., and J. J. Auer, *Discussion and Debate* (Appleton-Century-Crofts, 1951).

Hodnett, Edward, *The Art of Problem-Solving* (Harper, 1955).

Oliver, Robert T., *The Psychology of Persuasive Speech* (Rev. ed.; Longmans, Green, 1957), Chap. 18, "The Speech to Convince."

Winans, James A., *Public Speaking* (Appleton-Century-Crofts, 1915), especially Chap. 9, "Persuasion and Belief."

ILLUSTRATIVE SPEECH

At Bowdoin College, Brunswick, Maine, a senior, Pierre R. Paradis, member of Phi Beta Kappa, delivered the following speech to induce belief in November, 1959. Note how well he adapts to his audience and his frequent use of "audience-centered" illustrations. Note also how strongly his own personal convictions shine through his words. Does this, in your opinion, add to or detract from the effect he wishes to secure?

Stereotypes

BY PIERRE R. PARADIS

A few years ago, I won first prize in a national essay contest. . . . You see, when I was in high school, I wrote the best letter, in twenty-five words or less, on who my favorite character in *Sky Ranger* comics was and why.

Now, I want you to think back over what has just happened in your mind. It probably went something like this. When I stated that I'd won a national essay contest, you reacted mentally with the concept "author." Then, suddenly, a whole train of associations was set up: my wearing glasses seemed proper; you wondered if I had any strange avocations; and you probably labeled me an "odd ball," or, at least, "different."

Then, when I revealed the exact nature of the competition, this preconceived notion, this stereotype, was rapidly broken down. The words "high school" immediately decreased the accomplishment, since most of you, being college students, look down upon the intellectual prowess of the high school without stopping to ask whether I went to Boston Latin or dear, old Benedict Arnold High. Finally, the words "*Sky Ranger* comics" shattered what little was left of the illusion, since, having learned that it's fashionable to disdain comic books, you therefore as quickly dismissed the value of my essay as you had accepted its merit after my opening statement.

All this happened despite the fact that both instances stated the same truth, and in neither case had you actually read my essay to judge it on its merit. Like most people, you were reacting without thinking, relying on set ideas to avoid mental effort. In short, you were using stereotypes.

What is a stereotype? I believe we can say that it consists of a preconceived network of ideas brought to bear whenever one or several filaments of that network are stimulated. For example, I say the word "Italian" and this starts a whole pattern of associations. Words like "black hair," "olive skin," "cunning," maybe even "gangster," flash through your mind and you suddenly find yourself enmeshed in a paralyzing web of ideas to which you mold the situation, rather than vice versa.

Of course, when it comes to your own ethnic group, the stereotype is most likely to be a favorable one. This is why I prefer the company of the Franco-American boy down the hall to that of his Swedish roommate; and why I can overlook the hypodermic needle and white powder on my friend's desk and curse the Swede's sneaky way of smoking.

This brings me to the central part of this discussion. On the whole, are stereotypes good or bad? Are they a help or a hindrance in the modern world? As in most cases, there are two sides to the story. Let's examine the favorable points first.

The first of these is that a stereotype makes thinking easier. Clearly, no one man can master such diverse fields as international politics, guided-missile design, modern agriculture, and the effect of the Plato of the blue-jean set, Dick Clark, on the American teen-ager. Yet all these areas of human activity have a direct impact on what you and I do tomorrow and what kind of a world our children will inhabit.

Therefore, since they are all very important, and we can't acquire knowledge in depth in all these areas, we put labels on those which least interest us in order that we may pursue in a more effective fashion those areas of learning which interest us most. The result is that if I mention "American missiles" most of us will respond with the picture painted by this country's news services. However, to the rocket expert who helped design the Vanguard, there are no pat labels that fit. He realizes the complexity of the field and seldom thinks of it in terms of generalizations.

And so it goes for each of us, each concerned with certain aspects of life and, for sanity's sake, neatly filing away what doesn't fascinate us. The danger here, of course, is of filing everything away without retaining anything in the way of unbridled, mature thought. The danger is that we become a sterile filing cabinet.

The second advantage of stereotypes is that they allow us to cover mentally a lot of ground very fast, and thereby communicate with each other with a relatively high speed. For example, a few moments ago, I spoke of the American Plato, Dick Clark. By doing this, I could convey information and humor both in a few seconds by evoking the stereotype "infallible thinker," whereas to have done the same thing in straight explanatory style would have taken minutes. From the historian's point of view, such labels contain gross inaccuracies; but for my workaday convenience, they provide pegs on which I can swing into your mind without having to put up every peg myself.

Advertisers, especially, know this and therefore spend millions to create stereotypes: for example, "Viceroy." The word is hardly out of my mouth before you mentally counter with the phrase: "a thinking man's filter," and have visions of police chiefs who grow roses and bus drivers who build models of the moon. Once this reaction sets in, the advertiser has you confidently thinking of this brand as a thinking man's cigarette, despite the fact that you've never actually thought out, what, if anything, is so intellectually appealing about a Viceroy. This sort of stereotype not only sells cigarettes, but also provides a frame of reference for conversations and discussions such as this one.

Now, let's look at the other side of the ledger. When we do, we see that the first danger of letting stereotypes dominate our thinking is that they set up roadblocks to creative thought and the proper reaction to a given situation. I tell you I'm bringing my friend Herman Goldberg over for an interview about that job you have open. Now Goldberg may be just the man you've been looking for, and with a little creative imagination you can probably find uses for his talents you hadn't even contemplated. But, if you allow yourself to founder on the word "Jewish," you both lose. If this word doesn't allow you to see the man for what he is rather than what you think he has to be, then you've missed an opportunity to get yourself the right man; and, moreover, you've judged him on a basis that you yourself would be very quick to complain against were it used against you.

The second major drawback to thinking in terms of preconceived notions is that this is the sure way to the bitterest, most inane race prejudices, which lead, as it's been this country's misfortune to see, to the most hateful, hurtful and senseless kind of clashes—wherein a white man leads the attack to oust his Negro neighbor and then relaxes by going to the beach to get a good suntan. If you blandly accept the fact that people look and look again when a Halo girl walks by and that real men have tattoos on the back of their hands, then you're a set-up for your neighborhood segregation committee. All they have to do is pump in new facts on your old thought patterns, just as any electromagnetic signal follows the same circuit in a radio or any trash follows the same path down a gutter.

Third, stereotypes can rob life of much of its flavor. Most of us enjoy the view from a high mountain; but, first, we have to climb that mountain to get the view. It's the same way in our personal relations. When your new neighbor tells you that he's a research physicist, don't consign him under the sterile label "scientist," and think that he therefore must wear a white coat, be uninterested in women, and listen only to the opera. Make the effort to know him as a person. Sure, like climbing the mountain, it'll take a little effort; but when you're done you'll have a real friend who probably enjoys *Maverick* as much as you do and can't balance his checkbook any better than you can.

Don't let a stone image block your view of the living one behind it. Putting freshness and objectivity into our new acquaintances is what makes them worth while. And the fact of their newness, if we don't let a stereotype get in our way, can make our whole lives an exciting mixture of new stimuli rather than an insipid rehash of the past.

Finally, we come to a statement which is the very antithesis of the point I made some minutes ago when I was speaking on the pro side of the stereotype. I now tell you that stereotypes hinder the communication of ideas. How do I reconcile this with my previous statement? The answer is that they help in communicating simple ideas and humor with labels like "the American Shakespeare" and "the George

Washington of South America." But when a subject requires a more detailed treatment, popular stereotypes present a well-nigh insurmountable obstacle. For example, let us suppose that I'm a history teacher and I'm talking about Benedict Arnold. You'll recall that I mentioned his name at the beginning of this talk to produce a certain effect, based on the fact that his name would be synonymous with "traitor." If I now want to give you some serious information about him, however, how can I convey to you the full importance of his military services to the United States before his defection since I know that, in your mind, the word "traitor" rises above all else and you subordinate and twist your new information to fit this stereotype? How can I convince you that Wyatt Earp enforced law in only part of Dodge City, that below the so-called "deadline" vice pretty much took its own course? Hugh O'Brian looms in my way and communication breaks down.

We see, then, that stereotypes rob life of its freshness, vitality, fairness, and spontaneity—a high price to pay for the limited area in which they speed thought. Therefore, we should try to avoid stereotyped thinking wherever we can, realizing that the sheer bulk of known fact alone tends to force us into traditional rather than original thought. However, if you're still listening to me and haven't filed me away under "odd ball" or "orator" or some other neat heading, then you've taken the first step.

And, as you leave this hall tonight and reach for a Viceroy, as you light up, ask yourself: "If it really is the thinking man's cigarette, how come that of the five undergraduate Phi Beta Kappas on campus, not one smokes Viceroy?" As a matter of fact, only one of them smokes.

CHAPTER 20

CONTENTS

Speaker at a religious rally in an outdoor evening meeting in Franklin Park, Washington, D.C. (Library of Congress.)

THE SPEECH TO MOVE TO ACTION

> The fool tries to convince me with his reasons; the
> wise man persuades me with my own.—OLD PROVERB

THERE are numerous occasions when something ought to be done which will be left undone unless a speaker finds an effective means of influencing listeners to undertake the task or to accept the responsibility. The Red Cross needs blood—not abstractly, but concretely, not just in general but specifically: now, today and tomorrow, here in this community as well as elsewhere. A candidate needs votes—yours, if he can get it. A merchant needs to sell his wares—to you as well as to others. A club needs to have representatives in various activities—you, as well as others. There is need for speech designed to secure action whenever there is a job that has to be done.

It is not always true that the speech to induce action is unselfishly motivated or directed necessarily to the public good. A roommate tries to induce you to leave your studies for a week-end trip when you ought to remain concentrated on the writing of a term paper. An irresponsible radical tries to organize a mob action against some minority group in the community. An unethical businessman launches a campaign to sell worthless or even harmful drugs. A totalitarian regime directs a "brain-washing" program of mingled propaganda and terrorism against its own captive population. There is need to understand the principles and methods of the speech to induce action, both because of its values and because of its dangers.

In this chapter the problem dealt with is how to convert indifference or disbelief into action. As you study the means of doing this, it is hoped that you may increase your skill both in inducing action and in guarding yourself against appeals that are used for wrong ends.

Without persuasion men are not inspired to progress, new ideas die unused, truth lacks power and is impotent. This is well illustrated in the story of the early discovery and delayed use of penicillin. Dr. Alexander Fleming originally discovered the drug in 1928. But the factual report of it collected dust in a British biological journal for more than a dozen years—until a desperate and anxious British government sent Dr. Fleming by special plane to Cairo to save

Winston Churchill from death by pneumonia on his way back from the Teheran Conference. Dr. Fleming was knighted by a grateful government. At one of the numerous occasions honoring him Dr. Fleming said, "On such occasions I cannot help thinking of the thousands now dead who would still be alive had interest in penicillin been aroused when I first discovered it in 1928." No incident can more dramatically portray the great positive function which should be served by men skilled in the art of persuasion. Surely there is no study more deserving of the best efforts of that select group expected to be the determiners of tomorrow—the college men and women of today.

There is much point to the opinion expressed by Thomas Mann that "speech is civilization itself." Of all the means by which human behavior may be coordinated or controlled—including fear, force, bribery, and punishment—speech is the most civilized. By persuasive appeals, like-mindedness is achieved and programs of action are set in motion. Whether the action is ultimately good or bad depends primarily upon the quality of the leaders and of the people whom they lead. In either event, of all the tools available for social control, persuasive speech has come to be preferred by the most highly developed peoples.

SETTING THE GOAL OF ACTION

Occasions are frequent for using speech designed to persuade others to do as you wish, varying all the way from "Oh, come on, let's go to the movies" to political campaigns involving hundreds of speakers giving thousands of speeches over a period of many months, all designed to induce voters to cast ballots for a particular candidate for the Presidency. "How can I get him (or them) to do as I wish?" is a question that often occurs to each of us.

Of course, there is always an essential prior question: "How do I know that what I want others to do is good for them—or even for me?" Is the goal selected wisely and ethically? There have been many times when you have advocated something to your later regret. Perhaps, for instance, you once may have urged your parents to let you take a hitchhiking trip around the United States—only to be honestly relieved when they refused. Perhaps you have urged your roommate to go with you to the movies, half hoping that he would instead persuade you to spend the evening doing the studying you knew should be done. Before undertaking to persuade an audience to do something, you should first consider very thoughtfully whether what you advocate is really wise. For persuasive speech is not merely a form of academic exercise; it is influence exerted upon human beings.

If your classroom experience is to have maximum helpfulness in developing your persuasive skills, you should take care to select the goals for your speeches as realistically as possible. As a student, you are a member of the college community. The campus has its own rules and set of values. You may like some of them; you may feel some are in need of revision. Some forms of student behavior you may feel ought to be altered. Some relations between the campus and the town may be less than ideal. For example, when you think of automobiles you may be inclined to speak persuasively concerning a better plan for parking, the adoption of new rules governing permission for students to bring cars to college, or practices that might reduce traffic hazards. Perhaps you would like to see action taken to change graduation requirements, or to modify examination methods, or to change fraternity rushing rules, or to amend eligibility rules for student participation in activities. These particular problems are less vital than, say, those of international disarmament—but they are matters on which many students feel deeply; accordingly they pose very real tests for persuasive skills. From your own conversations on campus, you know what broader questions are of most concern to your student audience: Is it a religious obligation to attend Sabbath services? Should dormitory room assignments be made without consideration of race or religion? Should every student affiliate actively with a political party? Is it better to volunteer for military service or await the draft?

The essential considerations for formulating your goal for a speech to secure action are these:

1. The speech should aim to induce your listeners to do something that lies within their present capability: to give blood to the Red Cross, to make a contribution to UNICEF, or to practice more systematic study habits. If you wish to discuss national or international questions, or generalized philosophical questions, the test of persuasiveness is whether you can focus your topic on some action that your immediate listeners have it within their power to perform.

2. The speech should try to accomplish something that you earnestly want to see done, that you have considered thoughtfully and that seems to be both practically wise and ethically sound.

3. The speech should deal with a sufficiently limited goal so that you may accomplish it within the allotted time. This limitation may

require you to select only a portion of the larger goal you have in mind. For example, if you wish your listeners to broaden their appreciation of modern art, you might do your best to persuade them to attend a current exhibition of paintings; or if you wish them to extend their knowledge of religious thought you might try to persuade them to read Alan Watt's discussion of Buddhism in *The Way of Zen.*

THE MEANING OF THE SPEECH TO PERSUADE

In a sense, all communication seeks an action response—for simple knowledge presented in an expository manner must to some degree change our understanding, and a speech which uses humor may relax tensions and create a more tolerant attitude toward a serious problem. However, as was summarized in the second paragraph of this chapter, there is a difference between talk that presents information, leaving the interpretation or significance to be decided by the listener, and talk that identifies a specific action and urges the listeners to engage in it. *The speech to persuade is designed to change conduct in a particular way, to achieve a particular effect.* The test of whether a speech should be classified as persuasive is whether or not the speaker asks his immediate listeners to do something specific that lies within their capabilities. In preparing your persuasive talks, write at the top of your outline sheet a simple declarative sentence which begins: "I want my audience to (go, give, buy, do, undertake, commence, stop) . . . ." "Smoking has harmful effects" might be a topic for an informative speech. "Smoking is a habit that can be broken" might be suitable for a speech to induce belief. "I want my listeners to stop smoking from now on" is a topic for a speech to induce action.

THE ROLES OF AUTHORITY, EXPERIENCE, AND REASON

You need only to look back through the history of the race to learn the various means of persuasion and their relative strength. Primitive man was influenced primarily by authority—such as that of the medicine man or the tribal chief. Frequently the most effective type of missionary work has been medical service, by means of which the authority of the medicine man has been counteracted. When the medical missionary is able to restore a native's sick child to health, that native has an *experience* by which to judge the missionary, and that experience will tend to break down the authority of a contrary judgment urged by the chief or the tribal medicine man. Finally, as man has become more civilized, he has learned to formulate conclusions not only on the basis of authority and experience but by *reasoning*, or logic. If you will frankly take stock of opinions you now hold, you will be able to trace each one back to authority, to experience, or to reasoning—and unless you are indeed a rare person you will be able to trace very few to reasoning. Moreover, it will be pointed out later in this chapter that even what reasoning we do is largely a sort of pseudo reasoning, actually more emotional than logical, known as rationalization.

Since authority is the oldest means of persuasion known to man, it is not surprising that it is also the most universally effective. This suggests the advisability of including in your speeches many references to recognized authorities in support of your facts, your opinions, and your appeals to action. Of course, you will also do all that good taste permits to improve your personal prestige, citing any research or reading you have done or any personal experiences you have had which give you a right to speak with some authority. It is the acceptance of the authority by the audience which is important. If there is a possibility that your audience will fail to realize the value of the authorities you cite, your first task is to make them aware of that value.

If authority is against you, or if you wish to supplement it, you may count upon the appeal of experience—your audience's experience, the experience of others, your own experience. Even the best of authorities can be wrong; and the faith of democracy is deep in the experience and judgment of the common man.

In the history of man, reason is the most recently acquired means of persuasion. As the newest it is also the weakest. It is weakest of all among primitive men, children, and persons who have had little educational opportunity. Reasoning is a difficult art. Very few are capable of reasoning without error. These facts are pointed out not to belittle its power, nor to discourage its use by the persuasive speaker. The most effective persuasive speakers have learned to have high regard for their audiences' capacities for reasoning. *But,* they have also learned never to rely upon reasoning alone. It is vitally necessary for the student of speech to understand the relative values of the appeals to reason and to emotion. Our task as speakers is to work with people as they are.

Each of us tends to overrate the degree to which he relies upon reason. That man is an intellectual creature is a proposition which may be considerably overemphasized. Probably thinking plays a far less important part in our daily living than most of us realize. H. L. Hollingworth, in *The Psychology of the Audience,* presents the facts very accurately when he says:

It is not quite true that the average man reasons scarcely at all. On the contrary, he has a passion for argument, and prides himself in it; but he reasons stupidly. He mistakes coincidence for proof, correlation for causality, confidence for necessity, publicity for expertness, and appearance for reality. Habit, suggestion, and imitation constitute his instruments of thinking, as distinguished from his emotional reactions, and his inadequate background of knowledge, coupled with the urgency of his needs, makes him the ready prey of the fakir and the charlatan.

One need only cite the continuous succession of the illogical acts of individuals, communities, and nations in order to verify Hollingworth's analysis.

Yet reason is a human attribute. To reach a reasonable conclusion, two things are necessary: the unadulterated facts of the situation, and the logical correlation of those facts. Thus the great scientific thinkers, to whom we chiefly owe the development of civilization as we know it, have been close and accurate observers as well as dispassionate and objective logicians in considering the data resulting from their observation. Prejudice, personal desires, and traditional beliefs must be excluded from consideration, and the only question asked of a given hypothesis must be "Is it true?" rather than "Should we consider it true?"

You should always try to reach your own conclusions by a strictly reasonable process. Before urging others to accept an idea or a point of view, you should make every effort to determine whether the idea or point of view is factually and logically sound. Furthermore, you should present your ideas to the audience in as factual and logical a manner as it is able to accept. But every speech need not be composed strictly of facts and logic, and every speaker who uses other methods to influence his audience need not be demagogic. To the extent that people cannot be influenced by reason, other means must be used. The persuasive speech at its best is balanced in its intellectual and emotional appeal. It must be neither so factual and logical that it becomes pedagogical, pedantic, and dull nor so purely emotional as to omit all factual and logical appeals.

A good procedure to follow is to present a reasonable case for your proposal, based on a logical presentation of the pertinent facts, and to interweave with the argument such other forms of appeal as are presented in this chapter, in order to motivate those listeners who are not influenced by the reasoning. There must, by all means, be a strong emotional appeal in the final demand for action.

RATIONALIZATION

Too frequently when people think they are reasoning they are only rationalizing. Rationalization has been variously defined as "self-justification," presenting "good reasons" rather than "real reasons," offering "a reason" instead of "the reason," "false or pseudo logic," "covering our desires with the mantle of reasonableness," and "finding arguments for going on believing as we already do." We are coming to see how small a part reason plays in the decisions which men make, but since we have learned to respect and admire—indeed, almost venerate—reason, we insist upon going through mental processes that are at least superficially reasonable. We play at thinking as seriously as children play at "keeping house," and we are just as irritated when an observer points out that it is only a game. To a great extent we act emotionally, but at the same time we insist upon pretending, to ourselves as well as to others, that we are acting reasonably. Rationalization is the means by which the gap is bridged; it is a process of delivering emotion in the wrappings and under the label of logic. As such it ought to be combated by a "pure-speech law." Rationalizations are vastly more dangerous than emotional appeals, for, although the latter result in a great deal of action, they are at least recognized for what they are, whereas rationalizations are strenuously defended as being truly logical and are likely to deceive those who use them as well as those who accept them.

The whole process of rationalization may be very strongly condemned on strictly academic grounds, but this judgment should be modified by one all-important fact. As has been pointed out earlier in this chapter, rationalization does have an important function to perform. The typical man acts only because of emotional considerations. This is true whether his action is self-induced or is the result of external persuasion. But he has a higher ambition than this. He wants to be, and to be considered, a creature of logical thinking. He spurns an emotional appeal that is frankly and openly presented as such. He demands that it be camouflaged as logic. As a result, he rationalizes a great deal. As a public speaker, however, you should use rationalization cautiously: be sure that your speech is solidly based on a factual and logical examination of the problem you are considering, and present to your audience just as reasonable a discussion as it is capable of receiving.

Rationalization is indulged in so extensively because people tend to believe only what they wish to believe. In an article called "The Psychology of Belief," printed in the *Journal of Abnormal Psychology* for April, 1925, F. H. Lund reported the striking results of a series of experiments which verify this conclusion. Several hundred individuals, most of whom were college students, were given a list of propositions to judge. On one occasion they were asked to rate each for its degree of desirability; in other words, how strongly did they wish it to be true? On another occasion, when they would presumably no longer recall the results of their first rating, they were asked to list the propositions in the order in which they were credible; in other words, what degree of truth was there in the statements? A comparison of the two ratings showed that there was a very close correlation between them. These several hundred individuals, of better than average education and intelligence, had clearly demonstrated that they believed what they wished to believe.

The types and methods of rationalization vary greatly. No complete list can be presented, but, for guidance in detecting specious reasoning and rationalization in your own speaking and in the speeches and writings of others the following list of the principal types of rationalization is offered. The list is presented on the theory that if rationalization must be used it should at least be recognized and labeled as such.

1. *Argument by affirmation of the consequent.* If anyone declared, "X is true because X is true," nobody would accept this statement as being logical. But when he says, "If Y is true, X is true; Y is true; therefore, X is true," his statement sounds sufficiently logical to be widely accepted. "If justice is on our side, victory is assured; justice is on our side; therefore, we are certain to win."

2. *Argument based on sympathy.* Frequently an appeal to sympathy is thinly veiled as argument. "Enlist now! Bleeding Laos needs your help!" "Think of the unemployed men, the hopeless women, the undernourished children, the families without homes. The industrial system which is responsible for these conditions must be destroyed."

3. *Argument by applying labels.* A *New York Times* editorial for August 24, 1938, contained the following description of argument by use of labels: "Mild liberals find themselves damned as Communists. Decent conservatives who believe in the Bill of Rights are con-

demned as Fascists. It is well to remember that this game was invented by extremists who could not think of the world in any other terms than as a struggle between extremes." Such labels are short cuts which deny all possible shadings of opinion. You do not logically dispose of an argument by labeling its proponent a conservative.

4. *Argument from antiquity.* An appeal may be made to age. "The old-time religion [or political or economic system] is good enough for me." "Our ancestors got along under this system and I guess we can too." "George Washington warned against foreign entanglements." "We take our stand on the Declaration of Independence, which was hallowed by the blood of our ancestors."

5. *Argument from ignorance.* An assertion may be made that a proposition is proved by the fact that it cannot be refuted. "No one can successfully deny the possibility of communicating with the spirits of the dead. There is not an iota of direct evidence that such communication is impossible."

6. *Argument from novelty.* An appeal may be made to recency or newness. "The latest theory, you know, contradicts your point of view." "Your idea is old-fashioned; it goes back to the horse-and-buggy days. Mine is in accord with the newest theories."

7. *Argument from popularity.* "Fifty million Frenchmen can't be wrong." "Buy the car that leads the field!" "More people smoke X——— than any other cigarette."

8. *Argumentum ad hominem.* An argument is often transferred from principles to personalities. "The Governor's road-building program must be defeated because he is a notorious grafter." "How can 'The Prisoner of Chillon' be a good poem when it is well known how scandalously Byron lived?"

9. *Use of obscureness.* H. L. Hollingworth calls this practice "depending upon the impressiveness of words." The ability to clothe platitudes or asininity in a robe of glittering rhetoric has long been a priceless political asset. An excellent brief example is furnished in a speech made by a member of Congress: "Democratic freedom means the general agreement to stay out of each other's light by respecting privacy for the sake of perfection and to humanize power by compounding that of each into the mutual catharsis furnished by compromise of interests. Here is the only social pathway to individuality."

10. *Citation of authorities out of their fields of specialization.* Many advertisements will cite the opinions of movie stars, baseball players, and deep-sea divers on religion, tobacco, and the relative merits of automobiles; speakers will cite the authority of Abraham Lincoln,

Thomas Jefferson, and Andrew Jackson in discussions of the industrial and social problems of the twentieth century. An authority is an authority only in his own field.

11. *Confusion of correlation with cause.* Because two things happen together or in immediate succession, it is assumed that one is the cause and the other the effect. "He has never lost a game while wearing his mother's wedding ring. It always brings him luck." After Hoover was elected a depression occurred is no reason for assuming that the depression occurred because of his election, any more than the fact that wars occurred during the administrations of Woodrow Wilson and Franklin D. Roosevelt is a reason for assuming that the wars occurred because these men were in office.

12. *Explanation intended to confuse or mislead.* A common device is the spreading of a film of words over a situation to save the embarrassment of making a direct answer. In *The Confidence Man,* Herman Melville represents a character, in the days just before the Civil War, who avoids any revelation of his views on the touchy subject of slavery:

> "If by abolitionist you mean a zealot," said the herb-doctor, "I am none; but if you mean a man, who, being a man, feels for all men, slaves included, and by any lawful act, opposed to nobody's interest, and therefore rousing nobody's enmity, would willingly abolish suffering (supposing it, in its degree, to exist) from among mankind, irrespective of colour, then am I what you say."

13. *Use of irrelevant or nonpertinent analogies, illustrations, facts, or arguments.* A speech may sometimes appear very convincing because of the great quantity of specific examples, facts, and closely knit arguments it contains, but examination may show that they are irrelevant. Notice, for example, how a speaker "refuted" the charge that the use of loss-leaders by chain stores and large department stores has harmed the small retailers: ". . . the census tells the essential truth. In 1929, there were 96,900 stores in Illinois; in 1933, shortly after the bottom of the worst depression in modern history, they numbered 98,870." This, of course, does not consider whether the stores increased in number *despite* the allegedly harmful loss-leaders. Note the use of an illustration instead of an argument in the following advertisement: "Enroll in our short-story-writing course and earn big money! Last week one of our students sold a short story for $100. Signing your name on our enrollment blank is like signing a blank check. You can fill in the figures yourself!"

14. *Use of ridicule and sarcasm.* Belittling an opponent's argument

is often easier than refuting it. An example is found in Edmund Burke's comments on the King's ministers, in his speech on American taxation: "They never had any kind of system, right or wrong; but only invented occasionally some miserable tale for the day, in order meanly to sneak out of difficulties, into which they had proudly strutted." Franklin D. Roosevelt in 1932 disposed of the Republican prohibition plank by describing it as "high and dry at one end and moisterous at the other."

These fourteen types of specious reasoning indicate the main forms which rationalization may take. Whenever you find any of them, in your own speeches or in the speeches or writings of others, note whether it is not self-interest rather than the cause of truth which is being served.

EMOTIONS AND THEIR USE

The importance of emotions in determining human conduct is readily granted, but their precise nature is not easily defined. An emotion consists of a combination of a mental concept and a state of physiological disturbance. Among psychologists there has been considerable disagreement as to which initiates the emotion. The "common-sense" view, and for long the orthodox view among psychologists, is that an emotionally stirring situation is perceived, and the perception of it precipitates the bodily disturbance. Thus, we see a bear, become frightened, and run. Or, we learn that a friend has died, feel sorry, and weep. However, another view, developed more than a half century ago by Carl Lange in Germany and William James in America, has won widespread acceptance as the James-Lange theory of the emotions. James and Lange observed that the physiological disturbance comes first and contributes to causing and strengthening the mental concept. Thus, James insisted that "we feel sorry because we cry, angry because we strike, afraid because we tremble." For this view he cited the evidence of his observation;

In rage it is notorious how we "work ourselves up" to a climax by repeated outbursts of expression. Refuse to express the passion and it dies. Count ten before venting your anger, and its occasion seems ridiculous. Whistling to keep up courage is no mere figure of speech. On the other hand, sit all day in a moping posture, sigh, and reply to everything with a dismal voice, and your melancholy lingers. . . . Smooth the brow, brighten the eye, contract the dorsal rather than the ventral aspect of the frame, and speak in a major key, pass the genial compliment, and your heart must be frigid indeed if it does not gradually thaw.

The chief value of the James-Lange theory to public speakers is that it suggests a means for the control of emotions. It frequently happens, for example, that a subject is selected in which the speaker takes an earnest and enthusiastic interest. During the preparation of his speech, his emotional reaction to the subject is marked. He feels himself filled with the force and drive needed to make a rousing and effective speech. Then several days pass while he is awaiting the date for his speech. His emotion cools; he has become "cold" on the subject. His delivery is almost certain to be phlegmatic and his speech dull and uninspired. It is this experience, perhaps repeated several times, which persuades some beginning speakers to make no preparation at all until just before the time for their speech, at which time, of course, the development of their ideas is necessarily brief and haphazard. Yet the speech seems to them much more satisfactory than a speech delivered in the former type of situation. They find that they have much more spontaneous energy and animation for the delivery. But force and enthusiasm alone are not enough; their very reason for existing is to carry an idea into the minds of the audience. The idea remains the most important consideration, and its development should be carefully worked out. You will find that you are able to combine the advantages of careful preparation with the effectiveness of emotional force if you will observe the principle of the James-Lange theory of the emotions: act as though you have the emotion, and you will have it. You can be a self-starter; you can generate within yourself the emotion that you need for the effective delivery of your speech. This is one of the great values of the James-Lange theory.

ADAPTING TO THE AUDIENCE

Just as a salesman must analyze his prospect, so the persuasive speaker must analyze his audience. He must know his listeners as well as possible in order that he may know how best to appeal to them. Of particular importance will be information as to the range of their ages, their educational background, vocational and avocational interests, religious affiliations, political prejudices, club and organizational memberships—anything, in fact, which will assist the speaker to find common interests and likely points of agreement from which to begin.

For it is the speaker's task to adapt to his audience. He must have respect for his listeners, and respect comes from an appreciation of their own qualities. Realizing that there are different types of intelligence (artistic, mechanical, social, and verbal) the wise persuasive speaker will choose his illustrations and materials so as to appeal to the artist, the mechanical worker, the salesman, and the political-campaign manager as well as to the professional man or the college student. Rather than thinking of listeners as intelligent or unintelligent, the speaker should be asking: in which types of intelligence are they superior?

The primary purpose served by the speaker's information concerning his audience is that it will give him a good indication of the attitudes which will be held toward his purpose. Varying prejudices and a great variety of attitudes may exist within one audience and the speaker will attempt to deal with as many of these as possible within his limited time. Yet generally, and more importantly, each audience will tend to fall within one of three classifications as to attitude: favorable, apathetic, or hostile.

The Favorable Audience

When the listeners are favorable, the speaker's task is relatively easy. His chief concern is not to disappoint them by being too mild, too indifferent, or too purely logical. The enthusiasm of the favorable audience must be increased. This requires the re-emphasizing of arguments already known, the introduction of new supporting evidence, and the use of emotional appeals. Moreover, favorable audiences are not likely to be satisfied without some vigorous attack upon holders of the opposing point of view. They also expect praise for themselves and their leaders and specific suggestions as to what they may be able to do to aid the cause.

The Apathetic Audience

When the audience is apathetic, the persuasive speaker's obstacle is inertia or indifference. This calls for particular emphasis upon motivation and vividness. The social motives are likely to have the greatest force. Advertisers, whether over the radio, on television, or in newspapers and magazines, are aiming at an apathetic audience which they must stir to a desired action. They do this by stressing that "the trend is to . . . ," "this year everybody's buying . . . ," or "by three to one it's. . . ." In other words, the appeal is to be with the majority. Or it may be to take leadership or to best some rival group. Obviously, since concern must be aroused, vividness is essential.

A speaker may do many things to increase the likelihood of favorable response from his audience. He may use what psychologists call *the principle of suggestion.* Human beings tend normally to do and believe whatever is suggested to them. Thus the persuasive speaker avoids negative suggestion and seeks to phrase his demands in language that will induce favorable response. A salesman does not ask, "Have you ever used this product?" That would be to risk a negative answer. His question is more likely to be, "Would you like to save some money?"

Another principle which increases the likelihood of favorable response was mentioned in Chapter 3: *anything which increases the speaker's prestige or makes him liked by the audience makes it easier for him to win acceptance also for his ideas.*

The persuasive speaker should also give special consideration to the following principle, which is based on the idea that repetition is not only a stylistic device but has psychological advantage: *an idea which is repeated with frequency and persistence tends to become increasingly acceptable with each rehearing.*[1] Thus, in "Which Knew Not Joseph," Bruce Barton points out that the makers of Ivory Soap spend more than a million dollars a year repeating over and over the simple fact that Ivory Soap floats. It should be remembered, too, that *figurative language has psychological as well as literary value.* Notice the power of "A reactionary is like a crab that moves backward in order to go forward," of Carlyle's "What is hope?—a smiling rainbow children follow through the wet," of Southey's "It is with words as with sunbeams—the more they are condensed, the deeper they burn." And of Ruskin's "Imagination is a pilgrim on the earth, and her home is in heaven." The lecturer Thomas De Witt Talmage knew the persuasive power of the figure of speech: "In many eyes success is a crime. 'I do not like you,' said the snowflake to the snowbird. 'Why?' asked the snowbird. 'Because,' said the snowflake, 'You are going up but I am coming down.' "

No less important are the details that may well make the difference between favorable and unfavorable response, particularly from the apathetic audience. The speaker's dress is one of these. If it is too informal or careless it tends to increase the audience's indifference to

---

[1] Experimental proof of the persuasive value of repetition was established by A. T. Jersild in 1928, and his general conclusions were verified in a study published by Dr. Ray Ehrensberger in the 1945 issue of *Speech Monographs.*

him. Listeners who are scattered and far removed from the speaker will be much less responsive than if they are near the speaker and seated close to each other. Getting everyone to laugh together, applaud together, or sing together also makes the task of the persuasive speaker easier.

The Hostile Audience

When the audience is hostile, the situation calls for all the speaker's tact and persuasiveness. Usually he will use the indirect rather than the direct approach, because argument more often solidifies than weakens opposition. Remember that people believe what they believe because they wish to believe it—because of emotional and often prejudiced rationalizations. The first essential in reaching a hostile audience is to recognize the causes of its hostility.

An indirect approach frequently conceals the speaker's real purpose during the early part of the speech. The beginning must be made upon common ground. President Truman, winning his "hopeless" fight for re-election in 1948, relied chiefly upon a "whistle stop" campaign, going to the voters and speaking to them as a humble fellow American —a simple "man from Missouri." He knew that he must identify himself as one of them. Many political speakers, expecting at least some in their audience to be opposed to them, frequently begin by talking about the flag, the Constitution, or some choice bit of our historical heritage, for these are almost certain to win a common favorable response. To conciliate and win over to your point of view those who disagree with you, never begin with disagreements but always with points upon which there is accord; then seek gradually to expand this area of agreement.

The appeals to human wants, as means of *making the idea attractive,* are essential where there is a hostile audience. Since most of the reasons for opposition are themselves emotional, the speaker must find still stronger emotional reasons to overcome them. What has been said here concerning the roles of authority and experience should also be applied.

DELIVERY OF THE SPEECH TO PERSUADE

The persuasive speaker should have these four qualities:

1. *He must be confident.* He must forge ahead without vacillation or hesitancy. To be a leader, one must actually lead. An audience will

scarcely be swayed by a speaker whose manner reveals that he lacks assurance and whose speech is peppered with "probably," "perhaps," and "on the whole."

2. *He must be forceful.* To arouse an audience to action demands enthusiasm, vitality, and animation. The speaker must show by his own earnestness that what he has to say is truly important. He must himself set the example of strongly responding to the challenge of his proposal.

3. *He must be positive.* A negative attitude seldom stirs an audience to action. Bold, ringing statements telling the audience what it should do are much more effective than denunciations of the listeners for what they may have failed to do. Note the positive tone of the speech by William Jennings Bryan to the Democratic Convention of 1896, when he said:

Our war is not a war of conquest; we are fighting in the defense of our homes, our families and posterity. We have petitioned, and our petitions have been scorned; we have entreated, and our entreaties have been disregarded; we have begged, and they have mocked when our calamity came. We beg no longer; we entreat no more; we petition no more. We defy them.

4. *He must be definite.* He must clearly and specifically point out the kind of response which he desires. It is not enough merely to stress, for example, the need of money for the community chest. There should be a definite appeal for funds. It would be better to name an amount which should be donated by each listener; and it would be best of all to request that the funds be given or pledged right now, at this meeting. A tray should be provided at the door, so that the pledges and money may be received before the audience leaves.

These qualities of positiveness, forcefulness, confidence, and definiteness are in President Franklin D. Roosevelt's "Victory Dinner Speech," of March 4, 1937:

If we do not have the courage to lead the American people where they want to go, someone else will.

Here is one-third of a nation ill-nourished, ill-clad, ill-housed—now!

Here are thousands upon thousands of farmers wondering whether next year's prices will meet their mortgage interest—now! Here are thousands upon thousands of men and women laboring for long hours in factories for inadequate pay—now!

Here are thousands upon thousands of children who should be at school, working in mines and mills—now!

Here are strikes more far-reaching than we have ever known, costing millions of dollars—now!

Here are spring floods threatening to roll again down upon our river valleys—now! Here is the dust bowl beginning to blow again—now!

If we would keep faith—faith with those who had faith in us—if we would make democracy succeed, I say we must act—now!

PERSUASIVE SPEECHES IN THE BUSINESS WORLD

The purpose of business is to produce and sell goods or services. Business speeches are generally designed to promote the latter aim. For these sales talks, five rules that have been well tested in practice may be suggested:

1. *Use the "yes technique."* The sales talk may be delivered to a group of people or to an audience of only one. In both cases, it is designed either to arouse in the audience a desire for the article or service which is to be sold or to call attention to and emphasize the desire, if it already exists. You should decide first which of these conditions is true. If you are selling an electric razor, is it already desired by your listeners or must you first make them dissatisfied with other methods of shaving? If the latter is the case, your approach should be positive rather than negative. Do not attack other shaving methods; instead, concentrate upon a favorable presentation of the superior advantages of electric shavers. This is the first rule of salesmanship. Get your audience to begin saying, "Yes, yes," instead of "No, no." Do not try to arouse a negative attitude toward your competitors' products, but stimulate a positive attitude toward your own. It is appropriate that businessmen's luncheon clubs have as their motto "Don't knock; boost!" for that is the primary rule for the conduct of all business—including salesmanship. Other techniques are allied to this one.

2. *Do not sell the article itself, but sell its utility.* It is not an automobile that people want to buy, but the enjoyment, prestige, usefulness, and convenience of owning an automobile. Similarly, they do not buy hair tonic, but more attractive hair; not apples, but the pleasure of eating apples; not a railway ticket, but the excitement and change of a journey. In trying to sell to city dwellers an old, abandoned farmhouse in the country, the successful realtor does not expatiate upon the value of the land or the sturdy construction of the house—at least not until the final stages of the sale. He paints glowing pictures of the calm and peace of the countryside, the healthfulness of the fresh air and sunshine, the prestige of owning a "country place." Successful salesmen of all kinds follow the principle of not

telling the potential buyer what an article *is* until he has become enthusiastic over what it *will do*.

3. *Always keep the customer's point of view in mind.* People buy articles to please themselves, not to please salesmen. If this principle seems to be contradicted by the practice of many house-to-house salesmen, who always introduce a story about their own poverty or need as a standard part of their sales talk, you should remember that this is not selling but begging. In such cases the people who buy are not really buying; they are giving alms. But only a small percentage of all selling is conducted in this way. In the vast majority of cases, the salesman must visualize the customer's desires and needs; he must be aware of the customer's point of view; and he must hold it continually in mind while conducting his sales talk.

4. *Be confident.* Do not entertain any fears about the value of your product, about the price being too high, or about the possibility that the individual or group you are speaking to may not want or need your product. If you have such fears, you are either trying to sell the wrong product or you are aiming at the wrong customers.

5. *Stop when the sale is made!* This is the only answer to the question of how long a sales talk should be. Of course, a salesman cannot always realize this goal; if he proves unable to make the sale, he nevertheless must stop eventually. The rule must often be broken simply by the customer's refusal to buy. But one of the cardinal sins of salesmanship is to break the rule when the talk has been effective—for the salesman to keep on with his sales talk after the customer has made up his mind to buy. This not only involves a waste of time but may well result in the loss of innumerable sales. The customer may become irritated and change his mind, and the sale is lost. A primary requisite for successful selling is a great sensitivity to the reactions of potential buyers, so that the speech (that is, the sale) can be closed at precisely the right moment.

FUNCTIONAL PLAN FOR THE PERSUASIVE SPEECH

To say that a speech must have an introduction, a body, and a conclusion is true but often of small help. If the persuasive speech is considered from the standpoint of its purpose, the following steps must be made in order to attain it:

The persuasive speech must (1) obtain and hold attention; (2) arouse dissatisfaction with the present situation or a sense of need for change; (3) present clearly and appealingly the recommended change; (4) motivate the audience to desire to do what is asked; (5) use vivid imagery throughout; and (6) make a specific appeal for action.

Add effective delivery to a speech composition which does these six things well and you have achieved the fundamentals of persuasion.

1. Chapter 11 has already presented the essentials of *obtaining* and *holding attention*. Bear in mind, however, that attention fluctuates. As you sit in the classroom you are aware of the way in which your attention is constantly shifting. Unless the speaker continuously does or says things which bring the attention back to him and his subject, he will be wasting his time upon an inattentive audience.

2. The automobile salesman who invites you to step in and take a drive around the block in his new model is trying to make you dissatisfied with the old car, *to make you aware of the need for a change.* You must find some way of arousing in your audience such a sense of need for the action you seek of them. One way is to contrast the advantages of your plan with the disadvantages of the *status quo.*

3. *The clear statement of your precise objective and of exactly how you hope to have it attained* requires audience-centered exposition. In persuasive speaking, it is important to weave into the exposition any statements which will increase its appeal or attractiveness.

4. *Motivating the audience to desire to do what is asked* involves achieving what is really self-persuasion. It is probably true that you cannot persuade another person to do anything: you can only induce him to persuade himself. Thus *a basic problem in persuasion is how to induce an audience to want or desire to do what the speaker wishes it to do.* The technique of doing this involves motivation—an appeal to human needs, wants, and desires. Sometimes you may most readily discover how to appeal to others by analyzing the evolution of your own increasing interest in the subject. But you must be sure that the reasons for your interest will also grip others. You may be interested in giving a talk on Brazilian stamps because you are an enthusiastic collector of stamps, but your audience may not be entirely made up of stamp collectors.

Nevertheless, there are some fundamental and universal wants. These are sometimes classified as *protective, acquisitive, social,* and *sensuous*. Self-preservation is the strongest urge of man. Anything which can be shown to involve the protection of life or health, whether of self or of others, will win ready attention. Also strong is the desire to acquire personal possessions; talk of better wages, bargains, free offers, or higher dividends will receive a quick hearing. Among the social wants are prestige, the favorable regard of friends and loved ones, acceptance into desired associations or groups, and leadership. The sensuous wants are those which appeal directly to the various sense perceptors: tastes, smells, sounds, all types of beauty and artistic desires, and sex in the broad sense which underlies the ideals of love, marriage, and family. Fraternity pins, honor-society emblems, military decorations, and athletic awards are common examples of devices for motivation. A critic ridiculing decorations of the Legion of Honor drew this reply from Napoleon: "You call these toys—I tell you men are governed by toys." It is clear that men are motivated to action only through their needs, wants, and desires. Tell your listeners how your proposal will help them to obtain what they want, and you will probably win their acceptance of that proposal.

5. In a very real sense a speech is for an audience what schooling is for a young person: a briefer, quicker substitute for the otherwise slow or even impossible process of experience; as such, *it must be vivid*. A speech seeks to give the audience the value of the speaker's experience, whether it recounts a trip, describes a surgical operation, or tells of conditions of poverty and want which the speaker has witnessed. This substitute for experience can never be as vivid as the original experience. It must, however, call up all possible images. Although most persons are predominantly visual-minded, there are some for whom auditory, olfactory, kinesthetic, or other images may be even more effective. Whether describing present conditions or future possibilities, you must make them vivid. The judge in traffic court is utilizing this principle when he orders that traffic violators be taken on a tour of the morgue and the receiving hospital to see the victims of careless driving. As it is expressed in the Book of Proverbs, "Where there is no vision, the people cast off restraint." Persons who visualize the possible consequences of fast driving tend to be more cautious.

6. That your appeal for action must be *specific and definite* has been stressed earlier in this chapter, in the section "Delivery of the Speech to Persuade." What is chiefly to be noted is the fact that this definiteness must characterize both the manner of delivery and the subject matter being discussed. Tell your audience *precisely* what you wish it to do and how and when this action is to be performed. There should be no occasion for your listeners to say, "We agree, but what can we do?" The persuasive speech is primarily aimed at unfolding in a compelling manner the exact action the audience is expected to take.

CONCLUSION

From time to time you will hear in one form or another charges that it is unethical to use techniques of persuasion—that to do so is somehow taking improper advantages of human beings. There are some who feel that truth needs no persuasive presentation. Nevertheless, we live in an age unrivaled in the amount and vigor of propaganda. Error is being assiduously propagated within nations and across national boundary lines. Your own experience has doubtless demonstrated the need of persuasive speech to "help the truth along." As for the all-too-frequent misuse of persuasion for socially harmful ends, Professor James A. Winans has wisely pointed out, "The man who is unscrupulous off the platform will be unscrupulous on the platform." We cannot remake the nature of men, but we can try to counteract evil with good. The more persuasion is utilized by zealots and demagogues, the more important it becomes that men of good will should succeed in making their knowledge, their opinions, and their purposes accepted.

This chapter has pointed out what persuasion is; how it is achieved through use of authority, experience, reason, rationalization, and emotional appeals; and how you as a speaker can improve your own persuasive powers by skillful adaptation to your audience, by effective delivery, and by appropriate organization of your ideas.

EXERCISES AND BIBLIOGRAPHY

Exercises

1. Present a four-minute talk to persuade your audience to some action through utilization of the functional plan outlined in this chapter.
2. Present a four-minute talk intended for an average audience, making something particularly vivid. Make the audience feel horror, admiration, enjoyment, or some other emotion.
3. Present a seven-minute talk designed for a hostile audience. Tell your classroom audience what specific group they are supposed to imagine themselves: for example, a faculty meeting before which you are advocating lower salaries for teachers or a brewers' convention before which you advocate the elimination of all liquor advertising from the radio.
4. Bring to class ten full-page magazine advertisements which seem to you

to illustrate particularly effective use of principles of persuasion. Use these to illustrate a talk on the use of some principle in advertising.

5. Present a talk to your class on how you believe the principles of persuasion may serve some specific field: politics, religion, industrial management, social work, medicine, organized labor, industrial-safety work, personnel work, and the like.

6. Prepare a speech designed to win some specific action from an apathetic audience: to persuade a neighborhood group to develop a playground for the children in the community, to get students to attend some university function, to get voters to the polls on Election Day, and so on.

7. Prepare a talk in which you will expect to be interrupted by the class. Take a definite position on some controversial subject and attempt to persuade your audience to accept your point of view. After the first minute, members of the class may freely interrupt you with questions, demands for proof, or objections. You are to go as far as you can toward your goal, answering, avoiding, utilizing, or dealing with the interruptions in the best way you can.

8. Listen to a persuasive speech outside class and report on the kinds of appeals used by the speaker. Show how his organization was or was not functional. Criticize the speaker's delivery and adaptation to his audience. Indicate how well he met the requirements for a specific and definite conclusion.

Bibliography

Hovland, Carl I., "Major Factors Influencing Effects," pp. 1071–1103 in *Handbook of Social Psychology,* Vol. II, Gardner Lindzey, ed. (Addison-Wesley, 1954).

Oliver, Robert T., *The Psychology of Persuasive Speech* (Rev. ed.; Longmans, Green, 1958).

Packard, Vance, *The Hidden Persuaders* (McKay, 1957).

CHAPTER 21

CONTENTS

The speech to inspire is an essential function of social living, helping to establish and maintain traditions, create group unity and loyalty, and clarify human feelings. (Wide World Photos, Inc.)

THE SPEECH TO INSPIRE

So long as human beings confront difficulties, are conscious of their limitations and failures, and require spiritual and emotional stimulation, there will be a continuing need for speeches of inspiration. Whenever groups of people meet to engage in a common enterprise, to celebrate a victory or an achievement, to worship or to give thanks, appropriate inspirational speeches are in demand. On occasions in which vigorous action of some kind is required, inspiring speeches are expected to furnish the necessary stimulus. One of the shortest and most forceful inspirational speeches on record is that supposed to have been uttered by a sergeant to his men just before the charge in the battle of Château-Thierry in World War I: "Come on you ————! Do you want to live forever?" Also noteworthy was the appeal addressed by George Washington to the members of the Constitutional Convention in 1789: "If we offer to the people something of which we do not ourselves approve, how can we afterwards defend our work? Let us raise a standard to which the wise and the honest may gladly repair. The event is in the hands of God."

In all other kinds of speaking the essential function of the speaker is to change in some manner the thoughts, attitudes, or actions of his audience. Essentially, the function of the inspirational speaker is to express effectively and impressively what his audience already feels, thinks, has done, or is determined to do. The speech to inspire is the speaker's utterance of what the audience itself wishes to say. The speaker is his listeners' spokesman, rendering on their behalf sentiments appropriate to the occasion, in language fitting to the emotions they all share.

Being a spokesman does not, however, in any degree lessen the dignity or lighten the task of the inspirational speaker. He has the duty to sense the spirit and mood of the occasion. He must devise a speech that will satisfy the listeners' expectation and yet be sufficiently original to engage their interest. Far from being trite, stilted, or hum-

506

drum, speeches of inspiration comprise perhaps the largest single category in the world's history of great oratory.

Religion, patriotism, ethics, brotherhood, social unity, group loyalty, sacrificial endeavor, pride in the past, and hope for the future all depend to a high degree upon effective inspirational speeches. There is no kind of speaking in which the speaker must more surely possess the two requirements of leadership: to be fundamentally like his associates, but at the same time to be sufficiently superior to transcend them. There is no other kind of speaking that makes so great a demand for dignity and for emotional rapport with the audience. And there is no other kind that requires such excellence of style. Any consideration of the functions and requirements of the speech to inspire leads to the conclusion that it should be considered the capstone of public speaking. Winston Churchill's speech on accepting the prime ministry, Daniel Webster's first Bunker Hill oration, and Abraham Lincoln's Gettysburg Address and second Inaugural Address are superior examples of the speech to inspire. Inspirational speeches may be said to represent the best speaking of the best speakers.

The speech student should not feel unable to meet the standards this type of speaking requires. In every community there are so many occasions for commemorative and inspirational addresses that anyone who is a community leader or who is regarded as a "good speaker" can expect to be asked to give them.

It is advisable for everyone to have a basic knowledge of what is expected of inspirational speeches and to have had some practice in delivering them.

THE NATURE OF THE SPEECH TO INSPIRE

It should be evident from what has been said of the wide variety of occasions for inspirational speeches that this type of speaking cannot be defined narrowly. It may include the pregame talks of the football coach to the men on the team, a large proportion of sermons, "booster" speeches at sales conventions or chamber-of-commerce luncheons, keynote addresses at political conventions, commencement addresses, speeches for such holidays as Memorial Day, Labor Day, and the Fourth of July and for such occasions as father-and-son banquets, annual reunions, anniversaries, and dedications. The list of suitable occasions for the inspirational speech might be lengthened considerably. On the other hand, not all speeches given on the occasions mentioned are necessarily speeches to inspire, although such occasions typically call for one. For it takes more than the nature of the occasion to make an inspirational speech. Despite the very wide variations between inspirational pep talks before sports events and inspirational commemorative addresses on national holidays, there are certain essentials to which these and all other speeches to inspire must conform.

These qualities distinguish the speech to inspire from speeches to explain, induce belief, persuade, and entertain: (1) it expresses the general feelings of the audience; (2) it heightens, uplifts, or makes more meaningful the feelings of the audience; (3) it conforms in content, style, and delivery to the normal expectations for the occasion on which it is delivered; (4) it expresses confidence and authority unrelieved by doubt or qualifications; and (5) it has a level of style and delivery that commands the respect and admiration of the audience.

A small fireside group engaging in religious worship and discussion offers an opportunity for the inspirational speech. Note the complete accord which marks the relationship of the speaker and his audience.

EXPRESSING AUDIENCE REACTIONS

The inspirational speaker, as noted above, is a spokesman for the common aspirations, feelings, and beliefs of the audience. It is conceivable that at a football rally or a political convention a speaker might try to allay the emotions of his listeners by assuring them that their desire to win the contest is unreasonable, that whether they win or lose is of little real consequence, and that it would be better for them to devote themselves to more important concerns. But if he gave that kind of speech, he would unquestionably be trying to persuade or induce belief rather than to inspire. A body of partisans gathered on the eve of a contest expects a speech that will express its own desire for victory, that will praise its heroes and denounce its foes, that will provide unifying slogans and simplified appeals. Similarly, an unorthodox preacher or patriot might denounce the orthodoxies of religion or nationalism, but if he does so he will have to convince his listeners that his views are really their own before he can begin to inspire them with the virtues of the new ideas he propounds. The speech will not even begin to have an inspirational effect until the audience feels that the speaker is uttering truths it fully accepts.

In order to express the feelings of his audience, the speaker must, of course, understand clearly what those feelings are. Of successful politicians we are likely to say, "They know what the public wants." Or, if we wish to express the same thought in somewhat more flattering terms, as applied to a political leader we greatly admire, we say, "He has the common touch" or "He is a man of the people." The great inspirational speakers are those united by bonds of sympathy, understanding, and common experiences with the members of their audiences. It follows as a matter of course that a speech which is highly inspirational for one audience will appear ridiculous or subversive to people whose feelings are vastly different. Thus Hitler seemed almost a demigod to the massed thousands of Nazis listening to his addresses at Nuremburg rallies and a veritable madman to the opponents of Nazism who heard or read the same speeches. The deeper the feelings of the audience and the more nearly the inspirational speaker conforms to them, the more definitely contradictory will be the responses of followers and foes. During World War II Winston Churchill expressed the common English determination to survive and to fight; but after the war he apparently failed to express the general desire for economic and social reform, so that for the majority of Englishmen his speeches lost their deep emotional appeal. Wherever and by whomever they are delivered, inspirational speeches draw their chief power from their expression of the general feelings of the audience.

MAKING AUDIENCE REACTIONS MORE MEANINGFUL

It should not be assumed from what has been said that an audience always knows fully what its own general feelings are. At a football rally held the evening before the annual home-coming game, it may be assumed that the desire to win is general and clearly defined. But in a typical Sunday-morning church service, it may be assumed that the congregation will contain members varying from the deeply religious, through those who merely feel a desire to conform to the general pattern of church attendance, to a few who come from idle curiosity or lack of anything else to do. Inspirational sermons typically are based on the presumption that the congregation will be religious, but not religious enough. If a "spiritual thermometer" could measure the warmth of the congregation's religious ardor, it might register 50° or 60°. The purpose of the minister would be to heighten, uplift, or make more meaningful these religious feelings, so that a spiritual warmth of 75° or 80° might be attained. Similarly, an audience of typical Americans gathered for Memorial Day or Fourth of July services may be assumed to have real feelings of patriotism; but the speaker's function is to inspire deeper and richer feelings.

Often the inspirational speech to deepen and uplift the already existing feelings of the audience will take the form of reinterpreting those feelings in somewhat different and more commendable form. At the weekly meeting of his salesmen, for example, the sales manager may heighten the pride of his men in the work they are doing by pointing out that the more sales they make the more jobs there will be for men in the factories and the more satisfaction for the buyers who have the goods to use. A minister may tell his congregation that the desire for personal salvation should be a subordinate part of willing acceptance of whatever may prove the ultimate will of God. Thus the function of the inspirational speech to express the feelings of the audience does not preclude the possibility of improving upon the quality of those feelings. The best inspirational speeches, in fact, always aim to make better the very feelings which it is their primary purpose to express.

At campus rallies, student sentiment is often clarified and unified. Note that this speaker is utilizing humor to draw his large audience into one closely knit group. (Wide World Photos, Inc.)

CONFORMING TO THE OCCASION

The dominant theme of this book is that good speaking most successfully conforms to the demands and opportunities of the broad social setting in which it occurs. Speech always is a part of its *context*. It is inconceivable that there could be a "good" speech wholly independent of the specific circumstances in which it would be delivered. If this is true of other kinds of speaking, it is even more indisputably true of those speeches which express the feelings of their audience—that is, the speeches to inspire.

Many speeches to inspire are delivered under circumstances calling for a dignified and perhaps lofty style. This would be true of funeral eulogies and of most other formal inspirational addresses, such as those delivered on commemorative or anniversary occasions, at commencement exercises, or in churches. The dignified bearing and appearance of the speaker, the seriousness of the tone of his speech, and the formality of his speech style all help to express the listeners' sense of the importance of the occasion. The speaker who violates this anticipation can hardly expect his speech to have an inspirational effect. On still other occasions, however—notably at pep rallies, political conventions, "booster" luncheons, and sales meetings—formality and a too careful dignity would prevent the very uninhibited enthusiasm the meetings are designed to achieve. The same individuals, hearing a political speech on Friday evening and a church service on Sunday morning, may be inspired on both occasions, but in vastly different ways. In each instance the speaker must adapt himself and his speech to what the audience considers a proper atmosphere for the particular kind of inspiration that is offered.

Even the speech occasions that seem to violate the principle of conformity to the expectations of the audience will be seen upon examination actually to confirm it. If, for example, the comedian Bob Hope were invited to give a commencement address, his listeners would—despite the otherwise serious nature of the occasion—fully expect a humorous speech and would be disturbed and disappointed if they did not get it. Sales conventions of some firms (such as the International Business Machines Corporation) are likely to assume more of the character of a service of dedication than of a pep rally—for such is the tone of the company's management. Similarly, you may have attended church services distinguished by rollicking good humor and considerable informality. But all these seeming deviations from the rule of conformity actually emphasize the fact that the speaker must adjust his inspirational speaking to the fundamental characteristics his audience really expects, rather than to what, from lack of sufficient information, he may think they expect. In all instances, the inspirational speech picks up the audience where it is, expresses feelings that are fundamentally those of the audience, and moves the audience along toward the goal of its own choosing.

EXPRESSING CONFIDENCE AND AUTHORITY

There are many speech occasions on which a speaker should be tentative in his conclusions, qualify his arguments, defer to contrary judgments, and make evident to his audience that it is impossible to be dogmatic on the subject under consideration. The inspirational talk, however, is not in this category of speeches. It need only be recalled that the function of the inspirational speaker is to give superior expression to what is already felt and believed. We believe in God but inspirational sermons make that belief more meaningful. We may be persuaded, convinced, amused, or enlightened—but hardly inspired to stronger belief—by a speech which in content or delivery shows uncertainty, doubt, or confusion concerning the existence of God.

STYLE AND DELIVERY

Considering the interrelations of speaker, subject, and audience, we see that good speech style (1) expresses the thought or content of the speech; (2) reveals the nature of the speaker; and (3) conforms to and influences the audience. All three of these characteristics determine the style of the inspirational speech.

In the speech to inspire, the content consists primarily of beliefs and feelings already shared by speaker and audience. The aim is not to amuse, exhort, or inform the listeners, but to heighten and deepen the feelings they already have. Therefore the speaker must strive not for originality of opinion but for originality and superiority of illustration and phrasing. Vividness and pungency will be the stylistic qualities of some kinds of inspirational speeches, beauty and impressiveness those of other kinds.

The inspirational speaker makes of himself an appropriate medium for the expression of audience sentiments. Thus the aspects of his personality which should be most evident are those of conformity to the group's feelings and convictions. Instead of trying to lead the group from its own position to a different one which he is expounding, the inspirational speaker makes it clear that no difference exists except one of degree. He assumes agreement and speaks as the agent, rather than trying to become the master, of the audience.

Finally, since the audience is to be influenced primarily by accentuation of its existing feelings, the inspirational speech will normally be marked by liberal use of such phrases as "we all realize," "our experience has shown," and "as you well know." Since the speaker is largely confined to telling the audience what it already believes, he can only avoid triteness and boredom by making his expression of these old ideas exceptionally pleasing and vivid. What the informative speech can accomplish with facts, the speech to induce belief with argument, the speech to persuade with emotional appeals, and the speech to entertain with humor or dramatic narrative, the speech to inspire must achieve largely with superior style and delivery.

PREPARATION OF THE SPEECH TO INSPIRE

Since every speech must be adapted to its audience, the speaker must, of course, give close consideration to his audience while he is preparing the speech. It is perhaps even more important for the inspirational speaker to bear this in mind than for a speaker having any other purpose. No one can really serve as a spokesman for an audience unless he knows thoroughly its beliefs and feelings. Whereas in much speaking the speaker primarily wishes to deliver a message or point of view that is peculiarly his own, in inspirational speaking he is delivering back to the audience its own emotions and convictions.

The fundamental preparation, then, of the speech to inspire, is the achievement of a close identity with the audience. This is why we properly think of a politician as "having his ear to the ground." This is why the great preachers—Henry Ward Beecher and Harry Emerson Fosdick, to name but two—customarily prepared their sermons by thinking of the needs and characteristics of members of their own congregations. This is why leadership is defined not only as superiority to one's fellows but also as fundamental similarity to them.

In preparing the inspirational speech, you should first of all turn your mind *outward* to your audience, in order to determine what its basic expectations will be. After that, you should turn your thinking *inward* to find what you already know and what additional materials you must accumulate in order to satisfy those expectations. Once again it should be emphasized that this process is not basically different from what you do in any speech preparation. It does differ in degree, however, for in the inspirational speech you are trying to move the audience farther along on courses it has already selected for itself.

CONCLUSION

It has been pointed out that inspirational speaking is in a real sense the acme of all public speech, having especially high requirements in audience understanding and in speech style. Nevertheless, speeches to inspire are so much in demand that even relatively inexperienced speakers—particularly if they occupy conspicuous public positions—may expect to be called upon occasionally to give them. Consequently, it is advisable for the student of speech to learn its five characteristics and to gain practice in its composition and delivery. Above all, it should be kept in mind that the function of the inspirational speech is to help the audience to achieve a heightened and more meaningful appreciation of its own best thoughts and feelings.

EXERCISES AND BIBLIOGRAPHY

Exercises

1. Prepare a five-minute eulogy of someone who is particularly admired by your prospective listeners; include in the speech material designed to clarify and heighten their respect for him.
2. Prepare a five-minute speech of commemoration for a holiday, such as Mothers' Day, Good Friday, Arbor Day, Memorial Day, Labor Day, or the Fourth of July. Develop facts and ideas that will deepen and make more meaningful your listeners' appreciation of the significance of the occasion.
3. Prepare a five-minute speech of inspiration suitable for a banquet honoring your football team or for a testimonial dinner to the president or dean of your college.
4. Prepare a five-minute speech suitable for a sports rally, for a sales convention, or for a political meeting. Note in what respects this speech will differ in style and atmosphere from the kinds of inspirational speech called for in the first three exercises; but also note that, like them, it must express the mood and feelings of the audience.
5. Listen to an inspirational address and write a report on it, indicating the speaker's degree of success in identifying himself with his audience in mood, in purpose, and in belief; either the means by which the speaker succeeded in avoiding platitudes or ways in which he might have done so; and stylistic characteristics of the speech which were (or were not) suitable to the occasion.

Bibliography

Beecher, Henry Ward, "Lecture on Oratory," delivered in Philadelphia, May 29, 1876.

Emerson, Ralph Waldo, "Eloquence," in Society and Solitude.

ILLUSTRATIVE SPEECH

The address made by William Faulkner at Stockholm, on December 10, 1950, is regarded as a classical statement of the feelings of modern man. Particularly appropriate is his reference to the fear of being blown up, since Alfred Nobel, inventor of dynamite, established his series of awards primarily from remorse at the destructive uses to which his invention had been put. Learning only the preceding evening that he would be expected to make an address when receiving the award, Mr. Faulkner drew upon his lifetime of meditation on the functions of the writer. Deeply personal as his statement is, its fame depends largely on the fact that it also expresses feelings held very widely in our time.

On Accepting the Nobel Award

WILLIAM FAULKNER

Reprinted from *The Faulkner Reader* (Random House, 1954).

I feel that this award was not made to me as a man but to my work —a life's work in the agony and sweat of the human spirit, not for glory and least of all for profit, but to create out of the materials of the human spirit something which did not exist before. So this award is only mine in trust. It will not be difficult to find a dedication for the money part of it commensurate with the purpose and significance of its origin. But I would like to do the same with the acclaim, too, by using this moment as a pinnacle from which I might be listened to by the young men and women already dedicated to the same anguish and travail, among whom is already that one who will some day stand here where I am standing.

Our tragedy today is a general and universal physical fear so long sustained by now that we can even bear it. There are no longer problems of the spirit. There is only the question: when will I be blown up? Because of this, the young man or woman writing today has forgotten the problems of the human heart in conflict with itself which alone can make good writing because only that is worth writing about, worth the agony and the sweat.

He must learn them again. He must teach himself that the basest of all things is to be afraid; and, teaching himself that, forget it forever, leaving no room in his workshop for anything but the old verities and truths of the heart, the old universal truths lacking which any story is ephemeral and doomed—love and honor and pity and pride and compassion and sacrifice. Until he does so he labors under a curse. He writes not of love but of lust, of defeats in which nobody loses anything of value, of victories without hope and worst of all without pity or compassion. His griefs grieve on no universal bones, leaving no scars. He writes not of the heart but of the glands.

Until he relearns these things he will write as though he stood among and watched the end of man. I decline to accept the end of man. It is easy enough to say that man is immortal simply because he will endure; that when the last ding-dong of doom has clanged and faded from the last worthless rock hanging tideless in the last red and dying evening, that even then there will still be one more sound: that of his puny inexhaustible voice, still talking. I refuse to accept this. I believe that man will not merely endure: he will prevail. He is immortal, not because he alone among creatures has an inexhaustible voice, but because he has a soul, a spirit capable of compassion and sacrifice and endurance. The poet's, the writer's, duty is to write about these things. It is his privilege to help man endure by lifting his heart, by reminding him of the courage and honor and hope and pride and compassion and pity and sacrifice which have been the glory of his past. The poet's voice need not merely be the record of man; it can be one of the props, the pillars to help him endure and prevail.

CHAPTER 22

CONTENTS

At a banquet during the "Debate Day Program" at Wayne State University, debaters indicate their enjoyment of an after-dinner talk. (Allen Stross)

THE SPEECH TO
ENTERTAIN

A SPEECH to entertain should lead its listeners into an experience of unalloyed enjoyment, to dismiss them rested and refreshed. This is its purpose: not to change the destiny of men, but to relax and rejuvenate them. The standard by which it should be prepared and later evaluated is none other than its capacity to amuse or please.

Entertainment may be a means to any one of the chief purposes of speech, but it is the total purpose of the speech to entertain. Humor is frequently used by the persuasive speaker to relax and disarm the audience, thus minimizing opposition and creating a mood of good fellowship which facilitates acceptance of his proposition. One contemporary lecturer, for example, delivers an hour-long address composed almost entirely of dramatic and humorous anecdotes about famous authors, so that the listeners derive almost continuous entertainment with no particular awareness on their part of a serious motive. Yet the net effect of the speech is to leave them with a new determination to read some of the classics they had formerly considered rather forbidding. Such a speech is not entirely an entertaining speech; rather, it uses entertaining content to achieve persuasion. Similarly, a speech of complicated exposition may be intermingled with relaxing spots of humor or may be developed within an entertainingly dramatic framework. Thus, a speaker wishing to explain to his audience how to distill fresh water from the ocean might dramatize his topic by telling of the plight of sailors adrift at sea on a raft. The attention-compelling narrative ensures close attention to the key expository material.

As contrasted with the foregoing examples, the speech to entertain is not intended to intrigue the audience through entertainment to acquire new knowledge or to accept new points of view. Nonetheless, the range of the entertaining speech is very wide. Much fiction and poetry and many familiar essays are intended for entertainment; so are many motion pictures and radio and television shows. So is a great deal of music and a wide variety of social games, from bridge to the sack race at a community picnic. It is obvious that human beings crave entertainment and that public speaking is one of the many forms through which it may be provided.

TYPES OF HUMOROUS SPEECH

Any kind of entertainment adaptable to the public-speaking situation may constitute a speech to entertain. Humor is a common, in fact nearly universal, ingredient, and its uses for speeches of entertainment are manifold. However, humor is no more the sole province of the entertaining speaker than it is of the writer or the motion-picture producer. The speech to entertain may be developed around original humor, the humorous story, the dramatic narrative, the fantasy, unusual experiences, startling facts, or the travelogue. This range is sufficiently broad so that any speaker may select a type suitable to his own interests and capabilities.

Original Humor

It is undeniable that some temperaments are much better suited than others to creating original humor. However, whether you are "a born humorist" or cannot tell a joke without ruining it, you should find it helpful to consider the basic ingredients of which humor is composed. The many serious-minded attempts to define humor generally arrive at a definition more or less like this one: *Humor arises from a sudden perception of incongruity accompanied by a sense of well-being.*

Does the principle sound complex? Incongruity consists of any situation in which the parts do not properly fit together. Thus a one-legged man is incongruous. But he is not funny—for looking at him arouses pity rather than a feeling of well-being. If you see a child run down the street, trip, and fall into a puddle of water, making a big splash, your first reaction may be to laugh. But if the child lies still and you realize he has been hurt, the humor changes at once to concern. If you are standing before a cage of monkeys at the zoo, and suddenly perceive that one monkey closely resembles a friend of yours, the fact appears inordinately funny. You may laugh uproariously at the time, and chuckle over it for weeks thereafter. But if someone else points out that another monkey resembles you, you may fail to notice any humor in the situation. These are all examples of humor based upon "situation."

Another type of humorous incongruity arises from ill-matched or poorly balanced "characters." Stories of timid men with domineering wives are of this type. So are the Dog Patch girls' hopeless but persistent pursuit of Al Capp's comic-strip males. The comedian Red Skelton seeks by burlesque and exaggeration to deflate pomposity and demonstrate the innate superiority of the simple-minded. His audiences enjoy a sense of well-being because they feel themselves superior to the weak-minded dupes who finally win out and they are glad to witness the humiliation of the comedian's self-important stooges.

Nothing has been said thus far of the first part of the principle of humor—the perception of incongruity must be *sudden*. There is nothing funny about a joke which is so clumsily told that the audience sees the point long before the speaker gets to it. There is little humor about any situation which becomes apparent gradually. For example, it is almost useless to explain a joke to someone who missed its point. By the time your explanation has succeeded in making the incongruity clear, all the humor has been strained out. Humor needs to crackle and sparkle to be most effective. According to one theory, it is necessarily dependent upon surprised expectation. That is, the listener is led to expect one outcome, but finds that one suddenly replaced by an unexpected one. This is a means of ensuring that the crux of the humor shall burst upon him suddenly—that the point of the joke shall be concealed until the proper moment of surprise.

Another method of misleading the expectation of an audience, and thereby creating humor, is to begin to repeat a common saying and then to twist the latter part of it. This constitutes a humor of incongruous language. For example, "He is a gentleman and a dullard," "Spare the rod and spoil the batting arm," "Honesty is the worst politics," or "A little over three hundred years ago the Pilgrims came to establish a land where every man could worship his Maker according to the dictates of his wife's conscience." A similar method of achieving surprise in the portrayal of an incongruity and at the same time giving the audience a sense of well-being is to begin a statement in apparent seriousness and finish it with a ridiculous, exaggerated, or farfetched conclusion. As examples, "All married couples may be divided into two classes: those who believe in divorce, and those who prefer to fight it out to the bitter end," and "If all the politicians were

laid end to end, it would be a good thing." This method is also illustrated in the following parody of a well-known verse:

> Mary had a little lamb,
> Its fleece was white as snow;
> It followed her to Pittsburgh one day,
> And now look at it.

Among the types of incongruity which lend themselves readily to
use in speeches, exaggeration, understatement, and the device of
anticlimax are outstanding. Mark Twain's works are filled with examples of exaggeration. Describing the death of a citizen of Virginia
City, he wrote:

> On the inquest it was shown that Buck Fanshaw, in the delirium of a
> wasting typhoid fever, had taken arsenic, shot himself through the body,
> cut his throat, and jumped out of a four-story window and broken his
> neck—and after due deliberation, the jury, sad and tearful, but with intelli-
> gence unblinded by its sorrow, brought a verdict of "death by the visitation
> of God."

Understatement is illustrated in the following description of Ad-
miral Byrd's eight-month solitary sojourn in a little hut near the
South Pole:

> During the best part of a year, the admiral was all alone. Nobody
> dropped in for a social call on Saturday night. Nobody chatted with him
> across the back fence when he hung out the wash on a Monday morning.
> There was nobody to sit with him, and smoke a pipe, and talk about the
> weather. He was as deserted as a kindergarten teacher at recess.

Anticlimax results from the building up of an impression which is
punctured rather than capped at the end. Thus Frederick Landis, in
introducing Will Hayes, declared, "We are mighty proud of Bill.
There is absolutely nothing the people would not give him—unless
they wanted it themselves."

The sense of well-being is fostered by good-humored irreverence
for anything that normally is held in high esteem. Perhaps this explains the prevalence of mother-in-law jokes. It certainly explains why
women are frequent objects of jests. It seems that man needs some
escape from the strain of his generally chivalrous attitude. Thus
Horace Porter, speaking about the toast "To Woman," aroused
laughter when he said, "At public dinners this toast is habitually
placed last on the list. It seems to be a benevolent provision of the
Committee on Toasts in order to give man in replying to Woman

It is a heart-warming experience to speak to a group which responds as heartily and happily as this one. Although the speech of entertainment solves no great problems, it deserves high regard for its ability to wash away worries and reanimate jaded spirits.

one chance at least in life of having the last word." Similar in intent are the numerous jokes about ministers, such as the one which represents a minister, who has been replaced by a rival after a struggle to retain his position, as preaching a farewell sermon on the text: "Tarry ye here with the ass while I go yonder." The irreverent joke often is directed at those who are in positions of authority. There is always, for example, a stock of jokes directed at the President, whoever he may be at the time. The irreverence sometimes expresses itself in good-humored disparagement of individuals who are present. Thus Edward C. Elliot, speaking at the inauguration of President Louis B. Hopkins of Wabash College, turned toward his host and said:

This afternoon, as you ended your notable address, Sir, there was loud and enthusiastic applause. For a moment I wondered why. [*Laughter.*] First I thought it was because you had finished. [*Renewed laughter.*] Then I thought it was because of the things you had said. But these were not good reasons. [*Laughter and applause.*]

Of course, if the irreverence loses its tone of genial good humor, it ceases to be funny and becomes bitter or satiric.

Humorous incongruity may also result from punning, as in the comment that "soft soap is ninety per cent lye"; from the use of dialect, as in Negro, Irish, Jewish, Scottish, and Pennsylvania Dutch stories; and from verbal peculiarities, as in deliberate mispronunciation, alliterative phrases, and the representation of drunken speech. It may also result from the use of analogies that are obviously untrue and ridiculous, as in the example "as hard-boiled as a baby-beating politician during an election campaign."

The methods of producing humor mentioned here by no means comprise a complete catalogue. But if the speaker observes the principle of creating in one of a variety of ways a sudden perception of incongruity accompanied by a sense of well-being, he will find that his perception of humorous possibilities and his skill in utilizing them will be greatly sharpened.

Humorous Stories

Reference was made earlier in the chapter to a lecture composed of anecdotes about famous writers. Whenever a speaker tells true or apocryphal humorous stories about famous personages, the interest derived from the humor itself is heightened by the satisfaction the audience feels in having intimate and harmlessly disparaging glimpses into lives of the great. Wide reading of biographies or reference to some of the collections of anecdotes about famous people will supply humorous stories of this type which may be woven together in a common theme.

Least satisfactory of the speeches built around humorous stories are those that substitute the banal phrase "That reminds me" for a more careful planning to introduce the stories naturally. When a speaker's purpose obviously is sheer entertainment, an audience gladly will allow him wide latitude with the presumed facts he presents. The comedian Cliff Arquette (Charlie Weaver) for example, introduces all his humorous stories as though the characters in them were his own relatives. Other speakers tell their stories as though they were personal experiences or as though they happened to prominent members of the audience or the community. The chief caution to be observed in identifying actual people with your fictionalized anecdotes is to remember that humor depends upon a sense of well-being. You must make sure both in the content of what you say and in your manner of saying it that there will be no embarrassment for the people who are being introduced into your stories. Mark Twain, great humorist though he was, forgot this vital principle when he made a speech at an occasion honoring Ralph Waldo Emerson, Henry Wadsworth Longfellow, Oliver Wendell Holmes, and John Greenleaf Whittier. Both the audience and the distinguished authors were astounded when Twain described the four guests of honor as disreputable poker players in a Western mining town. Their reaction was similar to that of Queen Victoria when she icily responded to a story she considered in poor taste, "We are not amused." Humor can be dangerous as well as helpful. The story must always be in good taste, must be tactful, and must radiate good will.

The following story is an example of poking good-natured fun, yet leaving the object of the story in a most favorable light. When Ignace Jan Paderewski was visiting Boston some years ago, he was approached by a bootblack who asked, "Shine?" The great pianist looked down at the lad, whose face was dirty and grimy, and answered, "No, my boy, but if you will wash your face, I will give you a quarter." The boy looked at him closely, then said, "O.K." He ran to a nearby fountain and hurriedly scrubbed his face. When he returned, Paderewski gave him the promised quarter. The boy again looked at him closely, took it, and then returned it quickly, saying, "Gee, mister, you take it yourself, and get your hair cut."

Since humorous stories are an excellent source of speech entertainment, the speaker should build up a file of them. It is surprising how many good stories are forgotten by the next day. By writing them down and filing them, the speaker can have them available whenever an appropriate speech occasion arises. In making such a collection, the speaker should bear in mind that the more obscure and little known the source, the greater the chance that the story will be new to the audience. Jokes from so widely read a publication as *The Reader's Digest* are likely to be as well known to the audience as to the speaker. Thus the speaker needs to make his own collection of humorous stories, including in it, of course, only the best of those he reads and hears. As a further guarantee against their being already known to his audience, he will do well to personalize each story, adding individual touches which give it an original flavor. Listeners are not likely to be annoyed at hearing an old story if it is better told than when they first heard it.

DELIVERY OF HUMOROUS STORIES

Whether a speech is composed of original humor or of humorous stories, its delivery is a major factor in determining its effect. The speaker must have an easy and confident command of himself, of his material, and of his audience. No audience can be cajoled into a mood of relaxed jollity if it senses that the speaker is uncertain of himself or is struggling to recall the point of his own joke. It is as true of the humorous speech as of any other kind that it must be planned and prepared very carefully in advance. But humorous speaking at its best is characterized by frequent and close references to the situation and circumstances in which the speech is delivered. The humorous speaker must therefore know his material well enough to permit himself impromptu variations from it.

Mark Twain's excellent essay "How to Tell a Story" recommends that the humorous speaker remain "dead-pan" as he convulses his audience with hilarity. Actually this is only one means of delivering the humorous speech. Many speakers are quite incapable of it. What is to be avoided above all is the tendency of the speaker to "lead the laughs" and to exceed the audience in his enjoyment of his own quips and stories. It is a rare person who can be both performer and cheerleader at the same time. The audience may laugh till it loses control of itself, but the speaker must always maintain self-control. This does not mean, as Mark Twain felt, that the speaker *must* fail to react to his own humor; rather, it means that his own laughter should follow instead of precede that of the audience, should be more restrained, and should be the first to subside, so that the speaker is ready to pick up the threads of the speech and carry it on as soon as the audience is ready for him to do so.

Many humorous speakers find pantomime an excellent aid to delivery. A humorous story or situation can be built to its highest crescendo of ludicrous effect by facial grimaces and bodily posturing. For no other type of speaking is full and free bodily action so important. Many a gale of laughter is set off by a meaningful shrug of the shoulders or a bashful squirm. The best of humor can be spoiled if the speaker is tense, awkward, and visibly nervous. Ole Olsen, explaining the success of the Olsen and Johnson comedy team, said, "Mister, you can't stand still. Even when we make mistakes we make them enthusiastically."

From what has already been said, it should be apparent that the sequence of a humorous speech must be mastered. As in other kinds of speaking, notes may be used only if they are not permitted to come between the speaker and his audience. If the speaker stands behind a table or beside a rostrum, he would do well to place on it brief notes written in large and conspicuous script, so that he can refer to them quickly and easily. If he is standing before the audience with no support for his notes, he should devise some means of supplying himself with humorous "props" which will have the effect of notes without appearing as such. One student speaker, for instance, gave a very effective, entertaining speech on how to classify people according to the kind of shoes they wear. His "notes" consisted of several pairs of shoes, which he placed on a chair in the front row and picked up—one pair at a time—as he described the types of individuals who would wear them. In any event, obvious reference to notes is not in keeping with that spontaneity which should be a characteristic of the entertaining speech.

Perhaps the most important of all considerations in delivering humorous speeches is the quality of good-fellowship. There must be no question in the minds of the audience that the speech is filled with good will. The entertaining speech has no place for sharp or bitter satire. The atmosphere of the entertaining speech should be such that the question "Is everybody happy?" would bring back the hearty and unanimous response "Yea, man!"

NONHUMOROUS ENTERTAINING SPEECHES

As this chapter pointed out earlier, we too often think of the entertaining speech as being necessarily humorous, whereas, as a matter of fact, the test of an entertaining speech is not at all limited to whether it is funny. The more universal test is whether its purpose and effect are to amuse and please the listeners, rather than to influence their judgment or action. Nonhumorous speeches often may prove to be more entertaining than humorous ones. This may be especially true for speakers who are inept at handling humor. Speakers should familiarize themselves with the following nonhumorous types of entertaining speech.

Dramatic Narrative

There is as much variety in oral storytelling and narrative speaking as there is in written fictional and nonfictional narrative. A public speaker whose purpose is to entertain may occasionally wish to tell his listeners a story—making clear to them that it is fiction and adapting the characters and the plot somewhat to his audience, just as he would adapt his materials in any other kind of speaking. Far more frequently, however, the entertaining speaker may relate an actual dramatic experience, either of his own or garnered from his reading or acquaintances. Readily apparent, for example, are the entertainment possibilities of such topics as these:

How We Transported a Basketball Team in a Volkswagen
Hunting for the Abominable Snowman
Riding Out a Japanese Typhoon on a Destroyer
A Photographic Safari in Central Africa
A Trip up the Nile to the Aswan Dam Site
How a News Reporter Broke up a Graft Ring
A Summer Job at Cape Canaveral
My Week behind the Iron Curtain

In relating a dramatic narrative the speaker must give careful attention to creating a *mood* of excitement, suspense, and tension. He must make clear and vivid the *setting* in which the narrative occurs. The *characters* must be clearly defined, with the sympathies of the audience directed toward the "heroes" and away from the "villains." And the *struggle* must be presented as a series of difficulties leading toward an unexpected *climax*. Selecting a good narrative to relate is, of course, the first requirement. After that has been done, narrative skill, like any other, will improve through conscientious attention to each of the essential factors just mentioned and through practice.

Fantasy

Audiences will gladly grant to the speaker what S. T. Coleridge called "a willing suspension of disbelief" if he makes clear to them that he is going to let imagination carry them into a pleasant land of make-believe. Topics that student speakers have used successfully in entertaining speeches include:

A Trip to the Moon
Life on Mars
College in A.D. 2060
Men in Petticoats—The Housekeeping Husbands of Career Girls
Underground Cities in the Atomic Age
How to Be Happy on a Million Dollars a Year

Since the speaker is creating for his audience a world of fantasy, he must be sure to include the specific details that will make clear for his listeners the significant differences between his make-believe world and the real one.

Unusual Experiences

Some examples of unusual experiences which can provide excellent material for the entertaining speech include the following:

An Encounter with the Police in Yugoslavia
The Time I Persuaded My Professor to Change a Grade
Baby-Sitting a St. Bernard Dog
Substituting for Water-Boy at a Football Game
A Ride into the Grand Canyon by Muleback
How I Wandered by Mistake into the Delegates' Lounge at the United Nations
My Experience with a Recruiting Sergeant

The tone may be humorous, exciting, or lightly satiric. One speaker combined humor, pathos, and a surprise ending in a speech on how he discovered that a professor can have a kind heart. A married student used good-natured satire effectively in explaining how his views of parent-child relationships changed after he became a father. In relating an unusual experience, the speaker should emphasize the unexpected elements and their effects.

Startling Facts

The popularity of the late Robert Ripley's "Believe It or Not" and of John Hix's "Strange As It Seems" has demonstrated how interested people are in useless but odd or exciting facts. A speaker can deliver a speech with real entertainment value on "Life in an Anthill" or "Initiation Rites of an African Tribe." Dale Carnegie discovered that "little-known facts about well-known people" have considerable public appeal. "Milk can be as strong as iron, as soft as silk, and as flexible as rubber," one speaker pointed out in a talk on plastics. So vast is the range of modern knowledge and so limited is the typical person's understanding of it that specialized reading in almost any field will provide a body of surprising facts that will contribute to the entertainment of an audience.

The Travelogue

Probably at no other time in history have audiences been so deeply interested in all parts of the world as they are today. The millions of men and women who served in the armed forces have had unparalleled opportunities to become acquainted with hitherto unfamiliar portions of the United States and foreign countries. Such an experience is a vast reserve of material from which to construct entertaining speeches. In most instances, even if you have spent a year or so in Korea, or Bavaria, or England's lake country, you will need to supplement your own recollections with some fresh reading to provide details you never noticed or have forgotten. Reading of this sort, however, is buttressed by the fact that you were there, talked with the people, saw much for yourself, and formed your own impressions. For an entertaining speech, you will wish to keep the attention of your audience focused upon the picturesque and unusual elements in the country you are describing. The very fact that so many have in our time traveled so much has sharpened the curiosity and interest of the great majority who stayed at home. Your principal aim will be to give your listeners something of the pleasure and stimulation they might secure from the trip itself.

ORGANIZING THE SPEECH TO ENTERTAIN

Like every other talk, the speech to entertain has a beginning, a middle, and an end—or an introduction, a body, and a conclusion. However, the similarity of construction between the entertaining speech and other types ends at this point.

The Introduction

Whether for humorous or nonhumorous speeches of entertainment, the introduction should aim primarily at creating the desired mood and at making clear that nothing more momentous is to be expected than a period of unalloyed enjoyment. It is advisable to be explicit on the latter point, for members of the audience may be confused and even irritated if they keep expecting the speech to "get somewhere" and the speaker continues to provide entertainment and nothing more.

The Body

Chapter 10, "Organizing the Speech," stressed the necessity for limiting and carefully integrating the main ideas as well as the fact that they must in combination support the speaker's specific purpose

In the speech to entertain, these requirements are considerably relaxed. The entertaining speech must "hang together," with natural transitions from one point to another, but in humorous speaking there often may be no need for any unity except the essential unity of mood. In a narrative speech, the main ideas are replaced by a series of incidents, each leading in its turn toward the climax. The structure of a speech to entertain may be loose and extremely casual. But it should never be careless. The speaker must plan the sequence of his material so that he is always in command of his information, knowing what is coming next and making clear its connection with what has preceded and what will follow. In entertaining speaking, the most essential structural considerations are good transitions and swift and sure movement to the climax.

The Conclusion

The conclusion for the entertaining speech usually is brief, but it should be distinct, definite, and appropriate. If you are simply telling a series of humorous stories or startling facts, you must not merely end with a recital of a final one, as though you have suddenly decided that you have entertained long enough and should stop. Since your purpose is merely to entertain, you do not conclude by drawing a moral or pointing a judgment from what has been said. In narrative speaking or in the travelogue, the speech reaches a natural conclusion with the end of the story or with some stopping point of your trip. The collection of humorous stories may be concluded with, "The best story of all, however—for me the story to end all stories—is . . . ." The speech composed of startling facts may end with, "Among all these unusual facts the one that most strongly symbolizes for me the strange relationship between health and disease [or the odd attitudes of the African tribesmen; or the exciting new developments in physics] is . . . ." The chief thing to remember is that the audience must be given a definite sense that the speaker's intention has been accomplished and that the speech is therefore completed.

CONCLUSION

Entertainment is one of the important and popular uses of public speaking. There are so many occasions for it and so many differences in speakers and in entertaining subject matter that the speech to entertain has many types and varied characteristics. Regardless of the type, however, the primary factor is that the purpose of the speaker is none other than to provide his listeners with a period of amusement or enjoyment. This purpose must be made clear to the audience and should dominate the mood in which the speech is presented. The chief requirements of the entertaining speaker are deftness and sureness of touch and complete control over himself, his material, and his audience. The fact that the speech is "merely entertaining" does not mean that it is easily prepared or delivered. Masters of the entertaining speech are rare. But so frequently is it in demand that most public speakers should make determined efforts to gain a respectable proficiency in one or more of its forms.

EXERCISES AND BIBLIOGRAPHY

Exercises

1. Reread Chapter 11, "Adapting to the Audience," and note how helpful, in preparing the speech to entertain, it will be to make use of the elements and types of interest.
2. Phrase one topic for each of the types of entertaining speech discussed in this chapter.
3. Make a list of occasions or situations in which speeches of entertainment are appropriate.
4. If possible, find an occasion outside class at which you can deliver an entertaining speech. Prepare the speech under your instructor's direction and deliver it in class before you present it to the outside audience. Make such revisions of it as are desirable in the light of class discussion and criticism.
5. Outline (a) a narrative speech, travelogue, or fantasy and (b) a speech based on humorous stories or startling facts. If time permits, the outlines may be discussed and criticized in a class session.
6. Write a comparative analysis of two entertaining speeches heard in class: one that seemed particularly good and one that seemed relatively ineffective. Try to determine to what extent the success and the failure resulted from content, organization, and delivery.

Bibliography

Boatright, Mody C., *Folk Laughter on the American Frontier* (Macmillan, 1949).

Botkin, B. A., *A Treasury of Western Folklore* (Crown, 1951).

Clough, Ben C., *The American Imagination at Work* (Knopf, 1947).

Hertz, Emanuel, *Lincoln Talks* (Viking, 1939).

House, Boyce, *Tall Talk from Texas* (Naylor [San Antonio], 1944).

Randolph, Vance, *The Devil's Pretty Daughter and Other Ozark Folk Tales* (Columbia University Press, 1955).

ILLUSTRATIVE SPEECH

America's greatest humorist, Mark Twain—or Samuel Langhorne Clemens—excelled not only as a writer but also as an entertaining speaker on the lecture platform and on after-dinner occasions. On December 23, 1876, at the 71st annual dinner of the New England Society in the City of New York, Mark Twain was introduced to respond to a toast to "The Oldest Inhabitant—the Weather of New England." The audience was composed mainly of distinguished men, descended from families long prominent in New England. Twain's problem was to achieve entertainment without violating their severe code of propriety; also he had to combat the inevitable weariness that resulted from several hours of dining and listening to the seven speeches that had preceded his. The result is a combination of felicitous style and original humor that has established this short talk as a model for after-dinner speaking.

New England Weather

BY MARK TWAIN

Gentlemen:—I reverently believe that the Maker who made us all, makes everything in New England—but the weather. [*Laughter.*] I don't know who makes that, but I think it must be raw apprentices in the Weather Clerk's factory, who experiment and learn how in New England for board and clothes, and then are promoted to make weather for countries that require a good article and will take their custom elsewhere if they don't get it. [*Laughter.*] There is a sumptuous variety about the New England weather that compels the stranger's admiration—and regret. [*Laughter.*] The weather is always doing something there; always attending strictly to business; always getting up new designs and trying them on the people to see how they will go. [*Laughter.*] But it gets through more business in spring than in any other season. In the spring I have counted one hundred and thirty-six different kinds of weather inside of four and twenty hours. [*Laughter*.] It was I that made the fame and fortune of that man that had that marvelous collection of weather on exhibition at the Centennial that so astounded the foreigners. He was going to travel all over the world and get specimens from all the climes. I said: "Don't you do it; you come to New England on a favorable spring day." I told him what we could do, in the way of style, variety, and quantity. [*Laughter*.] Well, he came, and he made his collection in four days. [*Laughter*.] As to variety—why, he confessed that he got hundreds of kinds of weather that he had never heard of before. And as to quantity—well, after he had picked out and discarded all that was blemished in any way, he not only had weather enough, but weather to spare; weather to hire out; weather to sell; to deposit; weather to invest; weather to give to the poor.

The people of New England are by nature patient and forebearing; but there are some things which they will not stand. Every year they kill a lot of poets for writing about "Beautiful Spring." These are generally casual visitors, who bring their notions of spring from somewhere else, and cannot, of course, know how the natives feel about spring. And so, the first thing they know, the opportunity to inquire how they feel has permanently gone by.

Old Probabilities has a mighty reputation for accurate prophecy, and thoroughly well deserves it. You take up the papers and observe how crisply and confidently he checks off what to-day's weather is going to be on the Pacific, down South, in the Middle States, in the Wisconsin region; see him sail along in the joy and pride of his power till he gets to New England, and then—see his tail drop. He doesn't know what the weather is going to be in New England. He can't any more tell than he can tell how many Presidents of the United States there's going to be next year.[1] Well, he mulls over it, and by and by he gets out something about like this: Probable nor'-east to sou'-west winds, varying to the southard and westard and eastard and points between; high and low barometer, sweeping around from place to place; probable areas of rain, snow, hail, and drought, succeeded or preceded by earthquakes, with thunder and lightning. Then he jots down this postscript from his wandering mind to cover accidents: "But it is possible that the programme may be wholly changed in the mean time."

Yes, one of the brightest gems in the New England weather is the dazzling uncertainty of it. There is only one thing certain about it, you are certain that there is going to be plenty of weather—a perfect grand

[1] Reference is to the dispute over the election results of the Hayes-Tilden campaign.

review; but you never can tell which end of the procession is going to move first. You fix up for the drought; you leave your umbrella in the house and sally out with your sprinkling pot, and ten to one you get drowned. You make up your mind that the earthquake is due; you stand from under and take hold of something to steady yourself, and the first thing you know, you get struck by lightning. These are great disappointments. But they can't be helped. The lightning there is peculiar; it is so convincing! When it strikes a thing, it doesn't leave enough of that thing behind for you to tell whether—well, you'd think it was something valuable, and a Congressman had been there.

And the thunder. When the thunder commences to merely tune up, and scrape, and saw, and key up the instruments for the performance, strangers say: "Why, what awful thunder you have here!" But when the baton is raised and the real concert begins you'll find that stranger down in the cellar, with his head in the ash-barrel.

Now, as to the size of the weather in New England—lengthways, I mean. It is utterly disproportioned to the size of that little country. Half the time, when it is packed as full as it can stick, you will see New England weather sticking out beyond the edges and projecting around hundreds and hundreds of miles over the neighboring States. She can't hold a tenth part of her weather. You can see cracks all about, where she has strained herself trying to do it.

I could speak volumes about the inhuman perversity of the New England weather, but I will give but a single specimen. I like to hear rain on a tin roof, so I covered part of my roof with tin, with an eye to that luxury. Well, sir, do you think it ever rains on the tin? No, sir; skips it every time.

Mind, in this speech I have been trying merely to do honor to the New England weather; no language could do it justice. But after all, there are at least one or two things about that weather (or, if you please, effects produced by it) which we residents would not like to part with. If we had not our bewitching autumn foliage, we should still have to credit the weather with one ice-storm—when a leafless tree is clothed with ice from the bottom to the top—ice that is bright and clear as crystal; every bough and twig is strung with ice-beads, frozen dew-drops, and the whole tree sparkles, cold and white, like the Shah of Persia's diamond plume. Then the wind waves the branches, and the sun comes out and turns all those myriads of beads and drops to prisms, that glow and hum and lash with all manner of colored fires, which change and change again, with inconceivable rapidity, from blue to red, from red to green, and green to gold; the tree becomes a sparkling fountain, a very explosion of dazzling jewels; and it stands there the acme, the climax, the supremest possibility in art or nature of bewildering, intoxicating, intolerable magnificence! One cannot make the words too strong.

Month after month I lay up hate and grudge against the New England weather; but when the ice-storm comes at last, I say: "There, I forgive you now; the books are square between us; you don't owe me a cent; go and sin some more; your little faults and foibles count for nothing; you are the most enchanting weather in the world!"

CHAPTER 23

CONTENTS

At Provincetown, Massachusetts, the city fathers assemble for a meeting. In the background is a painting of the signing of the Mayflower Compact. (Library of Congress)

THE SPEECH FOR
A SPECIAL OCCASION

ANY speech that you give will be a speech for a "special occasion." Up to this point in this book we have sought to present the basic guidance needed for any kind of speaking, whether it be in conversation, discussion, or conference; in public speeches intended to inform, inspire, entertain, induce belief, or move to action; in a small room or a large auditorium, face-to-face with your listeners, or before a radio microphone or a television camera. All forms of oral communication have much in common, and a speaker whose thinking is quick and direct, whose diction and voice are good, and whose action while speaking is appropriate, should be able to utilize these skills in any speech situation.

Yet one dismal fact about education remains: transfer of learning is not automatic. Students whose courses in psychology have included the study of personality find it difficult to transfer what they have learned to the study of interpersonal relationships in their courses in social psychology. Indeed, it appears difficult even to transfer the ability to write a theme for English composition to the writing of a term paper for a class in history.

Hence it is not surprising that a student may complete a course in speech and then—when called upon to "make a few remarks" at a football pep rally—feel that he just doesn't know how to go about it. "Too bad we didn't study this in speech class," he may think. Once again, all your life, every time you make use of any form of oral communication, the situation will be "special," with its own peculiar characteristics and requirements. If the fundamentals have been really learned, you should, with continuing practice, gain increasing facility in successful communication, whatever the occasion.

VARIETY OF OCCASIONS

No list of the types of speeches for special occasions could ever be complete. If a friend dies, you may be called upon to speak a few appropriate words of tribute at the next meeting of a club in which you and he were members; you may wish to go to his home to speak whatever words of comfort you can to his family; you may be asked to join in a more formal obituary service, or to offer a suitable prayer at the cemetery. If a friend starts a new business, you may be called upon at a dinner honoring the occasion to make a congratulatory speech. Similar remarks may be called for at a wedding reception, or upon the award of a prize, or on the occasion of a twenty-fifth or a fiftieth wedding anniversary, or on the election of someone to a public office. At a parent-teacher meeting, or at a banquet held for a winning football team, or in a committee meeting, or in a Sunday school class, or at a community rally to launch a drive for funds for a local YMCA building—in innumerable situations, you will from time to time find need to use your ability to speak effectively and appropriately.

No matter how varied the situations may be, the essential factors are always the ones you have encountered in these pages. There is, first of all, *you*—the speaker—with a *specific purpose* to be *developed* into an appropriate *message* that will be *adapted* to the *time limits,* to the *nature of the occasion,* and to the *audience.* You will need to make use of all you have learned about how to *analyze* your own thinking (to determine your purpose and to discover what resources you already have and which you must supplement with additional information); to *organize* your ideas so that they will serve that purpose through sequential stages of the *introduction, discussion,* and *conclusion; to develop* your ideas with clarity, conviction, and appeal; to *phrase* your ideas extemporaneously and appropriately in a style that fits the needs of the occasion; and to *deliver* the talk with directness in a vocal pattern and with bodily action that helps you to achieve your aim.

In addition to factors which apply to all speaking, you should also always keep in mind that every talk you may ever present has its own requirements. One situation—such as nominating a friend for the presidency of a local club, where he will have no real opposition and in which a spirit of camaraderie prevails—calls for seriousness combined with good humor and unpretentious formality. Another situation —such as replying in a public meeting to a speaker who is known and liked, but whose ideas on the topic you feel are wrong—demands clarity of analysis and soundness in the use of facts and logic, combined with fairness and friendliness of manner. Still other situations call for other variations of mood and manner. For example, you are to present the annual award offered by the Kiwanis Club to the outstanding high school senior. There are many possibilities: everyone realizes the recipient is far superior to other candidates; or there is a narrow choice between two potential recipients; or the award goes to the son of the town's most prominent citizen in a narrow choice between him and the son of that same citizen's gardener, or vice versa. Obviously, although in each case the occasion is "presentation of an award," the occasions are essentially different. There is no substitute for using your best judgment in analyzing the whole complex of factors which determine the nature of each "special occasion."

There are recurrent needs in any community for longer speeches than any you have been able to present in your speech class—but normally these addresses are given by experienced speakers. "Occasional speeches" are usually no longer than the three- or five-minute talks to which you have become accustomed in meeting your class assignments. These talks for special occasions may for convenience be grouped into a series of categories—with the reminder, however, that each occasion has its own particular requirements. To the extent that you exercise any degree of expanding leadership, you will be called upon for the kinds of brief remarks indicated in the following categories.

ANNOUNCEMENTS

Announcements are of two kinds: those which merely give information concerning a forthcoming event; and those which urge the audience to attend and patronize it. For the former, accuracy, completeness, and brevity are the chief requirements. Clearly and correctly name the occasion and give the place and date. Like the news reporter, you should tell the audience essential facts on the *who, what, where, when,* and *why* elements of the event. If tickets are to be sold, tell their price and where they may be obtained. If there is a sponsor and a special purpose for the event, identify them. In other words, be sure to include all essential information, clearly, briefly, and without error.

The second type of announcement includes the material of the first and adds an appeal for participation by the listeners. It should stress the importance of the occasion and the nature of the attraction which it holds for the audience. If the occasion is philanthropic, appeal to the charitable sentiments of the listeners; if it is planned especially for their enjoyment, make them realize how much fun it will be. This type of announcement requires close analysis of the audience to ensure the kind of appeal that will prove most effective. Since all announcements should be short, they demand the utmost in careful planning so that every word will count.

INTRODUCTIONS

The speech introducing a speaker should provide a link between the speaker and his audience, not a separation. It should never be used by the introducer as an opportunity to make a speech of his own, to demonstrate his own cleverness, or to show his superior knowledge of the subject the speaker will discuss. Its purpose is to inform the audience of the qualifications of the speaker, so that his views will be received with respect, and to establish a harmonious speaker-audience relationship in accord with the nature and tone of the occasion. It is considerate to learn from the speaker beforehand whether there are any special things he may wish the introducer to say in order to prepare the way for a more favorable reception by the audience of both speaker and subject.

When you introduce one of your friends to another, you say in effect, "I like this man, trust him, and am glad to recommend him to you." This function is performed by the speech of introduction. It aims to secure for the speaker the highest possible degree of respectful attention. The introduction should contain a brief, objective description of the speaker's career, presented tactfully so as not to embarrass him; a statement of his subject, but not a speech on it; and a clearly audible pronunciation of his name, so all will understand it. In addition, the introduction may contain some remarks about the nature and importance of the occasion and a few words of congratulation upon the size of the audience—but an apology for a small audience is rarely in good taste.

Speeches of introduction are often unsuccessful. Frequently delivered by inexperienced speakers, they are often poorly prepared and are sometimes misconceived as an occasion for honoring some local dignitary by inviting him to make the introduction. Traveling lecturers have had many fantastic experiences with local chairmen—so many, indeed, that Mark Twain finally insisted that he never be introduced at all. Wilson MacDonald, poet laureate of Canada, was given the following introduction by a farmer-chairman in a little town in Nova Scotia: "Ladies and gentlemen, here's a put. Now, I don't like putry, I don't read putry, and putry ain't in my line. But here he is, so let him go ahead."

In preparing a speech of introduction, be sure that you have all pertinent information about the speaker and that you have mastered it sufficiently to be able to transmit it correctly to the audience without using notes. Be cordial, be forthright, and be brief. Be humorous, solemn, or factual, as the nature of the occasion requires. And organize your remarks so that they lead to the climax of stating the speaker's name and topic. Then stop!

SPEECHES OF WELCOME

A speech of welcome may be given for a single individual, as at a reception held for a returning military hero, a statesman, or a new officer or employee of an organization; or it may be given for an organization, such as the American Legion or Rotary International, which may be arriving for a convention. Sometimes a school or a lodge holds a welcoming reception, with speeches included on the program, for returning members. In any of these instances, the speeches should refer to the occasion and to the status or achievements of those being welcomed. It should express sincere cordiality and perhaps pride in the relationship between the honored guests and the audience. And it should be brief.

SPEECHES OF RESPONSE

The speech of response is made in reply to a welcoming address. It should express the speaker's appreciation of the honor being extended to him. It should be modest and sincerely appreciative of the spirit and purpose of the organization that tenders the welcome. If the recipient of the welcome is being honored not for what he himself has done but because of what he represents, as a returning general hailed for the victories of his army, he may well reply with praise of those who have served under him and with appreciation for the support given them by the citizenry at home. Sometimes the speech of response is a brief "Thank you." At other times it may be a lengthy expression of views that the speaker deems appropriate for the occasion. There should be a clear understanding between the committee in charge and the honored guest as to the type of response desired.

SPEECHES OF PRESENTATION

The speech of presentation should identify the person or organization making the presentation, the nature of the gift or award, and the reasons for its being given. The speaker should be truly appreciative of the merit which has led to the conferring of the honor. The value of the award itself should be subordinated to the sincerity of the tribute and the admiration and respect it represents. If the presentation is being made to an institution or an organization—for example, if a building is being donated to a university or a boat to a troop of sea scouts—the speech may include a discussion of the character of the organization and the purpose the gift will serve. But in most circumstances the speech is brief and is chiefly marked by sincere appreciation of the qualities of the recipient that led to the presentation of the gift or award.

SPEECHES OF ACCEPTANCE

On accepting a gift, honor, or award the recipient should express his appreciation and, if appropriate, his surprise. He may modestly disclaim any special merit, at the same time expressing appreciation for the spirit that motivated the presentation. For example, if a special honor has been conferred upon an athletic director, he may pass over the honor to himself and praise the group for the recognition it has given to the sportsmanship, courage, loyalty, and resourcefulness of the team. Like the other speeches we have been discussing, the acceptance should be marked by brevity and sincerity. The recipient will be judged most ungrateful if he fails to show proper appreciation.

SPEECHES OF FAREWELL

Speeches of farewell are ordinarily given upon two kinds of occasion: when an officer of an institution retires after a long and notable service; and when the speaker, about to depart on a journey, is tendered an expression of esteem by his friends and associates. The former (well illustrated by George Washington's Farewell Address) may be a long address of reminiscence, advice, and final formulation of policy. The latter is brief and marked by personal expressions of friendship; it usually refers to the purpose of the journey about to be undertaken. An excellent model is the speech of farewell which Abraham Lincoln delivered from the rear platform of his train to his fellow townsmen of Springfield, Illinois, as he was departing for Washington to assume the Presidency:

My Friends: No one, not in my situation, can appreciate my feeling of sadness at this parting. To this place, and the kindness of these people, I owe everything. Here I have lived a quarter of a century, and have passed from a young to an old man. Here my children have been born, and one is buried. I now leave, not knowing when or whether ever I may return, with a task before me greater than that which rested upon Washington. Without the assistance of that divine Being who ever attended him, I cannot succeed. With that assistance, I cannot fail. Trusting in Him, who can go with me, and remain with you, and be everywhere for good, let us confidently hope that all will yet be well. To His care commending you, as I hope in your prayers you will commend me, I bid you an affectionate farewell.

AFTER-DINNER SPEECHES

After-dinner speaking has become increasingly important. This type of speech has characteristically been short, genial, and humorous, with no particular purpose beyond the entertainment of the audience. There is still much speaking of this sort. In recent years, however, there has been a great increase in the number of long and serious speeches delivered after a dinner, while the audience is still gathered at the banquet table. These speeches serve a variety of purposes. Political rallies are frequently held at dinners, with keynote speeches afterward. Community-chest drives feature breakfast or luncheon meetings, with inspirational speeches. Conventions of businessmen and of scholars often hold some of their chief meetings at the banquet table, with important addresses given after the dinner. All this threatens to change the traditional character of after-dinner speaking (unless a distinction is made between after-dinner speeches and speeches that are given after dinner); nevertheless, a dinner still provides a valuable speech situation.

Its value consists of the effect which a good meal, eaten in congenial company, has upon a group of people. Dr. Samuel Johnson neatly expressed it when he said, "Sir, a good meal lubricates business." An atmosphere of friendliness, of tolerance, and of good humor is almost inevitable in such a situation. It is inevitable, too, that the digestive processes interfere to a degree with the intellectual function of the diners, who become less critical, less logical, and less capable of close and sustained attention than they are on other occasions. The combination of these factors makes it relatively easy to amuse, inspire, or stimulate them, but difficult to lead their minds through any process of complex reasoning to a logical conclusion.

The speech by John Ise called "Values in a Crazy World" (at the end of Chapter 11) illustrates very well the ways in which these factors should influence any after-dinner speaker who has a serious message to deliver. Professor Ise incorporated into his speech, especially in the introduction, the qualities of geniality and good humor which the after-dinner situation demands. Then, as the speech progressed, he gradually swung the attention of his listeners from humor to the serious problem he wished to present; without any complex analysis, he gave them ideas that were both concrete and interesting enough to hold their attention at the time and vital and striking enough to remain in their memories for serious consideration later. This is a technique that any after-dinner speaker who wishes to discuss a serious problem would do well to follow.

Whether the purpose of the after-dinner speaker is serious or light, he will find the following rules of value:

1. *Be good-humored.* Bitterness and denunciation are seldom forgivable in an after-dinner speech. They run directly counter to the spirit of good-fellowship, geniality, and tolerance induced by the meal. They deny the instinct of gregariousness which brought the diners together. Not least, they interfere with the diners' digestion and thus make them physically uncomfortable. For good after-dinner speaking, the tone of good humor is indispensable.

2. *Be brief.* No speech should ever last longer than the attention and interest of the audience can be held. After a heavy dinner, this attention span is brief. Furthermore, it frequently happens that several speeches are to be given. Take these considerations into account in preparing your speech. Make it brief, and be prepared to cut it even shorter if you find your audience restless and ill at ease.

3. *Be affirmative.* A positive approach to a subject is usually better than a negative one. Tell your audience what to like, what to do, what to be; not what to dislike, what not to do, and what to stop being. This affirmative attitude should exist in the delivery as well as in the composition of your speech. Be confident and forthright. Take it for granted that your audience will agree with what you have to say. Remember, of course, that your point of view should be reasonable and should conform fairly closely to the experience and attitudes of your audience.

4. *Be clear and simple in your expression.* An after-dinner speech is not an occasion for complexity or profundity. If your ideas cannot be easily understood, they will not be understood at all. They should be developed with an abundance of sprightly, interesting illustrations, but they should not be elaborated into a maze of fine distinctions.

5. *Be prepared*. Be so well prepared that there will be no hesitancy, no groping for thoughts, no use of notes. Any of these is fatal to the lightness and spontaneity which the after-dinner speech demands. The speech should be so well prepared, so thoroughly in the speaker's mind, that he will be able to deliver it with ease, confidence, and a ready adaptation to the audience which will make it appear absolutely spontaneous.

COMMEMORATIVE SPEECHES

Speeches which celebrate the memory of an event, an institution, or a man are called commemorative. Their chief distinguishing feature is the fact that they are planned to celebrate the "remembrance of things past." Within this general class of speeches are found anniversary addresses, dedicatory addresses, and eulogies, all of which are strictly commemorative. Most nomination speeches and inaugural addresses and some commencement speeches have enough characteristics in common with these to be included on the fringes of the group.

Practice in the composition and delivery of commemorative speeches is of great practical value in developing general speech skills, for it provides several types of experience which beginning speakers are likely to get in no other way. The preparation of a commemorative speech is excellent practice, first of all, in analysis of and adaptation to an audience, for the speaker is not expected to express himself but to serve as the spokesman for the thoughts and sentiments of his listeners. He says for them what they would like to say for themselves. He makes articulate the feelings of loyalty and reverence which they feel. He is like a man who draws up a petition to be presented in the name of and representing the thoughts of the entire group. Thus he fulfills the function of the poet of Alexander Pope's time, who dealt not with new material, but with "what oft was thought, but ne'er so well express'd."

Second, the preparation of a commemorative speech is good experience because this type of speech requires special attention to style. Since the subject matter is not new, the style must provide the distinguishing excellence of the speech. And since the occasion calls for a dignified, exalted utterance, the style must be the very best of which the speaker is capable. The words must be selected to fit a speech rhythm and for their connotative as well as their denotative values.

Word pictures must be frequently and carefully drawn. The structure of sentences and of paragraphs must be closely knit. Indeed, in no other kind of speaking is it so necessary to strive to achieve all the marks of good speech style. Since the general trend of modern speaking is toward a colloquial informality, some practice in this kind of speech composition is especially needed to counteract the usual carelessness in matters of style.

Third, there is a special value to be sought in the delivery of commemorative speeches. Their exalted and dignified tone calls for a dignified and formal type of delivery. The speaker must be especially well poised, for any awkwardness is particularly glaring in contrast to the composition of the speech. Gestures should neither be omitted entirely nor used carelessly. The highest correlation of body, voice, and composition is required for effectiveness in commemorative speaking.

The beginning speaker may quail at the difficulties involved in this type of speaking. In fact, it is the type in which the greatest orators have displayed their highest powers. But it is nonetheless a valuable medium of study for beginners. After the basic principles of effective speech have been studied—organization, style, voice, and action— the presentation of a commemorative speech gives an unrivaled opportunity to bring together all the principles that have been learned and to demonstrate the best speaking of which the individual is capable. It serves as a practical examination, testing how thoroughly the qualities of good speech have been incorporated into the speaker's practice. It also serves as a diagnosis, to indicate what special types of study and practice should be emphasized in the further development of the speaker.

Although they have so much in common, the various types of commemorative speech also have their individual characteristics.

Anniversary Addresses

Delivered upon such occasions as Columbus Day, the birthdays of Washington, Lincoln, and other notables, the Fourth of July, and dates having special significance for particular audiences, the anniversary address stresses (1) the significance of the institution or event being commemorated; (2) the lessons to be drawn from it to govern present and future conduct; (3) the feelings that are appropriate in considering it; and (4) the character of the men and women who participated in it. The function of anniversary addresses was well stated by Daniel Webster, in the introduction of his Plymouth Oration, delivered on the two-hundredth anniversary of the landing of the Pilgrims:

It is a noble faculty of our nature which enables us to connect our thoughts, our sympathies, and our happiness with what is distant in place or time; and, looking before and after, to hold communion at once with our ancestors and our posterity. Human and mortal although we are, we are nevertheless not mere insulated beings, without relation to the past or the future. Neither the point of time, nor the spot of earth, in which we physically live, bounds our rational and intellectual enjoyments. We live in the past by a knowledge of its history; and in the future, by hope and anticipation. By ascending to an association with our ancestors; by contemplating their example and studying their character; by partaking their sentiments, and imbibing their spirit; by accompanying them in their toils, by sympathizing in their sufferings, and rejoicing in their successes and their triumphs, we seem to belong to their age, and to mingle our own existence with theirs.

Dedicatory Addresses

As the anniversary address deals commonly with the past, the dedicatory address generally links the past with the future. It is delivered on such occasions as the dedication of monuments, parks, and new buildings. Lincoln's speech at the dedication of the new cemetery at Gettysburg is justly the most famous example of this kind of speaking. Webster's address at the laying of the cornerstone for the Bunker Hill Monument is a good example of a longer speech of dedication. Both speeches stress the duties and opportunities of the present generation, because of the sacrifices of those who went before. This theme—"To you from failing hands we throw the torch; be yours to hold it high"—is frequent in many commemorative speeches. But the most common of all themes for dedicatory addresses is that chosen by John Lancaster Spalding as his title, in a speech dedicating an educational institute in Peoria, Illinois. It was "Opportunity!" and it dealt with the uses to which the institute would be put and the results in richer and happier lives that would flow from it. Dedicatory addresses often cite the great need that existed for the building being dedicated, point out the difficulties that had to be overcome in making possible its erection, and praise its sponsors for their loyalty and devotion.

Eulogies

A eulogy is a speech of praise for an individual, usually for one who is dead. Funerals are the most common occasions for such speeches, although they are also frequently given upon the anniversary of the subject's birth. Eulogies should be marked by sincerity and a certain amount of restraint. They should contain a concrete presentation of the achievements of the subject, so that the praise will be amply justified.

Eulogies may take two forms: chronological and topical. The latter is usually preferred. The *chronological* type too easily degenerates into a simple recital of the year-by-year course of the subject's life: parentage, childhood, education, and then, in order, his achievements. This uninspired procedure should be avoided. However, the eulogist can use the chronological method to good effect by dividing the man's life into periods—such as preparation, achievement, and recognition —making each period a well-rounded unit. The *topical* method is much more elastic. It permits a greater degree of selectivity of subject matter. Topical eulogies concern themselves with such questions as the following: Why was the subject a great man? What did he accomplish? What unusual difficulties did he have to overcome? What admirable qualities did he possess? To what agencies or sources, other than his own efforts, did he owe his success? What dramatic or interesting incidents from his life best reveal his personality and character? What did his contemporaries think of him? What benefits do we reap from his labors? What lessons can we learn from his manner of living? What should be our final judgment of him?

Nomination Speeches

Nomination speeches are often closely akin to eulogies, except that their subjects are always living. The procedure often followed in nomination speeches is to give in some detail the requirements of the office that is to be filled and then to describe in eulogistic terms the qualities of the man being nominated for that office. An excellent example is the presidential nomination of Alfred E. Smith, in 1928, by Franklin D. Roosevelt, whose speech not only followed the form just described but added a third common element, a prophecy of victory under the leadership of the man being nominated. All these characteristics are combined in the concluding paragraph of that speech:

America needs not only an administrator but a leader—a pathfinder, a blazer of the trail to the high road that will avoid the bottomless morass of crass materialism that has engulfed so many of the great civilizations of the past. It is the privilege of Democracy not only to offer such a man but to offer him as the surest leader to victory. To stand upon the ramparts and die for our principles is something more than heroic. We offer one who has the will to win—who not only deserves success but commands it. Victory is his habit—the happy warrior, Alfred E. Smith.

Inaugural Addresses

Formal inaugural addresses are given by individuals who are being inducted into such high office as the presidency of the United States or of a college or other institution. Informal inaugural speeches may be delivered by presidents of fraternities and other college organizations as they are installed in their new offices. These speeches offer an opportunity for examination of the principles upon which the institution has been governed, of the nature of the task confronting the new president, and of the policies he intends to follow during his term of office. Lincoln's second Inaugural Address is perhaps the noblest example we have of this kind of speech. It dealt with the problem then paramount, the Civil War, and with the union of kindly tolerance and firm resolve with which the war had to be prosecuted until its object was achieved.

An inaugural address generally follows a political campaign, during which factionalism was emphasized and bitterness developed. One function of the speech is to heal the wounds of dissension and to make it clear that the new officer represents not only his own faction but the entire electoral body. Thus the tone is usually conciliatory and friendly. Since the speech is generally given as part of a lengthy ceremony, it should be brief and pointed. An example worthy of study is the inaugural address by President Kennedy printed at the end of the chapter on style.

CONCLUSION

As has been emphasized in this chapter, the occasion—as well as the speaker's purpose or the nature of the audience—may be the determining element in deciding what kind of speech to prepare. Certain occasions, such as the presentation or acceptance of an award, practically prescribe the content and method of the speech. Others, such as commemorative occasions, have a special tone and general pattern to which the speaker normally is expected to conform. For all the speech occasions that have been described, the speaker should satisfy both the demands of good speaking in general and of the particular occasion upon which his speech will be presented.

EXERCISES AND BIBLIOGRAPHY

Exercises

1. Select any one of the occasions suggested for a commemorative speech and prepare a "miniature" address of five minutes in length, making sure to conform to the tone and general point of view that the occasion requires.

2. The class may be divided into pairs of speakers, for brief welcome-response and presentation-acceptance speeches. Some students may instead deliver speeches of introduction and others speeches of farewell.

3. When circumstances permit, the class holds a session at a restaurant or in a private dining room. After the meal, each member delivers a three-minute after-dinner speech. The class is divided into two groups, each of which elects its own toastmaster and presents a unified program. One group, for example, may present a series of talks on phases of American life "when grandpa was a boy"; the other group may give speeches on what life in America will be like "when grandson grows up." If circumstances do not favor the meeting of the class around a real dinner table, the speeches may be delivered in class.

4. Draw up a list of ten living individuals who, in your opinion, are most deserving of speeches of eulogy. These lists should be discussed in class, with each student defending his list and explaining the particular merits of the individuals he has named. Prepare and deliver a five-minute eulogy of one of the men or women on your list.

5. Draw up a list of five important historic dates, trying to find for your list events that no one else will think of including. Join in a class discussion of the dates listed, following which each student will prepare and deliver a five-minute commemorative speech on one of the events he has selected.

6. Assume that Congress is about to be organized for a new session, and give a five-minute speech nominating your choice for Speaker of the House; or that the United Nations is to begin a new session, and present a speech for your nominee as President of the General Assembly; or that a Citizens' Good-Government Committee is being formed in your college community, and nominate the person you would prefer as chairman.

Bibliography

Baird, A. Craig, *Representative American Speeches* (annual volumes; H. W. Wilson).

Baker, James Thompson, *The Short Speech* (Prentice-Hall, 1932).

Brigance, William Norwood, *Classified Speech Models* (Appleton-Century-Crofts, 1930).

Copeland, Lewis, and Lawrence Lamm, *The World's Great Speeches* (Rev. ed.; Dover Publications, 1958).

Harding, Harold F., *The Age of Danger* (Random House, 1952).

O'Neill, James M., *Models of Speech Composition* (Appleton-Century-Crofts, 1921).

Peterson, Houston, *A Treasury of the World's Great Speeches* (Simon and Schuster, 1954).

INDEX